From Angels TO ALIENS

From Angels TO ALIENS

TEENAGERS, THE MEDIA,

AND THE SUPERNATURAL

LYNN SCHOFIELD CLARK

OXFORD

UNIVERSITY PRESS

2003

OXFORD
UNIVERSITY PRESS

Oxford   New York
Auckland   Bangkok   Buenos Aires   Cape Town   Chennai
Dar es Salaam   Delhi   Hong Kong   Istanbul   Karachi   Kolkata
Kuala Lumpur   Madrid   Melbourne   Mexico City   Mumbai   Nairobi
São Paulo   Shanghai   Taipei   Tokyo   Toronto

Copyright © 2003 by Oxford University Press, Inc.

Published by Oxford University Press, Inc.
198 Madison Avenue, New York, New York 10016

www.oup.com

Oxford is a registered trademark of Oxford University Press

An earlier, shorter version of this work was published as "U.S. Adolescents, the Media, and the
'Funky' Side of Religion," *Journal of Communication* 52, no. 4 (2000).

Library of Congress Cataloging-in-Publication Data
Clark, Lynn Schofield.
From angels to aliens : teenagers, the media, and the supernatural /
Lynn Schofield Clark
    p. cm.
Includes bibliographical references and index.
ISBN 0-19-515609-9
1. Teenagers—Religious life—Southwestern States. 2. Mass media and teenagers—
Southwestern States. 3. Teenagers—Southwestern States—Attitudes. 4. Public opinion—
Southwestern States. 5. Mass media—Religious aspects. 6. Occultism—Religious aspects.
7. Occultism—Public opinion. 8. Religion—Public opinion. I. Title.
BL2527 .S68   C57   2003
200'.835'0979—dc21   2002010397

9 8 7 6 5 4 3 2

Printed in the United States of America
on acid-free paper

When I was eleven, I bought my first and only book of witchcraft spells at a Winn-Dixie supermarket in western Florida. The pink pocket-sized booklet with a fluffy white cat and a red candle on its cover shared a display rack with glossy teen magazines, mini-cookbooks, and candy bars. My grandparents, who were taking care of me and my cousin Linda while my parents were on vacation, were in another part of the store when I plunked down my allowance money and quietly pocketed the purchase.

Later that evening, Linda and I huddled together on a worn chaise lounge, first intensely absorbed and then dissolving in laughter as we read the spells. We finally settled on one we could cast on Joey, a ten-year-old who lived next door and teased us incessantly. We sneaked around surreptitiously gathering the necessary materials, which included a branch of a tree and a candle. We performed our spell and then, gleeful from the experience, went on to choose another, and then another. After a while our interest waned and we turned to watching television in the living room, my sleeping grandparents none the wiser.

The next morning at the neighbor's door, Joey's older brother told us that Joey didn't feel well and wouldn't be playing with us that day. Linda and I giggled and exchanged knowing glances. Could it be that our spell had caused his illness? We didn't really believe that—but then again, it was a delicious coincidence for a couple of preteens anxious to harness any kind of power in a time of life when one feels particularly powerless.

Although my family was actively involved in a church at the time, it never occurred to me that worshiping God and my experiments with witchcraft had anything to do with one another, much less that they might be considered by some to be contradictory. Of course, I don't remember ever mentioning the witchcraft episode to my Sunday school teachers, either.

As a young person, I learned about these "superstitions" from various sources: in addition to friends and their stories shared from the insides of sleeping bags as a preteen, I voraciously read novels like *A Wrinkle in Time, Mrs. Coverlet's Magicians,* and *The Witch's Garden.* Later, I came to love the supernatural thrillers I saw on television years after their release, such as *Carrie, The Shining, The Omen,* and *The Exorcist.* While I screamed gleefully at the horrific, I was also drawn to positive and silly depictions of the supernatural, in films like *E. T.* and *Ghostbusters.* If Harry Potter had been around when I was eleven, I'm sure I would have been a fan, regardless of what my church or school had to say about it. And what young woman wouldn't love Patrick Swayze as the prototypical pin-up guardian angel in *Ghost*?

While I loved the stuff of the supernatural realm, as a preteen I knew that the story lines and practices that came out of the folk traditions of magic, witchcraft, vampires, ghosts, aliens, and paranormal experiences were not about "religion." Today, some might still see such dabblings as the harmless antics of teens, as my friends and I did then. But others would probably wonder about the possible harms of experimenting with witchcraft. In large part, this anxiety is fueled by the increasingly vocal protests of conservative Protestant and Catholic Christians, including those who are concerned that everything from Pokemon to Halloween might be opportunities for the spread of what they would call satanism and the occult. Among these people, there is a real nervousness that simply did not exist a few decades ago, when such talk about the Devil and other supernatural evils was largely the province of the relatively small and marginalized fundamentalist circles. Today, those holding such anxieties, as well as those who eschew them, are important to consider in a study of teens and teen culture. These views can be seen as placeholders for what can be characterized as the two extremes of contemporary religious life: on the one hand, the growth of various fundamentalisms, and on the other, the growing number of persons who claim indifference to religious or spiritual life. Teens are aware of these differences on an unconscious if not a conscious level, and this context of religious change inevitably plays a role in how teens come to understand and experience themselves as "religious" or "spiritual."

Given the rise of fundamentalisms and of indifference, why is it that so many people in the United States seem fascinated with the supernatural, the afterlife, the paranormal, and even the extraterrestrial? Moreover, why does there seem to be a connection between religious belief or spirituality and interests in the paranormal and supernatural? I want to explore what this fascination means, how it plays itself out in the lives of individuals and the culture, and why it is occurring at this point in history. In particular, I want to examine the role of the entertainment media in this fascination. And because young people are perceived as both the most vulnerable to the compelling stories of the entertainment media and the most likely to abandon traditional religions, I focus on their experiences with this fascination.

I was brought up in a liberal Protestant household. I had no contact with evangelicals or fundamentalists growing up, and no opportunity to form an opinion about them one way or another. But I was taught to be tolerant of the religious beliefs of others, and I have tried to carry that tolerance with me in my adult life. I first became acquainted with evangelicalism when I was in college, and although I disagreed with their politics (now as then), I was attracted to evangelicalism's vitality and the optimism that suggested that young people could change the world. "You can make a difference!" evangelical speaker and comedian Tony Campolo had cheered at my college and at others across the nation in the "Moral Majority" Reagan years of the mid-1980s. This was the era when evangelicalism had become a major news story, with its prominence in American political life and in televangelism. One added bonus to my own interest in evangelicalism was that it was completely annoying to my parents. As such, it was quite effective as a form of late adolescent rebellion. At some level, then, this book is a part of my own search to understand the relationship between religion and culture as a media scholar, as a teacher and mentor of young people, and as a parent. I believe that it is especially important to understand this relationship in the post–September 11 world. We now live in a society where religion is an issue on the front page and, for some, in the forefront of our minds. We have become increasingly aware of fundamentalisms and of the relationship between religious heritage, politics, and social practices. Yet there is still much that we don't understand. I think that part of our misunderstandings stem from the fact that as a society, we only rarely consider religion's role in our own country critically, looking at both its positive and negative attributes. Instead, we tend to live along the dividing lines of fundamentalism and indifference to religion, defending religion, ignoring it, or—especially when it's someone else's religion—blaming it.

In order to better understand religion's relationship to culture, I examine a very particular case: the relationship between teens, religious identity, and the supernatural in popular culture. Relying on in-depth interviews with teens from a variety of backgrounds, I present a theory of different ways that young people incorporate, dismiss, play with, reject, and wonder about what they see in the media, and I describe what I believe is an emergent approach to religion that seems well suited to the highly mediated, religiously plural, and diverse environment teens live in today. I build this theory by reflecting on the country's religions heritage and the contemporary representations of religions in popular culture, while considering how parents and peers also play a role in the strategies young people adopt. Clearly, there is no single, unitary way that religions and culture intersect for all people and at all times. My hope is that this study can extend the fruitful critical discussions of religion and culture, so that we can all become more aware of what's at stake and can play a positive role in creating a more equitable world for our young people.

This book is therefore not meant to disparage evangelicalism or to promote what evangelicals believe is its opposite, what they would call "secular humanism." In fact, I hope that people who consider themselves evangelical might find something of interest in the stories of young people and the way they relate media to their experiences of faith. I think these stories will be of interest to people outside those circles, as well. In the increasingly religiously plural environment of the contemporary United States, we owe it to our young people to try to understand their spiritual journeys and how these intersect with other facets of their lives, including the entertainment media. It is to the teens whose stories formed the basis of the theories presented here that this book is dedicated.

ACKNOWLEDGMENTS

This book could not have been written without many people who assisted at various stages of the project. I thank those who participated in the interviews, both those who shared the life stories that are analyzed here and the many others who provided important insights and background material. I also want to thank Cynthia Read, senior editor at Oxford, who was able to see the possibilities in this manuscript even at its earliest, unfocused stages, and Christi Stanforth, production editor, who shepherded it into a much better work. I am thankful to have been a part of a research team at the University of Colorado where, under the direction of Stewart Hoover, so many interesting conversations concerning the intersection of religion and the media were generated. Diane Alters, Joseph Champ, and Lee Hood generously shared their transcripts and analyses with me. Scott Webber provided exemplary help with the securing of permissions for the book's illustrations. Michelle Miles, Zala Volcic, Nicole DeJarnatt, and Shane Chastang shared their expertise on young people. Anna-Maria Russo brought me wonderful news clippings, while Christof Demont-Heinrich and Helga Tawil provided invaluable knowledge of the Web. Crystal Atkinson's apt formatting and proofreading skills made this a much better manuscript. Thanks also to Michael Abeyta, Rae Ann Armijo, Josh Hernandez, Nicole Houston, Josh Ortega, Melanie Salazar, Sofia Sellers, Daniel Walsh, and David Martinez for their assistance.

The research discussed here could not have been conducted without the generous support of the Lilly Endowment, Inc., and the Louisville Institute. I am thankful in particular to Craig Dykstra and Jim Lewis, as well as members of the International Study Commission on Media, Religion, and Culture and the Stichting Porticus foundation; Dorothy Bass, Don Richter, and the Practicing Our Faith project; Stephen Warner, Rhys Williams, and the Roundtable on Youth and Religion; and the Research Services offices of the Presbyterian Church (U.S.A.), all of whom provided avenues for discussion that assisted in this project's development. Thanks are due those who read and commented upon early versions of this work, including Stewart Hoover, Janice Peck, Andrew Calabrese, Erika Doss, Janet Jacobs, Alf and Gun Linderman, Richa Nagar, and Dennis McGilvray. Thanks also to Horace Newcomb, Diane Alters, David Morgan, and another reader who provided detailed and insightful comments on this manuscript's first drafts. I am grateful for feedback offered on various parts of the book that came from Nancy Ammerman, Mark Andrejevic, Elizabeth Bird, Mark and Karen Borchert, Brenda Brasher, Scott Carmode, Joy Charlton, Roz Dauber, Carl Dudley, Lynne Edwards, Mara Einstein, Jan Fernback, Ron Grimes, Larry Grossberg, Ingunn Hagen, Mary Hess, Annette Hill, Birgitta Hoijer, Jane Iwamura, Klaus Bruhn Jensen, Shawn Landres, Mia Lovheim, James Lull, Knut Lundby, Carol Lytch, Bill MacDonald, Jeffrey Mahan, Joel Martin, Carolyn Marvin, William McKinney, Adan Medrano, Don Roberts, Wade Clark Roof, Michele Rosenthal, Alan Segal, Christian Smith, Sam Smith, Judith Stacey, Rebecca Sullivan, Len Sweet, Hillary Warren, Robert White, Diane Winston, Robert Wuthnow, and Mark Yaconelli. Dennis Benson, Tom Boomershine, Ken Bedell, and Gregg Hartung provided ongoing inspiration and reminded me of the importance of good storytelling throughout this project. Julie Clark, Jennifer and Michael Olin-Hitt, Carrie and Jim Borer, Ann, Ryan, and Sarah Kampf, Joan Cattanach, Karen MacDonald Johnson, Shelly and Sarah Pinkernell, Katrina Sarsen, Gia Medeiros, Patty Gassaway, Risa Kerns, and members of the "Power Women," "Renaissance Babes," and "Playgroup" generously provided support as the project unfolded. The Schofield, Clark, Ramey, Bucey, and Pardridge families provided support as well. Special thanks are due to my father, father-in-law, and brother-in-law, all of whom read drafts and provided helpful insights, my "Gen X" brother, who has always shared my interests in all things spiritual and supernatural, and my mother, whose enthusiasm for well-written prose and wry wit inspired me. Jon, my husband and life partner, not only gave ongoing, patient feedback and insights from his experiences as a television producer but also provided the gentle prodding necessary to get a project like this completed. He and Jonathan and Allison gave love, support, and joy throughout, surely among my own most mystical, spiritual, and treasured experiences of this life.

CONTENTS

Part III
CONTEXTS AND CONCLUSIONS

Part I
THE SUPERNATURAL TODAY

WHY THE FASCINATION?

Introduction

When God made woman from man, he didn't want Adam to be lonely. He doesn't want us to be alone either. Now some of us are bored with what we've seen in our lives and want to see new things. Therefore, I think God will relieve our boredom with aliens. I don't think God would make them look like green, glowing blobs, because, like us, He would make them in His own image.
—Greg Norby, age eleven, Bloomington, Ind., home schooled

The only place I believe life exists other than on Earth is heaven.
—Emily Nelson, Andover, Mass., McKinley School

A few years ago, in an effort to encourage young people to read their daily newspaper, the *Star Tribune* of Minneapolis began a write-in program called MindWorks. Each month, the newspaper posted a question and invited responses from young people aged six to eighteen. When they asked for a short statement in response to the question "What do aliens think of us?," nearly five thousand wrote in, including Greg and Emily, quoted above. By a ratio of two to one in this revealing yet unscientific exploration, young people said they believed in the possibility of extraterrestrial life. They cited a variety of evidence for their views, including television programs or films such as *Unsolved Mysteries*, *Contact*, *Independence Day*, and *The X-Files*. They mentioned docudramas on alien autopsies, alien abductions, and Area 51. They also reasoned that space beyond earth was simply too big to be completely empty. Many noted that they had friends, relatives, or acquaintances who claimed to have seen UFOs.

Religious beliefs came up with surprising frequency among their responses. Some, like the preteen Greg, used religious beliefs to justify the existence of aliens. Aliens, like humans, are made in the image of God, he wrote. Others, like Emily, concluded that because the Bible makes no mention of aliens, they must not be real. Sure, life exists beyond the earth, she conceded, but only in heaven.[1]

If aliens, like Greg writes, are made in the image of God, as humans presumably are, do they then have an afterlife in heaven, as well? For young people like Emily, such musings are preposterous. But for some young people like Greg, perhaps all kinds of beliefs, from angels to aliens, are possible and not necessarily in conflict. Other young people, like fourteen-year-old Andrea Zimmerman of Brooklyn Park, may just prefer to avoid the subject altogether. As she wrote: "If there are aliens and they ever decided to come to Earth, I don't think they'd spend much time here. It's too confusing."

Certainly, the teenage years are a time of confusion, as significant physical, emotional, social, and sometimes even spiritual changes define the period that marks the transition from childhood to adulthood. Yet today's teens experience a host of other changes that also affect how they perceive this world, the realm beyond it, and their own relationship to both.

On the one hand, research into young people and their beliefs has often assumed that they have learned of and formed their beliefs about angels, God or Allah, and the Devil—the more traditionally "religious" supernatural beings— in the context of church, the synagogue, or the mosque.[2] (Presumably, they might also learn that aliens are not a part of their religion's tradition.) On the other hand, teens are immersed in a culture that extends beyond traditional religion in its fascination with the realm beyond. The Pagan Federation reports that it has been "swamped" by young people's requests for information about witchcraft in the wake of Harry Potter and television programs like UPN's *Buffy the Vampire Slayer* (formerly on the WB Network).[3] Belief in angels has also increased substantially in the past decade among people of all ages.[4] With more than three out of four teens and adults claiming such belief, it is no wonder that by the end of the last millennium, the sale of angel books had exceeded 5 million copies and one of the top-rated television dramas of the period was CBS's feel-good program *Touched by an Angel*.[5] But apparently angels are not the only beings that visit us from the realm beyond. Experiences with other supernatural phenomena are reported with increasing frequency in the United States, as well. Among teens, belief in ghosts is on the increase, as is the belief, among adults, that they have had a personal contact from a person who has died.[6] By the beginning of the new millennium, books about angels were increasingly sharing the best-seller lists with titles such as *Life on the Other Side* by psychic Sylvia Brown. Meanwhile, the television program *Crossing Over*, featuring psychic John Edwards, became the first program to garner significant ratings for the emergent Sci Fi channel—and eventually "crossed over" to syndication.

Compared to angels and spirits of the deceased, belief in aliens is much less prevalent, but it is also a more recent phenomenon, with stories of alien visitations first surfacing in the 1940s. Just over five decades later, only (only!) 27 percent of people in the United States believed that aliens had visited us.[7]

Not long ago, scholars and public leaders were convinced that interests in the realm beyond were on the wane and would continue to fall out of favor as Western culture became increasingly secularized.[8] Many believed that this was evidenced by the declining attendance figures among the formerly prominent religious organizations of North America and western Europe (particularly within mainline Protestantism).[9] More recently, numerous studies have shown that overall levels of religious involvement (including subjective reports of levels of belief, personal prayer, and religious experience) remain strong in the United States—and have actually been relatively stable over the last century.[10] Scholars working within what has been called the "new paradigm" of religious studies point to the rise of fundamentalisms, the immigration trends that have changed the religious landscape, and even the rise of alternative spiritual practices both within and outside formal religion that have brought new forms of religious vitality to the United States.[11] Historians have been debating the secularization process as well. It may be that western Europe and the colonial United States were not as religious as was once assumed. This makes it difficult to establish that the influence of formal religions on everyday life was any greater then, or less now.[12]

Still, the proportion of young people who are affiliated with a particular religious tradition has declined over the past decades.[13] Yet religion seems to have remained important in the lives of many young people, at least according to their self-reports.[14] Rather than asking about religion's decline among young people, therefore, more and more people are interested in how religion and spirituality are continuing in an increasingly religiously plural world, and how they are changing in relation to the highly mediated cultural and historical context in which they are found.[15]

Relatively little is known about how the encounters with the supernatural in popular culture relate to spiritual and religious identities and practices. In part, as sociologist William MacDonald explains, this is because of a possible reporting bias in sociological research. People know that experiences with clairvoyance, telepathy, and other encounters with the supernatural are generally considered by the broader population to be deviant. Thus, they are less likely to report them, and as a result, the prevalence of such phenomena or even interest in it is difficult to establish and compare with the past for evidence of increases or decreases in interest.[16] Popular magazines, books, television programs, films, and Web pages devoted to such phenomena often draw wide audiences, however, attesting to the widespread appeal of such things among all age groups in contemporary society.[17]

While the proliferation of such materials might seem rather recent, teen culture has long been linked to the supernatural fare associated with certain traditions of alternative spirituality, particularly those that challenge authority either overtly or indirectly. These teen interests in the supernatural have had varying connections with religion as it is formally conceived. On the side closer to traditional religion, we might consider the many Marian apparition stories that have involved European young people, whose religious leaders must verify or challenge such claims in the face of tremendous popular pressure. At some distance from traditional religion are the séances, Ouija boards, and levitation that have long been a part of teen girl sleepovers, and "legend tripping" (visiting cemeteries, purportedly haunted houses, and other creepy places) that has been an established practice in teen boy life since the introduction of the automobile gave them increased mobility and autonomy.[18] All of these practices serve as challenges to the ways in which authorities like teachers, parents, and the police oversee and discipline public spaces for young people. Also, they each play with (and to some extent rebel against) the definitions and practices of the afterlife that have long been the concerns of traditional monotheistic religions.

Why have these differing kinds of encounters with the supernatural been so prevalent among young people? Some have suggested, with sociologist Andrew Greeley, that young people may be more open to experiences with the supernatural than those who are older.[19] Psychologists have demonstrated that, compared with their adult counterparts, young people have greater "eidetic ability," defined by Miriam Lambouras as the ability to conjure "vivid visual images of specific objects that are not present in actuality, but are present to their conscious or sub-conscious imagination."[20] Lambouras notes a famous study by psychologist C. M. Staehlin, who demonstrated that through the power of suggestion, young people can experience imagined phenomena as real. Other connections might be drawn between experiments with the supernatural and the importance of rites of passage for the adolescent. As anthropologist Arnold Van Gennep noted in his analysis of rites of passage for adolescents, the facing of fears was an important aspect of communal rituals that symbolically ushered adolescent males and females from childhood into adulthood.[21] As anthropologist Victor Turner argued, in modern society the experience of watching films together can, in some ways, serve the same functions as the older rituals that marked rites of passage. Specifically, he wrote of the ability of film to call forth in its audiences a sense of liminal moments, that time of transition in rituals where the past is forgotten and the participants are able to envision a new future.[22] An important appeal of confronting the stories of the supernatural in teen culture, then, may have references to a need to feel competent and powerful in the face of powers beyond one's control. In today's situation, this occurs in the context of peers who share similar fears and are bonded together as those fears are invoked and symbolically overcome. Thus, perhaps the séance or the late-night communal television-viewing of horror films gives adolescent boys an opportunity to demonstrate their fearlessness while girls, due to changing gender conventions, can either demonstrate their own fearlessness or their need for reassurance from the boys.[23]

Experimenting with such things in the context of one's peers provides emotional titillation and a means for strengthening peer relationships. As teens ride the tension between fear and faith that characterizes the question of whether something unearthly might happen in their presence, they can heighten the emotional intensity, and hence the possible intimacy, among group members.

While teens undoubtedly spend time preparing for the future roles of adulthood, they also live in a culture that celebrates youth and its distinctions from adulthood. Thus, part of the appeal of the supernatural and alternative spiritualities can be explained in direct relation to the desire for teens to explore aspects of life in ways apart from those sanctioned by adults. Some practices associated with the supernatural are understood as distinct from the more accepted practices of adulthood, as well as those of official religion. As such, they appeal to the teenage desire to rebel against parental and societal norms.[24]

Parents remain an important source of information and influence when it comes to what young people believe, however. According to several national surveys, most teens feel that their ideas are similar to their parents' when it comes to values they consider important in their lives.[25] Most teens report that they talk about religion with their parents at least once a month.[26] Yet today's young people are experiencing family life much differently than their parents did. More young people are growing up in a home with a single parent, or one in which a parent has remarried or lives with a partner. More young people are also biracial and multiethnic (figure I.1).[27] Families and their teens are also strapped for time, largely as a result of changes in the postindustrial economy. More parents now work in service positions that offer lower pay and less security (and hence encourage multiple simultaneous jobs), and the few who are fortunate enough to have higher-paying positions regularly work long hours. This, combined with the fact that more mothers work outside the home, means that a great number of parents are away from their homes and their teenage children—more than was the case for the previous generation of teens—making them "a tribe apart," as author Patricia Hersch has described them.[28] Parents have a tremendous influence on the choices a young person makes because they can directly limit or coerce activities, but perhaps more centrally because they can indirectly influence the other social networks in which their teenage children participate.[29] This is especially important, as friendships among peers form the basis for the social groups that informally establish norms for how young people dress, how they act in different situations, and when they might articulate certain beliefs or participate in certain practices of religion, alternative spirituality, or supernaturalism. "You are who you hang around with," as one young person said.[30] Whether they are regular participants in religious organizations, "marginal members," or nonattenders, young people are constantly engaged in a kind of a cost-benefit analysis to determine how they will express themselves religiously in the contexts of differing social groups.[31] Since

FIGURE I.1
Today's young people are more diverse than any previous generation. Photo by author.

their generation is more religiously diverse than any previous generation, the challenge of identifying with a religious tradition is often perceived as marking out a way to live among relative truths.[32]

TEENS, RELIGION, AND SPIRITUALITY

What do religion and spirituality mean to young people? Certainly, the religious context encountered by young people today is different from that of their parents and grandparents. Fifty years ago, religious identity was something a young person was born into. It was taken for granted, like racial/ethnic identity, closely related to one's geographic home and shared by people who went to the same schools and participated in many of the same social activities. Over the past few decades, we have come to see religious identity as something we choose for ourselves—even when we choose to take on an identity that is consistent with the traditions with which we grew up. It is the choice of the individual that is emphasized, not the institution and its preferred construction of what it means to be religious. Sociologist Philip Hammond has identified this change as a rise in "personal autonomy," one in which, as sociologist Wade Clark Roof has noted, "the boundaries of popular religious communities are now being redrawn, encouraged by the [religious or spiritual] quests of the large, post–World War II generations, and facilitated by the rise of an expanded spiritual marketplace."[33] Sociologist Robert Wuthnow has further noted the changes in identification that relate to this shift as a move away from religious "dwelling," where we understand religious identity in relation to the social connections found in organizations, toward religious "seeking," as individuals see themselves as the final arbiters of what they will believe and how they will embrace practices related to those beliefs.[34] This has altered even understandings of religious conversions, which occur more frequently during the teen years than at any other time in life. Once an event viewed as a mystical experience beyond rational explanation, conversion is now understood as something that happens as a person tests the faith claims of the new set of religious beliefs, examining how well they fit into the practical experiences of her everyday life while discarding the older beliefs that no longer fit as well.[35]

Amid this reorientation toward the self, religion has become less exclusively associated with the traditions of organized religion.[36] As a result, while attendance at religious worship services was once relatively common, many now view such regular participation as a practice that is optional.[37] One national study of teens who had recently become members of Protestant churches found that 58 percent agreed or strongly agreed with the statement, "An individual should arrive at his or her own religious beliefs independent of any church." Nearly a third in the same study reported that they never read the Bible. It is instructive to note that these findings reflect not the general population of teens, but a group of new church members, or young people we might assume to be *particularly likely* to place an emphasis on the church, tradition, or the Bible as sources of information about beliefs.[38] Teens, like their parents and other adults today, do not seem to be very interested in learning about ultimate truths from authoritative sources like the Bible or religious traditions. They consider *themselves* to be the ultimate authority on what it might mean for them to be religious or spiritual.[39] *How* they assume this authority in the realm of constructing their own beliefs is difficult to measure with standardized surveys, but in-depth interviews and observations such as those that formed the basis of this book may be especially well suited to the examination of how this happens.

While more young people than ever claim to have no religion, there seems to be a growing interest in "spirituality" among them.[40] Yet what do young people understand spirituality to be? Ever since the emergence of the term in the nineteenth century, spirituality has meant something different than, but not altogether separate from, religion as it was more formally and institutionally conceived.[41] As sociologist Robert Wuthnow has argued, practices of spirituality seem to appeal to people because they offer more guidance than institutional religion in the human need to cope with existing challenge.[42] Their appeal is in their seeming practicality and accessibility, particularly in the therapeutic and commercial realms. Spirituality is often articulated as a lifestyle choice, adopted and signified through the purchase of such things as votive candles, weekend retreats, esoteric and self-help literature, and angel lapel pins.[43]

"Alternative" spirituality, a term that first came into use with the many social changes of the 1960s and 1970s, pushed the practices of spirituality even further away from religious institutions, making it possible for more people to claim to be "spiritual but not religious."[44]

CLAIMING A RELIGIOUS IDENTITY

Religion's increasingly individualistic and choice-oriented nature echoes larger societal trends of the late modern era that shape the experiences of today's teens. As sociologist Anthony Giddens has argued in his analysis of self-identity, individuals today are constantly confronted by change and uncertainty, and hence are forced to make conscious choices that affect the direction of their lives. Giddens argues that this is a condition of what he calls a "risk society." For Giddens, risk is a condition of late modern society, and it means more than an increased exposure to new forms of danger. It implies that "no aspects of our activities follow a predestined course, and all are open to contingent happenings." Giddens argues that people must therefore learn to be strategic in their approach to the "open possibilities of action" that confront them continuously.[45] As part of their coming-of-age tasks, therefore, young people need to develop the skills necessary to envision various possible outcomes to their actions. They may believe that they have some autonomy in making their life choices, but these choices often come about as a result of occurrences over which they have no control, such as divorce, job changes or losses, changes in their family's financial picture, or even changes in their family's geographical location.

Among sociologists, there has been a great deal of discussion about how to explain the relationship between identity, individual actions (or strategic life choices), and large-scale social change in religion and society. One promising approach focuses on how culture is like a "tool kit" of habits, stories, and worldviews for the individuals who live within it.[46] This theory argues that in order to live competently in everyday life, individuals must assemble certain patterns of acting, or "strategies of action."[47] These strategies are not completely shaped by either a person's socioeconomic position in society, nor are they the result of an individual's conscious, rational choice-making. Rather, these strategies are shaped by the capacities of the culture in which the individual is located. Ultimately, people choose to do things less because of the perceived ends they are trying to achieve, and more out of an often taken-for-granted understanding of how things should be done. People acquire this sense of how things should be done mostly as a result of their relationships with other people. This, in turn, has a lot to do with where they are located socioeconomically, geographically, and in terms of such categories as age, status, gender, racial/ethnic group, and so on.

In this view, culture is the store of public symbols and stories that flesh out and reinforce these taken-for-granted understandings of how things should be done, making those strategies of action seem sensible—even meaningful to people.[48] In fact, as Giddens has pointed out, what is important is not that a person consciously finds an appropriate response to a given situation, but that any response allows a person to "keep a particular narrative (of identity) going."[49] In other words, we know who we are by our location in relation to the strategies of action we adopt and identify with. As sociologist Nancy Ammerman writes, "Agency is located, then, not in freedom from constraint but in our ability to invoke those patterns in non-prescribed ways, enabled in large measure by the very multiplicity of solidarities in which we participate."[50]

Identity is understood as the way in which we adopt certain strategies of action to maintain a connection with others, with our past, and with our own aspirations. It is also constructed in relation to how we articulate these strategies in the form of narratives that are meaningful among different social groups. Identity construction is an ongoing process guided by the need each of us have to consciously make sense of our choices, and the often unconscious ways in which these choices create a form of social solidarity with (or distinction from) others. Identities emerge, as Ammerman argues, "at the everyday intersections of autobiographical and public narratives. We tell stories about ourselves (both literally and through our behavior) that signal both our uniqueness and our membership, that exhibit the consistent themes that characterize us and the unfolding improvisation of the given situation."[51]

What makes a particular identity narrative "religious" has to do with how "'religious' actors, ideas, institutions and experiences play a role in the story of who we are and who I am," Ammerman writes. She argues that an identity narrative takes on a religious dimension when it invokes an experience of transcendence or a sensed connection with what she terms a "Sacred Other."[52] These references can be explicit to one's own actions or experiences with a Sacred Other. Yet there can be implicit references to a Sacred Other as well, since "experiences of transcendence have been institutionalized in rituals, stories, moral prescriptions and traditions."[53] Thus, religious narratives of identity may include stories of direct personal experiences with a Sacred Other, as well as practices that are "recognized as religious" because they have been handed down through a religious tradition that recognizes transcendence. They may draw upon language and narratives from religious traditions, or they may be drawn from other publicly available narratives. What is worth noting is that this definition of religious identity is not based in any presumed relationship between affiliation and identity narratives. Moreover, there is no assumed religious "core" related to religious affiliation that is either affirmed or challenged by external forces. Instead, Ammerman writes, religious narratives come into being in the context of conversations where people discuss "whatever unpredictable Sacred experience they recognize in their midst," using whatever resources are available to them at the moment. To understand religious identity narratives, therefore, we need to abandon our categorical assumptions about affiliation and look instead at the dynamic processes of these conversations, recognizing that religious identity narratives may not fall neatly into conversations about religious traditions, nor may they be limited to private or personal domains.[54] This means that every identity narrative of religion has the potential to include references that are personal or public, sacred or secular. Religious identity narratives need not include references to transcendence, and certainly they may not reference the supernatural realm—but on the other hand, under certain circumstances, they might.[55]

Certainly, religious organizations supply some of what might be called the "public narratives" of religion, and they give a certain legitimacy to certain stories and practices while delegitimizing others. The point, however, is that the individual sees himself or herself as the authority over what is to be considered "religious" or "spiritual"—and these definitions sometimes include beliefs and practices that might be surprising to those who anticipate a more direct connection between institutional religion and a "religious" or "spiritual" identity.

RELIGIOUS IDENTITY AND THE MEDIA

The "culture as tool kit" model underlying the theories of Ammerman, Swidler, and others has gained in popularity because of the way it challenges two inadequate theories of individual action, belief, and identity narratives that preceded it. First, it offers a correction to approaches that have tended to reduce the actions and beliefs of individuals to "interests" predetermined by their socioeconomic position in society. Second, it attempts to counter the assumption that beliefs and values are primarily what shape a person's actions or choices for identity narratives.[56] It suggests instead that actions need to be understood in relation to practices, or habits—not only those of the individual, but those shared by many because they are consistent with ways of seeing the world that we take for granted.[57]

For religious groups and the parents who are affiliated with them, part of the appeal of the "culture as tool kit" approach is more practical. It suggests that cultural products might play an important role in socializing young people into faith traditions. In the past few decades, more and more religious organizations have sought to contribute to the "cultural tool kit" of their specific religious tradition by modeling products after those available in popular culture. Some products, like the popular WWJD bracelets ("What Would Jesus Do?"), are worn by teens as a means of reinforcing their identification with Christian evangelical teen culture. Other similar products, referred to as "resacralized," reinforce the distinctiveness of a particular religious group's identity, offering alternatives to materials available in the broader culture while in some cases reinforcing lessons about that group's traditions.[58]

The weakness of the "culture as tool kit" metaphor, however, is that it can focus our attention too heavily on individuals as actors who "use" elements of culture to solve problems or construct identities.[59] This allows us to think of culture as somehow separate from us instead of something that might better be described, as cultural theorist Raymond Williams has written, as the "relationships between elements in a whole way of life."[60] There are elements of culture, after all, that we cannot control or use to our individual advantage, just as there are questions of culture's relationship to existing power structures that get overlooked if we focus only on individual uses of cultural products.[61] How culture participates in the continuation of racism, unjust labor arrangements, and other inequitable social practices has been an important area of consideration for critical theorists of culture.[62] These theorists remind us that culture is more than simply a set of rules, habits, and artifacts. It is a "structure of feeling," a historically patterned collective identity that is ritualized and celebrated through its religions and rhetorics. To understand a culture, we must explore how its people express what they value, recognizing that such expressions often emerge unconsciously. Popular culture's narratives, like those of its religions, often embody meanings that its members cannot bring themselves to express.[63]

Of course, U.S. culture is increasingly commodified. We live in an era where "feelings are for sale," as historian Walter Kendrick points out.[64] A sophisticated set of entertainment industries exists to elicit excitement, fear, and titillation in exchange for profit. Because of this, what U.S. culture considers important—both the values it consciously recognizes and those that reside in the collective unconscious—are often expressed on a film, television, or computer screen. Films, as well as television programs and other forms of fictional entertainment, offer satisfaction because they symbolically resolve conflicts that are deeply troubling to our society. They offer these resolutions within stories that seem familiar, for the stories are told within the conventions of recognizable genres (horror, science fiction, gangster, and others in film; and in television, the melodrama or sitcom). As film critic Judith Hess Wright notes of genre films: "These films came into being and were financially successful because they temporarily relieved the fears aroused by a recognition of social and political conflicts. . . . Genre films produce satisfaction rather than action, pity and fear rather than revolt. . . . When we return to the complexities of the society in which we live, the same conflicts assert themselves, so we return to genre films for easy comfort and solace—hence their popularity."[65] We are not conscious of these conflicts, or of the way that films, television programs, and other forms of fiction resolve them. Yet these entertainment media—particularly the horror genre and its variations—express a societal unease. This unease is often related to the perceived crisis in masculinity, the contradictions of capitalism, or the disparate and contradictory ways of problem solving in late modernity (one based on rational science, the other based on faith and tradition).

Horror is an interesting genre to consider, therefore, both for its relation to teen culture and in some cases even the crises of religion. Both horror and religious stories express an "anxiety of metamorphosis," as cultural critic Edward J. Ingebretsen writes, a fear of possession and the loss of self, and a sense that little can be known with certainty—especially when it comes to death and the realm beyond.

Once they entered the mass media beginning in the nineteenth century, the stories and symbols that are the basis of much in the horror genre that I will refer to as the "dark side of evangelicalism"—stories of evil, demons, and apocalyptic battles—were themselves changed. They took on their own lives as referents for other stories that do not have targeted religious outcomes in mind. This is because they contain elements that may be dramatic and highly entertaining, and thus their use extends beyond the pedagogical goals of religious conversion. Moreover, as they are incorporated into stories that speak to unresolved contemporary conflicts, these narratives come to be about more than religion. They may still be a resource for identification, but with their prevalence in media culture, the connection between these cultural products and their usefulness becomes a highly contested issue. Attempting to use cultural resources in the purposeful construction of religion and religious identity narratives therefore forces us to struggle with the relationship between religion and commercialism, and between religion and entertainment.

TEENS AND THEIR LIVES AT HOME

This is a generation that some claim is defined by its interest in spirituality.[66] Yet this is also a generation defined by alienation and high school shootings, increases in sexually transmitted diseases, heightened awareness of terrorist activities, and prominent hate crimes based in prejudices of racial/ethnic identity and sexual orientation. Add to these the perennial concerns of teen pregnancy, delinquency, and drug and alcohol abuse, and the heightened attention to young people and their safety is highly understandable.

As a result of these concerns, parents often encourage young people to be at home, either with their siblings or with a small number of peers. In this context, home-based media, including television, personal computers with Internet access, video games, "home theater," and stereo systems become an important yet not completely unproblematic alternative for young people's leisure time.

Courting and cultivating the lucrative youth market has been an important part of the work of the media industries for decades. In recent years, however, the desire to appeal to teens has become even more intense. This is because today's teens represent the largest demographic group of young people ever—even surpassing their parents' generation, the baby boomers.[67] A large amount of disposable income jingles in the "echo boom's" pockets as they visit the malls, music stores, Internet sites, and theaters near their homes.

Even with the increasing importance of the Internet in teen culture, television and films remain the two most prevalent media forms in teen life. For young people, the rise of home theater systems built around video rentals, cable movie channels, and pay-per-view has made movies as pervasive to home life as television has been for decades. Two-thirds of all U.S. children aged two to eighteen watch at least an hour of television a day, and more than a quarter of U.S. "tweens"—those eight- to thirteen-year-olds who are just entering adolescence—watch five hours of television or more each day. In contrast, only 5 percent of the same age group spend an hour or more online.[68] Of course, some of the most popular Web sites for this age group are those dedicated to

FIGURE I.2

Among the 17 million teens who are online, the top three most popular uses of the Internet include sending e-mail, surfing the Web for fun, and visiting entertainment sites. Photo by Sofia Sellers.

popular teen films and television, thus pointing again to the importance of visual media in the lives of young people. In fact, the top Web site at the turn of the millennium, according to the youth- and young-adult-oriented magazine *Yahoo! Internet Live,* was dedicated to Sarah Michelle Gellar, star of *Buffy the Vampire Slayer* (figure I.2).[69]

Because teens are an audience with significant spending power and leisure time, they are appealing to the advertisers who provide financial support for television programs, radio, films, and Web sites, among other things. Thus, as the avenues for the delivery of entertainment materials have proliferated in recent years and as increased competition has created niche markets for media designed to appeal to specific audiences, entertainment designed especially for teens has also gained a stronger presence in the media marketplace. The 1980s were marked with the beginning of MTV and the rise of the Fox network; the 1990s saw the proliferation of the World Federation of Wrestling, the emergence of hip hop, and the inauguration of the WB Network; and the new millennium has ushered in cell phones, instant messaging, and several new forms of "reality" television programming designed to attract younger audiences.[70] At the same time, we have seen an increase in the number of television programs, films, and Web sites dedicated to issues of the supernatural and paranormal—long popular topics for the plots and subplots of teen culture stories.

A great deal of evidence suggests that the media play an important role in how young people form and articulate their identities. Young people learn

FIGURE I.3
Teens talk about their interest in media as a way of expressing both their individuality and their shared tastes. Photo by author.

from and identify with characters they watch and with celebrities they admire.[71] Their choices for media consumption have a lot to do with the identifications they hold according to their participation in different racial, class, gender, and friendship groups.[72] Teens make selections from the media that they believe fit with their own "style." They share their interests in media with their friends as a means of expressing both their own individuality and their shared tastes (figure I.3).[73] This sharing then informs teens' individual tastes, as well, for the two processes of using the media in individual and collective identity construction reinforce one another.

Based on research into the role of media in identity formation, we would expect that there would be different approaches to media based on how important religion or spirituality is to young people, but little research has demonstrated what those approaches might be.[74] Research on adults who identify themselves as Southern Baptists, fundamentalists, and conservative evangelicals has noted that the most involved members of these groups are interested in seeing themselves and their views as quite distinct from what they see in the mainstream media, even as they believe that their religious worldview informs what and how they consume materials from the entertainment realm.[75] Drawing such lines of distinction is also an important aspect of group identity for other religious groups, including conservative Jews and the fast-growing population of Sunni Muslims in the United States.[76] In chapter 6, I discuss some of the young people and their parents I interviewed whom I term Traditionalists, seeking to provide more insights into how this approach emphasizing distinction and separation from media (and from U.S. culture more generally) informs teen interpretations of the supernatural.

Still, many teens do not fit within the more traditional subcultures of religious beliefs and practices. Do the stories of the supernatural have anything to do with how these young people and their friends think about religion? According to the stories of alien belief cited at the beginning of this chapter, this certainly seems possible. Given the significance of the entertainment media in the lives of teens, it's worth exploring what teens mean when they identify themselves as religious, and what such identifications might have to do with what they see, hear, and consume in the media.

METHODOLOGY AND AN EMERGING THEORY OF MEDIA AND RELIGION

There are limits to the "cultural repertoire" that cause some actions and beliefs to seem unfeasible, even while others are taken for granted as the "common-sense" approach. What we need to do, and in fact what this book attempts to do, is explore further what some scholars term a historical materialist understanding of culture and its relationship to individual action. We must look not only at how young people approach cultural materials, or at how artifacts and practices of culture tend to articulate certain ways of seeing the world over others in ways that tend to benefit certain groups and positions over others, although both of these are important steps along the way. Ultimately, we need to consider how cultural products—and specifically, what is presented and accepted as taken for granted within them—are related to, and offer support to, the social practices and social relations in the contemporary world (practices and relations that themselves have histories).[77] We will then be able to understand young people's "strategies of action" not as the result of rational decision-makers, but as the actions of persons who are located in relation to others in a network of historically and economically specific social relations.

We will come to better understand the context in which young people find themselves through an analysis of contemporary American religion and its expression (both overt and indirect) in popular culture. In the following chapter, I argue that one of the reasons we seem to see stories of the supernatural everywhere these days is the ascendance of evangelicalism. I argue that when evangelical Protestants have attempted to use popular culture for their own ends, they have met with mixed results. Extending back to the writings of Jonathan Edwards, there has been a long tradition of using horror to introduce those they refer to as the "unchurched" to the gospel. Ultimately, I argue that despite their clear intentions, evangelicals are unable to control how the stories of hell and demons—the "dark side of evangelicalism"—are interpreted or used by others for the purposes of entertainment and profit. The cultural position of the stories of the dark side of evangelicalism is further illustrated in chapter 3, where we turn to the specific issue of contemporary supernatural stories in teen media. Exploring the way in which religion was articulated in the popular teen television series *Buffy the Vampire Slayer*—ambiguously, with infrequent yet often humorous references to formal religion—enables us to better understand the cultural environment and its assumptions, which shape how teens make meaning about the entertainment they consume, and possibly also about spirituality and religion, and the place of each of these in contemporary society and in their own identity narratives.

Understanding how teens claim a "religious" or "spiritual" identity is best understood through an examination of rich identity narratives. For this reason, the data for this book were collected using a method of in-depth repeated interviewing of young people by themselves, with their families, and, when possible, among their friends. There were 269 people interviewed, 100 of whom were teens.[78]

I wish to mention a few important points that shaped this book. First, when I began my interviews with teens and their parents, they focused on representations of religion in popular culture and on religious identity. As the research evolved, experiences with the transcendent and with the supernatural, along with representations of these through stories in the entertainment media, came to the forefront in conversations. The relationship between these things eventually became the centerpiece of inquiry. Second, the research project's design was informed by my experiences with young people, which began long before the formal interviewing stage. Before embarking on this project, I spent more than a decade serving as a volunteer with various educational, civic, and religious organizations in the northeastern, midwestern, and southwestern parts of the United States, tutoring and/or mentoring young people of varied racial/ethnic and socioeconomic backgrounds. These experiences provided me with anecdotal evidence of the importance of the supernatural and paranormal within teen culture, the centrality of the media in their identity narratives, and the relatively respectful if distant relationship many teens had with organized religion. My prior experiences both enabled me to gain the trust of the parents of teens (important in obtaining consent to interview minors) and helped me to foster relationships with the teens themselves. I also conversed regularly with others who were knowledgeable about the day-to-day lives of teens. This included not only researchers, but also parents, junior and senior public high school teachers, church and synagogue youth group leaders, teens and young adults who had served my family as babysitters, and the teens I interact with daily in my own neighborhood.

While those interviewed were not selected completely at random, they encompass a diversity that mirrors that of the general U.S. population.[79] They included persons of varying socioeconomic and racial/ethnic backgrounds, families led by a single parent and parents who were either married and sharing a household, divorced, remarried, or same-sex partners.[80] The level of commitment to religious organizations among teens and their parents ranged from high to marginal to none.

In this study, I defined teens broadly, as those between the ages of eleven (technically, preteens) and approximately twenty-one.[81] I wanted to explore the group that included junior high students and young persons up until the age when they left the home of their parent(s), either for college or for military service, or to live on their own with a spouse, friends, or their own children. Most young people at this age spend a great deal of time with their peers, in school and in peer-related activities. Yet most also live in a home with a parental figure of some kind. The people interviewed for this study reflect some of the changes in family life noted earlier, and all interviewed have experienced these changes indirectly through their peers and extended family members, if not in their own homes.

All of those interviewed were living in the southwestern part of the United States during the time of their participation in the study. People from western and southwestern states tend to have more interest in and acceptance of mysticism and other spiritual alternatives than people from other parts of the country.[82] According to national surveys, they are also more supportive of individualistic approaches to religion.[83] There is a lower incidence of religious affiliation in this part of the country than in the southern, midwestern, or northeastern regions.[84] This means that even those in my study who identified themselves as religious would be more likely to interact on a daily basis with those who did not share their interest in or experiences with organized religion.

The Southwest has also been the fastest-growing part of the United States in recent years, with many people, from younger high-tech workers to older retirees, migrating from other parts of the country and the world to its urban centers, some bringing their religious commitments with them. Migration has long been associated with departure from traditional religions. In our increasingly mobile society, the youth discussed might be seen as a bellwether for trends that will continue to blossom in other parts of the country. The geographical concentration on the Southwest, while limiting the generalizability of the study (indeed, it would be difficult to claim generalizability based on such small numbers), may have made it easier to locate young people who consider themselves spiritual or religious outside a formal or regular commitment to religious organizations.

Employing the analysis of data generated from in-depth interviews and observations with teens, their friends, and their family members, supplemented by national survey data when possible, this book suggests that there are at least five different ways in which young people approach and incorporate what they learn from the media into their beliefs and practices related to religion and spirituality. First, there are young people who view the media and religion as completely distinct from one another. This group includes the growing two extremes of young people: those who are very committed to their religious tradition, and those who make no claim of a religious identity at all.

In the first group, I found young people who echoed the concerns that evangelicals and others have voiced about the "secular" nature of American culture.

They believed that their tradition, and the morality they believed it supported, was in danger of being undermined by what they took to be the powerfully negative and seductive influences of the entertainment media. This is how media—traditionally viewed as an unquestionably secular realm—entered into their discussions. While many of the young people I refer to as Traditionalists spoke of a need to see their tradition as separate from the entertainment media, some claimed that they were able to view the entertainment media through a lens of faith.[85] This made it possible for them to enjoy the media without personally changing their views in ways that they believed it changed the views of others. In a sense, they believed that their religion inoculated them against the media's negative effects.[86]

The other group of young people who assumed that the media had nothing to do with religion had little interest in religion. "There's religion in *The Simpsons*?!," one such teen asked incredulously. When it was pointed out that several *Simpsons* episodes include references to baptism, sin, churchgoing, and even prayers to God, this teen—and others who made similar objections—expressed views that ranged from skepticism to mild interest.[87] For these young people, religion rarely surfaced as an area of interest, and hence any references to religion broadly or narrowly defined had simply flown beneath their radar screens.

When these young people were questioned about whether entertainment programs of the supernatural were of interest to them, differing responses emerged. This was also the case for those who described themselves as somewhat interested in religion or spirituality. Four different patterns of media interpretation emerged.

First, there were the Resisters, introduced in chapter 3. These were teens who might be expected to fall into the secular camp. They were not only uninterested in organized religion, but in fact they expressed a certain amount of vehemence toward it. This did not mean that they rejected all things supernatural or spiritual, however. These teens made some of the boldest and most intriguing statements of belief, such as equating God with aliens. Were they more influenced by the media than their peers, or are there other explanations for why they chose to embrace such seemingly idiosyncratic approaches to the supernatural realm? We look at the question in light of the stories of two Anglo-American teens, one male and one female.

In chapter 4 we review the stories of young people who, like the Resisters, have no interest in organized religion yet are familiar with it. The teens in this chapter unconsciously embrace stories and beliefs that are related to organized religion's historical relationship to Sacred Others, and for this reason I call them the Mysticals. We hear the stories of three teens: an Anglo-American female, an African American female, and an Anglo-American male, all of whom have had some previous experience with conservative Protestantism, abandoned in their childhood. The different racial/ethnic backgrounds of the teens discussed in this chapter give us an opportunity to reflect on how these differences play a role in the interpretation of such stories and their relation to alternative spiritualities.

Chapter 5 describes teens who, like the Mysticals and the Resisters, are highly interested in the realm beyond. These teens, the Experimenters, took these interests a step further, trying out different ways of tapping into the supernatural realm. One of the interesting things about these teens is that each identifies with a religious tradition and, perhaps surprisingly, attempts to relate their experiments with the supernatural realm to those traditions. Of all of the teens interviewed, they come closest to the "seekers" described by Wade Clark Roof and others, as they are the only ones who seem to consciously seek experiences with the supernatural realm out of a process of religious and self-identity construction. The chapter includes the stories of three teen girls: a biracial Native American/Anglo-American mainline Protestant and two Anglo-American Wiccans. Because this is the only chapter that features the voices of teen girls exclusively, I also address the relationships between gender and the appeal of the supernatural.

In chapter 6, I discuss the Traditionalist young people and their parents, seeking to provide more insights into how this approach emphasizing distinction and separation from media (and from U.S. culture more generally) informs teen interpretations of the supernatural. Employing case studies of a biracial Arab American/Anglo-American Muslim teen boy, two evangelical Anglo-American teen girls, and an Anglo-American Mormon teen boy, the chapter explores the question of whether teens who expressed a serious level of religious commitment were at all interested in supernatural beings, powers, or practices. In particular, the chapter looks at the tendency of these young people to be guided by an overarching concern with personal morality that framed their understandings of religion and of the media.

Chapter 7 then turns to teens who were highly committed to their religious traditions, yet were intrigued by the realm represented in the legends of the supernatural. How do such teens, whom I call the Intrigued, negotiate between these different traditions, especially in light of the clear distinctions articulated by the teens of chapter 6? Were they less aware of their traditions, confused by differing stories, or more open than the Traditionalists to the possibilities of the realm beyond that were presented in the media? How is this blurring of the sacred/secular boundary to be understood? In this chapter, we meet an Anglo-American female from mainline Protestantism, an African American male affiliated with conservative Protestantism, and a Mexican American, Catholic male.

None of the chapters of teen stories deal explicitly with so-called secular teens, or those who expressed no interest in either religion or the supernatural realm. There are several reasons for this omission. First, there was evidence that some teens, such as the Mysticals and Resisters, might characterize themselves as secularists under certain circumstances. Each of those chapters addresses the interesting examples of young people with no interest in organized religion who nevertheless embrace supernatural stories—and who also use language that may be characterized as referencing spirituality or traditionally "religious" categories. These chapters problematize the easy equation of secularization with a lack of religious affiliation, and more fulsome discussions of this issue are raised there. Second, while I found teens who seemed uninterested in the supernatural realm and in religion, I also interviewed a number of teens with varying levels of commitment to religious organizations who were not interested in mystical or spiritual concerns at all. No clear pattern emerged that distinguished the teens in these two groups. Part of this may have been due to the limitations involved in the methodology. Many young people and their parents know that stories of the supernatural are delegitimated, as noted earlier. They may not have considered such interests worth mentioning, and they may have opted not to share those interests with a researcher. I therefore chose to focus only on young people who expressed interest in the religious, spiritual, or supernatural realm or who actively resisted it, and must leave those with little interest in it to future research.

The final section of the book addresses areas that might be called contextualizing issues in the relationship between young people, the media, and their beliefs. In chapter 8, I look at the extent to which parents intentionally approached the media in relation to what they hoped to teach their teenage children about religion and spirituality. I note that what parents emphasize in the media-religion relationship grows out of how they define religion to begin with. Is religion primarily understood in relation to its formal institutions, the morality it is believed to support, its therapeutic potential, its possibilities for civic engagement, or its existential questions of ultimate meaning and purpose? Using data from three focus groups of parents of teens, I note that parents differed on their approaches to the media according to the perspective on religion they adopted. I then discuss two very different expectations that emerged regarding the media: the sense that the media should raise social issues for some young people, and the expectation that the media provides viable role models for others. I explore these two approaches in relation both to earlier discussions of religion and the supernatural and to the socioeconomic backgrounds of these families.

In chapter 9, I foreground issues of class and taste, employing analytical frameworks suggested by social theorists Pierre Bourdieu and Antonio Gramsci. In particular I explore the possible relationship between lower socioeconomic status and a preference for certain supernatural stories, such as those of aliens. I use case studies of two families from somewhat different socioeconomic positions to highlight the appeal of aliens among both families, and then I draw comparisons between aliens, with their delegitimated status in relation to the broader culture, and angels, with their acceptable and even elevated or inspirational status.

The book concludes by reviewing themes that have emerged, including a discussion that presents a theory of what I term "the religion of the possible." I consider the role of media in religious change and the context of religious pluralism. I question how active young people are as religious meaning-makers, offering a plea for a better understanding of the limitations on this activity. I offer some conclusions about the book's observations, along with a review of what I believe are its implications for those who work with young people today.

I have not written this book in an effort to provide the definitive word on teenage spirituality, supernaturalism, or the role of the media in religious or spiritual formation. This work is meant to be provisional and provocative rather than definitive and comprehensive. I am hoping this book may help you consider the relationship between teens, their beliefs, their role in society, and their love of entertainment media so that together we can better understand this intriguing relationship and work to address some of its implications for all of us.

1
ANGELS, ALIENS, AND THE DARK SIDE OF EVANGELICALISM

"Allure of the Occult!" blares a headline for one evangelical publication.[1] Another evangelical magazine, focusing on television programs that appeal to youth, such as *Buffy the Vampire Slayer, Charmed,* and *The X-Files,* proclaims *Buffy* to be "one of the most popular occult-based programs on television."[2] An authoritative-sounding Web site, offering film reviews that claim to "tell you the truth about the content of popular entertainment," says of *Lord of the Rings: The Fellowship of the Ring,* "This movie is likely another maneuver to capitalize on the new found infatuation of visually oriented youth with bright and dazzling display of the occult, witchcraft and evil."[3] In a similar vein, an earnest pastor offers these words of warning on his Web site: "*Pokemon* and *Harry Potter* have the right . . . methods to ease children in to the occult."[4] Through an impressive network of pulpits, popular magazines, newsletters, Web sites, and word-of-mouth communication, today's evangelical Christians are expressing a great deal of concern about what they view as the harmful influences of popular culture on the beliefs of young people. Many of these critics have suggested that today's youth-oriented supernatural thrillers are entirely unprecedented.

In a certain sense, these critics are right. Over the course of the past decade, commercial entertainment media outlets have discovered that stories of the supernatural that include young characters in leading roles, from *Lord of the Rings* to *Buffy the Vampire Slayer,* hold widespread appeal with youth and among older audiences, as well. However, these programs and their audiences did not materialize out of nowhere.[5] Teens have long been interested in stories and practices that have to do with the supernatural. And by the same token, leaders in religious organizations, notably within Christianity, have long been concerned about these interests and their representations in entertainment. What may be relatively new is the relationship of these teen-oriented programs and films to increasingly public evangelical concerns about the practices of esoteric religions, including those now called "New Age" (positive thinking, miraculous healings, mind/body connection) as well as those defined as "occult."[6] In many circles, "occult" has become synonymous with "satanic," thus making the current complaints about teen supernatural fare all the more dire.

It took me quite a while to realize how very important evangelicalism is to the question of the ascendance of interest in the supernatural in the contemporary United States. Yet despite the evangelical insistence upon the dichotomy between orthodox religious beliefs and fictional stories of the supernatural that highlight witchcraft, demon possession, and gruesome death scenes, the latter might not have existed, or at least not gained widespread popularity, without the former. How outraged can evangelicals be that young people enjoy the gory *Scream* horror movies or the frightening scenes in *Lord of the Rings*, after all, when teens can witness a reenactment of the Columbine High School shootings at the Abundant Life Christian Center's Halloween Hell House? Horror, as religious and cultural critic Edward J. Ingebretsen has pointed out, has long been a part of the Protestant tradition, marshaled for the purposes of encouraging moral fortitude among the faithful.[7] Little wonder that contemporary American writers, filmmakers, and television producers are able to extract intriguing, grotesque, and fearsome material directly from the country's religious heritage.

Despite the increasingly plural nature of religious life in the United States, "religion" is still often equated with Protestantism, and in recent decades, with Protestant evangelicalism in particular. It is important to consider, therefore, the way in which the writings of American Protestantism gave a very specific frame of reference to the topics of evil, hell, the Rapture, and, more generally, the realm beyond this world. More recently, evangelicalism's acceptance as a legitimate religious identifier, combined with an increasingly sophisticated understanding of the media, placed its concerns in the public imagination. To understand the contemporary attitudes toward the supernatural, we must understand evangelicalism's role in bringing such matters to the fore, and hence their role in providing some of the "publicly available stock of symbols and narratives" that are incorporated into the entertainment media.

EVANGELICALS AND THE RISE OF INTEREST IN EVERYTHING FROM ANGELS TO ALIENS

I am aware that the claimed relationship between the rise in interest in the far-out aspects of the supernatural and the success of evangelicalism itself is counterintuitive. After all, evangelicals are the ones who voice such strong objections to Ouija boards, tarot cards, witchcraft, and the rest. How could they be responsible for the growth in such interests? Evangelicals are not responsible for this growth, at least not directly. In part, I think the interest in the supernatural is related to increasing concerns about evil throughout the last decade of the twentieth century and the beginning of the twenty-first. The shootings at Columbine High School and in other schools across the country brought questions of evil close to home for many young people. These questions became even more urgent and widespread with the tragedies of September 11, 2001. What could cause people to participate in such horrendous, intentional acts of harm toward others, we wonder? We have all been forced to grapple with the fact that there are no easy ways to answer or address ourselves to this question. This is a deeply troubling frustration that becomes recast in our popular culture. Often, the deepest concerns of our culture are expressed in popular cultural forms. While the media do not provide us with answers, they do provide the comfort and satisfaction of resolving problems at a symbolic level that cannot be so easily addressed in "real life."

Evangelicalism has not provided the cause for our concerns with evil, but due to the often unacknowledged connections between culture and the religious heritage of the United States, evangelicalism has inadvertently provided a framework for thinking about and representing evil in popular culture. Evangelicals have long been concerned with the pervasiveness of evil in the world, and with the belief in a transcendent God who will eventually triumph over evil. Evangelical traditions, like other groups' traditions, are therefore seeking not only to fight evil, but to *define* it. As evangelicals have gained an increasingly strong presence in public life, their concerns have in turn received more attention.

But even as concerns about evil and the realm beyond become more widespread, evangelicals are not in control of how these concerns will be understood or addressed.[8] This has in fact been a long-standing problem for Christianity, for of course the question of evil has always been a concern for humanity. In the seventeenth-century writings of the preachers Cotton and Increase Mather there is evidence that religious leaders were concerned about the way laypersons were using amulets to ward off evil spirits.[9] The Mathers' writings were widely read and provided a moral indictment against occult practices—as well as perhaps the most detailed description available concerning how such practices might be engaged. Historian Jon Butler has argued that, contrary to the assumption that Christian values and beliefs largely defined early American culture and that witchcraft was confined to Salem, occult practices were widespread in the colonies. As evidenced by the Mathers' repeated warnings of the dangers of occult practices, New Englanders, as well as Pennsylvanians and Virginians, often drew from the occult as well as from Christianity when confronted with issues of ill health, misfortune, or "evil intentions."[10] Preachers like Mather were influential in their communities, but they were often frustrated by the way that the faithful failed to limit their practices to those prescribed by the faith.

Concerns about unexplained evil in the world continue to find resonance with many people, far beyond the evangelical fold. Even in this supposedly postmodern era, when all claims to authority and truth are increasingly questioned, people still experience terrible things.[11] No matter how ironic or playful we may seem in other avenues of our lives, when truly bad things happen to us, they occur in ways that are deeply personal. Evangelicalism, like other religions, offers explanations for why terrible things happen in our world, relating it to the ubiquity of evil.

Of course, we don't always consciously seek explanations for terrible events that occur in our lives. We want things that will help us guard against evil, things that offer protection and support when we are in the midst of them. Rituals, prayers, novenas, and other devotions do this. Evangelicalism and other religious traditions not only offer explanations for why evil occurs but also suggest that practices such as prayer can help us through the worst of it. Religious practices thus have some talismanlike functions. We hold onto them both as a means to solidify our connection with the good and with God, and to distance ourselves from the inexplicably bad. For many, religious communities and their practices offer a sanctuary against evil, a haven of security in a world filled with uncertainty. This ability to claim allegiance with the good becomes central to contemporary religious identity narratives of people from all age groups, encompassing the desire to act ethically, the wish to respond faithfully, and the practices that become meaningful as one is faced with the reality of evil in everyday life.

Religious communities, of course, use different language to talk about why they participate in rituals and prayers. Most believers would emphasize that there are important differences between their practices and those that rely on things like charms or crystals in the attempt to ward off evil. Asking God for grace and protection as part of a faithful life is not the same as doing certain things in order to cause grace and protection to come to us.[12]

But at least for some, the lines between these things may not be so clear. Some religious communities, such as Pentecostals and fundamentalists, have historically emphasized that supernatural power is available for all believers because of faith, and that power may be expressed in miraculous manifestations of the Holy Spirit. Thus, there is a sense in which individuals, believing that they are claiming access to a holy power, are able to bring about healing or prophesy, for instance. Moreover, while believers may see vast distinctions even between these practices and those deemed superstitions, the differences may not be quite as apparent to those who are outside these religious traditions. Thus, while there may be real differences, these may be obscured in the eye of the beholder.

I can give an example. Years ago, when I was a volunteer with young people at a moderate Presbyterian church in conservative western Pennsylvania, a controversy broke out over this very issue. Gail, a sophomore in college who had been attending a Pentecostal church before joining the Presbyterians, was a fellow volunteer working with young people. Gail became concerned that Jessica, one of the girls in the junior high group, was suffering from some sort of satanic influence. Gail decided that the best course of action was to engage Jessica in a ritual and prayer at Jessica's house. Jessica agreed, hoping that such a ritual would help her to avoid participating in activities that tempted her, such as smoking and getting sexually involved with her boyfriend. Gail decided to anoint Jessica's room with oil so as to ward off any demons and reclaim the space for God. Finding no oil in the house, she settled for the Crisco she and Jessica found in the kitchen cupboard. Jessica's mom arrived home from work a short while later and found Gail on a ladder, holding a cross in one hand and smearing Crisco on the oak moldings around the door to her daughter's room with the other. Jessica's mother was outraged and asked Gail to leave immediately, while Jessica first cried, then stomped away and slammed the door—and refused to talk with anyone about what had happened. Jessica's mother stormed to the church, angry that this youth volunteer had involved her daughter in such a strange and exotic ritual. She demanded an explanation from the pastor. The pastor of the church tried to assure Jessica's mother that Gail's intentions were good. But he also decided it was probably best for Gail to find another church for which she could volunteer. While Gail's ritual may have seemed appropriate in some (although not all) Pentecostal churches, it was clearly viewed with suspicion and alarm in the context of a sister Protestant congregation. What looks like a sincere and faithful response to one can look an awful lot like superstitious, strange, and even possibly dangerous practices to another.

These kinds of practices are not embraced by many who would claim to be evangelical. In their identity narratives, most evangelicals today stress the literal interpretation of the Bible and connect its interpretation with a certain code of morality that has political dimensions. Thus, evangelicals are often active in the fights against legalized abortion, pornography, and civil rights for gays and lesbians while supporting prayer in public schools and programs such as vouchers that provide financial support for private church-related or "Christian" schools. Despite the fact that many in the United States disagree with these stances and challenge them on ethical and moral grounds, evangelicals have successfully defined each of these as moral issues, and acceptance of them as such is widespread throughout their constituencies.

I believe that evangelical definitions of evil began to gain such credence in the 1970s and 1980s in part because of this increased political presence. But a second reason relates directly to the supernatural concerns of this book. Evangelical Christians see themselves as engaged in a battle of good versus evil on this earth; evil is a real presence that must be resisted by the faithful at every turn. With its emphasis on a battle against evil, evangelicalism holds a great deal of appeal for persons who are alienated or distanced from other faith traditions. This may be one reason for its growth. It also provides a reason for why its categories of evil and the "End Times" continue to provide taken-for-granted frameworks that often are found in popular entertainment and even news stories.

The way evil is understood in the United States has a great deal to do with the country's evangelical heritage and its continuing importance in the lives of many people. Consider how mentions of evil, and specifically the Devil, abounded in the wake of the World Trade Center tragedy of September 11, 2001. This specifically Christian way of understanding evil was frequently offered in news and commentary and was presumably widely accepted. Such definitions were often presented as unquestioned, and even unquestionable.[13] This is an example of a taken-for-granted framework rather than a consciously sought explanation concerning evil's existence in the world.

EVANGELICALISM AS A DOMINANT STRAND IN THE RELIGIOUS LIFE OF THE UNITED STATES

Today, evangelicalism is suffused throughout mainstream U.S. culture. Not only are evangelicals a recognized presence in the political arena due to their sophisticated lobbying and grassroots mobilization efforts; they are also present in local public school battles over curriculum and prayer, and they increasingly have a place at the table in discussions both public and private. Evangelicals can certainly believe that they are "winning": more people know about their tradition and about their concerns. This sets up a certain tension within evangelicalism. On the one hand, the movement relies heavily on its identification as a beleaguered subculture. Evangelicals readily complain about the secularism that surrounds them and about the discrimination they believe that they and fellow believers suffer. Yet on the other hand, there is a great deal of evidence to suggest that religion, and evangelicalism in particular, is not only accepted but is in fact close to the expected norms of our society, and that evangelicalism is an important supplier of America's "cultural tool kit."[14] Certainly, the president of the United States must declare his respect for Protestantism, if not his allegiance. Billy Graham, one of the founding leaders of American evangelicalism, is widely viewed as the "nation's pastor," having prayed with every U.S. president since Truman. It was no accident that when former President Bill Clinton admitted his "inappropriate relationship" with Monica Lewinsky, he did so at a prayer breakfast—and he later asked a group of evangelical ministers to serve as his "spiritual advisors." But consider more recent examples, such as the fact that all of the major television networks and newsmagazines in the past few years have offered fare similar to Peter Jennings's 1997 ABC special report, *The Search for Jesus*. Or the popularity of Stephen Carter's book *The Culture of Disbelief*, which affirms the need for more, not less, religion in public life, asserting—in agreement with the evangelical position—that religion is to be equated with virtue, a force for moral good.[15] Moreover, religious depictions in prime-time television have experienced a fivefold increase in the last decade. CBS's *Touched by an Angel* ranked in the top ten of the most-watched programs for more than five years, and the WB Network's teen program about a minister and his family, *7th Heaven*, served as that station's flagship for ratings shortly after its initial launch.[16] In the last few decades, we have even witnessed business leaders like Stephen Covey advocating an active spiritual life as a key to business success, while alternative and country music regularly highlighted religious subjects. Even a recording of Gregorian chant, featuring the monks of the Santo Domingo de Silos monastery, became a chart topper that signaled for many a growth in spirituality among young people.[17]

While these examples are described as being about religion, they are actually focused rather narrowly on the U.S. Christian experience, and in most cases the specifically Protestant version of it. With this level of acceptability, those who identify with evangelicalism are bound to find it increasingly difficult to draw distinctions between that religious tradition and the culture in which it finds itself.

EVANGELICALISM: DEFINITIONS AND DISTINCTIONS

Contemporary evangelicalism is somewhat difficult to define, for it comprises nearly as many varieties as there are groups that identify themselves with its label. At least 20 million Americans identify themselves as evangelical. Some estimate that as much as 40 percent of the U.S. population would identify with at least four of the key beliefs associated with this movement. These include the idea that humans are sinful and therefore in need of personal salvation; the belief that Christians are charged with bringing others to the faith through evangelism; the belief that the Bible is inspired by God, free of errors, and is a primary source for teachings about morality; and the belief in the Rapture, or the Second Coming of Jesus Christ that will mark the end of time.[18]

Fundamentalism is a historical predecessor and important subgroup of contemporary conservative Protestantism, although it does not share fundamentalism's strong separatist traditions. Despite their differences, the fundamentalist roots of contemporary evangelicalism are still influential in how evangelicals think about the supernatural and the realm beyond this world, and about the popular media that so often portray them. Two beliefs in particular are relevant here: the End Times and the Second Coming, and the ongoing supernatural battle between God and Satan or, more generally, between good and evil.

THE END TIMES AND THE APOCALYPSE

Most fundamentalists assert that we are living in the End Times, meaning that the Rapture might occur at any time. Dramatic prophecies concerning the end of time have been the basis for many sermons that sought to persuade people of the urgency of conversion to Christianity. This urgency figures prominently on the numerous contemporary Web sites devoted to End Times prophecies. On one such Web page, titled "The Second Coming of Jesus Christ," the following line is boldfaced, underlined, and flashing: "It is time to prepare the Bride for the Second Coming of Christ!!"[19] The page urges Christians to recognize that the day of the End Times is fast approaching, offering suggestions on how to prepare for the event. On another page, www.virtualchurch.org, a writer presented several arguments for why he believed the End Times would begin at the turn of the millennium. The author first noted several world events that seemed to him to correspond to the Bible's prophecies and thus indicate an imminent apocalypse. He also defended his right to offer a prediction (this is a debated issue within fundamentalism, as Scripture asserts that no one knows the day or hour of Christ's return). He then offered five stories of angel appearances that had been told to him. In each case, the angel appeared as a stranger (hitchhiker, loiterer, etc.), made a pronouncement about the imminent return of Christ, and then disappeared.[20] The author argued that these visitations, too, were evidence that the End Times were quickly approaching. He had even thought about those who would not be taken up with Christ in the Rapture, offering a link titled "A Letter to Those Left Behind." Unfortunately, however, on the day I visited the site the link was broken. I certainly hope the writer fixes that link soon, before he is raptured away.

While I might make light of the lost link, there is a tremendous earnestness that accompanies concern about the End Times among the faithful of all ages. Young people who accept these views are anxious that their friends, like them, learn what they believe is the truth about the need for salvation, and they discuss the Rapture with great urgency. As one teen wrote on a prayer chat board at a site called Teens Living for Christ: "I ask you all to please pray for my friend J. Ferry. She's a sweet girl and she believes that when the Rapture comes, she's not gonna make it with Jesus. I know that with everyone's help, we can get all of our friends to make it. With strength and courage and God on our side, I know we can do it!!"[21] In a language that combines team spirit, issues of self-esteem, and a fervent belief in the power of prayer, this young person expressed a concern for others' souls in a way that would warm the hearts of many in today's conservative Christian circles.

End Times predictions extend as far back as Christ himself, who told his followers that "this generation will not pass away" before his return (making this one of the passages fundamentalists interpret as cryptic and metaphorical rather than "literal," since they believe we are still awaiting his return).[22] During most of the twentieth century, the imminence of End Times has been a reigning idea within conservative Protestantism and among fundamentalists in particular. But at least since the 1925 Scopes trial, when William Jennings Bryan famously won courtroom approval for the fundamentalist views of creationism, the battle of public opinion has been lost. After that time, fundamentalists were increasingly viewed by the press and other cultural leaders as marginal, and in response, fundamentalists viewed the larger culture as hopelessly apostate. They needed to separate themselves from the culture in order to stay morally pure and thus ready for the coming apocalypse. This strategy was only confirmed for fundamentalists in the many social upheavals of the 1960s and early 1970s, when the civil rights movement, the women's movement, protests against the Vietnam War, and Watergate all challenged traditional views. If the End Times meant chaos and the feeling that traditional values were under siege, then those who deplored the revolutions, even those not inclined toward fundamentalist religious belief, were now finding common ground with fundamentalists.

But even as fundamentalism's claims to besiegement seemed to find resonance among those who identified with counterrevolutionary views, the cultural ground for fundamentalist and evangelical Christianity began to shift. Fundamentalism appealed to those actively opposed to the social revolutions of the past decade, as well as to those seeking clearer answers in the wake of those changes. Fundamentalist and evangelical ranks swelled, and their institutions of higher learning, grassroots protest organizations, publishing houses, televangelism, and parachurch organizations experienced parallel growth. The press began to take notice of this shift with the election of Jimmy Carter as U.S. president, naming 1976 the "Year of the Evangelical." While Carter did not govern according to the interests of what was to become the Moral Majority that brought Reagan into office four years later, this emergence of religion into public consciousness did introduce (to the press, politicians, and believers themselves) the idea that conservative Christians were a politically important constituency.

This emergence of evangelical political and social power coincided with an interesting development in beliefs regarding the End Times. Among other things, religious leaders who voiced evangelical traditions argued from a much more optimistic viewpoint than that of the separatist fundamentalists. They felt that God was working through contemporary believers to redeem the world. Thus, while they still believed in the Rapture, attention was more clearly focused on bringing the nation into alignment with Christian values. This, moreover, fed into an existing emphasis within some segments of fundamentalism that saw the United States as playing a special role in God's plan to evangelize the world. Rather than separation from that world, therefore, "infiltration" became the watchword, particularly for evangelicals. Evangelicals sought to insert their views and themselves into the "secular" worlds of national and local government at the legislative and judicial levels. They organized sophisticated lobbying efforts. They ran for membership on public school boards and sought to influence curricular issues at that level. They offered training programs and support groups for evangelicals seeking to work in the business world, and even in Hollywood. All of these efforts were deemed important, part of the Christian's responsibility to bring about God's reign at the end of time.

THE END TIMES AND EVANGELISM

Like their fundamentalist counterparts, therefore, evangelicals await the Rapture. But rather than interpreting its story as a reason for withdrawal from U.S. culture, they were drawn to its potential for evangelism.

The evocation of horror has long been a strategy for conversion among conservative Christians, and the dramatic narrative of the End Times makes a riveting story. While fundamentalists and evangelicals take it as a literal interpretation of the biblical accounts, its appeal also stems from its entertainment value. It has elements of human drama and futuristic imaginings, a battle between good and evil, horrific consequences for some, and a happy ending for the "good guys." It is a story that evangelicals believe might convince the "unchurched" of the urgent need for salvation (and might caution the faithful against backsliding). For this reason, the apocalypse has been a topic of great interest among Christian filmmakers and fiction writers seeking to communicate the Christian message.

One of the most important premillennial films in evangelical circles was and continues to be *A Thief in the Night*, produced by Mark IV Pictures, Inc., and directed by Donald W. Thompson (figure 1.1). Originally released in 1973, the story of this film centers on a married couple. While the man becomes a born-again Christian as the result of a brush with death, the wife remains in her theologically liberal church, despite the many clues in the film that Christ's return is imminent (and the implication that what fundamentalists would define as a casual affiliation with Christianity is not enough). One day, she awakens and finds that her husband is gone; the radio is reporting strange disappearances while the electric shaver her husband had been using is buzzing in the sink where he left it. The plot that unfolds is increasingly terrifying and consistent with premillennialist visions of Tribulation. A worldwide government appears, and all the people remaining are admonished to have the mark of the beast placed upon their skin. When the woman refuses this, she is denied food and betrayed by her friends. Running frantically from a helicopter that searches for her, she is finally trapped, slipping downward into a pounding waterfall. Suddenly, she awakens from the nightmare. But the opening scene happens again: upon arising from her bed, she hears the radio reports and discovers her husband's shaver, abandoned in the sink.

The film, dubbed into three different languages and subtitled in many others, saw a resurgence in popularity with the increased presence of the VCR in the homes and churches of the 1980s and 1990s. It was followed by *A Distant Thunder, Image of the Beast*, and *Prodigal Planet*, all by the same production company, all further dramatizing the story of Tribulation that the fundamentalists believe is foretold. Despite their age, these films have retained their ability to draw audiences. Twenty years after its initial release, the original version of *A Thief in the Night* was named as the best-selling Christian video for the years 1990–95 on lists compiled by *Christian Bookstore Journal*, and it continues to have strong sales and rental receipts. *A Distant Thunder, Image of the Beast*, and *Prodigal Planet* also remained among the top ten best-sellers during those years.[23]

A Thief in the Night was seen as a watershed for the Christian entertainment industry as it combined drama with production values that, while low budget, mimicked those of Hollywood. Recent films such as *The Omega Code* (1999)

FIGURE 1.1
With its suspenseful plotline and successful distribution, *A Thief in the Night*, released in 1973, marked an important turning point in the use of film entertainment among evangelicals. Reprinted with permission from Russ Doughten Films, Inc.

and *Left Behind: The Movie* (2001) were based on books that achieved best-seller status among Christian bookstores. Both films were well received among Christian groups despite poor critical reviews. *The Omega Code* raked in $12.5 million at the box office, while *Left Behind*, released on video prior to its theatrical release, sold 2.5 million copies by the date of its theatrical opening and was 2000's best-selling independent video.[24] Churches received advance notice of the commercial release of both films, and many participated in their active promotion among congregations, in parachurch organizations, and through Internet list-serves. Young people in the fundamentalist and evangelical folds were encouraged to bring their "unbelieving" friends to these films as a way of bringing them to salvation, out of the fear that they, in the title of the best-selling Christian apocalyptic novel series and the 2001 film of the same name, might be "left behind."

Apocalyptic films and fiction achieved great success at the turn of the millennium, no doubt assisted by the many prophecies of history's imminent demise. At some churches, these films were shown in the aftermath of the September 11, 2001, attacks, ostensibly to give an interpretation of world events in light of conservative Christian beliefs. Some, like Jerry Falwell, drew connections between the real-life horror and the predictions of the apocalypse. The producers of the sequel to the film *The Omega Code* even decided to release their story within a week of September 11, 2001, a move that cost them dearly in terms of poor critical reviews and criticisms for poor taste.

SATAN, DEMONS, AND THE EXPERIENCES OF EVIL

Along with the apocalypse, one might say that Satan has enjoyed a resurgence of popularity in recent years, as well. This is a little more surprising, for from the 1950s into the 1990s, while Satan was still a concern for fundamentalists, others in the Christian fold had abandoned their interest in such discussions in favor of other things. Commenting on modernism's role in eliminating superstitions from contemporary life, for instance, one writer noted in 1951: "For the most part, orthodox religious groups are emphasizing the importance of character development and there are fewer references to theological abstractions. We no longer believe that our misfortunes are due to malevolent spirits or that our neighbors are practicing satanism. Except in remote communities, demonology and witchcraft survive only as lore, and the spirits and goblins of the past are remembered only at Halloween festivals."[25] Talk of Satan had become one of the marks of separation that was consistent with Protestant fundamentalism but presented a problem for the emergent evangelical movement and its interest in infiltration and transformation. This situation changed with the entertainment industry's introduction of Satan in contemporary fiction and horror films of the 1970s.

In 1971, the best-selling book *The Exorcist*, followed three years later by the groundbreaking movie of the same name, introduced the Roman Catholic practice of exorcism to a wide and diverse audience. This film gave a public platform to practices that had been previously considered marginal in several religious traditions but that had recently gained ascendance within the Pentecostal deliverance movement. At the same time, psychotherapy and the self-help movement were achieving greater acceptance, and Christian counseling emerged as a movement within these. The idea of Satan's presence in the world, especially through demon possession, no longer seemed so far-fetched. Exorcism and counseling joined forces in the attempt to combat the problem. As one practicing exorcist told a journalist, "In the early days, we would cast out demons, but we would find they would come right back again. The counseling approach gets to the root of the problems."[26]

In the past few years, conservative Christian organizations like Demon Stompers have emerged to offer counseling about possession and exorcism over toll-free phone lines. Radio talk show host Bob Larson began translating his exorcism programs into self-help books, audiocassettes, and videotapes. For $69, you could order his three videos on demons and their removal, titled

The Six Entries of Evil, The Six Strongholds of Satan, and *The Six Ways Demons Dominate.*[27] Consistent with the Pentecostal emphasis on the religious author-ity that is available to all believers, these tapes ostensibly allow any practicing Christian to do what had previously been reserved for the experts. At the same time, the Roman Catholic Church quietly increased the number of authorized exorcists in the United States, and a number of seminaries began discussing how to deal with the issue. At Fuller Theological Seminary—one of the flagship evangelical schools for ministerial training—exorcism is related to the concept of "spiritual warfare," the battle between good and evil that is believed to be a product of living in the End Times.[28]

Pentecostals, fundamentalists, and evangelicals believe that the End Times will usher in a battle between God and Satan. Fundamentalists believe that the battle is taking place today, and the earth itself is the battleground. Thus, they believe they must remain separate from the world and its influences, as we are living in "Satan's territory," as one fundamentalist explained to an interviewer.[29]

Evangelicals also believe that there is a battle going on in the world, but they tend to describe it instead as a clash of ideologies between a Christian and sec-ular worldview. The battle itself is no less urgent, however, for evangelicals fear that their right to live as they desire is impinged upon by the secular control op-erating in public institutions such as the government and public schools. As one Presbyterian man said:

> There are two opposing views, a Christian worldview and a secular world-view. And one is going to be crowded out and denied their freedom to live by the standards they hold to. They might say "Well just leave us alone," but the thing is they won't leave the Christian community alone. They are impinging on us. There is a war going on, and when you're in warfare, you battle to take ground, not just to hold it. They're not just trying to hold ground, they are trying to take ground, which is our right to live in a Christian society. There are a lot of people that would deny us any rights. They aren't passive, they are active.[30]

While evangelicals distance themselves somewhat from the fundamentalist talk of Satan, they do acknowledge that Satan is responsible for the tempta-tions that must be overcome as individuals seek to live a morally upright life. Many also share with fundamentalists the concern about evil supernatural forces at work in today's world, particularly in the face of inexplicable tragedies. This was the focus of an analysis of the shootings at Columbine High School in *Christianity Today.*[31] Four of the shooting victims in that tragedy were evangelical Christians, including Cassie Bernall, who was said to have answered yes when one of the killers asked her, "Do you believe in God?" Cassie's story has held special resonance for evangelical teens and was report-edly a model for role-playing in youth groups around the country. When faced with the inevitable question of why this horrific event occurred, the author of an article in *Christianity Today* cited a student who had been in the Columbine library, where several students had been injured and others lost their lives. The student said, "There was like—I don't know if I can explain it very well—but like a spiritual battle you could feel going on. As soon as the killers came in you could feel evil in the room. Yet, I also felt God's presence, or maybe it was just angels, also with me in the room." Another described the killings as "the work of Satan," while the author described the teen killers Dylan Klebold and Eric Harris as "at the epicenter of evil, totally disconnected from their community, [from] their families, [and from] the Author of all that is good." According to this evangelical account, evil entered the world, taking the form of two teenage boys armed to the teeth. Whether or not Satan is named, evangelicals believe firmly in the power of evil. But they also believe emphatically that good will triumph in the end.

SATAN, EVIL, AND HELL HOUSES

The reality of evil in the world, like the apocalypse, can and should be marshaled for purposes of evangelism, according to contemporary evangelicals. The story of Columbine was written and performed as a morality play at the Victory Fellowship Church in a suburb of New Orleans. Titled *Beyond the Grave: The Class of 2000*, the play reenacts the shootings with the use of video, special effects lighting and makeup, and pulsating music. Although the play had its beginnings as a one-weekend alternative to Halloween in 1999, the performance was drawing more than a thousand spectators a week for months afterward and was still being presented every Friday evening two years later. In 2000 and 2001, the cast took the play to various churches around the country. With its high school setting and a script that personified the tensions between preps, geeks, Goths, and Christians, the production held special appeal for young people. Each performance ended with an altar call and an invitation to join in a full-immersion baptism.[32]

The idea of a confrontation with evil as a means to introduce the gospel to nonbelievers was also behind the so-called Hell Houses that began to emerge as a part of the evangelical response to Halloween in the 1990s. Earlier, organizations like Campus Crusade for Christ, along with other civic organizations, had held haunted houses as holiday fund-raisers, offering a popular program for young people in their communities. Organizations may have passed out tracts at the tour's conclusion, but that was largely the end of the evangelistic efforts.[33] In the 1990s, however, evangelical and Pentecostal ministers began to see Halloween as an occasion to carry a more potent message to the "unchurched." In 1995, Keenan Roberts, an associate pastor of the Abundant Life Christian Center in a suburb of Denver, packaged and sold a seven-scene morality play he'd begun two years earlier, which he had called *Hell House*. Each room of the Hell House features a scene that depicts the negative consequences for teenagers involved in sin. Drunken teens die in a fiery car crash. Others die in gang-related shootings, by suicide as a result of incest, in an abortion clinic, or of a drug overdose at a rave party (as shown in figure 1.2). And most controversially, a homosexual teen dies of AIDS. Similar attractions have

FIGURE 1.2

Teens practice a rave party scene at Abundant Christian Life Center's Hell House. Demons tempt a young woman to take drugs, and she dies of an overdose. Photo by Ahmad Terry. Reprinted with permission of the *Rocky Mountain News.*

appeared across the country, going by such names as "The Nightmare," "The Judgment House," and "Heaven and Hell House." In the last room, an actor portraying Jesus Christ emerges from the tomb and offers participants an opportunity to accept Christ. Volunteers are then available outside to talk with those who are interested.

The dangers evoked are "real," as those involved emphasize, and this is why these events have evangelical potential, particularly for young people. As one youth minister who volunteered at such a house in a Los Angeles suburb noted, "Just being scared for the fun of it doesn't do anything but give you nightmares. Proverbs says the fear of the Lord is the beginning of wisdom. What we want them to do is to start thinking about life."[34] And about death, apparently, for the message these organizations communicate is that Hell and Tribulation are the consequences of not accepting Christ. This is an old message for fundamentalists, who have long been known for their sermons of hellfire and brimstone. But it is new to an audience from the more mainstream traditions of contemporary evangelicalism.

Hell Houses are part of a larger trend within evangelical, Pentecostal, and fundamentalist churches that has begun to change the connotation of Halloween from a harmless night of ghosts and goblins to a night connected to the Devil. Some churches even go so far as to urge young people to avoid trick-ortreating, arguing that Halloween is not a Christian holiday and therefore should not be celebrated. While Hell Houses offer evangelical churches a way to introduce young people to the urgent need for salvation, other churches offer "Harvest Festivals" or other events meant as alternatives to Halloween. The effect is the same, however: Halloween now serves as a dividing point between believers and nonbelievers, but for evangelicals the urgency centers on the reality of evil, rather than of Satan, in this world. It is now the task of evangelicals not only to boycott the holiday themselves, but to alert others to its dangers and to use its evil connotations as a tool for evangelism.

EVANGELICALISM'S DARK SIDE
AND POPULAR CULTURE

Evangelicalism's emergence as a cultural force has, to an unprecedented degree, placed the concept of the battle between good and evil on the public agenda. Once concerns with evil entered the public imagination, evangelicals could no longer control how people chose to respond to the evil that many agreed existed. It was not only the responses that could not be controlled, however. While evangelicals have long recognized the potential for evangelism in film, filmmakers have similarly seen the entertainment possibilities in the stories of evangelicalism's dark side.[35] Thus, while evangelicals and other conservative Christians may feel that stories and images of supernatural battles between good and evil in some sense belong to them, they cannot control how these stories will be used, and reconfigured, once they enter the realm of the media—and particularly the entertainment media.

Stories of the End Times may have been popularized recently with the rise of evangelicalism, but the ideas go back to the roots of Christianity. While conservative religion has employed the narratives of the End Times in the context of updated images and story lines, the images most often used in popular cultural representations of the End Times—notably, those of demons, hell, and the afterlife—date to medieval depictions such as that of Pieter Bruegel the Elder (figure 1.3). At that point in history, religious scholars were devoted to explanations of the supernatural realm that they believed was very much a reality. As scientific knowledge increased in the age of the Enlightenment, however, cosmological definitions fell out of favor in both formal theology and in religious artwork. The fictional depictions of demons and hell found in popular culture therefore visually refer to the point in history when the "truth" of supernatural beings was very much a part of Christian orthodoxy. Yet as Max Weber argued, with modernity the world became "disenchanted": people no longer viewed the world as a place where spirits and forces freely roamed.[36] The unexplained mysteries that were once ascribed to the supernatural realm had increasingly come to be the subjects of scientific debunking. Supernatural wonders were transformed into vehicles of amusement, repackaged as entertainment for the skeptical yet curious urban public of the nineteenth century.[37]

FIGURE 1.3

Pieter Bruegel the Elder, *The Fall of the Rebel Angels*, 1562. Reprinted with permission from the Royal Museum of Fine Arts, Brussels, Belgium.

Some instances of the contemporary borrowing and reconfiguring of religious elements in popular culture are more obvious than others. One recent example of this appears in a popular computer game, Diablo II. When this game first hit the stores in July 2000, it sold 184,000 copies in a single day and sold more than a million by the end of its first month.[38] On the Web page devoted to this game, the following origin myth is offered:

> Since the beginning of time, the forces of Order and Chaos have been engaged in an eternal struggle to decide the fate of all creation. That struggle has now come to the Mortal Realm . . . and neither Man, Demon, nor Angel will be left unscathed. In Diablo II: Lord of Destruction, you will return to follow the path of Baal, the last of the Prime Evils, into the Barbarian Highlands of the North. Travelling with hordes of demonic minions, Baal intends to corrupt the powerful Worldstone, which protects the whole of the mortal plane from the forces of Hell. You will face a new series of quests and challenges to prevent the vile minions of the underworld from destroying the world of sanctuary.[39]

Demons, hell, and of course Diablo and Baal all draw upon what we have identified as the "dark side" of evangelicalism. Here, preteens are invited to participate in a role-playing spiritual battle in the realm of entertainment. They seek to defeat evil beings in a battle that, despite its Christian overtones, makes no reference to Christian categories that are central to evangelicals, such as Jesus Christ and personal salvation.

Of course, evangelicals are savvy to the appeal and entertainment value of evangelicalism's dark side, as well. A company that competes with that of Diablo II's creators is called, appropriately enough, Eternal Warriors. They released their computer game, The War In Heaven, a full year earlier than Blizzard Entertainment's Diablo II. Like Diablo II, The War in Heaven engages young people in a first-person, role-playing battle, complete with rapid-fire gunfighting and hand-to-hand combat.[40] The game Archangel, released in 2001, while it is less violent, is another variation on the theme, allowing young people to participate in the battle against Lucifer while adopting different characters.

While many in evangelical circles see a clear difference between Diablo II and its evangelical competitors The War in Heaven and Archangel, the distinctions may not be so obvious to all. As noted, the imagery and narrative share some distinct similarities. Moreover, all of these games are available for purchase on eBay. Christian gaming discussion groups, newsletters, and magazines devote far more time to discussing GameBoy, WarCraft III, and Diablo II than The War in Heaven or other "Christian" games. Some on Christian gaming discussion groups even make it a point to claim the more popular games for evangelism purposes. As one fan writes, "If you're like me, a Christian that enjoys Dungeons and Dragons and other RPGs [role-playing games], you've probably talked to friends and gotten a response like, 'D&D? Isn't that satanic?' It's my opinion that that is not inherently true. This club's purpose is to meet other Christian RPG players and talk of ways to get Jesus more into the game to reach our fellow gamers, as well as other gaming topics."[41] The young man who manages the site on which this statement is posted seeks to lay claim to games like Dungeons and Dragons, transforming them into vehicles for evangelism. For him and for others in evangelicalism, Dungeons and Dragons is not so far removed from A Thief in the Night: both are vehicles that may open the door to the presentation of a salvation message for unbelievers. But of course, there are many in evangelicalism who are at least as interested in drawing distinctions between what is truly consistent with the faith and what is not, and for whom popular culture is itself a battleground. This is illustrated by the following exchange on an AOL Teen Chat site called CyberChristians.

"Seven was awesome," wrote Sarah of the commercially released murder mystery/horror film Seven, which starred Brad Pitt and Morgan Freeman. In full, she wrote: "Seven was awesome it was about the 7 deadly sins. It got pretty nasty in parts, though! It is a must see. If anybody out there has seen it I would love to talk to them about it." Her statement was answered within a half hour with the following not-so-subtle rebuttal:

Sarah,
Seems like we're talking to each other a lot ha? I didn't see "7" and don't plan to. The reason why is because it's full of all the things I'm trying to stay away from. Mainly "sin," which is what it's based on ironically. Just be

careful what you recommend—sometimes we lead each other astray in things and don't even know it. I guess, if you could picture it—do you think you could bring someone young to a movie like that and expect them to shrug off those things? Probably not. That's why it's rated R, so younger minds won't be subject to that stuff. Take a look at Romans 1:28–32—it basically lists off all those things that are in that movie. God lists those as bad. I'm a fan of movies, don't get me wrong—I just don't want to see people being spiritually brought down through the things we hold as good. Look also at 1 Corinthians 8:9–13.

In his Grace, Rob

Unconvinced and undeterred, Sarah replied to Rob the next day:

I do not think there is any thing wrong with the movie 7. It really explains why you should not perform these sins or other sins. Although I do not believe that the language they use is appropriate the movie in general is good. I really think you should give the movie a second chance it is not as bad as most people think. Please write back I would appreciate it!

Peace, Love and Christianity, Sarah[42]

Sarah asserts her own evangelical interpretation of this commercially released film. Like the Dungeons and Dragons fan, Sarah claims that the horror film *Seven* could alert people to the harrowing consequences of a sinful life. As such, it holds potential for evangelism. She underscores her own religious commitment both in her recognition that the language may be "inappropriate," as well as in her new signature line: "Peace, Love and Christianity." In this way, she identifies herself as an "insider," on the same side of the "battle" as Rob is. Yet despite Sarah's closing invitation, Rob chose not to reply.

The argument between Rob and Sarah echoes the tensions in evangelicalism, and in other parts of Christendom as well, that make it difficult for adherents to decide how to view popular culture. The entertainment media often borrow stories and elements from Christianity. Whether or not they value its potential for evangelism (and some actually do), they clearly value its ability to entertain and hence to draw audiences and profits.[43]

Recently, similar discussions about films highlighting the supernatural have divided adherents within Christianity. The films *Harry Potter and the Sorcerer's Stone*, *Harry Potter and the Chamber of Secrets*, and *Lord of the Rings: I and II* have each been fertile areas for the discussion of the role of story, myth, and supernatural powers in relation to faith and practices. Some evangelicals and fundamentalists, like those cited in this chapter's opening paragraph, view these recent films as highly troublesome. As one evangelical wrote on a listserve devoted to the discussion of media, culture, and religion: "The Potter books . . . are based on the practice of witchcraft as a way of life. It's very dark stuff, sweetly packaged."[44] The problem, according to this writer, is that the Harry Potter books and films assume that witchcraft is good or at least benign, and evangelicals take the supernatural realm far too seriously to dismiss these things lightly. Others within the Christian fold may have been similarly convinced of the reality of evil and of supernatural powers, yet they remained unconvinced that a fictional film could influence peoples' beliefs and practices. "As far as the book being a kiddie manual for witchcraft," wrote one youth minister from Australia, "I suspect that we'll see about as many serious attempts from kids to get into witchcraft as we saw attempts from kids to fly around England on giant peaches in the seventies. Kids actually understand imagination." Clearly, this position is more trusting of the largely preteen audience, a group that has been often acknowledged as highly sophisticated with regard to the entertainment media. A third position stems from the second, arguing that there are ways to view the films metaphorically, connecting them with the values affirmed in young people's own religious/spiritual traditions, whatever those might be. Such popular cultural stories like *Harry Potter* and *Lord of the Rings* might be used as, in the words of one young woman, "entry points to discussions about life, meaning, spirituality, etc." She writes of *Lord of the Rings*: "The corrupting power of the ring for even the best of intentions [is one such entry point that raises questions, such as:] Where do I find the strength for resisting corruption exhibited by Gandalf and Galadriel? When might I be in danger of becoming ensnared by the desire for power like Borimir? What can Borimir tell us about Judas and ourselves?" In this way, she offers an illustration of how popular cultural texts can be interpreted through a lens of faith or tradition. This stance rests upon the assumptions that viewers interpret fantasy as fantasy, that there are many possible interpretations for media symbols and narratives, and that young people might reaffirm their own traditions and beliefs as they learn to apply this lens to all popular cultural texts. Affirming this position and that of Sarah (the *Seven* fan), some have argued that such "reframing" of cultural materials is actually a sign of religious vitality.[45] Many, however, were uneasy with the centrality of supernatural power, witchcraft, and sorcery depicted in both *Harry Potter* and *Lord of the Rings*.

RELIGION AND THE INSTRUMENTAL USES OF THE MEDIA: AN AFTERTHOUGHT

As I have noted, evangelical Christians have sought to harness the power of the media for their own ends, with mixed results. The desire to create popular cultural references that reinforce religious beliefs is not limited to evangelicalism, however. One of the most unusual of such products comes in the form of religious board games. To those outside a particular tradition, games such as *Redemption* and *Chicken Soup for the Kids' Soul* may range from the unusual to the downright absurd. In a review offered by Beliefnet.com, one can learn of games such as *Kosherland*, which has a *Candyland*-like board that requires children to recite prayers while learning the rules of kashruth (being kosher), or *Leela*, a Hindu-based game for adults (which comes complete with a 133-page instruction book that covers the Theater of Karma and the Fundamentals of Being). Roman Catholic "tweens" can play *Communion of Saints*, in which they receive credit for praying the rosary and lose credit for daydreaming during Mass. Beliefnet.com's reviewers of this game had some reservations: "Players were surprised at how close a death square was at every turn, even in the very early stages of the game. As one player poetically noted, 'The grace and sin cards would have more of an impact if we didn't die so quickly.' Another agreed, saying, 'I wanted to sin and go to hell just so the game would last longer.'" My favorite preteen game, however, was *Left Behind: The Game*. Based on the book and film that have been enormously popular in evangelical Protestant circles, the game has players competing to bring about the Rapture and defeat the Antichrist by answering Bible trivia and truth-or-dare, or through the performance of "Tribulation" tasks. Players of the game roll for themselves and also for the Antichrist. When this game was put to the test by reviewers at Beliefnet.com, one reviewer, identified as a "non-Christian," felt that it was "kind of weird that the Antichrist was chasing us around, and all we could do was run and bribe him [with tokens]."[46]

Religious groups of all kinds have been attempting to emulate popular culture artifacts and entertainment stories in their efforts to add to the cultural "tool kit" available to their young constituents. They have realized the value of viewing cultural products as markers for identity and have sought to make products look like they come from Hollywood—at the same time that the products of Hollywood and other commercial ventures continue to draw upon ever new variations and combinations of religious beliefs and representations. Religion imitates and borrows from popular culture, which in turn imitates and borrows from religion. This is an important aspect of the relationship of religion and culture as both exist and are shaped by the highly commercialized context in which they find themselves.

CONCLUSION

The evangelical approach to the supernatural in popular culture reflects broader contradictions regarding culture that are inherent to evangelicalism. Contemporary evangelicals inherit a separatist impulse from their fundamentalist heritage, yet they want to infiltrate the culture as a way to transform it. Thus, evangelicals tend to view the culture as something that they are not completely a part of: "We are in the world but not of it," as a popular Scripture verse says. Aspects of culture, even from their own store of beliefs, are therefore viewed in a somewhat utilitarian way: they can be helpful when they can be marshaled for evangelism's purposes and are to be eschewed when they cannot. Offerings from the entertainment media, a large concern given the amount of time young people devote to them, are viewed in much the same way: they may be helpful when they introduce potential converts to the Gospel, but they can be a dangerous distraction when they do not. Evangelicals therefore resist media views and representations that appear to them to be unorthodox, particularly when they stem from individuals who have marginal or no ties to evangelicalism. Such concerns go to the heart of the discussion about whether the music of U2, Jars of Clay, or even Amy Grant in her "crossover" (and recently divorced) status should be considered Christian music. Today's evangelicals apply the same test to people like Brenda Hampton, who produces the teen-oriented WB Network's popular and highly moralistic program, *7th Heaven,* and J. R. R. Tolkien, author of the *Lord of the Rings* books.

When I began writing this book, I at first avoided evangelicalism altogether. I wanted to study people who were not evangelicals, because I thought this was where I was most likely to find instances of interest in the supernatural realm, and thus I could come closer to explaining why there is such a fascination with it at this point in history. Eventually, I came to see that evangelicalism, with its resonance in contemporary U.S. culture, has introduced a concern about evil and has largely defined the terms of the conversation about evil and the realm beyond this world. Due to the cultural power evangelicalism has had over the past few decades to define what it means to be religious and to be moral, I eventually realized that what I was really studying was how young people who *are* and *are not* evangelical respond to this public face of evangelicalism. Among those who do not identify completely with evangelicalism's claims as outlined here, there seems to be a range of ways for identifying themselves as religious, often by drawing upon alternate discourses of religious beliefs and practices. On the other hand, some young people distance themselves from evangelicalism as a way of distancing themselves from religion. I found that it was impossible to talk about anyone's interest in or rejection of religion without recognizing the extent to which evangelicalism has permeated U.S. culture and become mainstream. Evangelical frames of reference, in fact, seem to structure the way that people experience and identify with religion today, which is surprising given the increasing religious pluralism of U.S. society.

The contemporary impulse to draw a line in the sand between Christian and secular, or authentic and demonic, is part of a very long tradition, and young people have always been right at that line. They are the center of concern for those who would preserve the traditions because teens challenge that line in ways more visible and more permanent than other age groups. These challenges have been encoded in popular culture that appeals to teens, as we will see in the next chapter.

TOUCHED BY A VAMPIRE
NAMED ANGEL

THE SUPERNATURAL

IN CONTEMPORARY

TEEN POPULAR CULTURE

I don't know who sent me. They don't speak to me direct. I get visions—
which is to say great splitting migraines that come with pictures; a
name, a face. I don't know who sends them. I just know whoever sends
them is more powerful than you or me. They're just trying to make
things right. . . . It's not about fighting and gadgets and stuff. It's about
reaching out to people, showing them there's still love and hope in this
world. . . . It's about letting them into your heart. It's not just about
saving lives, it's about saving souls.
—Premiere, *Angel*, WB Network

Is this a speech from one of the angels in the popular CBS melodrama television program *Touched by an Angel*? Perhaps an excerpt from the popular evangelical book series and film *Left Behind*, or words from a fictional Billy Graham
film on conversion? None of the above. This dialogue came from the series premiere of *Angel*, the WB Network's hit melodrama spinoff from *Buffy the Vam-*
pire Slayer, first aired in 1999.[1] The lines were spoken by Doyle, who, until he
was killed off early in the first season, was the half-demon sidekick to Angel
(David Boreanaz), the over-200-year-old (20-something in appearance) hunky
vampire and erstwhile love interest of Buffy, the Slayer. *Buffy the Vampire Slayer*
and *Angel* were interesting and fresh innovations at the turn of the millennium
that merged elements of melodrama, horror, film noir, and hip teen comedy,
while appealing to teen and young adult audiences across racial/ethnic lines.

These programs were also groundbreaking in the way that they reintroduced otherworldly enemies into popular fictional television after a several-decade hiatus. In this way, they also did something else: they told stories of a spiritual battle between good and evil with an almost complete disinterest in organized religion. On the rare occasions when references to religion surfaced in these programs, they were approached with great ambivalence—echoing the current contradictions among young people who claim to believe fervently in God yet have rather lukewarm feelings about organized religion.[2]

Not many young people would think that the television programs *Buffy the Vampire Slayer* and its spinoff, *Angel,* have anything to do with religion, and certainly the program often doesn't address religion in a direct way as did programs airing in the same era, such as *Touched by an Angel.* In *Buffy* and *Angel,* religion is rarely mentioned overtly, and most people would agree that it is rather preposterous to think that young people might abandon their faiths and come to believe in vampires as a result of watching the program. It is more likely that some young people, hearing criticisms like those mentioned in the previous chapter, might think of such programs as trafficking in the "occult," or at least as a negative influence on young people. These criticisms echo other long-standing concerns about the role of the media in the lives of young people. In the twentieth and early twenty-first centuries, concerns about religious and moral values have often been addressed with reference to the influence of youth-oriented films, television programs, video games, and material available on the Internet.

While it is important to examine the relationship between popular entertainment and religious beliefs, the claim that one directly changes the other denies the way that media tend to reflect cultural values as well as shape them. This is not to say that the media are not influential. Still, we need to recognize that television programs and films are polysemic: that is, they are open to many levels of interpretation, from the obvious and literal to the metaphorical and mythical. The conflicts they resolve on a narrative level stand in for those societal conflicts that are much more difficult to resolve, such as the problem of how to balance the human desire for technological progress with the fact that technology's outcomes may not always turn out as planned (*Frankenstein*); or, from a more overtly conservative perspective, how to live in a tolerant, culturally plural society that requires more sophisticated codes to distinguish between the "aliens" who offer important contributions and those who threaten the society's stability (*Men in Black* and *Men in Black II*). The resolution that occurs on the symbolic level is one reason even the most horrific films and television programs are often reassuring: they reaffirm for us that "no matter how dreadful things look, there really is nothing to fear."[3] Thus, analyzing why certain stories in the media hold appeal, and how they relate to young people's beliefs, involves sorting out the obvious from the inferential meanings and pleasures that young people may draw from popular culture. The intersection of religion with the popular culture that appeals to teens, such as the Buffy phenomenon of the late twentieth and early twenty-first centuries, therefore needs to be viewed in the context of contemporary culture's unresolved conflicts over teenage life in general as well as religion's role in society: a culture struggling between its heritage of evangelicalism's proclaimed certainties and an increasingly plural religious and cultural environment. It also must be understood in relation to a stance of religious relativism that has been a natural outcome of an environment in which spiritual and religious identity are increasingly viewed as a personal choice.[4] Each of these themes is reflected in how religion, spirituality, and beliefs are represented in Buffy and its spinoff, which is what makes these examples so interesting for consideration.

In the previous chapter, I argued that evangelicalism's interest in transcendence and its concerns about evil have inadvertently played a role in popularizing the kinds of stories and myths that traffic in the supernatural and that are featured in teen popular culture. Evangelicalism's emergence as a cultural force has placed the language and symbolism of a supernatural battle between good and evil on the public agenda to an unprecedented degree. In this chapter, I look at religion's coding in *Buffy the Vampire Slayer* and *Angel*, highlighting three episodes and the end of a fourth for closer analysis. I explore how the programs refer to organized religion and to the lore of vampires, how they express a postmodern, relativistic approach to belief, and, paradoxically, how they ultimately embrace a romantic notion still central within Christianity: that of the individual's need for community and her capacity for transformation.

Before turning to the analyses of these programs, I want to note the perils of attempting to write about teen popular culture. Teen culture is nothing if not dynamic, and of course it is at its best when it shocks the adults it often parodies. Once it becomes a subject for a review such as this, it is already an artifact of history and must be approached as such. In other words, by the time a scholar or other adult leader notices it, it must be passé to teens. The television industry faces a parallel challenge: what to do when the teen or teens who are at the center of a phenomenon grows up. I was reminded of these dilemmas while finishing this chapter. I watched as Sarah Michelle Gellar, the star of *Buffy the Vampire Slayer*, was recognized as *Seventeen* Magazine's Role Model of the Year on the Teen Choice Awards television special.[5] Seated with her fiancé, teen heartthrob Freddie Prinze Jr., Gellar rose to take her award among a sea of fans, some of whom were ten years her junior.

Even as its star ages into "role model" status, and her character moves from high school to young adult life and, eventually, a series finale, her television program remains an important point in teen popular culture—especially with reference to the current discussion of the rise of interest in and visibility of the supernatural in teen culture. In addition to its pioneering teen "girl power" approach, the program illuminates changes in the way young people approach religion and the supernatural, while also reflecting concerns about teen life at the time of its popularity.

From its debut in 1997 on the WB Network, *Buffy the Vampire Slayer* was a postmodern mix of the film and television genres that preceded it, drawing upon the imagery and narratives of teen *Scream* thrillers, fantasy television sitcoms, and the ironic, pop-culture-literate, and self-referential style of teen culture staples like *Total Request Live* and the World Wrestling Federation.[6] A spin-off from the movie of the same name, *Buffy* centers around the fight against "real" demons and vampires who serve as a metaphor for the multiple horrors of high school and later young adult life. In Buffy's world, the high school principal may really be a demon seeking world domination, children turn into the demons their Halloween costumes portray, teen runaways age quickly as they travel through a literal hell, and a girl may discover that if she has sex, even her oh-so-nice boyfriend may become a monster.[7] As Buffy's star Sarah Michelle Gellar has said, "We basically just take high school and use horror as the metaphor for it."[8]

Buffy began the television series as a sixteen-year-old transfer to Sunnydale High in southern California. There, Giles (Anthony Stewart Head), the English-accented and tweed-wearing head librarian, serves as her Watcher, charged with training Buffy for her chosen role as the Vampire Slayer. Giles and Buffy's bookish friend Willow (Allyson Hannigan) research the legends behind the various vampires, aliens, and demons Buffy is to defeat, offering clues that complement her training and "natural" expertise in the martial arts. Xander (Nicholas Brendon), a hapless geek who is tongue-tied around his many attractive female peers, is the third member of the initial "Scooby Gang," although others join the cast through the years. Together, they assist Buffy in her mission to kill demons and secure the safety of the town and school.

Media critic Rhonda Wilcox has pointed out that much of the humor of the program turns on the adult misrecognition of teens' "true" wisdom and purposes.[9] Buffy's mother Joyce (Kristine Sutherland) worries that Buffy is bound for trouble, viewing her slaying activities—staying out late, missing classes, getting into fights—as signs of juvenile delinquency. When Buffy's true calling as a vampire slayer is revealed to her, Joyce struggles to be supportive while fretting over the dangers to which Buffy is exposed. The teens and adults also exhibit very different language styles in the program, Wilcox notes. "My spider sense is tingling," Buffy says to Giles, and then apologizes, saying, "Pop culture reference. Sorry."[10] While they sometimes reference other films and television programs, the field of reference is often to elements in contemporary teen culture, thus keeping the program appealing even as its characters age. For example, in a post–high school episode when Xander secures a job on a construction crew, his love interest, Anya (Emma Caulfield), comments to Willow, "So much sexier than the outfit from his last job." "Oh, I miss the free hot dogs on sticks," Willow replies, referencing the fast-food chain Hot Dog on a Stick, a popular teen workplace notorious for its ridiculous uniforms and hats.[11]

The program's irreverent approach to authority extends to its overt religious references. *Buffy the Vampire Slayer* is premised on the idea of an apocalyptic End Times, yet this point also becomes a source of humor, as literary critic Patricia Pender points out. "The dead rose!" exclaims Xander. "We should've at least had an assembly."[12] Or as Buffy tells her friends, "If the apocalypse comes—beep me."[13] As Angel fan Kristina writes, in these series "prophecies serve as nothing more than early warning devices—they let the forces of good/evil know a big event is coming, and this allows them to prepare for it." Thus, prophecies often set in motion the drama that results in confrontations between good and evil. At every turn, individual choice is emphasized, so that a person's (or monster's) actions can bring about or stop the prophecy.[14]

In their self-referential style, even the overuse of prophecies in their narratives becomes a source of parody:

> ANGEL: The end is not coming. Someone is always uncovering some ancient scroll, and they're always saying the same thing: that something terrible is coming. Do you know how many of these things I've seen in my very long life?
> CORDY: Four?
> ANGEL: Three. But there's nothing to worry about.[15]

Both Angel and Buffy's irreverent approach to the very end of time is what makes the television program a part of the "*Scream* meme," as Pender argues.[16] Referencing both Edvard Munch's painting *Scream* (1893) and the recent series of films of the same name by Wes Craven, literary theorist Mark Dery has argued:

> The *Scream* meme suggests that we're so ironic that we can't even take our own apocalypse—our lurking sense, on the eve of the future, of social disintegration and simmering discontent—seriously. This is the moment Walter Benjamin warned us of, when humankind's "self-alienation" reaches "such a degree that it can experience its own destruction as an aesthetic pleasure of the first order."[17]

Buffy is postmodern in the sense that the program "delights in depthlessness."[18] Religion—the ultimate serious and "deep" concern of U.S. culture—is here turned on its head, to the delight of a generation accustomed to questioning everything and turning all into irony. Of course, the horror of what may lie beyond is often equated with the fears of high school. When Buffy reflects on her lack of preparation for final exams, she notes flippantly, "I'll wing it. Of course if we go to Hell by then, I won't have to take them. [Sudden fear] Or maybe I'll have to take them forever."[19]

Religion in *Buffy* thus recurs largely through nuanced references to its traditional beliefs, notably those related to the battle of good and evil at the end of time. Its images of religion's dark side are borrowed in the tradition of nineteenth-century Victorian gothic novels, none more so than Bram Stoker's *Dracula*, the literary source to which it owes its most obvious debt. Supernatural fiction saw its greatest period of development and the establishment of both popular story lines and visuals at this time, when science and religion were each insisting on providing definitions of normalcy and advocating limits to the parameters of possibility. The fictional realm was one place where such issues could be explored metaphorically without being perceived as either directly threatening established religions or offering contradictions to scientific evidence.

Stoker's tale participated in this reframing as fiction stories that at one time had a more overt connection with religion, as literary critic Gregory Erickson notes. *Dracula* was built upon vampire legends that have their origins in eastern Europe. There, vampires were associated with the seductiveness of evil and the fear of its consequences after death, both important concerns within seventeenth-century Christianity. The earliest folktales of vampires in eastern Europe held that people became vampires as the result of a death touched with wrongdoing, such as excessive drinking or fighting. The need to seek revenge for a wrong done against them was believed to be another cause for the transformation to vampirism. Vampires were doomed to unnatural existences, extending their "lives" only through drinking the blood of others. Their carnal visits to the widows they left behind held the potential for the further spreading of evil, danger, and "dis-ease." Laurence Rickels notes in *The Vampire Lectures* that vampire lore directly connects fear of vampiric transformations with a fear of death and the afterlife. Crosses were originally put on grave sites not to commemorate the dead, he writes, but to keep them in the grave.[20] Of course, fear of sex is also implied in the original vampire stories and becomes an important theme in Stoker's fictionalization of the legends. Vampires are sensual and attractive, which is often the key to their ability to lure unsuspecting victims to their death. Thus, vampires combine dread and longing, embracing the desire of immortality through the earthly and erotic act that renders death.

In *Dracula*, crosses are used as a weapon against vampires, and the staking of a vampire is accompanied by a prayer. Moreover, the killing of a vampire was associated with saving its soul, returning it from the Devil to God.[21] Buffy wears a crucifix around her neck, but in this update of Stoker's story, it is the vampires and demons, rather than those staking them, who quote the Bible. [22] Often, the pop culture references in *Buffy* and *Angel* ironically comment on the supernatural legends that are the television program's precedents. In the 2000 season premiere, when Buffy is faced with the possibility of a confrontation with Dracula, the "original" vampire, she says skeptically, "You're sure this isn't some fanboy thing? 'Cause I've fought more than a couple pimply, overweight vamps that called themselves Lestat."[23] The program thus simultaneously references Stoker's legend and its more recent characterization (played by real-life superstar Tom Cruise in the film version) in Anne Rice's novel, *Interview with the Vampire*.

Literary critic Gregory Erickson further details the ways in which vampire killings on *Buffy* reflect the traditional lore yet also parody it: Xander accidentally kills a vampire when, holding a wooden stake, he is bumped from behind; Buffy defeats a vampire by tricking him into believing that a lamp is the rising sun.[24] In part perhaps reflecting postmodernism's depthlessness, and in part because this is television, staked vampires on Buffy immediately turn to dust, eliminating the horror of death's transformation that defined the earlier legends.

Of course, unlike the early folklore legends, both the story of Dracula and that of Buffy speak not only to death fears but also to the contemporary concerns of the time. As literary theorist Joel Feimer argued of Stoker's *Dracula*, "At the dawn of the age of psychiatry and the certitude of 'normalcy,' Bram Stoker was cautioning his contemporaries and their posterity against the too rigorous insistence on the rational against the tyranny and arrogance of the normal."[25] This fictional story articulated not only the challenge to religion that had been a part of earlier vampire legends, but also a rejection of the authoritative claims of science, particularly those that excluded the possibility of any realities beyond that which was knowable in the material world. Buffy's stories, as noted, reflect the contemporary fears of young people: fear of loneliness and ostracizing, fear of sex, fear of rejection, fear of the future.

Vampires in *Buffy* also reflect the turn to the "new" vampire in recent Hollywood stories. New vampires, according to literary critic Jules Zanger, commit evil as "expressions of individual personality," not because of a "cosmic conflict between God and Satan."[26] In movies like *The Lost Boys*, vampirism is metaphorically related to criminal activity and the nihilism that underlies it at its worst.[27] Yet in Buffy, as Erickson notes, vampirism takes a new turn.[28] Anyone can become a vampire simply by being in the wrong place at the wrong time. It is only after the transformation that a person loses his soul, and for that former person, in most cases there is no restoration possible. As Giles explains, "A vampire isn't a person at all. It may have the movements, the memories, even the personality of the person that it took over, but it's still a demon at the core."[29] When a person is "sired" into vampirism on *Buffy*, the soul leaves the body and is replaced by a demon. Staking kills a demon; the soul of the person is already long gone. Thus in *Buffy*, tales of vampires and those of demon possessions blur, with little hope for the redemption of the lost ones, as there was in earlier vampire lore such as *Dracula* and as there is in demon possession practices.

The prominent exception to this retelling of the vampire as demon-possession story in *Buffy* occurs in Angel (David Boreanaz). Angel, whose original life dated to the eighteenth century, killed viciously for a hundred years as "Angelus," the soulless vampire. But when he killed a young member of a tribe of gypsies, a curse was cast upon him that restored his soul. Thus Angel must now endure both the knowledge of his past misdeeds and the disgust at his continuing desire for blood (we later learn that he keeps a supply of pig's blood in his refrigerator in order to survive). He is a tragic, flawed romantic hero, with echoes of Stoker's *Dracula* as well as Dr. Jekyll, Dorian Gray, and even Milton's Satan from *Paradise Lost*. He is condemned to an eternal life (or, rather, undeath) spent searching for the atonement that will restore his humanity. He is a vampire, yet also a guardian angel and later, on his own series, a hip and weary Perry Mason–style private investigator for the unfortunate and haunted young people he finds on the streets of Los Angeles.[30]

Buffy and Angel have some striking differences. While Buffy's calling is of a supernatural purpose, she largely uses strategic knowledge and excellent martial arts skills to subdue her adversaries. She is not a supernatural being, but she calls upon supernatural power in the fight against evil. Angel, on the other hand, is more complicated. As a supernatural being himself, he relies upon his ability to call up his vampiric identity, signaled by his distorted vampire face, to fight supernatural evil. Buffy, as many media critics have noted, is a postfeminist heroine: she is strong, capable, and aggressive, while also feminine, loyal to her friends, and (hetero)sexually attractive (figure 2.1).[31] Her "girl power" comes in part from her ability to embrace her sexual allure. Angel, then, is her foil. He is in many ways traditionally masculine: a strong, brooding, and ominous figure dressed in black and wearing a flowing black trenchcoat. His power does not come from embracing his appeal so much as in controlling it; he must subdue the evil within him in order to maintain his humanity. Ultimately, of course, he is not a man but a monster, constantly on guard against the possibility that his body will betray him and deliver him to the dark side. The modern-day gothic tales of *Buffy the Vampire Slayer* and *Angel* therefore also draw upon nineteenth- and early-twentieth-century Victorian stories of the supernatural. Literary theorists Elton Smith and Robert Haas argue that as the Victorian reader became acquainted with the nascent field of psychology, the tragic flawed protagonist that had been popular in romantic and gothic writings became more brooding and consumed with inner conflict. Indeed, one of the defining features of the supernatural fiction of the Victorian era was "a progression in the Victorian concept of the supernatural from an exterior, often physically manifested force acting upon characters to an interior, psychological power often causing characters to act upon others."[32]

FIGURE 2.1
Sarah Michelle Gellar as Buffy the Vampire Slayer, postfeminist teen heroine who struggles with the obstacles of teen life by day and slays supernatural monsters by night (episode: "Puppet Show"). Buffy the Vampire Slayer, © 1997 Twentieth Century Fox Television. All rights reserved.

In other contemporary supernatural horror stories, deep experiences of repressed pain and rage may lead one to give in to unholy desires that, in turn, may cause young people to serve as "the Devil's portals," as film critic Carol Clover has noted.[33] This transformation is central to supernatural horror films such as *Carrie* (1976), *The Exorcist* (1973), and *Witchboard* (1987). Reversing previous gender conventions, Angel is the one open to the devil's influence, as he is already a monster whose temptations must be controlled. Appealing to his pride and seeking to enter through his unconscious mind, demons (and the lawyers with whom they collude on the spinoff program of his name) continually plot to pull him to the other side. Giving in to sexual temptations is completely out of the question: that alone can break the gypsy's curse, taking away his humanity and restoring his demon possession. As viewers learned in the episode "Surprise," such a "moment of pure happiness" causes him to lose his very soul.[34]

Unlike earlier protagonists of horror, Buffy does not open herself to supernatural evil but strikes out against it. In psychological terms, she turns the rage outward rather than inward. Buffy slays because she is Chosen; Angel slays because he wants to be human. Each has their own destiny, and when it becomes clear that those destinies conflict, they must separate from one another. This narrative hints at the changes in gender roles and related desires that define ideals of today's younger generation, especially for young women: a female protagonist who can attract yet limit others with the use of her body, and a repressed male protagonist who controls his body lest he endanger others.

Buffy and *Angel* are therefore largely about the struggles of the teenage years, using the metaphor of vampires—and thus, inadvertently, religion's dark side of demons and death fears—to express them. We turn to a close examination of one episode from *Buffy*'s first season to see this representation at work.

SEX AND RESURRECTION IN *BUFFY*

In the early years of the series, the conniving punk English vampire Spike (James Masters) serves as Buffy's nemesis, a dark evil force living in the city's sewers. Spike has already confronted and defeated two slayers before her, and hopes to add to his status as a menacing vampire by killing Buffy. Druscilla (Juliet Landau), Spike's girlfriend, seeks revenge on Angel, her former lover who sired her into vampirism after killing her entire family while she was confessing her sins in church.

In the two-part episode "What's My Line?," Spike has learned that the ailing Druscilla can regain her former strength through a spell that binds her with Angel.[35] The second episode contains some of the most overt references to organized religion in the series, although the church at first glance appears largely as "window dressing" as a site for Spike's spell. The episode also plays significantly on the theme of vampire feeding as related to both sexual initiation and desire. This occurs both in the narrative and in the episode's humor; when

Xander learns from Buffy that it was Angel who sired Druscilla, he replies enviously, "Man, that guy got major neck in his day." Scenes involving Angel, Spike, and Druscilla are laced with sexual innuendo and thus contrast with the innocent budding romances that emerge in the same episodes between Willow and Oz and Xander and Cordelia, and the collegiality that develops between Buffy and the exotically coded dark-skinned Kendra (Bianca Lawson), a fellow teen girl slayer who has arrived in Sunnydale to help stop the evil that Spike and Druscilla have planned.[36]

When Angel is captured by Spike, he is brought to Druscilla, who is lying across a lace canopied bed in white silk lingerie. Sexual tension between Angel and Druscilla still exists, despite their allegiances to opposite sides in the battle between good and evil. Druscilla uses this tension to attempt to control Angel; he uses it to limit both her power and Spike's. Druscilla taunts Angel, who is stripped to the waist, gagged, and tied to the bed. She sits between his legs, scorching his skin by pouring holy water on his bare chest while seductively retelling the story of how Angel mercilessly devoured her family. When Spike returns, Angel verbally taunts Spike with references to the former sensual relationship between Druscilla and himself, implying that Druscilla is not currently satisfied. Spike is angered to the point of almost staking Angel (the only way to annihilate a vampire, of course), but then he realizes that this is what Angel hopes for, as this would cause Druscilla to lose her means to a cure. Interestingly, the weakened Druscilla does not rush to defend Spike's damaged manliness in the face of Angel's taunts, but instead stands passively by as Spike realizes that he cannot kill Angel and save Druscilla at the same time. This is in marked contrast with Buffy, who in another scene expresses her determination to save Angel from the fate Spike has planned. Referencing her calling as a vanquisher of evil who is constantly under attack, while also drawing on a perennial theme of high school love, she declares, "You can attack me, send assassins, whatever. But nobody messes with my boyfriend."

In the episode's climactic scene, Spike has bound Angel and Druscilla to a common stake in a chapel located inside a large, gothic church structure. With stained-glass windows and lit votive candles in the background, Spike, in his vampire face, begins his chant by calling on the mythical Elegon while releasing incense into the air. The chapel in which this ceremony occurs is obviously in disrepair; curtains behind the Marian statues are faded and torn, dropcloths and old blankets cover the communion table and pews, and a broken candelabra sits in the corner near a decrepit and chipped mantled fireplace. Holding what at first looks like an ornate upside-down cross that turns out to be a knife cover, Spike ends his chant with the words, "From the blood of the sire she is risen, from the blood of the sire she shall rise again." With a slash of the knife, a flash of light, and appropriate pulsating sound effects, Angel's blood begins to flow into Druscilla.

Just then, Buffy enters the room, followed quickly by her friends, and the requisite violent brawl ensues between Spike and his vampire friends and Buffy and hers. Just as Buffy is nearly defeated, Kendra, Buffy's fellow vampire slayer, arrives and assists in overcoming Spike. When Spike attempts to escape with the wilting Druscilla, Buffy throws the incense holder at him, and Spike and Druscilla are thrown against a rotting wooden organ which collapses on top of them, setting the entire chapel on fire. Although the episode continues by tying up the loose plot ends involving the teen romances and friendships noted earlier, the last scene is of a newly empowered Druscilla, who with one hand lifts an injured Spike out of the rubble and carries him out of the burned-out wreckage of the former chapel.

The church setting functions as a counterpoint to both Buffy's association with vampire slaying and Kendra's association with (an unnamed) Island culture and hence "folk" religious traditions. Druscilla, the "resurrected" vampire, is the only person who claims a religious identity as a former Catholic (former only in the sense that her original soul is now gone). Here, an interesting parallel emerges between Druscilla and Kendra. When she was young, Druscilla had visions, which caused her mother to send (or abandon) her to a Catholic church, ultimately leaving her vulnerable to Angel. Similarly, Kendra was abandoned by her parents and left with Mr. Zaputo, her vampire slayer Watcher and guardian, when she exhibited the gift for slaying. In a subsequent episode, Druscilla hypnotizes and then murders Kendra, thus completing their narrative circle.[37]

The church structure is not the only explicit reference to Catholicism. The holy water that Druscilla pours onto Angel's body scalds him because its goodness is presumed to be in direct contrast with Angel's evil vampiric body. It is important to note that holy water is not joked about or dismissed in this episode, but instead is elevated; it has the power to burn Angel because of its relationship to presumed supernatural good. Similarly, the spell that will reinvigorate Druscilla must take place in a church, suggesting not that the church building is a neutral or unimportant location, but that in fact it is a source of power that can be marshaled, in this case for evil purposes. The ritual Spike performs resembles the Christian communion ritual, with blood as the symbol that restores and reunites the community in both instances, although in this case it is used for evil purposes: to bring a vampire back to full strength.

It is important, if obvious, to note that religion is not clearly on the side of the "good guys" here. An earlier exchange in which Giles expresses surprise at the fact that there are so many churches in Sunnydale suggests the infrequency with which Buffy and her allies might visit them. The episode implies that religion's rituals and locations may be made useful, but that such uses are not necessarily aligned with good.

Why would this particular representation of organized religion and its relation to supernatural forces be found in teen contemporary culture? To understand this, we must remember that today's young people are offspring of the children of the 1960s. Their parents learned to mistrust religious and other societal institutions for their oppressive roles in society. Moreover, the education of today's teens tends to underscore the need to question authority, another legacy of the 1960s. Ever since the supposedly neutral scientific discovery of atomic science was used to destroy Hiroshima and Nagasaki, science and its claims of neutrality and abstract truth have been questioned. Similarly, in school teens learn about how religion has been used throughout history to keep some people in their places, such as in the Salem witch trials and in the U.S. slavery system. Today's young people do not come to notions of religion with an empty slate; religion is not seen by them as an unquestioned good. The representations in teen popular culture reflect this. The implication is a far more relativist and tentative approach to religion, particularly of the organized, institutional kind: religion might be used by some for good, but religion's power can also be marshaled in ways that the "good guys" never intended. While much of the episode under discussion echoes an occult tradition that positions itself in marked contrast to Christianity and its rituals, what emerges again and again in the program is a recognition of the power of both good and evil, and of evil's inevitable defeat. Echoing a theme that encompasses numerous stories in popular culture throughout history, this struggle and victory is central to all the monotheistic religions and in fact dates to their earliest beginnings. It's important to point out, therefore, that while programs like *Buffy the Vampire Slayer* may be reflecting a certain relativism toward religious institutions, these programs are not without morals. While characters may change from good to evil as the result of experiences over time or curses with immediate effects, a strong contrast between good and evil *behavior* pervades their story lines, with social responsibility a taken-for-granted value that drives the characters to embrace danger out of concern for the welfare of others. Incidentally, this same value emerges clearly in other stories of teen culture, most notably those of Harry Potter.

DEMONS, DIFFERENCE, AND RELATIVISM

While religion's presence may be incidental, it is therefore not without meaning. The monsters, as well as the references to religion, become increasingly sophisticated with the passing seasons. In part, this has happened as a result of the demands of the television medium, and the fact that these programs draw upon two distinct television/film genres: horror and fantasy. Before *Buffy* and *Angel*, fantasy television programs like *Bewitched*, *Sabrina the Teenage Witch*, and *Xena: Warrior Princess* each used special effects to portray the invocation of supernatural power.[38] Drawing upon both traditions of the supernatural in television, in *Buffy* and *Angel*, magic and witchcraft "are open to a broader and more diverse set of meanings than those portrayed in traditional occult horror film and similar in format to multinovel cycles, such as those written by Anne Rice or J. K. Rowling," as literary critic Tanya Krzywinska writes.[39] This allows the series to combine spoofs of the fantasy and popular culture traditions of the supernatural along with irreverent humor that turns on a reference to religion. Nowhere is this better expressed than when Buffy's friend Willow, who practices "witchcraft" in the tradition of *Bewitched* or the film *Practical Magic*

(1998), attends a meeting of Wiccans at her college. She notes afterward in disgust: "Bunch of wanna blessed be's. Nowadays every girl with a henna tattoo and a spice rack thinks she's a sister to the dark ones."[40] Willow's comment places witchcraft and Wicca in playfully ironic relation to one another: she is frustrated that Wiccans have lost their connection with "real" witchcraft. This reference to the fantasy supernatural plays with the boundaries of real world and fiction, poking fun at the presumption in some circles that Wicca and witchcraft are the same thing while also giving viewers an opportunity to laugh at any supposed connections between Buffy and real-life interests in either alternative religion or the supernatural realm. The program therefore turns on its ear the long-standing Christian fears of women's folkloric practices that in Salem ignited moral panics over witchcraft. It inverts reality and fantasy, dramatizing as real Willow's "witchcraft" practices, long a standard in fantasy, while approaching contemporary Wiccanism with the same irreverence with which it approaches Christianity. Magic is thus contained in the realm of fantasy, parodying—rather than affirming, as some charge—the possibility that it might be related to alternative spirituality.

Another way in which audience interest in serial television is sustained is by maintaining a sense of the unexpected through the ability of characters to change. This, too, has implications for how the supernatural is represented. Mary Alice Money traces the development of characters in the series, noting that some characters that begin as caricatures—such as the evil punk vampire Spike (James Masters) or the wanton slayer Faith (Eliza Dushku)—change, and become more appealing and human, as they are made vulnerable in some way. This ability to change is central to the vampire and demon possession myth as it is told in *Buffy* and *Angel*. As Golden and Holder describe in *The Watcher's Guide*:

> What makes them human is their capacity for feeling emotion; what makes them demons is their inability to change; their emotions don't grow or lead to good as human emotions can. . . . In [series creator Joss] Whedon's universe, at least, there seems to be a continuum running between the opposite poles of human and demon; in other words, some demons are more human than others, and some humans behave like demons. Or, to put it another way, what makes us human is our capacity to change, to feel emotions, to choose good over evil.[41]

In short, demons can turn out to be good; "angels" can become evil.

Ambiguities between good and evil become a central part of the dramatic tensions in *Angel*. As already noted, in his very character Angel embodies both good and evil—he is a vampire with a soul, as we learned in the pilot episode. He has a mission: to help those whose distress is caused by supernatural forces. Sometimes those he helps are demons. In *Angel*, as well as in later episodes of *Buffy*, demons are not necessarily those who embrace bad behaviors; like the humans in the episode, they can change. Xander's love interest, Anya (Emma Caulfield), was a "vengeance demon" until her magical necklace and power center were crushed by Giles (she then became human). Doyle, Angel's sidekick for the first few episodes, was a half-demon (human "on my mother's side," he explains).

In the episode "Bachelor Party," which originally aired in fall 1999, we learn that Doyle's ex-wife, Harrie, is about to be remarried, but Angel learns just in time that Richard, her fiancé, is a demon. Angel watches as Richard, who owns a restaurant, leaves Harrie in one part of the kitchen while he puts something away in the refrigerator and pulls a large knife out of its holder. As Richard turns to rejoin Harrie, his face becomes red and horns extrude from the top of his head. Angel, witnessing this, jumps through a plate-glass window and lands on Richard, wrestling him to the ground. Harrie rushes to Richard on the floor and angrily demands to know why Angel was spying on them. "He's a demon!" Angel replies, and Harrie responds, "Well, yeah," and the following dialogue ensues:

HARRIE: Richard's family owns this restaurant. They're anamovic demons, peaceful clan, totally assimilated into our culture.

ANGEL: You knew about this?

RICHARD: Harrie's an ethnodemonologist, and a damn fine one, too. We met while she was scouting clans in North America.

ANGEL: You study demons? That's your profession?

HARRIE: You have a problem with that?

ANGEL: No, I just—Doyle said—

HARRIE: —that when he went through his change (and became a demon) I freaked. Which is true. But after, I adjusted, and I realized, here's this whole rich interesting world just waiting to be explored.

ANGEL: But you didn't tell him that.

HARRIE: Of course I did! I even tried to get him to go out, meet other demons, go to a mixer, you know? But he couldn't accept himself, or them. So then he was just angry, and pretty much a bitch to live with.

In this episode, prejudice against demons becomes a metaphor for other kinds of racially based prejudices. In this case, rather than having the building of a church as a representation of organized religion, we see religion's metanarratives implicitly linked with other oppressive narratives. Perhaps demons were only deemed evil because Christians had the power to define them this way, the story suggests. Demons are beings of different yet interesting cultures, worthy of respect and study, as Harrie's professional interests as an "ethnodemonologist" suggest. After exploring this idea through the narrative of this episode, the viewers learn that, in fact, Richard's family does intend to participate in the rather heinous "ancient" ritual of having the intended eat the ex-husband's brains. Rather than presented as a parallel of a religious ritual, however, this ritual more closely resembles a strip club visit by a group of rowdy young men in a bachelor party.

Acting as a guardian angel, Angel, resorting to his own supernatural powers, saves his friend from being devoured by demons and vampires (figure 2.2).

FIGURE 2.2

Acting as a guardian angel, Angel (David Boreanaz) saves his friend from being devoured by demons and vampires in a "primitive" ritual, a bachelor party (episode: "Bachelor Party"). *Angel,* © 2000 Twentieth Century Fox Television.

After Angel halts the ritual, Harrie breaks off her engagement with Richard, not because of the ritual but because he lied to her, concealing his true reason for wanting to invite Doyle to the party. After demons have been placed into the relativistic frame that acknowledges the positive attributes of differing cultural backgrounds, it would be metaphorically impossible, given the general direction of the program, to conclude the episode by reconfirming their "true" evil status. Instead, they are portrayed as hypocritical in their desire to embrace ancient traditions while also assimilating into acceptable middle-class culture. In addition to the implicit religious critique, therefore, this episode conservatively reaffirms that certain norms—those not coincidentally aligned with white, middle-class culture—are, indeed, deemed more acceptable than others. It also offers a liberal feminist criticism of men and the "barbaric" rituals surrounding bachelor parties.

While the demons in this episode ultimately are made unappealing by their desire to engage in a disgusting ritual, in other episodes demons are portrayed more sympathetically. In "Setting the Captives Free," which originally aired in winter 2000, Angel, along with several other demons, is enslaved by a pair of mercenary humans. These people have enslaved the demons and have scheduled a series of illegal fights, Gladiator-style. The demons must fight one another to the death, and if a demon kills twenty-one other demons, he gains his freedom.

Unlike the demons in the previous episode, who seemed able to maintain a human appearance except when engaging in traditional rituals, the demons in the prison are depicted as grotesque. With lizardlike markings on green or red skin, oddly shaped horned heads, and hoofed feet or hands, these beings more closely resemble the demons of medieval paintings. Rather than appearance, as was the case in the previous episode, the audience's sympathy for them is based on the fact that they are enslaved against their will and that some will die unjustly because of the mercenaries' interests.

In the prison, Angel attempts to fight the mercenaries to free himself and a few of the weaker demons who are destined to die. When Angel is at first thwarted, the owner of the slaves laughs and taunts him, saying, "Who do you think you are, Moses?" Of course, in the end, Angel's friends come through and they, along with a few of the demons who presumably have had a change of heart, are able to help him kill the mercenaries and free the enslaved demons.

As the episode ends, friends Cordelia (Charisma Carpenter) and Wesley (Alexis Denisoff) help an injured Angel out of the arena and into the dark, damp street. "I think we did a good thing here," Angel says with some pride. "We set the captives free," Wesley responds enthusiastically. The camera then turns from the three heroes to a group of demons, cackling mischievously as they skulk off into the shadows. There is a moment of awkward silence. "Actually, didn't we set a bunch of *demons* free?" Cordelia asks. As the scene cuts to black, Wesley replies, "Technically, yes" (figure 2.3).

In this episode, religion emerges not with reference to the power of supernatural good and evil or as a grand narrative aligned with oppression of certain

FIGURE 2.3
Angel (David Boreanaz) and his friends Cordelia (Charisma Carpenter) and Wesley (Alexis Denisoff) depart after another successful, if ambiguous, mission (episode: "Judgment"). *Angel,* © 2000 Twentieth Century Fox Television. All rights reserved.

viewpoints in favor of the status quo, but as a tradition that embodies ambiguities about good and evil. The writers rely on the fact that the audience will
share at least a general knowledge of who Moses is and his relation to freeing
the enslaved from their oppression. They also assume that most would expect
that demons would be categorically portrayed as evil and irredeemable. Yet in
this story, similar to the previous episode, demons are represented as oppressed
and at least some of them are assumed to be worthy of respect and freedom.
The humor of this episode, and indeed of much in *Buffy* and *Angel*, turns on
recognizing that sometimes even one's best efforts to combat evil do not yield
unequivocally good results. In this case, setting the captives free seemed an
honorable action—until it becomes clear that then the "captives" may very well
be expected to turn around and torment others. Here is where the racial/ethnic
metaphor becomes questionably retrogressive, as it did in the last episode, particularly for a generation that is increasingly multicultural and tolerant. On the
level of religious metaphor, however, there is a different conclusion that is actually more consistent with the episode's overall theme. The program beckons
the viewer to consider the implications of even one's most morally admirable
actions, raising the question of social responsibility in the context of a largely
individualistic society.

As the seasons progress, *Buffy* and *Angel* affirm that beings are to be evaluated not by their visible characteristics, but by their actions: an important
metaphorical theme for an increasingly multicultural society struggling with
a past steeped in racist prejudices. The relationship between good and evil is
portrayed as flexible and thus at times ambiguous. Coming to recognize and
appreciate difference is itself portrayed as an act of recognition and development: Riley (Marc Blucas), Buffy's boyfriend in season five, is an example of
this. When he learns that Willow's former boyfriend Oz (Seth Green) is a
werewolf, his reaction causes Buffy to call him a bigot. She explains, "It's just
different with different demons. There are creatures, vampires for instance,
that aren't evil at all." Later in the episode, Riley notes his new understanding: "I was in a totally black and white space, people versus monsters, and it
isn't like that."[42] As Buffy and Angel embrace the possibility of change in
both viewpoints and characters, the programs are able to sustain interest in
the audience: there is no ultimate closure at the end of each episode; there
will be new evils to be fought, and new learnings to be had, in ways that are
unexpected.

There are at least four ways in which religion emerges in *Buffy* and *Angel*,
none of which are dismissive of religion but instead problematize it in relation
to truth claims, fantasy fiction, prejudice, and history: (1) religion is referred to
obliquely, particularly with references to the apocalyptic end of the world, narratives of demon possession, and fears of death; (2) religion is referenced in re-
lief, consistent with religion's historical role in relation to vampire legends; (3)
religion emerges irreverently, in jokes about Christianity or Wicca or the relation between the two of them through references to previous fantastic stories of
the supernatural; and (4) religion, particularly the dualistic relationship be-

tween good and evil it affirms, is relativized both to accommodate the possibility for growth in the program's characters and to satirize the simplistic notion of duality itself.

HORROR AND RELIGION IN POPULAR CULTURE: OR, IS BUFFY A CELEBRATION OF THE OCCULT?

Why do programs like *Buffy the Vampire Slayer* and *Angel* appeal to young people? The most obvious answer, of course, has to do with the program's humorous approach, which nevertheless takes seriously the problems of teenage life, combined with the appeal of the program's young and attractive stars. Yet as this chapter notes, the programs stand in a long tradition of the supernatural's appeal in teen life. Experimentations with the supernatural—from the visits to cemeteries to sleepover séances—give young people a chance to encounter their fears (especially of what they cannot control) in the context of their peers. Such experimentations also, of course, challenge authority. Teens know that adults consider such actions to be deviant and even dangerous; that is part of their appeal. Like séances and other supernatural activities, horror films and television programs give young viewers a chance to vicariously participate in rebellion while also containing their fears through its symbolic defeat. In both cases, even as monsters are defeated or supernatural spirits subdued, the social order is ultimately restored, and teens can revel in the thrill they experienced with their peers, thus making the whole experience less an initiation into eventual adulthood than a celebration of the moment of youth. Horror, a genre that establishes important precedents for *Buffy* and *Angel*, generally embraces blatantly violent or bizarre sexual behaviors—exactly the elements many adults find objectionable. But as film theorist Jeffrey Cohen points out, such films and television programs serve an important purpose for young people. As they highlight the boundaries of acceptable activities, monsters "police the borders of the possible."[43] Horror films therefore allow their audiences to consider what is acceptable or troublesome for a society. Monsters, after all, are not countercultural so much as they symbolically mete out punishment for culturally defined transgressions (such as sexual promiscuity, lawlessness, or pretension).[44] Horror films—including slasher films, those dealing with the occult and possession, and rape-revenge films—traditionally appealed primarily to adolescent boys.[45] Recent horror variations, including *Buffy* and *Angel* and other stories in the "*Scream* meme," have young female protagonists and hence appeal to both genders. Others, such as *Blade I, Blade II,* and *Queen of the Damned,* resonate with young people across racial/ethnic lines. When the being causing the horror—monster, psychotic killer, demon—is defeated, society is restored and its members survive. Horror stories, particularly those with strong supernatural elements, allow young people to experience and relieve fears about death, the afterlife, and in general, the forces in life that they believe are beyond their control—which includes quite a bit, from the teen perspective. This suggests that looking at both supernatural stories and the patterns of interpretations that surface among their audiences offers important ways of understanding what matters most to the young people who view them.

Teen culture is a relatively recent phenomenon, with its roots in the early part of the twentieth century. But there are some who note that Christian beliefs and the genre of horror have much deeper connections. As noted in the previous chapter, religious and cultural critic Edward J. Ingebretsen makes what is perhaps the most startling claim in this regard. Ingebretsen argues that horror finds its initial impulse and articulation within the central stories of Christianity. "The theological mapping of the heavens not only made possible a map of Hell but made one necessary," he writes.[46] He argues that horror in the writings of such influential twentieth-century novelists as H. P. Lovecraft and Stephen King—both of which are predecessors to *Buffy*'s mythology—can be seen as inversions of the Incarnation: they examine the "horrific possibilities" of mixing supernatural and natural worlds. Look at the stories in the book of Genesis for a prototype, writes Ingebretsen. There, "sons of heaven" desire, "find beautiful," and "took for their wives" "daughters of men."[47] As with vampire legends and the Buffy/Angel romance, we see the themes of longing and dread, natural and supernatural. Centuries of piety and sentimentality about the Christmas story and about angelic appearances may mask the horrific possibilities within the sacred, Ingebretsen notes, but nevertheless they remain a part of the tradition. These stories are somewhat problematic within Christianity, which is why they wind up repressed—and reemergent—in the stories of popular culture.[48]

Employing religious categories of the supernatural for entertainment purposes is hardly a new phenomenon. It probably has its roots in the most unlikely place: the writings of early American Puritans, including those by Increase Mather and his son, Cotton Mather, as Ingebretsen argues.[49] The Mathers, as I noted in chapter 1, were especially vocal in their protests concerning the occult practices that were widespread in seventeenth-century New England. While their writings offered strict admonishment against such practices as witchcraft and the use of charms and potions, they also provided stories of these practices in lurid detail. Their sermons could therefore be heard and read for both the purposes of edification and—although usually unacknowledged—as entertainment. Cotton Mather's work often provided material that lent itself to the latter purposes. As Ingebretsen writes of Cotton Mather's *The Wonders of the Invisible World*, published in 1693:

> Mather was concerned with demonstrating the presence of witches in Salem; he knew well that discovering evil was a righteous religious duty, but that, in addition, its spectacular display in the courts and other public places gave it value as "entertainment." . . . The exempla that Mather gathered about the possessed witches of Salem and their lurid ways enabled a

reader to enjoy (surreptitiously, of course) the exotica of the immoral life while obediently repudiating them at the same time.[50]

Although Mather wrote his book on witchcraft in Boston in an effort to protect New England society from what he considered to be deviant social practices, the book was widely read at least in part because it was highly entertaining. And the entertainment value of witchcraft did not escape fictional writers such as Nathaniel Hawthorne. Within thirty years of the last recorded witch trials at the turn of the nineteenth century, Hawthorne was drawing upon the trials' narratives and symbols for his own stories.[51] It should be recognized, therefore, that such writings had an important, if inadvertent, relationship to the establishment of what we now consider the American supernatural fantasy genre and its related popular practices.

As Ingebretsen argues, evil, death, and punishment were popular themes in early American Protestant sermons delivered to the faithful. The reason for this, he notes, is that "the Holy could not be expressed in language at all except by negation: as absence, as ineffable—or by contrast and inversion, negation: as demonic."[52] In other words, it is easier to talk about the holy in relation to that with which it contrasts: evil, demons, and hell. Thus, American Protestant sermons highlighted the possible negative consequences of sin rather than the positive benefits of communion with God.

No one did this with greater success than Jonathan Edwards, the influential Calvinist minister of the eighteenth century.[53] Edwards is famous for his ability to link the urgent need for personal salvation with the language and images of the terror that would befall the unfaithful. In what may be his most famous sermon, delivered in 1741, Edwards intoned:

> O sinner! Consider the fearful danger you are in: it is a great furnace of wrath that you are held over in the hand of that God, whose wrath is provoked and incensed as much against you, as against many of the damned in hell. You hang by a slender thread, with the flames of divine wrath flashing about it, and ready every moment to singe it, and burn it asunder: and you have no interest in any mediator, and nothing to lay hold of to save yourself, nothing to keep off the flames of wrath, nothing of your own.[54]

With his interest in the wrath of God and the consequences of sin, Edwards is aptly described as "proto-Gothic": the terror he invokes is interiorized, a "telling of the rended soul."[55] He focused on spiritual anxieties about the dangers of divine judgment, affirming a terrifying supernatural realm that was well beyond human control. The contemporary American gothic tales of *Buffy the Vampire Slayer* and *Angel* are therefore important descendants of that earlier religious tradition.

Evangelical films of the apocalypse, such as *A Thief in the Night* and *Left Behind,* are clearly within the tradition of Jonathan Edwards. While they tell stories that invoke fear for the purpose of evangelism, other films invoke similar themes and images for the purposes of entertainment. Films like *Seven* (1995), *The Devil's Advocate* (1997), *End of Days* (1999), and *Frailty* (2002), as well as video games like Diablo II, have important roots in the series of horror films produced in the late 1960s and early 1970s. At that time, horror films began drawing rather explicitly on religious themes for definitions of evil. And much like today's controversies over the depictions of supernatural topics in the entertainment media, religious leaders took note then, too.[56] *Rosemary's Baby* (1968), the first film in this genre, used demon possession metaphorically to address the concerns of sexual reproduction and the newly introduced birth control pill, as well as the accompanying tensions of women's emergent recognition of themselves as sexual beings.[57] While these concerns would have been enough to gain the attention of the National Catholic Office for Motion Pictures, it was the perversion of religious beliefs that was focused upon in their condemnation of the film: "Much more serious . . . is the perverted use of fundamental Christian beliefs, especially surrounding the birth of Christ, and its mockery of religious persons and practices. The very technical excellence of the film serves to intensify its defamatory nature."[58]

Rosemary's Baby was the first film in the United States to provide a popular illustration of occult traditions, and as such it is an important film to consider in relation to the charges now made against *Buffy* and *Angel*. Occult traditions in the United States have their roots in esoteric practices that arose as alternatives to Christianity throughout the nineteenth century and continued to garner interest and followers throughout the twentieth. *Rosemary's Baby* had been developed in the shadow of a 1960s series of occult-based British horror films that had been popular among teens in the United Kingdom. One of the actors in a sister film, *The Devil Rides Out* (released in the United States as *The Devil's Bride*, 1967), commented that while popular with young people, these films, and the books by Dennis Wheatley upon which they were based, incited fear among British censors. He noted: "Rather than fantasy, these books dealt with the absolute reality of Black Magic. There are such cults and such people even today, at every level of society."[59] Books such as Wheatley's introduced a generation of British teens to fictionalized accounts of the occult that resonated with the same faith in supernatural good and evil advocated among evangelicals. In place of evangelistic efforts, however, information on ancient and medieval sources of secret practices became popular and increasingly available in alternative bookstores and similar locations.

Books with more serious intentions about practices in the occult and witchcraft had circulated among a much smaller audience before the fictional books and films of the occult gained popularity. One important work that was destined to become a classic in the contemporary neopagan movement was Gerald Gardner's 1954 publication, *Witchcraft Today*.[60] In this book, Gardner combined various medieval sources with writings from Aleister Crowley. Crowley had been a controversial leader in the late-nineteenth-century occult tradition.

He had welcomed, and in several instances even encouraged, the association journalists made between practices of the occult and those of satanism, claiming to be the "Great Beast" and associating himself with the numbers 666. For these reasons, Crowley—and the popular fictional treatments he received in Dennis Wheatley's books—contributed much to the understandings of a link between the secret traditions of the occult and satanism as it is understood by Christians.[61]

By the time *Rosemary's Baby* was released in the late 1960s, awareness of both satanic cults and witchcraft ceremonies had already become fairly widespread, if overstated in relation to actual participants. Yet the film played an important role in further adding to the fears these practices evoked among U.S. audiences. In an era when attendance and affiliation with some Christian and Jewish organizations had begun to decline among families in the United States, and adolescent behaviors were associated with rebellion and antiestablishment activities, horror films joined a host of other purported pop cultural influences as possible sources for both religion's cultural retreat and for what was believed to be the rising interest in the occult.

Certainly, *The Exorcist* was a watershed in this regard. That film took one of religion's own most horrifying experiences—that of demon possession—and placed it center stage with grotesque aplomb. But the film was also noteworthy for its foregrounding of teens within this genre. In *The Exorcist*, Regan (Linda Blair) symbolized the struggle between religious authority and occult practices as it was played out in the concerns about young people. The teen culture of the Ouija board was in this film directly related to the invocation of evil. Prior to this time, Ouija boards had largely been considered a kitsch amusement, akin to the supernatural references in the so-called Monster Culture of the late 1950s and early 1960s. Yet in the context of the early 1970s, concern about occult practices, long an undercurrent in conservative Christian circles, began to bubble to the surface, encouraging examination from the emergent fundamentalist and Pentecostal circles, as well as among serious scholars of American religion.[62]

In addition to its frightening special effects, *The Exorcist* introduced to a wide audience the idea that religious leaders could participate in combating supernatural evil. *The Exorcist* introduced into horror films a heightened realism that changed the direction of the horror genre.[63] The key narrative point of the movie was that a person's identity could be changed by something from beyond him- or herself, a theme that was picked up in several subsequent horror films with supernatural and religious connections, such as *The Omen* (1976) and *The Evil Dead* (1982).[64] In the box-office success *The Omen*, for example, one man was inadvertently responsible for giving the Anti-Christ a home, resulting from his own traffic in deception. The horror in *The Omen* rests upon fearsome aspects of religion's supernatural realm, much like its predecessor, *The Exorcist*. In the film, Father Brennan (Gregory Peck) warded off many dangers in his quest to ascertain whether young Damien was truly the son of the Devil (figure 2.4).

FIGURE 2.4
The Omen, © 1976 Twentieth Century Fox. All rights reserved.

After the 1970s, horror films with religious themes receded from the main-stream. The 1990s and the end of the millennium saw the genre's reemergence, with the possibly hallucinogenic demons and hell scenes in *Jacob's Ladder* and *Flatliners* (both 1990), the evildoers' descent to hell in the horror/murder mystery/romance *Ghost* (1990), and later and more subtly in the supernatural thriller *The Sixth Sense* (1999).

What is distinctive about the most recent films to engage supernatural themes is their central appeal to teens and preteens. This is why *Harry Potter and the Sorcerer's Stone* and *Lord of the Rings* tap into some of the earlier concerns about a purported rise of interest in the occult. Today, things like miraculous healing, mind-body energies and parapsychology belong to a kind of spirituality popularized by authors like Marianne Williamson and talk show host Oprah Winfrey.[65] Drawing upon ancient traditions associated with the esoterica popular in nineteenth-century occultism, these spiritual leaders advocate a "positive thinking" and personal empowerment approach that seeks to embrace the good.[66] On the other hand, the term "occult," as I noted, has come to be synonymous with evil and, specifically, with satanism. Protestant religious leaders have long been concerned about both types of practices, and fundamentalists have always described both as deviant. But the concern over evil that has come to play a role in public discussions of teen life means that the concern about the occult has reached new heights.

CONCLUSION

Because the media industries avidly pursue the leisure-oriented and disposable income–friendly world of youth, many programs and films pick up on these long traditions of supernatural interests in teen life. Buffy and Angel can be seen as a part of a host of teen heroes with supernatural or scientifically engineered powers, including Harry Potter, Frodo of *Lord of the Rings*, *Dark Angel*'s Max, *Smallville*'s Clark Kent, *Charmed*'s Piper, Phoebe, and Prue, *Roswell*'s teen aliens, *The Matrix*'s Neo, and even members of the short-lived *Dead Last* band. In each of these programs and films, the young people at their center have either inherited or stumbled upon their powers in their teen years, and they find that they have no choice but to use them. Having these powers is their "destiny," regardless of how much they may long for a normal teen life.

Despite the darkness and ambiguity in many of these popular culture stories, this concern with destiny may be an optimistic response to what young people observe about themselves, particularly with reference to their parents' lives. For generations, teens have embraced the celebration of youth that is at the heart of popular culture, voicing the concern that they do not want to grow up into a life they observe as the meaningless drudgery of adulthood. Yet in recent decades, that coding of how to achieve a desirable life has been along the lines of affluence: with wealth comes the ultimate prize, personal freedom. In the supernatural and science fiction stories appealing to today's teens, however, personal freedom is important yet also potentially lonely. Money may come and go, family may disappoint you, but friends will not (figure 2.5). Certainly, wealth is still desirable, particularly in light of the real economic difficulties encountered in many of today's families with young people. But what these stories suggest is that young people want more than just a good-paying job that supports their own interests. In an individualistic society, where evil tends to be thought of as something done to someone by another, these stories suggest that evil is dangerously large in its consequences. Fearless individuals with special powers, and indeed with an appreciation for difference in a multicultural society, are needed in order to address it.[67] Distinct from the selfish individualism that has been identified with their parent's generation, therefore, today's young people want to be a part of something that is bigger than themselves: they want a destiny, a calling, a challenge that is ultimately worthy of their time and energy. And they realize they cannot fulfill this calling alone.

Buffy the Vampire Slayer provided an excellent example of this in the 2001–2002 season finale.[68] In a season that was criticized by its detractors for its increasingly graphic sexual and violent content and by its fans for its lack of humor, the series concluded with a return to its earlier references to the battle between good and evil, and also, indirectly and surprisingly, to its references to religion. For this reason, I want to conclude this chapter with a review of that episode and its analysis in relation to earlier episodes.

FIGURE 2.5
Buffy (Sarah Michelle Gellar), along with her friends Xander (Nicholas Brendon) and
Angel (David Boreanaz), make plans to defeat the demons called forth by her enemies
(episode: "Prophecy"). *Buffy the Vampire Slayer,* © 1997, and *Angel,* © 2000, Twentieth
Century Fox Television. All rights reserved.

The battle of good and evil that is the heart of this episode takes place in the
form and body of Willow, Buffy's best friend. Over the past several seasons,
Willow has become accomplished in the art of witchcraft. While initially using
her powers for good (and occasionally producing a humorously botched spell),
Willow has increasingly experimented with using her powers as a means to fulfill her own interests.

When Willow's lover Tara is mistakenly killed by three teen boys who themselves have been developing skills in witchcraft, Willow is inconsolable. She is
also consumed by rage, and mercilessly and graphically murders the first of the
three assailants. As she stalks the other two, Buffy attempts to stop her, for Buffy
fears that Willow's evil acts will cause her to become increasingly and irre-
deemably evil. And indeed, Willow's power continues to grow and change her,
as represented by her eyes, which are devoid of expression (and pupils); her
darkened hair; her pallid and translucent skin; and the electrical force field that
seems to surround her ominously (figure 2.6).

Giles, who has returned from England for the purpose of stopping Willow,
is able to bind her briefly with a spell (he was granted powers by a coven ex-
pressly for this purpose). Giles, who is ultimately no match for her power, attempts to reason with her. He tells her to consider what Tara would think, noting that Tara would want her to turn to her friends for help through her grief.
Mentioning Tara only further enrages Willow, who finally draws all of Giles's
power away from him. Giles's powers, however, cause Willow to feel the pain of

FIGURE 2.6
Willow (Allyson Hannigan) increasingly used her powers as a means to fulfill her own interests, causing her to change from good to evil (episode: "Grave"). *Buffy the Vampire Slayer*, © 2002 Twentieth Century Fox Television. All rights reserved.

Tara's death that her vengeance has masked, as well as the pain of everyone in the world. To stop the pain, Willow decides to destroy the world. (As one person writes on a *Buffy* fan site, "What would a season finale be without the massive threat of apocalypse?")[69] Willow transports herself to Kingman's Bluff, where she raises a satanic temple that had been buried in the earthquake of 1932 (this is needed to bring about the world's destruction, she explains). Buffy, who is trapped in a grave site some distance from Willow, receives a telepathic communication from Willow, who tells her that a world that ceases to exist is better than one in which so many experience great suffering.

Xander goes to Willow and, admitting that he is powerless to stop her, simply says he wants to be with her during the destruction. He jokes with her and gradually wears down her resolve, saying to her, "The first day of kindergarten, you cried because you broke the yellow crayon . . . and you were too afraid to tell anyone. . . . You've come pretty far. Ending the world, not a terrific notion, but the thing is . . . yeah, I love you. I love crayon-breaky Willow and I love scary-veiny Willow. So if I'm going out, it's here. If you want to kill the world, then start with me. I've earned that." As Willow attempts to go about her task, Xander continues to draw closer to her, placing himself between Willow and the temple she has unearthed. Willow cannot strike Xander, so she eventually gives in to her grief and his support, and the apocalypse is (yet again) averted. Giles, who is suddenly recovered, explains that his "good magic" enabled her to feel pain, which in turn allowed Xander to tap into the "spark of humanity she had left."

Buffy also recovers, and the ordeal has granted her a sense of purpose and a renewed appreciation of the important relationships in her life. As *Buffy* critic Thomas Hibbs notes of the episode's conclusion, Buffy's new resolve serves as "a counterpoint to the metaphysics of evil. By contrast to goodness and in parasitic dependence on it, evil involves isolation from the rest of humanity, a closing off of the possibility of love, friendship, and communication; it is a will to raw, unconstrained power, a nihilistic drive to destroy all that is, including oneself."[70] In *Buffy*, we see once again that friendship and love are the ultimate powers that defeat evil. Moreover, while a sense of purpose and destiny is gained through difficult personal ordeals, the steadfast support of loved ones makes it possible to fulfill one's purpose: to continuously fight against evils, in the many forms that they take. Willow will suffer consequences as the result of her actions, but what is ultimately affirmed is the good of connectedness. Only in our connections can we find a way to resist the desire for power, claim a destiny, and fulfill the mission to change the world for the better. In this way, *Buffy* resolves the contradictions that arise between contemporary culture's individualism and drive toward nihilism, and our need to be in relationship with others.

Another important counterpoint to evil is found in the soundtrack that accompanies the episode's final scenes, and this is where we find an oblique reference to religion. The slow, soulful song playing in the background is called "Prayer of St. Francis" and is sung by Sarah McLachlan.[71] It seems a fitting conclusion to this chapter's discussion of how religion is represented to reprint part of this song's lyrics, which repeat the prayer attributed to St. Francis of Assisi. These passionate words, still important in may Catholic and other religious and spiritual traditions, were first popularized in song in the early Renaissance:

> Lord, make me an instrument of your peace.
> Where there is hatred, let me sow love;
> where there is injury, pardon;
> where there is doubt, faith;
> where there is despair, hope;
> where there is darkness, light;
> where there is sadness, joy!
>
> Grant that I may not so much seek
> to be consoled as to console;
> to be understood as to understand;
> to be loved as to love.
> For it is in giving that we receive;
> it is in pardoning that we are pardoned;
> and it is in dying that we are born to eternal life.

Once again, religion is not the point of the episode, but the program's references to supernatural evil that draw upon traditional religious representations also posit its opposite. Good is to be found in reference to all of those things that appeal to contemporary teens—friendships, destiny, power, and so forth—as well as in vague reference to traditions that come to our culture from religion.

The episodes reviewed in this chapter illustrate at least some of the ways in which religion is approached in contemporary teen culture in relation to fictionalized supernatural power. First, it is clear that these programs are not embracing evangelical definitions of good and evil, yet in important ways they serve as a counterpoint to the public debates about such definitions. The programs are built around certain aspects of what I call the dark side of evangelicalism, which includes the existence of demons, witchcraft, and manifestations of evil in the material world. Like most fictional stories in popular culture, however, they are not only at some distance from organized religion, but approach its claims and its traditions with irreverence and ambivalence.

Second, these stories also rely upon fictional conventions first put into place in the Enlightenment era. Like those stories, these comment upon the fact that both religion and science seemed to set limits on the possibilities of the unexplained realm beyond. Young people, like most adults, are fascinated with what lies beyond our knowledge, and explanations for evil in the world have always made for particularly compelling speculation. Set in the context of fiction, these stories make no claims to be true, yet their popularity suggests that the questioning of Enlightenment perspectives, especially as they relate to the claims of religion and of science, still holds important currency in contemporary culture.

Third, as these episodes illustrate, religion is approached relativistically in teen culture, as it may be aligned with purity and goodness (as in the case of the holy water), but its ability to gather power may also be marshaled for evil (as in the case of Spike's communionlike ritual). On a related note, religion is tainted by its association with its oppressive practices of the past, such as the support many religious organizations and leaders gave to the enslavement of African Americans in the United States, its complicity in the Holocaust in Germany, and its association with other historical atrocities. There is always a danger that courses of action identified as appropriate by religious organizations can come to appear much more like a contributor to social injustices than like actions that are actually "setting the captives free."

In spite of the recognition of religion's role in oppression, organized religion retains an important and even emancipatory role in the lives of many young people around the world. How is this contradiction possible? Programs like these suggest that while supernatural powers may be portrayed in fiction as clearly good or evil, for today's young people, religion and its claims often embody ambiguity.

This brief discussion, focused around episodes from *Buffy the Vampire Slayer* and *Angel* and the role of both religion and the occult in entertainment, form an important background to the exploration of how young people today describe their experiences with both the phenomena of the supernatural realm and the fictional stories that portray it. Although they may seem in many ways to be at a great distance from the traditions of organized religion, *Buffy* and *Angel* are far from anomalies in contemporary teen culture, or indeed in the popular cultural story forms of the past. They provide key insights into how the contemporary teens in the next section interpret the intersection of traditional religion and the popular beliefs about good and evil they encounter in the entertainment media and elsewhere. It is to these stories that we now turn.

Part II
ETHNOGRAPHIC STORIES

TEENS AND THEIR APPROACHES

TO MEDIA, RELIGION, AND

SUPERNATURAL BELIEFS

3

LOVING SUPERNATURAL

LEGENDS AND HATING

ORGANIZED RELIGION

"I watch a lot of extraterrestrial stuff," Jodie, a young Anglo-American woman from an impoverished economic background, told me as she puffed her cigarette. Her lip curled in defiance as she continued: "They're different. It's a new outlook on what could be happening, rather than on what already is happening, or what in the past has happened." Skeptical about the God she associated with organized religion, Jodie was fascinated instead by other forms of the supernatural, such as the paranormal, ghosts, and aliens. When I asked her which television program was most like her religious beliefs, she offered this intriguing answer: "It would have to be *X-Files*. Because, no matter what anybody says ... I've seen everything that everyone's compiled together about aliens. There's no doubt in my mind that we are not the only intelligent life ... God was a higher being. How do we know he wasn't an alien? On *X-Files*, Mulder, he would say something like that: how do we know God's not an alien?"

How, indeed? Some scholars in the studies of contemporary religion have questioned whether the entertainment media are to blame for what they might call the distorted beliefs of young people like Jodie.[1] In this era of irregular church attendance at religious organizations, stories like Jodie's suggest that while the local synagogue, mosque, or church might be a source of information about the realm beyond, so are television programs like *The X-Files*.

While few young people might declare that they believe God is an alien, Jodie's statement raises intriguing questions about religious beliefs among U.S. teens and the relationship of the media to those beliefs. One might assume that

Jodie illustrates what has been termed the postmodern idea of individual autonomy, as she seems to choose her beliefs from the media rather than from specific religious traditions.[2] Yet in this chapter, I hope to provide a more detailed analysis that demonstrates why such an argument is not adequate. Jodie never said she wasn't a religious or spiritual person. She simply made it clear that her religious beliefs were unconventional, to say the least. She was interested, as another teen termed the fictional stories of the supernatural, in the "funky" side of religion. As this term encompasses science fiction explanations and more traditionally religious categories of beings like angels and demons, it encompasses within it what I have earlier called the dark side of evangelicalism.

The stories of Jodie and Eric, who will also be introduced in this chapter, highlight some of the historic tensions between religious institutions and popular religious beliefs, and between the religious and the secular realms more generally.[3] With little formal background in organized religion and no stated interest in it, their stories suggest that some "secular" young people are nevertheless intrigued by the realm beyond the material world and often use surprising ways to talk about those interests. Jodie and Eric were friends, and others in their friendship circle were similarly either uninterested in or hostile toward organized religion. At age twenty, these young people were among the oldest of any interviewed. I begin with their stories because they raise important questions about the role of teen culture in belief formation. Ghost stories, horror movies, and experimenting with séances and spell-casting have all been popular as teen culture pursuits for a long time. We might assume that young people naturally abandon these things when they reach young adulthood. Yet this chapter explores the stories of two young people who seem to be carrying these interests forward in their lives. In part, this is because they are not fully adults, but see themselves in transition, or in the latter years of the extended adolescence phenomenon that increasingly defines the twenties in U.S. society. They were interviewed for this book because they remain financially and socially dependent on a parental figure even as they plan for their exit to adulthood. Because of their life experiences, however, they could discuss their views articulately while reflecting on their high school years with a dose of intentional irony. This made their stories provocative and, at times, especially poignant.

Jodie and Eric were not "seekers" of religious meaning. They didn't think it was important to have a set of beliefs that were coherent, let alone consistent, and they didn't consciously seek out ideas about the realm beyond from television or film. Like most people, they watched *The X-Files* and other programs for their entertainment value. When asked about their beliefs in the supernatural realm, and even their media preferences for programs and films featuring ghosts, demons, and aliens, they talked enthusiastically, expressing a deep sense of defiance toward the givens of organized religion and its relationship to the middle-class culture they felt rejected them. They animatedly resisted many of the terms and definitions that others might have considered the taken-for-granted, commonsense approach to religion and the realm beyond, such as "God loves everyone" or "God is good." In short, those beliefs that some have described as "civil religion" were resisted, sometimes even derisively, by these young people. This chapter considers how they came to this position and how their views related to their appreciation for supernatural stories in the entertainment media.

FINDING MORE PROOF FOR ALIENS THAN FOR GOD: JODIE OLSEN

It was a warm summer afternoon when I arrived for my first interview at Jodie's house. The front door was ajar (there was no screen) and four people were seated in the darkened living room on worn, mismatched couches, listening to loud heavy metal music. The front yard was fairly unkempt, and numerous large vehicles, most of which looked to be in disrepair, crowded the small driveway. Because I had arranged to interview a single mother and her teen-parent daughter (Nancy Donahue and her mother, whose stories are described in a later chapter), I was unsure who the other two people were and what their relationship was to Nancy and her mother. Yet obviously they were all waiting for me. One of the young women, who turned out to be Jodie, made room for me on her couch after I introduced myself.

I quickly learned that in addition to Nancy and her mother, the house was occupied by Cliff, Nancy's older brother; Mickey, the father of Nancy's two young children; Jodie and her husband, Carl (Jodie was Nancy's best friend in high school); and Eric, who was Nancy's friend and Jodie's ex-boyfriend. The seven of them, in addition to Nancy's two sons under the age of two, lived in a house of no more than 900 square feet. The home was not a permanent location for any of them, however, and in fact other young people had lived there before them and still others were to live there after some members of this group had moved on. At the time of the interview, however, all except Nancy's mother were living in this house as a result of various terrible circumstances, mostly involving crises of finances, job instabilities, imprisonment, and troubled familial relationships.

Jodie had a terrific sense of humor and a loud, raucous laugh that invited those in her presence to laugh with her. She also had a darker side, though, and had suffered for that: she left high school after getting in several fights with her peers, and she encountered even greater difficulties when she tried to return a few years later. Jodie exuded confidence—or, one might say, bravado—and enjoyed regaling her housemates with many stories, some of which were quite obviously exaggerated.

Jodie had lived in the house for eight months at the time of my first meeting with her. She and her husband had moved to another state to pursue job opportunities that turned out to be less lucrative than they had hoped. Upon their arrival back in their home area, Jodie and her husband, then high school dropouts, were told that they were not welcome in the home in which Jodie grew up. Her husband's parents had said that while he was welcome to live with them, his wife was not. With no money, no jobs, and no place to go, Nancy's mother offered them a place to stay "until they can get on their feet." Her husband had only recently been able to find a seasonal, low-paying job that enabled them to contribute toward the household's grocery bill, and Jodie had completed her GED but was unemployed.[4] She referred to Nancy's mother and the others in the house as "extended family."

The young people living in the house occasionally participated in social activities together, although more frequently they socialized in smaller groups that sometimes included housemates and others. A recent highlight for all had been OzzFest, a series of concerts featuring Ozzy Osbourne, Pantera, Marilyn Manson, and other heavy metal rock groups. Usually, however, they watched movies on cable television in the late evenings and listened to the radio during the day. They did not get a daily paper but instead purchased a Sunday paper primarily "for the TV Guide," as one household member explained, half-jokingly.

In her younger years, Jodie had some experiences with organized religion, although her mother participated without her father's support. She explained:

INTERVIEWER: Jodie, were you saying your family was religious?
JODIE: Mine? No, my dad always told me there's no such thing as God.
INTERVIEWER: And your mother? What did your mom say?
JODIE: My mom just told him to shut the hell up. Leave us alone. 'Cause we were going to church. I went up until almost seventh grade. And then I quit going. 'Cause, just some of the things in the Bible, and some of the things that are real, they just, they don't happen. No. There doesn't appear just two people on the earth, to inhabit the whole world. No, it doesn't happen that way.

Jodie discussed her rejection of religion in terms of what she later described as "scientific evidence" against the claims of the Bible. Yet the lack of proof, while it surfaced a number of times in our discussion, seemed to be one of two reasons for her rejection. The second reason emerged in later discussions and was related to the many frustrations she had experienced in her life, including depression and poverty, and being unable to have children: "I just figure, God doesn't want me to have any [children]. And then, the question of religion, is there a God, and why doesn't he like me now. The only thing I gotta say is if there's a God, he's very cruel." Her cynicism toward religion emerged as she referred to the difficulties she experienced in her own life. She was a fan of Marilyn Manson because, she said, his beliefs echoed her own: "His word about God is that there isn't one, and if there is, he's very cruel. And I agree, because I've had so many rough times where I don't think I deserved it, but He did it to me, anyway." She identified with the rage Marilyn Manson expressed, appreciating what she called his "outspoken" approach. She believed many people underestimated him simply because of his outrageousness:

I mean, a lot of people were [disgusted] when he did that [ripped up a Bible and wiped his backside with an American flag]. But he's saying that

America today isn't worth wiping his ass with. And it isn't, I mean—we're in debt, we used to be the richest continent in the world, and now, we're in debt billions and billions, and it's growing even more every second of the day. And he's saying, "We could do more." And by ripping up the Bible, he's saying, "That's a whole bunch of people getting together to make money, and if there was a God, why does he treat us like shit and why is our world going to hell like it is?"

Using what is perhaps a standard interpretation of Marilyn Manson's actions and lyrics, Jodie related her own rage to a cynical view of both the Christian tradition and the U.S. financial situation. She viewed both as related to the establishment and to the maintenance of the status quo.

Like some of the teens discussed in the following chapters, while she was skeptical about organized religion, Jodie had had what she considered both positive and frightening experiences with the supernatural realm. The frightening experiences were related to a young man who had lived with her and her husband, who had been experimenting with both drugs and witchcraft: "He was totally insane. He tripped fifty hits of acid and went totally nuts. Well, then he moved in with his girlfriend, she got pregnant. She moved out, 'cause she got afraid. And to tell you the truth, when we left, I was afraid of him. This guy was completely nuts, thinking that he was casting black magic spells on people, and making it rain, and killing people just by thinking about it. He was totally nuts." She and her husband discontinued contact with this former friend. Despite this experience, however, she has since ceased to think of people who make such claims to control supernatural powers as "totally nuts." Her change in opinion was the result of two factors: her husband's increasing involvement in Scientology, and her respect for Nancy's mother and her reported experiences with such powers. When her husband first tried to convince her of the power of mind control, she admitted that she was skeptical:

JODIE: He was telling me all the different things your body can do, and your mind, and I was like, "no way." I didn't believe half of it. And now that I've actually talked to people and—[Nancy's mother]. She's one person I could sit down and talk to for hours about this kind of thing. Because she actually knows what she can do, and she does it, and it's kinda weird, 'cause the things I've heard her say that she's done, just like, wow, I wish I could do some of those things.

INTERVIEWER: Like what?

JODIE: She says when she was a child she used to have this nose, and she hated it. So just by thinking about it, she changed her physical appearance. And it's been the same ever since. And I didn't believe her, until I saw a photo. And I asked if she'd had plastic surgery, it was so different and she said, "I did it myself." And I was like, "no way." I just could not believe that. And then I thought about what [her husband] said, that once you get up to the higher levels of Scientology you will be able to change your physical appearance. It's hard to believe, but it could happen . . . it was starting to make me believe that yeah, everything's created by us.

While Jodie remained skeptical that such events could occur and she herself had never experienced them, her respect for her husband and her friend's mother led her to an increased respect for the possibility that such powers were indeed accessible.

In contrast to experiences with conjuring, or calling forth supernatural powers, Jodie had had several experiences with ghosts and related them to her belief in reincarnation. One of her friends believed that she could access information about her past lives, something that intrigued Jodie, who believed that she "kind of remembers" her own past lives. Moreover, Jodie had read a book her husband gave her, titled *Have You Lived This Life Before?* by L. Ron Hubbard, founder of Scientology. These people and sources had been influential in how she had chosen to think about the supernatural realm.

Jodie's interests in the supernatural realm guided her preferences for science fiction and horror. While ghosts and past lives interested her, so did the legends surrounding alien abduction. She had never been abducted, but she wished that she could have had such an encounter. As I noted at the beginning of this chapter, when I asked her what television show was most like her own beliefs, she responded: "It would have to be *X-Files*. Because, no matter what anybody says. My dad's a real science fiction freak, he's the one that kind of got me into that, thinking about aliens. Well, I've seen everything that everyone's compiled together about aliens. There's no doubt in my mind that we are not the only intelligent life. . . . God was a higher being. How do we know he wasn't an alien? On *X-Files*, Mulder, he would say something like that: 'How do we know God's not an alien?'"

Jodie was aware of the fact that such a statement would be controversial, and indeed, I imagine she enjoyed "shocking" me. Yet such a melding of beliefs from popular television did not seem inconsistent with how she had come to accept various other beliefs, such as the books she had read and the stories she had heard from friends who shared their own experiences with the supernatural realm. Her conversations tended to draw upon and mix ideas from Christianity, popular conceptions of aliens, popular science, reports of friends' experiences, and other bits and pieces from Eastern spirituality. These all came together to some extent when she was describing her dreams about alien abductions and her experiences with the ghosts in the home where she grew up:

I believe that everybody has a soul, and it's put on earth for one thing, and it'll keep returning until that happens. Make different decisions in different lives, different things happen. I do remember some of my past lives, and I'd like to get into that, because I think if I do, I can remember all of them, what happened. . . . I believe more or less in aliens, because if aliens are real, they're coming from billions and billions of miles away. People say they have big eyes and big heads. What if that's just an outer shape that they take? It is kinda frightening, but to some people it wouldn't be. That's just the shape they take when they're here. And it's just an energy somewhere else. That's what I think our souls are, is just energy.

According to Jodie, aliens, like humans, were just souls of energy in a different form, perhaps even destined—like us—to repeat lives until they fulfill their purpose. Not only are we and aliens of similar substance, but according to Jodie we are intimately connected with alien life. In an interesting creation story that has been popularized by films such as *Chariots of the Gods,* Jodie noted:

> Me personally, I think we were put here by aliens. I think they brought down a certain number of people, stuck them on certain islands or whatever, and said, "Make something for yourselves." And we just evolved into what we are today. And now the aliens are coming back to check on us, see how we're doing. We've only been here a couple million years, and now they're getting more curious since we're getting more intelligent, and we're using our intelligence for something good rather than something bad, like warheads. We're using it for the good, like space exploration, things like that. They're getting interested in us again. "What are they doing?" Medicine's getting better. "They're all evolving."

Aliens seemed to appeal to Jodie because, as she noted, while there were "too many facts against the book [Bible]," belief in the possibility of aliens addressed her sense that there was much to the universe that remained unexplained. "There's no doubt in my mind that we are not the only intelligent life," she noted. I wondered how she might relate these beliefs to her own evaluation of what she saw on television or in movies regarding aliens:

> INTERVIEWER: So, when you have shows like *The X-Files,* or *Millennium,* or some movie that represents aliens, do you think that those are accurate representations? And why would that be? Are there some people who are descendants of aliens then, who are helping to produce the show, or who've had contact with alien life in some way?
>
> JODIE: See, that's what I keep wondering. I read an interview one time with Steven Spielberg. He says that he has been abducted by aliens, and that's where he gets most of his ideas from. Well, I mean, yeah, I do believe that *X-Files,* someone on the writing team has obviously seen something, or believes in it, to have such detail on some of their stories. I mean, the story about the two guys in the forest that they did, that was a true story. It did happen. And I think they mostly take stories of other people and just put 'em on their show and just add a couple things, you know? They say that the stories are mostly fiction. Well, I think they take stories from people and just add things, and make it fiction, rather than truth, so people don't think, "You're crazy, I'm not watching that show anymore." Yeah, some of the writers or producers

or whatever, I guess some of them would have to really be believing in that to be part of that show. I mean, if I didn't believe in it, I wouldn't have anything to do with it from what people say about it. Whether it's imagination or whether he heard it from a story, it just gives people a different view about what life could be like, or is like.

To restate, part of the appeal of fantasy and science fiction programs that deal with aliens, the paranormal, and other aspects of the supernatural reside in their ability to present, as Jodie said, "what life *could* be like, or *is* like." The emphasis was not on finding the "truth" in these programs (or elsewhere) but on being open to possibilities, an idea that emerges in several of the interviews with young people. It is an idea to which we will return.

THE FUNKY SIDE OF RELIGION: ERIC DAY

Eric had moved to Nancy's mother's house a few months before my first meeting with him, after he had completed a three-year prison sentence. He had been told that he was not welcome in the home of his parents, and, like Jodie, was offered a place to stay by Nancy's mother. Eric described Nancy's mother and the others in the house as a kind of extended family, echoing Jodie's description. He had been friends with Nancy since their high school days together and had even dated Jodie at one point.

Like Jodie, Eric had completed his GED in the previous year after having dropped out of the local high school. He had also been married, but then divorced after a year. He had recently found a job with a moving company and intended to move out of Nancy's mother's house as soon as he could afford to. With an attractive and mischievous smile, Eric noted that he enjoyed thinking of himself "like a kid" and did not have many plans beyond the immediate future.

In Nancy's mother's house, Eric slept on the couch in the living room, where the television was located. This meant that whether or not he wished to watch whatever television program or film others were watching, he often participated when not at work because he had nowhere else to go. While Eric protested that he did not like soap operas and game shows, for instance, both Nancy and Jodie pointed out that he never left the room when either of them chose to watch such programs. He also disliked the television program featuring black comedian Martin Lawrence because he felt it discriminated against white people. The only programs he objected to strenuously, however, were those involving real stories of police, such as *Cops* and *Highway Patrol*. His distaste for these grew out of his personal experience: "If you're going to jail, I don't think they need to be airing that on television. That's your own business. And if I was ever being arrested and somebody came up and stuck a camera in my face, I woulda let them have it." Eric's negative experiences with law enforcement and imprisonment caused him to identify with the perpetrators rather than the police, which, given the content and focus of many such programs, would seem to be a contradictory, or what television theorists Fiske and Hall have described as a "resistive" interpretation.[5] Eric particularly liked watching graphically violent horror films with his male housemates. Because the house mostly held older adolescents, there were no restrictions on the media use, other than those that arose when people could not agree on which programs or films to watch.

Eric, like Jodie, had little use for organized religion. While Jodie had described her mother as Baptist, Eric was less clear about his mother's religious background, identifying her as "just an orthodox Christian." Like Jodie's parents, Eric's parents were not in agreement about approaches to religion. Eric noted that he, like his father, rejected religion in his early teen years: "My mother's religious, my dad just kinda tolerates it. Along with everyone else in the family. I mean, it wasn't so bad when [I was] a kid, but when you start growing up. 'Cause we [he and his younger brother] got to be teenagers, and we started to get in trouble. My mom just totally changed. She was really, really cool and then as soon as I hit teenage years, it was like, 'You guys stay out of trouble'—and blah, blah, blah." Eric related his mother's religion to her "change," or perhaps strictness, in his teen years, when she became less understanding toward what she considered his deviant behavior. His rejection of organized religion was one of several ways in which he had chosen to rebel against his parents and other authority figures.

While his parents normally did not attend religious services, he and his younger brother had taken the bus to church while growing up. The religious experience of his youth that stood out in Eric's mind, however, had occurred not in the church but during a summer stay at what he called a "Bible camp," for which his church had sponsored his attendance. Each evening, the camp had held a worship service that Eric described as "pretty intense," with charismatic features such as speaking in tongues and jumping up in praise. Most of the time, he observed such behavior with some discomfort, but then one evening a preacher's message struck a chord for him:

> There was one night out of the entire week that something kinda hit me. It was like, "Slap! Wake up!" And we're walking out and I was just totally engrossed in what the preacher had just said. I turned around to say something to my brother, and then I looked up on the top of the chapel, and an angel's standing there. I grabbed my brother. "Do you see that?" "No." "There's an angel standing there." "No, there's not." "Yes, there is!" "No, there's not." I turned around and grabbed him. "Yes, there is!" But when I turned around to look, it was gone. Then it was like, "Nah, couldn't'a been."

Eric didn't say anything to anyone about this sighting until long after he had returned home from camp. Then, a young woman who had also been at the camp told him that she had seen an angel on top of the chapel: "I said, 'No shit. So did I.' I was like, 'But I thought it was just a hallucination.' She goes, 'Yeah, so did I.'"

The fact that they reported to each other that they had witnessed it served as evidence for both of them that what they had seen was indeed an angel. He also had an occasion, much later in his life, when he believed he had seen the Devil. This experience was more open to doubt, though, according to Eric:

> I coulda sworn on a stack of Bibles that I saw the devil himself. But that, you know I can't vouch for that, because I was kinda—after going to a very intense party, I was pretty drunk and stoned, and all that other funky stuff at the time. And I'm walking through my buddy's house toward the back bedroom, I was going to lay down, and I walked past the last window, and I heard a tap on the window. I turned around and there's his face, just— [makes an evil face]. I didn't even stick around long enough—I didn't even take a second look. I hit the bed and said, "Yikes!"

Instead of an intense worship service, this vision manifested itself to Eric after an "intense" party involving drugs and alcohol, behavior not condoned either by his "religious" mother or, for that matter, many other authority figures. With his discussion of the summer camp angel and his early years of church attendance, Eric had demonstrated that he held on to some of the tenets of Christianity even if he rejected many others. So it may not be surprising that while the experience after a worship service had been positive with the appearance of an angel, an experience after what Eric believed was deviant (if fun) behavior had resulted in the appearance of the Devil. While both reports reference religious phenomena, Eric said that neither changed him much. This was because he was not convinced that these events had actually occurred. As he said, there was not enough scientific evidence supporting it: "People go with this, 'I ain't gonna believe it unless I see it.' I'm sorry, but I'm not gonna believe it unless I see it, touch it, and taste it. . . . The way my analytical mind works, I won't believe it." The existence of such beings lacked empirical evidence, reasoning that was akin to Jodie's earlier comments about the "facts against the book."

While Jodie had rejected organized religion in part based upon her own belief in this lack of "facts," Eric's rejection rested much more firmly on his rebellion against his parents and authority in general. His thoughts about the beliefs of organized religion were in some ways much more clearly related to the Christian tradition than were Jodie's. Unlike Jodie, for instance, he did not agree with Marilyn Manson, explaining, "It's not okay to rip up a Bible, I'm sorry." He also saw a relationship between his favorite television program and his acceptance of some of Christianity's beliefs. His favorite television program was a graphically violent series called *Spawn,* based on a comic book character who, in a Faustian bargain, is able to avoid death by agreeing to serve in Satan's army as a "hellspawn." Eric described it as a television program that "dealt a lot with religion" in terms of what he called religion's "negative aspect":

> ERIC: There's a lot of evil stuff in it, and all. It deals a lot with evil, and hell, and Satan, and shit like that. And it also shows a lot of the corrupt sides of society.

INTERVIEWER: So, how is *Spawn* different from *Touched by an Angel*?
ERIC: Well, it covers the exact opposite. . . . I mean, in *Touched by an Angel*, they're like angels from God. And in *Spawn*, they're more like demons.
INTERVIEWER: So it's pretty much the same beliefs, just the other side of the coin?
ERIC: Yeah. Pretty much.

Each of Eric's favorite television programs and films echoed his interests in views that he seemed to see as challenging to the status quo and rebelling against authority: "I like all that science fiction and funky alien-type stuff," he told me. His own beliefs mixed Christianity with the legends of aliens told by Jodie and other members of their household. As he explained:

Yeah, I do believe that there are aliens out there. We had to get here some-how. I believe in God, I believe that God was an extraterrestrial. Which, when you think about it, He is. There's absolutely no way to avoid clas-sifying God as an extraterrestrial life form, because the term "extrater-restrial" means "not of this planet." And if God supposedly created this planet and everything in it, how can he be from here? My mom thinks that's just totally a sacrilegious way to look at it, you know. And every time we have a conversation about religion, it comes up. First she asks me, "What do you believe?" I'll tell her, and it's the same thing every time, that God was an alien. I don't know about heaven and hell. But if there is a hell? We're there. We're there.
INTERVIEWER: Yeah, let's hope it can't get any worse!
ERIC: Oh, but it will, it will! But the hell that we live in is what we made it. I mean, the only reason this planet is in the condition it's in is because of us. Nothing else but us.

For Eric as for Jodie, it seemed plausible to unite traditional Christian under-standings of God with the more "funky" idea that God was an alien. The fact that his mother, the arbiter of traditional Christianity for Eric, was frustrated by his equation of these two seemingly disparate belief systems only added to the appeal. As was the case with Jodie's assertion that scientific evidence demonstrated the existence of aliens, Eric used scientific logic to deduce that if God created humanity and the world, God must be separate from it. His beliefs of hell as existing on this earth also echoed Jodie's embrace of Marilyn Man-son's critique of what has become of the world. We have allowed the world to become tainted. This is not the result of an evil force outside of this universe, but it is from forces within society that Eric felt were beyond his control. One of Eric's housemates said it best: "Personal opinion has no relevance. At all. If you don't make a six-digit salary, you don't count in today's society. It's true. Even if you vote, you're still not making a big enough impact. You don't make a six-digit salary, then they're not gonna listen to you, 'cause you are nobody. You didn't work hard enough, I guess. Half of them didn't work either, though." Eric, Jodie, and their housemates all seemed to recognize that, on the one hand, they may have made choices that placed them at odds with the society that had made this world a hell for them. Yet on the other hand, they also recognized that there were forces beyond their control that held in place the distance between them and those with the "six-digit salary." Embracing aliens, the "funky" side of Christianity, and the offbeat experiences with the supernatural realm that they or their friends had both reinforced this separation and served as an act of resistance to society's norms.

Jodie and Eric, along with several of their housemates, resisted more conventional approaches to religion. In particular, they challenged what they believed were Christianity's claims to have complete and authoritative explanations for the workings of the universe and the realm beyond. Instead, each of them asserted that there was much that remained unexplained. This came up in Eric's conversation with reference to the truthfulness of what the entertainment media represented in the way of legends of the supernatural:

> INTERVIEWER: Okay, so when you see stuff in television or in the movies that's about angels or ghosts, or the Devil, do you sometimes feel like what they're portraying in television is authentic?
>
> ERIC: It depends. . . . Anything that's really fake like the *Nightmare on Elm Street* movies, or these dreams about the psychos who blow their head off and then the next year they're back—I don't believe it. No, it's fake. But there were a few—Stephen King, H. P. Lovecraft. The reason I like them so much is because things they write about could actually happen.
>
> INTERVIEWER: Could, or do you think they did?
>
> ERIC: There's a possibility, I mean, it's possible. Theologically, scientifically, and everything else, it's possible.

Eric, like Jodie and many other teens interviewed, did not say that he "believed" in aliens or in other supernatural or extraterrestrial phenomena represented in the media. What did his favorite television programs and films do? They represented what might be *possible* in the realm beyond. In Eric's view, Christianity wanted to close off options for what might be possible in the realm beyond. So enjoying programs that explored possibilities was another form of rebellion against the society and the religion that, to him, supported its worldview.

THE RESISTERS AND THEIR APPROACH TO THE SUPERNATURAL, RELIGION, AND THE MEDIA

The Resister teens of this chapter were in many ways the furthest removed from religious traditions of any of the teens discussed in this book. They were not at all concerned about separating the stories of religion from the legends of the entertainment media. Harboring a great deal of concern over the financial, relational, and job-related challenges of everyday life, Jodie, Eric, and their housemates viewed speculations about the realm beyond the material world primarily in terms of entertainment. These young people's explanations of the supernatural realm, and even of their beliefs, depended on the needs of the moment and did not seem to be related to either personal or social moral systems. They were also not viewed as resources to help them deal with their everyday lives.

Friends, parents, and personal experience figured significantly in how they interpreted their beliefs and experiences with the supernatural. Eric's belief that he had had an encounter with an angel was strengthened when another young woman shared her own experience, and Jodie credited her interest in possibly invoking supernatural power with her husband's convictions, the experiences of her friend's mother, and another friend's interest in past lives. Their friendship and kinship circles reinforced their desire to see themselves as rebelling against authority, and against what they understood to be dominant culture. This resistance to the status quo took various forms, including negative relationships with parents and law enforcement, and the enjoyment of music and visual media that is frequently dismissed in elite culture as tasteless or denigrating.

Interestingly, their resistance did not include complete rejection of either the idea that a Christian God might exist or that there might be forces and beings beyond the material world that could be interpreted through Christian frameworks. It may seem surprising, but their beliefs of the supernatural and religious realms sometimes overlapped. While their suturing of varying viewpoints may be unusual and perhaps even rare, such combinations must be understood within our earlier discussions of the relationship between religion and culture. Jodie and Eric associate Christianity with the authority they want to rebel against, and so they seek to resist dominant interpretations of the supernatural realm that come from that religion. But they are hard-pressed to come up with alternatives. What they hear and see all around them are ideas of evil and darkness that provide echoes, no matter how faint, of Christianity. Marilyn Manson is not desecrating the I Ching, after all. What these teens prefer in the entertainment media, as Eric said, is the "funky" side of religion. They like demons, "hellspawn," the stuff that was earlier described as the dark side of evangelicalism. Even science fiction, that genre that articulates concerns about scientific rather than religious authority, is interpreted by both Jodie and Eric as a challenge to religion: God could be an alien (figure 3.1).

The interests in alien life that Jodie and Eric expressed are hardly unusual in contemporary U.S. life. According to a 1996 Gallup poll of those living in the United States, 96 percent of respondents had heard of UFOs, and 46 percent of those believed UFOs were real.[6] An earlier poll found that 27 percent of people believed that aliens had visited the Earth, and a Roper poll reported that one in fifty believed that they had been abducted by aliens.[7] Scholars have found that there is no relation between alien belief and income, occupation, or level of education, and psychological tests have found no relation between belief in aliens and mental illness.[8] "True believers" in aliens, such as those who claim to have experienced abduction, may completely reject Christianity and other religious

FIGURE 3.1
"I want to believe": *The X-Files* begs the question of a possible conspiracy among the culturally powerful to conceal the fact that aliens exist, an intriguing idea for alienated teens like Jodie and Eric. Pictured: David Duchovny and Gillian Anderson as Agents Mulder and Scully. *The X-Files*, © Twentieth Century Fox Television. All rights reserved.

explanations. But there is evidence that many believers, like Jodie and Eric, do not find the two belief systems completely incompatible.[9]

The accommodation between Christianity and aliens that Jodie and Eric make is particularly interesting with respect to the very different positions these two belief systems occupy in relation to the hegemonic ideas, or "common sense," of Western culture. Belief in aliens, of course, is neither as common nor as acceptable as beliefs that are at least nominally Christian. Consider, for instance, how each are covered in the news media. While Peter Jennings regularly hosts ABC television specials such as *The Search for Jesus* to explore the roots of and controversies within Christian faith, questions of aliens only appear occasionally among newsmagazines (more frequently in television and radio talk shows), and they are always framed with questions of skepticism. Psychologists, journalists, and many hobbyists have devoted innumerable hours and publications to debunking theories of aliens, most noteworthy perhaps being popular scientist Carl Sagan.[10] Believers in aliens have responded that such efforts are only attempts to cover up what they see as the truth about aliens. Alien believers may be concerned about a cover-up. But in contrast, no one claims that anyone is trying to cover up the existence of God.[11] When Jodie and Eric talk about their interest in aliens, they realize that many people think of religion as "the truth" and aliens as "fictional." Mixing up these two categories is the point, and it is a source of entertainment for them. But it is also indicative of their positions in relation to the larger society.

There are some surprising features of this particular "blurring" between Christian and alien encounter stories. First there is the method by which people come to be convinced of alien encounters, which folklorist Bill Ellis likens to "an experience identical to that of a religious conversion."[12] Ellis analyzes a book that has become a central text for believers in alien encounters, Whitley Strieber's *Communion*. In this book, Strieber details the psychological stress he was under that caused him to contact Budd Hopkins, a known advocate for beliefs in alien encounters and abductions. After Hopkins assured him that his stress was similar to that experienced by others who had undergone alien abductions, Strieber began to reconsider certain events in his life as possibly paranormal. His storytelling of angst and enlightenment that led to his sense of mission about relating what he believed was the message of "communion" from aliens was "structurally identical to . . . the narratives of 'born-again' Christians," according to Ellis.[13] The fact that alien encounter leads to enlightenment and purpose for one's life parallels what many consider a primary function of Christianity. This suggests that when young people like Jodie and Eric talk about aliens, they are not so much rejecting Christianity altogether as they are unconsciously recognizing in it certain tropes, or themes, that have long been a part of that religious tradition with which they are most familiar. Christianity has established the terms of reference, and even aliens are understood by these young people within its terms.

Second, the stories of alien encounters and abduction have many similarities with other legends associated with Christianity. Another folklorist, Peter Rojcewicz, has pointed out that alien stories often follow a pattern of earlier tales of encounters with devils or demons.[14] These beings may change shape, read minds, prod and poke humans or otherwise wreak havoc on their environments, and generally inspire fear because of their stealth and invisible power. Richard Boylan, a psychologist who claims to have experienced alien abduction, for instance, draws upon these same fears of demons when arguing that attempting to track aliens is futile: "You're dealing with people who can read your minds. . . . If they don't want to be captured, they'll catch it while you're forming the plot," he has said.[15] Some in the more conservative branches of Protestant Christianity even see alien abduction as the work of demons.[16]

On the other hand, rather than demons, some have seen aliens in relation to the angels of the Christian tradition in particular.[17] Religious historian Geddes MacGregor, for instance, leaves open the possibility that angels have never been anything other than intelligent life forces from different universes. He writes:

> What I am suggesting (as a worthwhile hypothesis but obviously no more) is that angels as they are represented in the Bible and religious tradition might be such more advanced forms of intelligent life: extraterrestrial beings who (far from being the little green men of science fiction) could

have developed along another evolutionary line to a higher form than ours and be more rational, more benevolent, and so capable of helping humans in the way that angels in traditional religious lore are said to do. ... there is no scientific reason why it should not be a viable one and there are many indications of its plausibility.[18]

Certainly, some alien enthusiasts would agree with this approach. John Mack, who is known for his advocacy of alien encounters from the hallowed halls of Harvard, has written that alien abductions challenge the separation of the spiritual and physical realms.[19] Strieber, mentioned earlier, also related angels to aliens. He came to see the aliens he encountered as messengers who charged him to convey a message of hope to the world—a task that sounds very similar to that of the angels of Christianity.[20] While each of these examples comes from persons who have invested a great deal of time and effort into considering the role of aliens and their relationship to certain tenets of Christianity, the fact that they analyze such overlaps underscores how people like Jodie and Eric may take for granted a certain coherence between these seemingly disparate belief systems.

Another interesting facet of the simultaneous acceptance of Christianity and beliefs in aliens concerns the relation of both to science, specifically to "evidence" and "proof," as Jodie and Eric discussed this. All of the teens interviewed for this book have a respect for scientific knowledge, although some of the Traditionalist teens mentioned reservations about science's explanations and exclusive claims. Unlike any of the other teens, however, the Resisters viewed themselves as largely oriented toward scientific evidence and for the most part did not identify themselves as religious. Thus in some ways the Resisters discussed here embraced a "secular" identity despite their continued interest and belief in the possibility that explanations might rest in realities beyond the realms explorable by science.

Still, science and religion are not so distant from each other as they might have been in the times before the last few decades. In part, this is due to the widespread popularized accounts of physics and the cosmos, notably the writings of Stephen Hawking and Carl Sagan.[21] While both of these scientists discuss issues of the universe in scientific terms, they and their followers also use "God language" in their arguments. An example occurs in the writings of Paul Davies, a mathematical physicist, who writes: "I belong to the group of scientists who do not subscribe to a conventional religion but nevertheless deny that the universe is a purposeless accident. Through my scientific work I have come to believe more and more strongly that the physical universe is put together with an ingenuity so astonishing that I cannot accept it merely as brute fact. There must, it seems to me, be a deeper level of explanation. Whether one wishes to call that deeper level 'God' is a matter of taste and definition."[22] While some theologians have noted that the scientists' use of "God" to describe the workings of the universe may refer to a more abstract concept than that embraced by most people in the United States, the language nonetheless popularizes connections between scientific explanations of the universe and religious ones.[23] The languages of God and of science are both employed in a way that reconciles the increasing scientific knowledge of our era with the long-standing appeal of religious explanations. While this dialogue between science and religion continues in important circles of the public and the intelligentsia, it also inadvertently encourages the blurring of science and religion in less legitimated ways—particularly in the curiosity surrounding aliens.

Science and evidence have been a part of the alien tradition since its origins in the Cold War, as political scientist Jodi Dean has argued.[24] As she notes, the term "flying saucer" was coined in 1947 with the first of three highly publicized sightings of UFOs. In this same year, the Air Force initiated Project Sign, an effort to control information regarding UFOs primarily because it was believed at the time that they might be foreign (e.g., Soviet) invaders. Despite the fact that not all sighted objects were identifiable, the military took the position that it was in the best security interests of the country to demonstrate that it had the authority to rule out the possibility that such unidentified flying objects might be dangerous. Thus, there was a campaign waged to demonstrate that scientific, or psychological, explanations could account for all such occurrences. Those who had sighted unidentifiable objects were dismissed as confused (it may have been airplane lights or swamp gas) or worse, disturbed or hysterical. This strategy backfired, leaving people with the impression that the military had something to hide. Two influential books supporting this hypothesis were published at the time: *Flying Saucers are Real* and *Behind the Flying Saucers*.[25] In the meantime, amateur groups began investigating the occurrences on their own, challenging the military explanations and, because of the controversy, drawing increased public attention to UFOs through the media. From its earliest musings, stories of aliens have been defined in terms of debates about evidence (with the issue of the credibility of witnesses a central aspect), and in relation to mistrust of the government and military and its presumed "cover-up."

On the other hand, in its earliest days science itself arose as a challenge to religious leaders' claims to authoritatively speak about the universe and its workings. Religious explanations lacked proof, a fact that enabled scientists to separate themselves and their work from the auspices of church authority in the late sixteenth century. The growth of empirical knowledge throughout the following centuries led sociologist Max Weber to posit that the need for religious explanations, and hence for religion itself, would cease, leading to the disenchantment of the world. While many who study the vitality of religious faiths argue that scientific explanation has not reduced religion's hold on the majority of the population of the world (save, perhaps, in academia), the concept of a "secularized" worldview has tremendous influence on how people view both religion and its relationship to scientific evidence. Part of the appeal of alien stories for Jodie and Eric, therefore, was in their sense that they were aligning themselves with beliefs deemed less acceptable, less credible, and challenging to authority, while at the same time calling upon the authority of science to justify their own beliefs.

When I have presented the stories of Jodie and Eric to others, it has been suggested to me that perhaps they were not giving me a "true" representation about their beliefs, but instead were providing stories that would be entertaining or disturbing. Yet whether or not these were their actual beliefs, it is important that they chose to tell these delegitimated stories to a researcher they would have no doubt associated with the dominant values of middle-class culture and perhaps even of skeptical academia. The embrace of the possibility of aliens, at least for Jodie and Eric, was consistent with how they saw themselves and wanted to be seen by others, as at a distance to those very norms and yet also intelligent, as evidenced by their calling upon science and issues of evidence.

It is easy to see a relationship between the underprivileged economic positions held by Eric, Jodie, and their friends and their desire to question and challenge what they see as the views of an establishment that marginalizes them and legitimates certain approaches through religion. Yet like the working-class teens cultural theorist Paul Willis analyzed in *Learning to Labor* and the working-class readers of the *National Enquirer* interviewed by media audience ethnographer Elizabeth Bird, aligning themselves with the "funky" side of religion and its mediated representations is at least one aspect of a worldview that ultimately reinforces their lower social status by structurally resulting in limited access to what sociologist Pierre Bourdieu has termed social and economic capital.[26] Their beliefs alone do not keep them from such attainment, certainly, but they provide reinforcement for their continuing desire to remain marginal to what they view as the unsavory relationship of legitimated religion to the "snobs" of suburbia, as one teen from another family group put it.[27]

In the next chapter, we introduce other teens who have a marginal association with religious organizations. Yet this group is not as interested in resisting dominant authority as were Eric, Jodie, and their friends. How do they talk about the stories of the supernatural from the entertainment media, particularly when formal associations with religion no longer mediate their interpretations? We turn to their stories to find out.

BLURRING THE BOUNDARIES

BETWEEN RELIGIOUS

AND FICTIONAL LEGENDS

On the WB Network's *Charmed,* Prue Halliwell (played by Shannen Doherty) faced challenges that called upon her to make use of her special powers. Like her sisters Piper (Holly Marie Combs) and Phoebe (Alyssa Milano), Prue kept her connections to witchcraft hidden from mortal view. But when troubled and vulnerable Maggie made a suicidal jump from the roof of a skyscraper, Prue knew that she needed to do whatever she could to save the girl. After first grabbing for Prue's hand, but then slipping and falling several stories, Maggie was saved at the last moment as Prue moved her body so that it would land on a nearby awning, breaking the fall. Recovering from the incident at the police station, a rattled Maggie attempted to explain what happened:

> MAGGIE: I shouldn't be alive. If it hadn't been for that—angel . . .
> INSPECTOR: Excuse me?
> MAGGIE: She just—appeared. Out of thin air. When I was on the rooftop.
>   She reached out her hand, and then when I was falling, it was like
>   something slowed me down, like she guided me to that awning.
> INSPECTOR: The angel?
> MAGGIE: Yes, she saved me.
> INSPECTOR: Help me out here. What exactly did the angel look like?

Inspector Darryl Morris (Dorian Gregory), a friend of Prue's, immediately suspected that this "angel" was actually a witch. He called Prue to warn her that someone might have witnessed the incident, encouraging her to stay out of sight lest someone reveal her supernatural powers.

As this episode unfolded, the reason for the young woman's jump became evident: she was being pursued by a "darklighter": a supernatural being that was seeking to convince "whitelighters" to kill themselves before they had a chance to become powerful supernatural forces for good. Every Thursday in the first years of the twenty-first century, Prue and her sister witches battled "darklighters," demons, warlocks, and other supernatural beings, using their powers and calling upon the wisdom of the Book of Shadows. Drawing on Wiccan folklore in its imagery and plotlines, the charmed ones were also sent into distinctly Christian-inspired realms, fighting demons in the underworld and, in one episode, contemplating their actions while floating, clothed in white, through a cloud-filled mystical heaven.[1] With this mixing of religious imagery, perhaps it's no wonder that Maggie Murphy assumed that the do-gooder who helped her was an angel rather than a witch.

Angels, ghosts, demons, and witches: they are all supernatural beings, and they are all distinct from one another. Or are they? In this chapter, we meet a few young people who, like Maggie, aren't so sure. These young people are also not convinced that such distinctions matter much.

As has been noted already, the vast majority of teens in the United States claim to believe in God. Very few might be described as "secularists"—those with no interest in God, religion, or faith. Teens that surveys might categorize as secularists because of their lack of involvement in formal religion, therefore, are not necessarily uninterested in the mystical realm. This chapter sets out to explore these Mysticals. While not at all interested in organized religion, but not as interested in protesting organized religion as the Resister teens, the Mystical teens remain believers of a sort, particularly as they are intrigued by the realm beyond the material world.

Like the Resister teens, the teens highlighted here have little involvement, interest, or background in organized religion, although they had some limited exposure to Protestant Christianity when they were much younger. Given this lack of current commitment and interest, it comes as no surprise that they demonstrate little concern for whether the stories they see in the entertainment media are consistent with a particular religious system. Nevertheless, they each have had experiences that they believe have involved contact with the supernatural. Like the Resisters, their interests in stories of the supernatural do not rest upon a conscious "seeking" of meaning or a desire for a coherent belief system; in fact, the Mystical teens adamantly refuse such language and argue that their media choices are in no way related to how they interpret their own experiences with the supernatural realm. How they choose to interpret these events, and how these interpretations are related to their media choices as well as other factors, are the subjects of this chapter.

A SECULARIST WHO SPEAKS OF ANGELS
AND ALIENS: JAKE PICKERINGTON

Sixteen-year-old Jake was enthusiastic about drag-car racing. He and the other members of his Anglo-American, middle-class blended family spent many Friday nights at the track, cheering on his older stepbrothers, admiring the cars, and sometimes even working the pit crew. Drag racing was a family activity, and it was no small task to gather this energetic family of five teen boys and one teen girl, given that all were active in sports and other frequent outings with friends. In addition to racing, Jake worked at a fast-food outlet a few hours a week. He also spent some of his spare time on his artwork, as he and his mother shared an interest in freehand drawing.

Jake lived in a large, beautiful suburban home with his mother and stepfather. His older sister was at college, while his three half-brothers, his father's sons from a previous marriage, lived with their mother during the school year. During the summer months, however, all of the teens lived in the Pickerington house. Even during the school year, relations between the Pickeringtons and their ex-spouses were friendly, and Jake's half-brothers often spent the night with them on the weekends.

Other than drag racing, the family rarely had time for joint activities, especially television—except for the one program they all made time for: *The X-Files*. They were latecomers to the series, but after several weeks into the fourth season the family had become so intrigued by *The X-Files* that they rented and watched every episode that had aired before they began viewing.

Jake's family had few restrictions on their media use, although he and his sister recalled that their television watching was curtailed when they were either grounded or had received poor grades in school. While they had a large-screen television, they only subscribed to the basic cable package because they preferred to rent movies. One of Jake's stepbrothers who, according to Jake's stepfather, went through a "hip-hop phase," was told that he could not listen to his music when in the house because it was inappropriate. He later abandoned that style of music in favor of country music, which the family found much less objectionable. Jake himself liked to play computer games, including, as his stepfather said, games that were "gross, violent, bloody, shoot-em-up kinds of things." In general, as the parents pointed out, the tastes of the teens tended to reflect those of the parents—they were all appalled by crude language and overt sexuality, for instance. Because the young people tended to share their parents' tastes, and because all of the young people in the house were thirteen or older, the parents felt that restrictions on media use were generally unnecessary.

Jake tended to approach media content by viewing it in relation to issues of taste and class, as his parents did.[2] He did not like what he called "trashy" television talk shows or music that appealed to what he termed "gangster wannabes." He was also concerned about certain representations in the media that reflected his own position. Like his stepfather, Jake thought the media tended to discriminate against white males, depicting them as greedy, self-serving, or prejudiced, and he was personally angered by this. His approach to media, like other matters, was guided not so much by adherence to a philosophical, religious, or moral system but by the practical experiences of his everyday life. For instance, he did not object to bad language or sexual situations because they differed from what he believed. Nor did he object to violence in the media because it might persuade him to act in certain ways or because it misrepresented certain societal groups or conflicts. He made his choices based upon both what he liked and what seemed realistic to him at the time. While this could be said, to some extent, of all of the teens interviewed, Jake's approach seemed directly related to his view of his life as organized by routines (largely managed by his parents) rather than by reflection or conscious decision-making on his own part.

A somewhat reticent teen, Jake grew up with few experiences in formal religion. His mother, raised in the Methodist Church, had been active in a conservative Protestant organization until her divorce from Jake's father when Jake was eight years old. Jake's stepfather, raised a Catholic, had not been to mass at all since before his children were born. Jake was not hostile to religion, however, noting that he enjoyed it when his English class had read the story about "the guy with the coat of many colors" and another story about "the guy who parted the sea." Yet after a series of questions about his thoughts on religion, Jake expressed some exasperation, telling me: "I really don't think much about *religion*. I know there's people that believe in different Gods, and there probably is one. There's something, 'cause there's all these situations where, you don't know how you get out of 'em—like, you're about to get hit by a car or something, and then something happens, and it's like you're okay. I don't know, it's just weird." Jake noted that he hardly ever talked about religion with anyone. It just never came up among his family, friends, school, and extracurricular activities, again reflecting his focus on the practical, everyday requirements of life. Jake's lack of interest in religion did not preclude him from occasional speculations about guardian angels and the existence of aliens, however, as both were popular topics related to his family's television and movie-viewing preferences.

"My biggest complaint about *The X-Files* is that they're too damned short," Jake's stepfather had lamented. The Pickeringtons watched many programs on the supernatural, from *Unsolved Mysteries* to documentaries on Roswell, New Mexico. Jake's mother and stepfather expressed great enthusiasm for such programs, noting in particular that they rarely missed specials on the topics of UFOs, aliens, or prophecies of the future. The teens watched these programs as faithfully as their parents did. I asked the teens who they identified with more on *The X-Files*: the pragmatically minded female scientist Scully, or Mulder, the more offbeat male agent whose personal life was overturned by aliens. They each unhesitatingly volunteered that they were more like Mulder (figure 4.1):

FIGURE 4.1
The X-Files's Agent Mulder (David Duchovny) appeals to sixteen-year-old Jake and his family because they "like to think there's stuff out there that we don't know about" (episode: "Biogenesis"). *The X-Files,* © Twentieth Century Fox Television. All rights reserved.

> CURT (thirteen): [I'm more like] Mulder. I'm weird. I think of things most people wouldn't.
>
> JAKE (sixteen): [I'm more like] Mulder. 'Cause he believes in everything, that aliens exist, and that there's all these strange people around.
>
> WENDY (nineteen): I just like [Mulder] 'cause he's so open-minded, and he just seems, he's willing to believe further than she is.
>
> CURT (thirteen): That's what I—I forgot to say, he believes in a lot of stuff. I like to think there's stuff out there that we don't know about.

Given the fact that the narratives of *The X-Files* favored Agent Mulder's suspicious bent toward supernatural explanations for strange occurrences, it is not surprising that fans of the show would identify more with him than with Agent Scully. This openness to various explanations guided several of the media choices of the Pickeringtons, however.

Some of the Pickeringtons also watched the CBS program *Touched by an Angel* occasionally. It aired too early for them to see it every week. Jake's mother said she wished she could watch this program more frequently because "I truly know that there are angels out there, I believe there are." At a later point in the interview, the family continued:

> INTERVIEWER: So you started saying you liked *Touched by an Angel?*
>
> JAKE'S STEPFATHER: Well, I've seen it once or twice. It was good. But we believe in angels. We definitely believe in guardian angels.

JAKE'S MOTHER: Mm-hmm!

JAKE'S STEPFATHER: We've had an incident or two where, there's no explaining why we're still here. And that convinces you pretty quick.

JAKE'S MOTHER: Yeah, it really does.

JAKE'S STEPFATHER: That somebody's watching out for you.

CURT [Jake's thirteen-year-old stepbrother]: What convinced me is my arm still works. Well, I was wrestling one time, and I fell back, and when I landed, I landed like this [arm twisted back] instead of like falling. My elbow popped and I broke the plate in half, and I don't think I had a real surgeon, I think it was God or something—

JAKE'S MOTHER: [Laughs] He's a surgeon for the NFL, he probably is a God.

CURT: Yeah. Because now I have like one of the strongest arms on the baseball team, and everything. I can't believe it.

JAKE'S MOTHER: Probably used titanium or something special.

CURT: They used steel pins.

JAKE'S MOTHER: Oh, okay. I don't know, we do believe that there are guardian angels.

INTERVIEWER: Is that something that you talk about as a family together?

JAKE'S MOTHER: Mm, probably not.

JAKE'S STEPFATHER: No, but we've mentioned the occasions, when we've really felt like something, way outside of the normal.

JAKE'S MOTHER: I'm sure we told them about that time when we really should've been in that accident. Coming up Kipling.

JAKE: That semi that was in the road.

JAKE'S MOTHER: It was a pickup.

WENDY [Jake's nineteen-year-old sister]: Was that when you had the little white—?

JAKE'S MOTHER: Mm-hmm.

WENDY: Oh, yeah.

JAKE'S MOTHER: I don't know how we got out of that. It was unbelieveable. It was that guardian angel. And we have guardian angels that probably work overtime with our teenagers.

Despite the fact that Jake's parents noted that they rarely talk about either religion or guardian angels in the home, the teens were all familiar with several of the guardian angel stories of both the parents and of each other. Jake raised this issue again in our individual interview, as noted before. While he was clear that he was not interested in religion, he declared that he believed that there was "something" that accounted for the fact that, despite various near-mishaps he had experienced in addition to those mentioned by other family members, they had somehow escaped harm. Surprisingly, he also was favorably impressed with an episode of *Touched by an Angel* I'd asked him to watch with me and comment upon. The conversation about the program got off to a rough start, however:

INTERVIEWER: So, what did you think of the angels [in the program]?

JAKE: Uh—what do you mean?

INTERVIEWER: Okay, that might be a hard question. Did you know, first of all, that they were angels?

JAKE: Um—? [Laughs uncomfortably]

INTERVIEWER: You heard [the angel] Monica's speech, right, where she had the light come down on her head, when [the lead character] Jason was in the car. 'Cause you've never seen this show before.

JAKE: No.

INTERVIEWER: Did you get that they were angels?

JAKE: Not really. Like, if they wouldn't've told that they were [angels] in the beginning, like the little introduction where it says, "Touched by an Angel," you probably wouldn't've known.

At the time of this conversation, I knew that Jake did not have much knowledge of any religions despite his mother's stated interest in conservative Christianity. Still, given the widespread infusion of Christian imagery in U.S. media, I was surprised by the limits this placed on his ability to interpret what I believed was the overtly religious imagery in *Touched by an Angel*. Interestingly, despite this lack of recognition, Jake did not consider himself an outsider to the television program or the tradition to which it more or less refers.[3]

When I asked Jake to further describe what he thought angels were like, he noted, "Well, there's a lot of movies that have angels in them, so that's always what I thought they were like." "Like in the movies?" I asked. "Yeah. They're always coming down to help you in some way."

Then, however, a somewhat odd thing (at least, to me) happened in our conversation. When I asked him if he could think of a movie that featured an angel coming down to help a human, he volunteered *Ghost*, the popular 1990 mystery/thriller/love story/comedy starring Patrick Swayze, Demi Moore, and Whoopi Goldberg. I thought this was strange, because I hadn't remembered that Patrick Swayze's character was an angel; I had thought, as the title of the film indicated, that he was a ghost. Jake, however, did not seem to think that there was much difference between the two. Jake's assumption was far from idiosyncratic. In a representative national survey, 15 percent of those questioned reported that they believed that angels were spirits of the deceased.[4] Even Funk and Wagnall's dictionary defines angels in this way.[5] Moreover, Hollywood films often depict spirits of the deceased who return to earth to bring closure to events left hanging at the time of their death.[6] Needless to say, Jake was untroubled by this equation of angels and ghosts. We will return to explore how his approach to angels fit with his more practical orientation to everyday life and with his media practices. First, however, we meet another Mystical: Nancy Donahue.

RELIGION INFORMS THE TEEN CULTURE
EXPERIENCE: NANCY DONAHUE

The practice of visiting dark, deserted, and isolated areas to tell scary stories and to sometimes engage in illicit activities has been a part of youth culture for a long time. Nancy Donahue, an Anglo-American young woman from an underprivileged background, relished telling me of her experiences with these practices, which folklorists refer to as "legend trips."[7] "Legend trips" became an important, if underacknowledged, place of adolescent experimentation with the supernatural with the introduction of the car into adolescent life, along with the practices of illegally used alcohol and drugs.[8] As folklorist Bill Ellis noted, "Witches, werewolves, and the like at first seem incongruous with the desire to get high, but in fact both are means of escaping from the symbolically sterile world governed by school, parents, and police."[9] At once an intentional embrace of fear and exhilaration and a ritual of adolescent rebellion, a legend trip involves a late-night journey to a purported site of a gruesome death (or of some similarly unusual and ambiguous happening), usually in an isolated area.[10] Once there, the teens (usually boys) attempt to demonstrate their manhood by defying the superstitions associated with the site (by driving fast, kissing a statue in a graveyard, etc.), all in an effort to invoke—and then successfully escape—the wrath of the ghost or other creature. While in the light of day such legends and related practices are hardly believable even to the most ardent participants, the context of the journey is important. As Elizabeth Bird has noted, "Put those same people in a dark cemetery, add a few beers, the discourse of friends whose conversation centers on death and evil, and you have a very different situation."[11]

Such adolescent traditions have been explored as a means by which young people play out anxieties related to mortality and chaotic or tragic happenings, and the consequences of violating perceived moral rules or gender roles.[12] These are certainly valid explanations for why young people participate in these events, and they echo the psychological literature that addresses why horror films are perennially popular with adolescents.[13] For the purposes of this book, however, I wish to set aside the psychological and social reasons for participation for the moment and concentrate on some of the surprising ways in which one of these supernatural encounters was interpreted and talked about by a teen in my study.

Nancy had just turned twenty at the time I interviewed her, meaning that she was no longer technically a teen. However, she still lived in her single-parent mother's home and was dependent upon her for support, so that in many ways she had not entered adulthood either economically or socially.[14] She was, however, the mother of two sons aged two and six months, and they and their father also lived in Nancy's mother's house, along with Jodie and Eric, who were introduced in chapter 3. Nancy's early entrance into parenthood had delayed her high school graduation until just weeks before my interview with her, and caring for the two small children kept her at home most of the time while the children's father worked and, as she said, "went out" in the evenings.

While many of the friends with whom Nancy shared her home had encountered difficulties with their parents, Nancy's relationship with her mother was quite positive. Nancy had two other brothers: one lived with her father, and the other was in prison. Nancy's parents had been divorced during Nancy's late teen years. Her mother worked in a low-paying clerical job, often having to go into the office seven days a week to cover the phones. In recent years, rather than return to her own full house, Nancy's mother often elected to spend the night at the home of her boyfriend. Since her own youthful days, Nancy's mother had been surrounded by younger people for whom she'd given care, as she watched her five younger siblings while her own mother worked three jobs.

Nancy had never taken much interest in religion. Her mother, however, was deeply interested in religion and traced her journey as an occasional attendee of first the Lutheran, then Unity, and then a nondenominational church called Science of Mind (which bears some resemblance, but is unrelated, to the Church of Scientology). Nancy's mother believed that while church attendance was important, it needed to be tempered with one's own reflections: "See, I was always the type that, you listen to what it is, or you put it up on the shelf and save it for later. 'Cause you know, anything's possible. All of [the various religions] have, everything coincides with each other. Every [person] has [religion] because they need it for one reason or another. But they all, no matter what religion it is, have their good points. And they're there because [people] need them." She emphasized the importance of finding the good in all religions and of seeing all as related or at least as serving similar purposes, a common view among U.S. churchgoers who see all religions as the foundation for the "Golden Rule," as Ammerman has pointed out.[15] Nancy's mother argued for religious tolerance as well as tolerance for all kinds of societal groups, such as homosexuals: "What they [religious people who discriminate against homosexuals] don't realize is that they're people, too. And I seriously believe that they are born that way. You know, there's something in here that's more feminine and that's just the way they are. They're people, too, and you should just accept them as they are." Nancy's mother was unable to attend church regularly because of her work commitments and because she "got busy," arguing that attendance was secondary in her mind anyway: "It's what's in here that counts." Describing the practices of Science of Mind, she explained:

> It's the correlation of the laws of cause and effect . . . but it's more like a positive—. Everything you see and do is a prayer. So you have to be careful of what you ask for. So a lot of people go around saying they have a pain in the butt, they usually end up with hemorrhoids. There was a couple weeks that I would say, "That really burns me up," and then my son burnt the house down. I never said that again! My mom, at one point, when I was about twelve, she always used to say, "That drives me up the wall." Well, one time her brakes went out in the car and she had a choice of

whether to hit a tin shed or a brick wall and she hit the tin shed. She never
said that again, either. Della Reese [the actress who plays Tess, the "head
angel" on CBS's *Touched by an Angel*]—she came [to the church].

Nancy's mother's understanding of religion was infused with stories of coincidence and luck that were largely attributed to the actions she or other individuals performed, whether intentionally or not. She noted that she had won
money through a series of radio contests and bingo games, but she faulted
herself when she was not able to win the lottery: "Always got a couple numbers
away and just sat there. I guess my belief system wasn't high enough to win
that much." She related this to more conventional Christian teachings: "I've
just always believed that everybody has [the ability] to be able to do [things
like affect the outcome of a game or the weather]. I mean, that's kinda what
Jesus was trying to teach us, but we're all busy trying to think it's something
else, you know, it's so easy that people think it can't be that easy. You know, 'Ask
and it shall be given.' But I guess I don't believe enough in the lotto, 'cause I
haven't won that yet!"

Also connecting her beliefs with those associated with traditional Christianity, Nancy's mother noted that she has an angel that talks to her, although not
always to provide comfort or good fortune: "I have a little voice that tells me
things. That's how I knew [in advance] about the little girl that got kidnapped
[a highly publicized local news story]. But I try not to dwell on it because it's
kind of scary. And I don't want to—I mean, that's why I can't see things, because I have a block. I'm afraid. I mean, I don't sleep in the dark, I'm afraid of
night." In addition to this prophetic voice, she had experiences with ghosts who
had lived in her childhood home before she did. She recalled a ritual her
mother performed to "send them on their way" and noted that both her
mother and grandmother also had a "sensitivity" that enabled them to have experiences with spirits of the deceased.

Although she had taken Nancy to the Unity church when she was young,
Nancy and her mother only occasionally attended the Science of Mind church
together, which Nancy only "kinda" remembers, as she said. Nancy never talked
about religion with anyone, in fact. She scoffed when I asked her about religious institutions, noting that her judgmental aunt had become an evangelical
and that that had turned her off to organized religion.

While she had much less interest in organized religion than her mother,
Nancy was intrigued by the mystical realm. Like her mother, Nancy believed
that she had had numerous experiences with spirits of the deceased who had
lived in places prior to her arrival there. She also saw one shortly after her
grandfather died of a stroke.[16] Additionally, she had an encounter with an
angel:

NANCY: I've seen an angel.
INTERVIEWER: You've seen an angel? What was that like?
NANCY: Down by Deer Valley, at the creek. Oh my God, she was *beautiful.*

INTERVIEWER: Did she say something to you?

NANCY: She was too far away to say anything.

INTERVIEWER: Wow. How could you tell she was an angel?

NANCY: Well, 'cause, we were sitting there, and I don't know, Casey was saying something about there were demons there, you know. I could feel an evil presence. And I turned around and looked, and I just stood there and stared. [Laughs] I had no breath!

INTERVIEWER: So, have you seen demons, too?

NANCY: Uh-unh. Never. I've felt an evil presence, though. . . . I got that weird feeling when we were at the park one night, that really weird feeling. Seen a kid's shoe, like way up in a tree. But I felt like, "Let's go. I don't feel right here, let's go."

INTERVIEWER: Is that something your friends talk about, I mean, obviously when you were down at the creek, you did.

NANCY: I did with Casey, he was my boyfriend at the time, one of my ex-boyfriends. And Naomi. Naomi turned around and saw a totally different one, I guess. Casey told me it was probably my guardian angel. 'Cause he's hard-core Christian.

INTERVIEWER: Oh. So, he wouldn't've seen the demons, then? He'd see the angels instead?

NANCY: He didn't see 'em [the angels]. But he knew they were there.

INTERVIEWER: Wow. What were you all doing before that?

NANCY: [Long pause] We were at the Pancake House.

There's no telling what was happening just before Nancy and her friends arrived at the creekside, but based on similar legend trips that center on encountering fear, we could guess that Nancy's hesitation might suggest drinking, drugs, or some rebellious activity. Unlike her mother's experience of the prophetic angel who sometimes told her things she would rather not hear, Nancy's experience with an angel was laced with comfort rather than fear, an approach suggested by her "hard-core Christian" friend and yet not inconsistent with her mother's beliefs concerning the supernatural. This was particularly interesting, given that Nancy, a young person with few positive experiences with traditional religion, found her fears dispelled with the appearance of a being that her friend interpreted as a guardian angel. Nancy drew upon a religious category—that of a guardian angel—to explain and provide comfort in the context of the "secular" experience of a legend trip, the purpose of which is to induce fear and thus bring thrills and intimacy to those who have shared the experience.

Nancy's family had few restrictions on media use. In fact, their television was on almost constantly because, as Nancy explained, her two-year-old son would cry and throw a temper tantrum if it were turned off. While Nancy loved horror movies and science fiction programs like *Outer Limits* that delve into the mysteries of the supernatural realm, her mother loved stories of benevolent contacts with the supernatural, particularly those involving angels, ghosts, and aliens. Nancy's mother was a regular viewer of CBS's *Touched by an Angel* and its spinoff, *Promised Land*. When I asked Nancy's mother about whether she believed that some of the programs she watched represented authentic happenings of the realm beyond, she replied: "Well, it depends. I mean, I loved [the film] *Ghost*, because I could feel it in here, I mean, it was kinda gory in places but—. Also *ET*."

Nancy's mother relied on her emotional response to these films to verify their truthfulness, although this does not necessarily mean that she believed that the stories reflected what she believed had actually occurred, or could occur, in the realm beyond. However, these representations from the entertainment media were not completely separated from her own beliefs, as she continued, speaking of *ET*:

NANCY'S MOTHER: I know that there are 333 billion universes just like ours out there that have people in them, too. It's just that there's so many and it's so vast that they're not gonna figure that out for a long, long time. And the fact that the Egyptians, inside the temples, have pictures of outer space vehicles with people coming out of them. So, I know that they really exist, because how else could they come up with something like that?

INTERVIEWER: Now, where did you learn about that?

NANCY'S MOTHER: What, about the Aztecs?

INTERVIEWER: Yeah, I never heard about that before.

NANCY'S MOTHER: Or just like the Aztecs, how'd they build those big pyramids.

INTERVIEWER: Yeah, and pyramids having extraterrestrial signs, is that in a documentary somewhere, or a book or something?

NANCY'S MOTHER: Well, I'm not sure, I think maybe it was . . . Well, no, maybe it was. But yeah, well I *know*. I mean, it's like we were put here probably from somewhere else to see how we would survive and grow.

One of the interesting aspects of this conversation is that it didn't seem to matter whether Nancy's mother saw the program on aliens, nor did it matter whether it was in a documentary or a fictional source such as a book or popular film. The plotline she described follows that of the movie (often rebroadcast on cable television) *Chariots of the Gods*. Evidently the fact that this film was presented in the language of science packaged in a documentary style contributed to her assumption that the program carried a certain legitimacy. After all, she reasoned, if it weren't true how could someone have imagined it? It is also interesting to note that she did not draw a distinction between Aztec and Egyptian cultures; her "learning" was not about these cultures but about how anomalies within each of them supported the theory of alien intervention.

Nancy was less interested in discussing why horror films and programs of science fiction appealed to her. What really gave her joy was her participation in rock concerts, and a recent performance of Pantera during OzzFest was especially meaningful. She was not interested in discussing my questions about

why people tended to associate such musical groups with evil and even satanism, however, adamantly pointing out, "Ozzy [Osbourne]'s a Catholic!"
Prior to the fame incurred from his MTV reality series *The Osbournes*, of
course, Ozzy Osbourne was lead singer for the band Black Sabbath. The
group capitalized on their use of symbols and lyrics associated with what I
have termed the "dark side of evangelicalism." Black Sabbath and Ozzy Osbourne irreverently reference Christianity, from the band's name to their live
video titled "The Last Supper" to their cheeky promotions. "Now Hell has a
soundtrack, and it's been laid down for eternity!" reads the announcement
for the OzzFest 2001 live album released in 2002. Yet in Nancy's opinion,
rather than courting controversy through the use of such imagery, the association between heavy metal and evil was primarily a misunderstanding on the
part of those who are not fans. "Ozzy's from like the old hippie generation,"
she explained to me, apparently implying that he could not be associated
with evil either because of his tolerant ideas or because he was old. While she
refused my suggestions that perhaps Ozzy and other heavy metal groups were
either exploring evil in a way that was generally considered off limits or offering critiques of mainstream culture, she was unable to articulate its appeal
for her.

Nevertheless, her experience with an angel had made her feel better in the
moment of fear, as she acknowledged, although like Jake, this experience with
the supernatural was not an occasion to dwell upon, nor did it seem to have
much effect on the rest of her life. When I asked her what she would try to teach
her two-year-old son about her beliefs, she was ambiguous: "I don't know,
'cause I don't know what's right or what's wrong. For all I know, the evil could
be what's true."

RELIGION AND FOLKLORE COMBINE
IN RELIGIOUS IDENTITY: TAMMY PEARSON

Tammy Pearson's encounters with the supernatural, while still drawing importantly on peer culture as did Nancy's, took place in a different context and with
reference to a few important adult interpreters.

While Tammy's mother and brother attended a Church of Christ congregation and her mother fervently used "God-language" to speak of her faith and
life, nineteen-year-old Tammy, an African American teen from a low-income
neighborhood, was more ambivalent about her relationship with church, religion, and faith more generally. "I do believe in God, and whatever . . . I'm just
not practicing it myself, I guess you could say, right now," she told me. Like Jake
and Nancy, Tammy focused primarily on the practical realities of her day-to-
day life and its routines. She was, at the time of the interview, rather glumly
considering what to do to earn money now that she had graduated from high
school. While her mother had offered to support her in opening a beauty salon
in the family's basement, Tammy was not greatly enthused about this prospect.

She was considering taking some business classes at the nearby college while she pursued a part-time job.

Tammy's mother, a high-energy and high-achieving single parent, was less concerned with enforcing limitations on the entertainment media than on highlighting interpretations that could reinforce positive self-esteem. Like many African American families, Tammy's family sought out television programs and films that featured African Americans in lead roles. While Tammy enjoyed the few dramas that featured African Americans, she noted that most programs with African American actors were comedies. Moreover, African Americans were generally portrayed with reference to certain stereotypes, as she noted: "It's always to the extreme. Either they're super-rich or they're like dirt-poor and off the street, whatever. It's just like to the extreme, never normal people. Like Moesha, they try to make her look like she's a normal teenager, but then, her dad buys her, at the beginning of the show, he buys this great car, just to surprise her, and she says she doesn't want it, 'cause she wants a Jeep. I'm like, 'Oh, picky!' I'm like, 'If my mom bought me a bike, I'm gonna be happy!'" Tammy's mother stressed that she believed it was important to see African Americans in popular culture, and she noted her displeasure at her white coworkers who were unfamiliar with African American celebrities. Similarly, Tammy insightfully acknowledged that while she often felt obliged to be acquainted with the popular culture preferences of her Anglo-American acquaintances, they felt no such obligation to be aware of African American celebrities, music, or television programs and films. While interpreting this in light of societal issues, Tammy also saw this lack of racial/ethnic awareness on the part of her peers as yet another of the many challenges that faced her whenever she attempted to remain involved in activities outside her own neighborhood and school.

While Tammy's orientation to life echoed the practical approaches of Jake and Nancy, she gave reasons for why she had come to this view that were related to her living in an impoverished community that suffered from both discrimination and violence: "I feel that even with me, and a lot of my friends, there's so much violence, it's like, I don't know anybody that hasn't lost a good friend or brother or cousin or whatever to violence, so it's like, we don't try to get real deep in stuff. Everything's like, 'Whatever.' If something happens it's like, 'I don't care.'" Tammy related this "I don't care" attitude to her explanation for why extremely violent and gruesome films and television programs did not bother her: "Well, you can't really get that into it [concern for violence that's represented in the entertainment media], 'cause with the everyday thing, you'll just go crazy. You gotta kinda go with the flow." I wondered if Tammy's approach to life might be better understood as nihilistic or at least fatalistic rather than simply oriented toward practicalities. Yet she did have a sense of hope, although it was grounded in what some would consider a fairly unusual way: "I didn't like hang out with [gang members], but I see them in school, 'cause once in a while they actually go to class even though they haven't been all year. And I mean, a lot of them are really smart, 'cause I've seen some that haven't been in

class all year, and they come, and they answer questions. It's not like they're totally deranged people. So sometimes that can give you hope."

She hoped that perhaps the fact that gang members were "smart" might lead
them to reconsider their life choices. While she was not convinced that this
could happen to many, she thought perhaps a few could change. Maybe this
would even happen, her mother said, as Tammy and her brother and their
friends demonstrated alternative routes. Still, while Tammy was committed to
living an alternative to gang life, she said that it was challenging to grow up, as
she and her brother had, living "in the middle of the gang neighborhood, but
trying to stay out of it, but then having to deal with these people on an everyday
basis." An added challenge was the fact that, other than Tammy and her best
friend, most of her other girlfriends from her high school days had become
teen mothers, thus changing both their social needs and their availability for
socializing. These environmental factors meant that time spent with her
mother, brother, or boyfriend watching television programs or rented movies
was not seen as a "waste of time" or even a negative influence either by teens or
their parents, as was the case among some of the other teens interviewed. Instead, television and film-watching was family time, time in which she and her
brother and boyfriend lived out their ongoing decision not to be a part of either
the gang life or the early parenthood they felt surrounded them. Some might
see it as ironic that Tammy described her own behavior as immature or "silly"
when compared with those around her.

One event that had a significant influence on Tammy was the death of a peer
who attended the same church as her mother. While Tammy and some of her
other friends would often attempt to sneak out of church during the services,
Tammy noted that this young woman, who died suddenly of an undiagnosed
medical condition, had only rarely joined them. After the death, Tammy and
her friends discussed the inevitable "whys" of a sudden and tragic event, yet
Tammy was not motivated to seek answers through an increase in her religious
involvement, nor through deeper considerations of questions of life or the afterlife. When I asked her whether she considered herself a spiritual person, she
did not relate this to the discussions of her peer's death among her friends. Instead, she related spirituality to her love of dancing. Her dance teacher had told
her that she looked "like an angel" when she danced. Yet this reference to supernatural power did not comfort but rather unnerved Tammy:

A lot of times—kids are still scared of the dark—well, I'm still scared of
the dark, too. It's like, I don't know, you know how in the dark you kinda
like see stuff? I don't like to rehearse certain dances in a room by myself,
because I always see this man peeping in the window, and I'll be like, "Oh,
no! I am tripping!" And my dance teacher, she says, "That's probably just
one of your ancestors watching over you, just don't be scared of him, talk
to him." And I'm like, "Yeah, right! If my mom knew that you would have
me talk to spirits, do you know—!" ... And then what was really strange, I
was at my grandmother's house ... and I was looking in this photo album,

and I see this guy, and I was like, his face looked so familiar, like I had just seen him like, last week. And I was like, "Who's this old man, granny?" And she's like, "That's your grandfather's grandfather." And I'm like, "Yeah, right. I know this guy." She was like, Tammy, that man died before you were even thought about." . . . And I know if I talked to my teacher, she'd be like, "Because he's your ancestor, you *should* know him." And I'm like, "No, I don't!" It just really freaks me out. People say I'm in tune with stuff, and I'm like, "No, I'm not in tune. I'm not." That's why I say I'm spiritual, but I don't try to be. I try to like get away from it. It's spooky.

While it might be possible to interpret Tammy's experience with the supernatural as benign or even positive, particularly in light of the interpretation offered that the man watching over her was an ancestor interested in her welfare, Tammy's own emotional response was one of fear.[17] This is possibly why she sounded ambiguous when she talked about the efforts made by her dancing peers to comfort her after the untimely death of the young woman in her mother's church: "The African troupe kinda helped me. In the African tradition, one of the biggest things is like ancestors. You have to give total respect to them, and still talk to them. Like when my friend Ebony died, the troupe, everybody was still telling me, 'Well, talk to her.' You know, 'Ask her why did she leave.' And I was like, 'Yeah, right! If I talk to her and I hear somebody say something, I'm just—I'm out!' [Laughs]." This passage is interesting as Tammy's peers seemed to draw a connection between the ability of ancestors to continue to participate in life through their descendants—a legitimate religious practice in several traditions such as those of Africa and some forms of mystical Judaism—and Tammy's ability to speak to the ghost of the young woman who had died.[18] Drawing on the experiences of ghosts and ghost stories, then, perhaps it is no wonder that Tammy's experience of the supernatural was one laced with fear and ambivalence.

While Tammy and Nancy's stories illustrate the importance of the interpretation of personal experience in the context of peers with regard to beliefs about the supernatural, their stories also have connections to the mass mediated realm. Tammy in particular drew connections between her fears that she related to her understandings of God, and the fears she felt when viewing horror films: "I don't know, [religion]'s just scary for me. I get scared, when it starts to get deep, for some reason. It's just too much for me right now. And even though I know God is supposed to be good, you know, and all that kind of stuff, and when you die you go to heaven, and Judgment Day, and God's coming back, and I'm like, I'm scared. I just get scared. I still get scared off scary movies, I try to act like I don't but I do. I'm just—chicken. [Laughs]."

While her practical focus on life may have been an important aspect of Tammy's day-to-day concerns, her lack of interest in religion was also, interestingly, related to this sense that getting "deeper" into religion or spirituality might be "scary." Religion was related not so much to moral decision-making as to existential questions of death and the afterlife for Tammy. In this sense, religion shared common mythical ground with "scary movies" and their tales of death and the afterlife. Still, Tammy did not relate her fears to what she had seen in the media, but to her interpretation of the Christian tradition to which she was nominally committed. When I asked her whether she believed in psychic powers, she replied in such a way as to draw a distinction between the Christian faith she believed she embraced and the traditions of reading palms and tarot cards she equated with the African tradition her dancing peers and teacher had suggested:

> I don't believe in it the way that people are [engaging in psychic phenomena] now. I believe in it, like, in the Bible, way back or whatever, in the day of the prophets, people would pray to God and say God spoke to them or whatever. And this is the right thing to do. But I don't believe like, reading people's palms, and the cards, and all that kind of stuff. But see, that's one of the biggest problems I have, in the African tradition, they don't believe totally like the cards and stuff, but it's kinda more to that side to me, and I'm like, "No, that's not right." If I'm gonna know something, I want to know 'cause God told me, not because the cards said so. And I'm like, "If cards can rule my life, we are really in trouble." Let's hope there's a God and not just some cards because boy, we are in for it.

Despite the fact that she was dismissive of "the [tarot] cards" in favor of God and what she understood to be the biblical tradition, Tammy was still ambivalent about her own commitment. On the one hand, she said that she would prefer to "know because God told me" in spite of what she had said earlier about wishing to avoid such "knowledge." On the other hand, her commitment to her beliefs sounded rather agnostic when she stated, "Let's hope there's a God." Tammy saw herself as part of a religious tradition that invoked a great deal of fear. This invoking of fear became a justification for the fact that she distanced herself from it. Even guardian angels, those beings in which both Jake and Nancy had found comfort in their otherwise practical and "secular" lives, were more equivocal for Tammy. When I asked her how she felt about television programs and films that featured God or angels, she noted:

> TAMMY: *Touched by an Angel* is really good, and sometimes that's kind of scary, too. What if there really is somebody in my life that is an angel. And I'm not in church, and I'm not doing what I'm supposed to be doing. So I get kinda scared on both ends. You know I don't want to be there when it gets too deep, but what if I'm not there, what if something happens, like, with [the young woman at church], I know that she probably went to heaven, 'cause she was in the church. And I'm like, what if I'm not, and it just kinda happens to me. So I start feeling guilty about that. So I don't know. And I think maybe there is angels around like that. And I just wonder if they're around me.
>
> INTERVIEWER: You'd rather not have them around you?
>
> TAMMY: I don't know! 'Cause see, you like, want them there, but then you

would like not. The ones in there to protect you from bad things, but then you don't want them there to see the bad things that you do. So it's like a two-way street, and I just have to decide what I want.

Angels for Tammy were not protectors, even when viewed in the sentimentalized form represented in the popular television program *Touched by an Angel.* Instead, angels could issue God's judgment, a much more unconventional view of angels given the contemporary emphasis upon their goodness, but one not unrelated to concepts of strictness in conservative and fundamentalist churches. Of course, a judging angel could also be related to the vengeful ghosts of the cinema and perhaps even to African ancestors, as well. These beings served as reminders for Tammy that she believed she could suffer consequences because of her choices and actions—an idea not far from what her more orthodox and conservatively religious peers believed.

THE MYSTICALS AND THEIR APPROACH TO THE MEDIA

The Mystical teens of this chapter had several interesting characteristics that set them apart from other young people. On the one hand, each believed that they had had experiences with the supernatural, and each interpreted that experience in light of religion—despite a lack of religious background and experience. Yet on the other hand, Jake and Tammy voiced fairly conventional approaches to morality while also embracing a strong bond with their primary parent. Because of their lack of religious commitment, combined with their parents' interpretations, the Mystical teens expressed little concern about separating the stories of religion from the legends of the entertainment media. Referring back to the *Charmed* episode, they would have no difficulty believing that a witch could be a guardian angel. As far as they were concerned, an angel could be a ghost and vice versa, or a ghost could be an ancestor. Stories and symbols might be drawn from religious sources or from places like family stories of good fortune, "legend trips," the entertainment media, or popularized African traditions of ancestors. Each of these sources was potentially meaningful and useful, depending on the needs of the teen at the moment. Yet thoughts about these occurrences were fleeting and titillating rather than sources that served as markers for beliefs or foundations for moral systems that could be called upon repeatedly. Like their predecessors in early New England, the Mystical teens acknowledged supernatural powers as a means to explain why things happened when they were otherwise inexplicable.[19] But titillation was key to their responses, rather than religious fear. This speaks to the fact that they approached materials about the supernatural largely out of a desire for entertainment rather than for religious, cosmological, or existential information. In this sense, they continue a tradition of finding entertainment in the stories of the unusual and unexplained. In the nineteenth century, such stories were often presented as true, offering the same kind of entertaining titillation in the context of unanswered (and unanswerable) questions about the realm beyond. The story of the Cock Lane ghost, a purportedly "true" ghost story, was one such example (figure 4.2).[20] At that time, the reporting of such "true" occurrences served the emergent newspaper publishers' aspirations to "high culture" by seeming to mock superstition—while at the same time increasing circulation.[21]

In short, these teens were in some ways the antithesis of religious "seekers," interested in the practicalities of everyday life and only engaged in considering the possibilities of what lies beyond the material world when such possibilities presented themselves to the teens. Yet while they sound like the persons of "practical mastery" described by Giddens as persons primarily interested in a secular view of the world and with little incentive to engage more fully either in organized religion or its belief systems, it is important to make two points about these teens.[22] First, of course, they were not uninterested in the mystical realm and its many secrets and questions. They did not dismiss what they believed were encounters with the supernatural as "coincidence" or explainable through scientific means, along the line of the disenchantment Max Weber

FIGURE 4.2
Publications from the eighteenth century onward told of strange and unusual occurrences. Title page of the report on the Cock Lane ghost, anonymously penned by Oliver Goldsmith. Reprinted with permission from the Fortean Picture Library.

THE

Mystery Revealed;

Containing a Series of

TRANSACTIONS

AND

AUTHENTIC TESTIMONIALS,

Respecting the supposed

Cock-Lane GHOST;

Which have hitherto been concealed from the
PUBLIC.

—— *Since none the Living dare implead,*
Arraign him in the Person of the Dead.
DRYDEN.

LONDON:
Printed for W. BRISTOW, in St. Paul's Church-yard;
and C. ETHRINGTON, York.
MDCCXLII.

once suggested would be the secularizing result of increased scientific knowledge.[23] Second, despite their rather unorthodox approaches and even their lack of attention to the supernatural realm or to religion more generally conceived, each related their experiences to the Christian tradition which they believed they embraced. They were not looking to consciously build a worldview distinct from what they understood as the Christian tradition; rather, they believed they were drawing upon its resources when they needed them, unaware, of course, of how their own understandings of that tradition had been shaped by their parents, peers, and popular ideas from various cultural sources. Moreover, the analyses above also suggest that any consideration of secularization is complicated by racial and class positions, both of which, in the cases of Nancy and Tammy, contributed to feelings of distance from white middle-class norms generally associated with Christianity in the United States.

One factor that united each of these stories was the idea of the guardian angel. When asked in a survey whether they believed in angels, Jake, Nancy, and Tammy all probably would have responded that they did. An estimated 76 percent of young people in the United States report that they believe in angels, a figure that has increased over the past two decades and echoes increases seen in the adult population.[24] The angels often seen in popular television and film echo those described by Jake and Nancy in that they are largely sentimentalized.[25] Each seemed to view religion's function, as understood in relation to angels, as simply to provide positive, sentimental feelings that rarely interfered with the more practical issues of daily life. As noted in Jake's case, there also seem to be relationships between taste, class, and the interpretations of certain supernatural figures in the entertainment media as benevolent.

Tammy's more fearful approach to angels may have been related to her emphasis upon what she believed was the judgmental role of God. One study found that particularly when African American persons held such views of God as "judge," they had higher odds of believing that they had experienced contact with the dead, as Tammy reported.[26] The same study also found that females were more likely to have such experiences than men. Moreover, African American traditions, such as those of ancestors described by Tammy, suggest that rather than simply relating the appeal of the supernatural to a disadvantaged position in society, African Americans may learn of supernatural interpretations from persons and beliefs in African American culture itself.[27]

Each of the Mystical teens also allow further elaboration on the relationship between the entertainment media and religious questions of what lies beyond the material world. As noted, the Pickeringtons, Donahues, and Pearsons place few restrictions on the media use of their children, an approach attributable to the older age of the children in the house. Each household enjoyed watching television programs and films that featured fantasy, horror, and science fiction, all genres that commonly deal with aspects of the supernatural. Tammy's story in particular raised the connections between religion and the legends of the supernatural in the entertainment media, as she seemed to view religion primarily in terms of its role in ritualizing and explaining the existential questions of life, death, and the afterlife. Moreover, her conceptual connection of religion and its judgmental possibilities with the fear invoked through horror films and other sources points to a slightly different approach to the "what if?" element of science fiction and fantasy discussed in chapter 3. In Tammy's case, considering the possibilities of what lies beyond the material world was not necessarily intriguing but was troubling, a response she explained with reference to her feelings that she has made personal choices that might not be to God's liking. In this sense, Tammy's response echoes some of the importance of personal morality in religious understandings and their application to the media realm that we will observe among the Traditionalist teens, but it also relates to both her gender, race, and class position.

While neither Jake, Nancy, Tammy nor any of their parents were actively involved in fan communities, what Ben-Yehuda says of these groups also relates to the teens discussed in this chapter: "For most people, being part of the science fiction and/or occult subculture, even with relatively high degrees of involvement, means that they have a meaningful, controlled, enchanted alternative center towards which they can orient themselves whenever they so wish, with very little risk to their otherwise usual and conformist lifestyle in the disenchanted, pluralistic, centerless modern world."[28] Ben-Yehuda argues that entering such subcultures is relatively easy, given the accessibility of books and other media addressing science fiction and the occult. My analysis in this chapter points not so much to people who take these interests to the next level of commitment and practice, but to those who, like Jake, Nancy, and Tammy, are content to leave such explorations in the realm of entertainment. Thus, it is not quite accurate to state that the media stories replace religion as authoritative sources of information about the afterlife for these teens. Yet the way in which the teens address their existential (or, some would say, religious)[29] questions, and their sense that their interpretations are indeed consistent with ideas of traditional organized religion (specifically Christianity), are stances toward religion that unconsciously incorporate within them stories from various sources, including those reinforced by the entertainment media.

This chapter, therefore, has strengthened the argument that interpretations of the entertainment media among teens must be understood as such interpretations are mediated by personal experience, parents, peers, and the socioeconomic and racial positions of teens themselves. It further demonstrates the importance of interrogating the question of why Christianity appears to be a taken-for-granted religion for these teens. The willingness on the part of teens to identify themselves as Christian, despite their stated distance to those traditions and practices and their own preferences for orientations guided by the practicalities of daily life, raises further questions. For instance, we must consider further how the entertainment media relate to existential, "religious" questions of the ordering of the universe, looking for historical evidence of how Christianity has informed certain representations and ideas. Second, we also must explore the relationship between Christianity, the media, and processes of legitimation that place certain beliefs in the position of what may be assumed or taken for granted within a culture. This is a theme that continues as we consider young people who intentionally seek out experiences with the supernatural: the Experimenters.

5

THE EXPERIMENTERS

APPRECIATING BOTH

RELIGION AND THE LEGENDS

OF THE SUPERNATURAL

"I used to just leave my body, float around the room a little, and look down at my body lying there on my bed. Then I started floating around and out the windows of my room, looking down at my house, going higher and higher. At first it was really cool that I could do that. But then, the last time—it wasn't on purpose—I couldn't even lie down in my bed without leaving my body." The normally defiant eyes of sixteen-year-old Carter Farnsworth, self-proclaimed agnostic, were downcast as he gave a furtive glance to his friend Greg. Greg turned to me and said, "Can you tell him how to make it stop?" As a twenty-something volunteer mentor with young people at the time, I was speechless. Carter assumed that his body was being possessed by evil spirits, Greg continued, and so he had told Carter he should talk to me, as I was a member of Greg's church and I worked with young people. So, Greg wanted to know, could I talk to the evil spirits and make them leave him alone?

In all of those pamphlets and orientation meetings you get from the Boys and Girls Club and similar organizations, nothing had prepared me for this. I wasn't a psychologist and I wasn't a minister, much less an exorcist. Moreover, I was raised in the moderately liberal Presbyterian (U.S.A.) Church. In that organization, as a general rule, we don't talk to evil spirits. We barely talk to the people who show up in the pews next to us in church. In the end, I decided I wasn't qualified to talk with what they thought were evil spirits, but I did listen to and talk with Carter and Greg and did what I could to point them in directions where they might find more information.

117

Out-of-body experiences may not be terribly common among contemporary teens, but there is reason to believe that young people tend to be drawn to such experimentations with the supernatural. In earlier chapters, we have discussed the prominence of Ouija boards, séances, and legend trips in adolescent life. There, we related their appeal to the adolescent desire to rebel against parents and other authority figures. Many teens engage in these kinds of activities for amusement more than anything else. Still, there are some who are extremely interested in engaging supernatural power or being in contact with the realm beyond. For instance, more than 40 percent of U.S. teens have reported that they believe in extrasensory perception (the ability to communicate with another person through other than ordinary means) and nearly a third report that they have had some kind of experience with an otherworldly presence.[1] These kinds of experiences do not seem to be most prevalent among those who, like Carter, actively reject traditional religious organizations and beliefs. Instead, these experiences occur most frequently among those who identify themselves with some kind of religious organization.[2] In the United States, where a majority of people identify themselves with some kind of religion, this becomes particularly interesting. This chapter sets out to explore a few instances of such blurrings of boundaries among contemporary teens, to attempt to better understand why they happen and what they mean.

This chapter introduces three young Anglo-American women: Lily, Annae, and Katie. These young people are each affiliated with a religious tradition that they say is very important to them. Yet they do not define or limit their beliefs to those of their chosen religious affiliation. Instead, these teens are closer to what sociologist Wade Clark Roof has termed "seekers" or what sociologist Carol Lytch calls "customizers": individuals who actively select from various sources to make sense of their worlds and to meaningfully participate in them.[3] Unlike the engagement in "seeking" among baby boomers, for whom the term was coined, the teens described here were less interested in fostering individual spirituality in a coherent, conscious sense than in simply encountering God— or the mystical realm—in a way that was meaningful for them.

EVIL IN THIS LIFE AND BEYOND: LILY DEARBORN

Attractive and energetic, Lily had both a passion and enthusiasm for life as well as a darker, angrier side. While the passion spilled over into several areas of her life, the anger had a clear source and target: her mother. Her parents had undergone an extremely contentious divorce, and Lily was clearly scarred by it. At fifteen, the disagreements between Lily and her mother had escalated into distrust and violence. So Lily had been sent to live in her father's spare apartment, while her younger sister, Deniece, stayed with their mother. Their father had recently experienced several layoffs in his large-vehicle repair work, and Lily's move into his apartment further destabilized his already fragile financial situation. It also represented a financial change for Lily. After being raised in a lower-income urban area, she moved to a new and upscale suburban subdivision when their mother moved Lily and Deniece into her boyfriend's home. Lily viewed that move as a "liminal moment," a time in which she was forced to define herself because of her immersion in the new social and economic context of her high school and her mother's imminent remarriage.[4] While some teens might see such a change in economic fortune as positive, Lily expressed disgust for her soon-to-be stepfather's materialism, claiming he was "stuck on his money" and "a snob" who was "used to getting whatever he wants," while her mother was "a status-seeker." The changes in their family structure had been hard ones for Lily. Both she and her father blamed her falling grades and behavioral problems on the divorce.[5]

On one social occasion, after a dinner of pizza and pop, Lily cheerfully presented me with a large book of family photos. The photo album was old and nearly empty, with a few stray photos of Lily, her father, and her younger sister, Deniece. There were none of her mother. When I asked where the rest of the photos were, her father told me that his ex-wife had taken most of the photos when they split up. She grabbed the photos out of the album, he said, mimicking an angry ripping motion. It struck me as interesting that the remaining photos had not been moved to another, smaller album, or grouped together in the old album. It seemed symbolic of the way in which the family approached the divorce and ensuing struggles. Like the old album with its missing photos, the family was not so much reconstituted in a new form as it has continued to exist, with certain gaping holes and spots of grief, reminders of anger and loss in the midst of other snapshots of family celebration and joy.

Lily's father considered himself very protective of her, requiring that the many young men who were interested in her come to the apartment and meet him before sixteen-year-old Lily was allowed to go out on dates. While Lily appreciated and had a great respect for her father for the most part, she also expressed the common teen sentiment that he should "let me live my own life." She barely tolerated her mother, however, calling her an "old hag" and saying, "I want her out of my life." She told me that once she turned eighteen, her mother would no longer have any legal right to be in contact with her, and she planned to sever all of her ties with her at that point.

After the move to her father's apartment, Lily began to refer to herself as Chicana, although her father corrected her, noting that he was part Native American. He noted that while they both grew up in an area of their city that is largely Mexican American, they had no Mexican heritage. Still, Lily told me several times when we were not with her father that he was "a little bit Mexican," although "he denies it." She called her friends her "Chicana sisters" and also claimed Mexican heritage for them (although her father was skeptical about this, also). When she spoke of Chicanos/Chicanas, Lily adopted an appropriate accent as if to signify her connection with the culture.

Both Lily and her father were angered by disrespectful portrayals in the media of Native Americans and Mexican Americans. Lily's father also pointed out the rarity of finding African Americans portrayed as "role models." They emphasized tolerance as the most important value by which to judge media representations.

Lily's father had few restrictions on Lily's media use. Each of them had stereo units in their bedrooms, and Joe had a smaller television in his bedroom. While they usually agreed on television programs they would watch together, Lily occasionally asked to watch something different in his bedroom. They both preferred to watch in the living room, however, because that was the room where the phone was located, and they both received numerous phone calls from friends during the evenings. As they were both confined to the house in those hours, their primary social ties to friends were through such calls.

Both Lily and her father considered themselves to be religiously conservative. They both expressed a great deal of appreciation for their church, which they said was very supportive of them during their divorce. They attended an American Baptist church, and both were frequent participants.[6] Lily's father had been raised Methodist, but his family joined a Baptist congregation during the Vietnam era when the Methodist pastor "was preaching more politics than religion," as he explained it. As a young adult, Lily's father left that Baptist congregation in disgust, as he noted: "There was a lot of inner church politics, a lot of hypocrites, really. On Sunday, they'd be, 'Hey, brother,' like that, but come Monday they wouldn't talk to you. A lot of holier-than-thou people who'd look down their nose at you, but nine times out of ten they were doin' worse things than I was doing. And so one day I had it, and so I told the pastor what I thought of him, and what I thought of his church, and what I thought of his congregation and I left." After that encounter, his parents began attending the Baptist church that Lily, Joe, and her grandmother still attend. Lily's father liked the fact that this small congregation of mostly elderly members treated them "like family," a description with which Lily agreed.

Lily said that religion was "very important" to her, noting that the church treated her "like an adult," giving her responsibilities in child care and Sunday school teaching. During the year and a half I knew them, however, Lily had begun to attend Catholic mass with her close friends, pointedly noting that she had begun to do this because her father refused to drive her to the Baptist church. He was too tired to drive there on many Sundays, he told her.

While religion was very important to them, they also had a great deal of interest in paranormal, supernatural, and science fiction–related phenomena. Both Lily and her father had had paranormal experiences, for instance. Interestingly, neither saw any inconsistencies (or connections) between these experiences and their Baptist faith. Lily described her first paranormal experience, which occurred when she was young, as a seemingly pleasant and benign interaction with her grandfather shortly after he died violently in a fire: "When I was little, I'd wake up, and me and my grandfather would play games even though he was burned to death. My mom would come in, she'd say, 'Lily, what are you doing?' 'I'm playing games with Grandpa.' She'd look around the room and go, 'Where is he?' 'Look, he's floating through the vent.' There's been a lot of paranormal things in my family." Her father, too, had had paranormal experiences, Lily said. While Lily noted that she had "enjoyed" such paranormal encounters, her father's experience was more haunting. His single paranormal experience had occurred when he was a preteen after his father died of a heart attack while performing on stage. He described the occurrence after noting his inability to deal with his father's death at the time:

INTERVIEWER: Did it hit you later?

LILY'S FATHER: It hit me later, yeah, it did. [Pause] Then there—you probably think—this is really silly. [Pause] Ah, I don't know if I believe it
anymore. [Pause] Two weeks after his death I got the room that he used
to have, he and my mom used to have. It's a straight shot, I can look
out that bedroom door, and I can see the back door, straight shot
through the entire house. [Pause] And. About two o'clock, two-thirty
in the morning, you know I used to wake up and hear my dad come in
the back door [after performing with local bands]. And I woke up and
looked up and here—[slight laugh]—as God is my witness, I swear I
seen this. There was this black-and-white image of my father there.
And he doesn't open the door, he comes *through* the back door. And
he's tripping through, and he's walking. And it's a full body, black and
white—and I'm awake. I am, so help me God, I am awake. I didn't
dream it. I freaked, I watched right until he got to the beginning of the
hallway, which is about fifteen feet from my room, and I freaked, I just
pulled the covers over my head. Looking back in retrospect, I really
don't think the man would've hurt me. I think he was just so used to
coming home he was coming home. . . .

INTERVIEWER: Did he see you, or was there any kind of connection?

LILY'S FATHER: It was like you projected an image onto a cloud, like a holo-
graphic image. It wasn't like he was looking at me, it was like he just—
had a really weird look in his eye, this distant look. Like, you know it is
when someone's daydreaming, and they're looking at you, but they're
not really looking at you, they're looking *through* you. That's the way he
looked. It's like he just was walking like this, not really looking at me. I
was twelve years old, I mean, shoot. I was a horror fanatic. And here it
is in living color and I'm like, "Well, TV's one thing, this is real life.
We're outta here."

Lily's father noted that this was the only time he ever saw his father. Lily, on the other hand, described several paranormal experiences of her own, none of which echoed her father's fear. Also, she approached the topic much differently, seeming proud of and excited by her experiences while her father was tentative in describing his. This was not surprising, given that he might have expected me as a researcher to be skeptical about these occurrences. Lily, on the other hand, seemed delighted to tell me about how her paranormal experiences echoed the tumultuous experiences of her parents' divorce and her mother's hostility:

INTERVIEWER: Have you seen anything recently, like since you've moved here [to her father's home]?

LILY: Not recently. But back at the old house, I saw it all the time. It was great.

INTERVIEWER: And then did it stop when you went to Orchard Park [her mother's neighborhood]?

LILY: Yeah. I think something—when I moved to Orchard Park, I knew something was there but it wasn't a good feeling. I think it might have followed me from my neighbor's house. I used to mow his lawn all the time, and he was a trucker, and no one was in our neighborhood, and I was mowing his lawn and was almost done and I was just talking to myself and all of a sudden the lawn mower just died. It was full of gasoline, and all of a sudden I heard this really evil laughing from all around. Nobody was in the neighborhood except for me and my brother. And it sounded really evil, and then it kinda followed me down to Orchard Park. And I saw a figure . . . it wasn't like a full body, it was kinda like an aura around a face . . . really gruesome teeth, no nose, and that's the aura right there [pointing to a picture she'd drawn of it earlier]. And I saw it at school and when I went home, and in my nightmares, and I never got a full night's rest because of that.

INTERVIEWER: And so that started before you moved to Orchard Park and then was there?

LILY: Well, I didn't see too much of it but I saw it mainly when I was in Orchard Park. I'd go outside and it would follow me. I could feel its vicious paws go through my body. It felt like I had been torn in half and then put back together again. It was really scary. It followed me a little at night, and I haven't seen it since. [Pause] I don't know. Some people don't believe in ghosts, but I do.

Certainly we can draw connections between Lily's unhappiness and alienation in Orchard Park, her parents' divorce, and her interpretation of the experience of this evil manifestation, which tore her "in half and then put [her] back together again." The paranormal experience became a story that was helpful for her as she sought to dramatize just how miserable and horrible she felt. It also served as a validating experience, linking her with her father's family's similar experiences and providing her with something she felt was unique about her. Lily believed that something about her called forth these paranormal experiences, and she indicated an interest in learning how to encourage these encounters more intentionally. She entertained the possibility that she might pursue a career in the area as a "paranormal psychologist," as she termed it.

While Lily's father had not mentioned his paranormal experience to many people, Lily asked her Sunday school teacher about hers, a fact that her father seemed surprised to learn. She then related the occurrence of the evil laughter and aura to her father, and noted what her Sunday school teacher said: "She told me that she went to a seminar where people worshiped the devil. She said she heard the same thing." When I asked whether Lily thought that people who were religious might be more or less interested in life after death, she replied:

LILY: I don't think there is [any relation between beliefs in life after death and religion]. I mean, I got my religion, and I get into it [paranormal experiences], it's neat. It keeps you on the edge of your seat, keeps you living, keeps your heart beating.

INTERVIEWER: Your religion, you mean?

LILY: No, reading about [life after death and other paranormal experiences]

. . .

LILY'S FATHER: Buddy of mine—he's not what you'd call really religious, but he's had what you call paranormal experiences where he's seen a ghost when he was a kid. So I don't think religion [is related to paranormal experiences].

INTERVIEWER: So it's not, religion is not related. Or it's not in conflict. You can be religious and have experiences, or not be religious.

LILY: Yeah. It happens, whether you're religious or not.

LILY'S FATHER: Whether you want to admit to it or not, you know, if you don't want to believe what you saw then you can justify it off in any number of different directions. And if you want to believe what you saw, you can justify it in any number of directions. Until someone proves or disproves religion.

In this statement, both Lily and her father verified their beliefs that such paranormal experiences could and did actually occur. Furthermore, they both believed that such events happened to both religious and nonreligious people, although, as her father noted, some might want to "justify" the experience rather than believe that it had actually occurred. To them, the reality of paranormal experiences trumps any attempts to explain away such phenomena—whether those explanations come from religious or, presumably, scientific sources. As Lily said, such events "keep your heart beating" and are therefore worth pursuing whenever possible. A paranormal psychologist would presumably seek out such occurrences intentionally, while also seeking a meaningful context for them in everyday life.

As the conversation continued, Lily related a series of stories she had read that highlighted interventions from spirits of the deceased and from angels. Lily and her father both liked to watch documentaries and other programs about paranormal experiences, grouping these "strange phenomena" with "life-after-death experiences," "faith healing," and "ghost stories." Lily's father's use of the latter term was not meant to trivialize the stories, as he argued for at least the possibility that they *might* be true. This is not to say that he took them more seriously than others might. He was careful to tell me that it was "only entertainment," after all, and Lily agreed. However, he and Lily both claimed that they could tell when a particular portrayal of the paranormal was accurate and when the writers "don't have a clue of what they're talking about," as Lily's father said. He mentioned as particularly appealing the program *In Search Of*, which had been narrated by Leonard Nimoy, who played Dr. Spock in the original *Star Trek* series. They distinguished these shows from what they called the "science fiction" of *The X-Files* and *Outer Limits*, which they did not watch. Still, the two activities that they mentioned doing together regularly as a family were attending church every week and watching *Star Trek* every night at 10:30 P.M.

I had learned earlier in our time together that Lily and her father were loyal viewers of *Star Trek*. At one point, I asked Lily's father a rather rambling question about the connections between this program, their paranormal experiences, and their Baptist tradition: "Do you think there's any connection between your paranormal experiences, or religion, and your liking of *Star Trek* shows? Because people seem to think they're sort of religious, or uplifting, or whatever." Lily's father seemed to interpret what I was asking as, "Do you think *Star Trek* causes you to believe in paranormal phenomena?" To which he replied:

> I wouldn't say so. Even my pastor and I have gotten into debates over *Star Trek*, and Gene Rodenberry [the creator of the *Star Trek* series] in particular. Because he, my pastor believes that *Star Trek* is along the lines of the cults out there that are saying that Jesus Christ was actually an alien that landed on this planet. And I'm goin' . . . "Well, do you know he wasn't?" And I said, "Y'know, that is one man's point of view." I said, "There's too many things in this world that nobody can explain away, like the drawing on the pyramids with the ancient Egyptians, drawing what looks like a modern-day space suit. And too many other variables, y'know?" I said, "All I'm saying is, *what if?*" And he just, you can see the veins start to come out [motions to his neck], but him and I, we go at it. I don't think, as far as *Star Trek*, I'm just curious. I'm just a naturally curious person. I truly believe that we don't know a fraction of the things that go on in this world. So I don't think *Star Trek* is something that really pulls any weight on paranormal existence, I just think that it might offer some ideas on why it takes place . . . and y'know, what if life after death is nothing more than a different dimension? You go from, say, this dimension to another? I'm not saying we do that, I'm just saying, *what if.*

Echoing concerns about the distinctions between legitimately religious tradition and the representation of beliefs in supernatural phenomena at some distance from that tradition, Lily's father related his pastor's concern that *Star Trek* might encourage some unorthodox beliefs. Yet Lily's father, like most people in the United States, did not feel the need to rely upon the suggestions of "experts" to tell him what it was appropriate to believe. He saw himself as quite capable of making his own decisions concerning his religious beliefs and thus seemed to take his pastor's concerns in stride; the religious leader had some, but certainly not final, authority. Several experts in contemporary religion in the United States have noted this tendency for individuals to assume final authority over religious belief, linking it to our nation's historic support for freedom of religious expression and the context of our individualistic culture.[7] Lily, like her father, noted that she not only believed that phenomena such as ghost appearances and evil spirits were possible but actively sought out such occasions in her own life.

EXPERIMENTING JUST BEYOND THE BOUNDARY: KATIE AND ANNAE GARDNER

While the Dearborns were affiliated with the American Baptist Protestant religious tradition, Katie and Annae Gardner saw themselves at some distance to Christianity.[8] At fourteen and twelve, Annae and Katie were Anglo-American middle-class members of a family of committed and articulate Wiccans. Wiccanism, a religious system with a rather small number of adherents, has recently received legitimation by its recognition as a religion by the U.S. armed forces.[9] In the small city where the Gardners live, Wiccans are represented on the Interfaith Council and, the Gardners report, they often participate in joint projects with the local United Methodist Church, along with other members of their group. Despite this seeming increase in tolerance for Wiccan and pagan beliefs, the Gardner parents noted that the Wiccan community's cohesiveness rests to a large extent on the fact that persons of their belief system are often harassed, misunderstood, and even threatened.[10] Katie related one such uncomfortable occurrence with a friend of hers:

KATIE: There's this girl ... who's still my friend. But earlier, like last year, I found out she was Wiccan, and I'm like, cool, and everything. And then at the start of this year, or sometime, I mentioned something about it, and she's like, "Oh, my God, you're still that way? My mom took me to church and I got"— [to her mother] What is it called?

KATIE'S MOTHER: Baptized?

KATIE: Yeah. And she's like, "If you don't do that, I'm sorry but you're going to go to hell and everything." And I just told her, "Jackie, I'm what I am and you're not going to change me." And then, the other day, I was walking through the hall and she threw water on me! And I'm like, "Jackie, why did you do that?" And she goes, "It's holy water." And I just started laughing really hard!

KATIE'S FATHER: Either that, or she thought you might melt like the Wicked Witch of the West.

KATIE: I was tempted to say, "I'm melting!"

KATIE'S FATHER: That would have been great! That would have been funny. [Laughs]

Humor was one way that the Gardner family dealt with the challenges that came to them out of the ignorance of others, in this case, interestingly enough, referencing the Wicked Witch of the *Wizard of Oz* fantasy. Katie and Annae had learned from their parents that they needed to be careful regarding who they talked with about their religious tradition. For Katie and Annae's parents, the Internet has been an important means by which conversations among fellow believers could take place without much of the possibility for threat that might be encountered in more public arenas.[11] They noted that connections between participants in their religious group were maintained through Internet contacts, and in fact the Internet was used to organize local gatherings at public places. Few of the coworkers of the Gardner parents knew that they were Wiccan. Both Gardner parents worked, the father in a professional writing position and the mother as a nurse who was working to complete her BA degree.

Annae and Katie's mother grew up in Baptist and Quaker churches, while their father grew up in what he called the "country club" religions of Presbyterianism and United Methodism, which he described as religions where people attended services primarily to build their social and professional contacts. Both parents experimented with a variety of religious traditions separately and after they'd met and married, settling upon Wiccanism after being introduced to earth-centered religions in a class sponsored by an area Unitarian Universalist church. At the time, they were seeking a "connection," as they felt alienated from nature and its cycles, as well as from other people. Wicca appealed to them, as Annae and Katie's father stated, because "it gave us the background then to just be very aware of the cycles of the Earth and the energies of the Earth and how everything applies in our own lives. . . . It told us why we feel certain ways at certain times of the year, or in certain places. Why we were getting certain kinds of energies from certain things of the Earth. In a lot of ways, it tied everything together and made it all cohesive and made it a lot easier to work with and to use in our lives." While the entire family claimed that the Wiccan rituals and beliefs were important to them, they were not actively participating in a small group coven at the times of the interviews because, as the parents explained, the people involved in their coven were "no longer serious." Instead, they opted to continue the rituals as a family, occasionally attending the larger public rituals of the pagan community.

Another reason the Gardners joined the Wiccan community was out of a desire to give their daughters an understanding of a variety of religious traditions so that "they could decide what they wanted to do" and so that they would both understand and be tolerant of other people's religions. As with the Dearborns, this emphasis on tolerance also informed how the Gardner family formed their opinions and policies about media use. As Katie and Annae's parents explained:

KATIE AND ANNAE'S MOTHER: There are certain things I don't let them watch. But it's for certain reasons. As far as protecting them from seeing what real life is like, I'm not going to do that. They've got to live in it when they leave home. They've got to know what's really going on out there in the world.

KATIE AND ANNAE'S FATHER: And if we put too strict—you know, I'd rather watch something with them and talk about it than to say, "Don't watch it," because then it becomes forbidden fruit, and it becomes something that they're going to really try to watch.

While Katie and Annae's mother occasionally did watch films or television programs with her daughters, she indicated that she did not closely monitor what her daughters were watching, listening to, or reading. However, as she worked in the home, she was often near enough so that "I'll hear it [as I] go by and pay just enough attention to it to know what the content is." When the girls are interested in seeing a film at the theater, their parents look for movie reviews online so as to make the decision about whether they believe it will be appropriate for their daughters, in particular ruling out films deemed "exploitive" of women. Like the Dearborns, the Gardners were primarily concerned with how the media represented groups and persons that they believed were, like themselves, often discriminated against. Tolerance was a primary value by which they evaluated the media, as was clear in this exchange:

KATIE AND ANNAE'S FATHER: Shows like that [*The Simpsons*] are . . . taking on the misconceptions and really addressing them. *Ellen* is doing a wonderful job of that. I was really glad for [his daughters] to see *Ellen.* This week, on the first episode, there was just a real babe that was billed as being a lesbian, and Ellen said something like, "Oh yeah, she's the one they put on the recruiting posters." [Laughter]
KATIE AND ANNAE'S MOTHER: Yeah, the recruiting posters.
KATIE AND ANNAE'S FATHER: And last year, she made some comment about how she'd recruited [so many people, she ought to get] a toaster oven.
KATIE AND ANNAE'S MOTHER: At the end, they show them giving her a toaster oven, too. [Laughter]

In the Gardner family, where prejudice is often suffered due to their difference from the norms of Christianity, they sympathized with other social groups who similarly suffered criticisms that they believed arose out of ignorance. Katie and Annae's father explained, "I think there's a one in a hundred chance that either of our girls will be [homosexual], but they're going to meet people who are. And that's really important to recognize people for what they are instead of what you're told they are." Tolerance and acceptance of others were important values emphasized in the Gardner household.

Katie recognized that her parents' opinions regarding television and film viewing were based on standards that differed from those of her friends and colleagues at school, and she enjoyed pointing this out to them: "At school, I mentioned watching *Ellen.* I said, like to somebody, 'Did you see that *Ellen* show last night?' And they were like, 'Oh my God, you watched that? That show is so sick!' And I'm like, 'Why?' And they said, 'Because she's gay!' And I'm like, 'So? For all you know, I could be gay!' [Laughter] And they backed off." Not only did Katie enjoy challenging the stereotypes of her colleagues at school, but both she and Annae also relished the fact that due to their religious tradition, they were viewed as different, unpredictable, mysterious, or possibly even dangerous. How they were viewed by their friends and school colleagues influenced what they found appealing in the Wiccan tradition. This, however, formed a largely unspoken difference between the Wiccan tradition as embraced by the Gardner parents and that which was embraced by Katie and Annae.

In the family's interview, the young women and their parents all expressed frustration that their religion was so frequently represented as folklore, such as in the popular teen film about witchcraft, *The Craft*. Their criticism that such films portray "witches" as commanding evil powers and casting spells (rather than portraying the Wiccan respect for the free will of others and not willfully committing evil, the preferred definitions offered by their parents) suggested the wish for clearer boundaries between religion and the fictional representations of legend in popular culture. At the time of the group interview, the girls explained that they liked the film *The Craft* primarily for the fashion and glamour of its central teen characters (figure 5.1). In their family's discussion of the film, the parents took the opportunity of the interview to interject what they believed were the differences between their beliefs and the film's representation of their beliefs:

ANNAE: It's just like a really interesting movie.

ANNAE AND KATIE'S FATHER: How so?

ANNAE: Well, just like how they use their powers and stuff.

ANNAE AND KATIE'S FATHER: Would you ever want to use your powers that way?

KATIE: No.

ANNAE: [Except maybe that thing that changes your appearance.] That'd be cool.

ANNAE AND KATIE'S MOTHER: The glamour spell.

ANNAE AND KATIE'S FATHER: But what's wrong with a lot of the other things they did? [His daughters don't respond] It affects other people's free will and does evil.

ANNAE AND KATIE'S MOTHER: She [one of the lead characters] kills people, doesn't she?

ANNAE AND KATIE'S FATHER: Which tends to interfere with their free will.

ANNAE: Dad, one thing they did wrong— [Annae and Katie's mother laughs] One thing wrong with the movie, they kept—They kept saying, "culling the corners."

ANNAE AND KATIE'S FATHER: Culling? Culling the corners? Yeah, if you're in a circle, it's hard to have corners.

[Katie laughs]

ANNAE AND KATIE'S MOTHER: It's called quarters.

ANNAE AND KATIE'S FATHER: You call the quarters, the four elements, North, Earth; East, air; South, fire; West, water.

ANNAE AND KATIE'S MOTHER: Yeah, there's no corners in a circle. . . . They did a lot of things—a lot of these metaphysical movies do something that drives me absolutely up the wall! They've done it for years. They'll take a little bit of something that's really true. This is a classic for people who are also trying to get their point of view across without quite showing you the truth. Put a little bit of truth in it, mix it with a lie. And a lot of these movies do that. Some religious leaders have been known to do it, too. [laughs]

While the teen girls did not disagree with their parents' presentations of the differences between Wicca and the representations in the film, in her individual interview, Katie revealed that she saw more commonalities than differences regarding her Wiccan identity and practices and those she saw in the popular film:

INTERVIEWER: Last time, we were talking about *The Craft*. You and Annae really liked it, and your mom was saying, "It's not real." What do you like about *The Craft*?

KATIE: I just like the fact that some of it is actually real. They took some stuff that actually you can do.

INTERVIEWER: In Wicca?

KATIE: Yeah. In paganism.

INTERVIEWER: What's an example?

FIGURE 5.1

In *The Craft*, teen girls call upon powers from beyond to change their appearance. The Gardner girls copied this ritual with their friends. *The Craft*, © 1996 Columbia Pictures Industries, Inc. All rights reserved. Courtesy of Columbia Pictures.

KATIE: In *The Craft*, they change their appearance, like hair color or eye color. When my friends were over, we were down in the basement and ... we got Becky's hair to be about this long [chest-length] and black. ... Pretty much what happened is, while we were watching *The Craft*, we wrote down stuff which we might want to try later. And then we did.

INTERVIEWER: And it actually worked. Did you tell your mom?

KATIE: No, because we didn't know whether she would approve or be mad at us for trying that stuff.

Based on previous conversations with Katie's mother, it was clear that she would not be pleased that Katie embraced more of the practices she saw in the popular movie than those she witnessed in her parents' coven or larger pagan community. On the few occasions when Katie's mother has inadvertently become aware of her experiments with witchcraft, she has instructed Katie that it is not good to be disrespectful of the spirits when she calls upon them. Her father, in contrast, has laughed off such experiments.

Like Katie, Annae, too, bent the family's Wiccan religious tradition along the lines of popular culture, drawing connections between Wicca, *The Craft*, and the long-standing popular teen practices of the Ouija board. Annae, being a Wiccan, seemed to be consulted as an "expert" on these rituals by her friends:

INTERVIEWER: Do you see the stuff you've learned in Wicca in *The Craft*, or are those two separate things?

ANNAE: Yeah. Like when they call the quarters. ... And a lot of the ritual stuff they do is the same.

INTERVIEWER: Like what would be an example?

ANNAE: Like burning incense, putting up a circle, lots of other stuff. It's pretty interesting.

INTERVIEWER: And you've done that too, in your ritual?

ANNAE: Uh-huh. I do it whenever I'm with my friends, and do like the Ouija board, we always put up a circle, like smudge the room and everything.

INTERVIEWER: Why do you do that?

ANNAE: Because sometimes the Ouija board attracts negative energy. And it can get spirits like to tell you whatever you want to hear, or they'll tell you stuff just to hurt you. And, at one of my friends' parties, we're playing, we were like doing the Ouija board. We had one of the spirits in there that was obviously the spirit of an Indian [Native American] girl. We told her that we didn't really want her there because she was making all of us freaked out. And when she left, she just shattered the circle. After that, we didn't really sleep very well because we knew that there was other spirits there that were kind of attracted by what she did. ... Half the girls were freaked out because one of our friends had died last year. And we'd just had an encounter with her. She said that she like came on, and we were like, "Who is it?" And it said, "Cathy." And one of the girls was about to cry so we told Cathy that we had to let her go.

Then the spirit [of the Native American girl] just started playing with
us, and she thought that it was all funny . . .

INTERVIEWER: Is the way you use the Ouija board, do you connect that
with Wicca, or is that a separate thing?

ANNAE: Sort of. I mean it's a circle and everything. We just like usually
put up the circle, but before we put up the circle we usually like
cleanse the board, where we feel the energy in it, and if we perceive
faces, we get rid of the faces. So we like imagine like it's brand-new
and everything.

In this story, Annae mixed Wiccan rituals designated for the sacralizing of
space with the Ouija board "parlor game" traditions of "cleansing the board"
and calling forth spirits from the dead.[12] In this case, the practice, they believe, brought forth both the benign spirit of a deceased friend, an experience
upsetting enough, but also the mischievous spirit of a girl they did not know
who was ostensibly from another racial/ethnic, cultural, and religious tradition. While Wiccan rituals, like those of other religious traditions, are designed to bring a sense of peace and renewed vision to their participants,
those of the Ouija board "freak out" their participants, as Annae described
the ceremony.

Neither Annae nor Katie seemed particularly concerned that combining
Wicca with more popular practices might be at some distance from the way
their parents preferred to think about their Wiccan tradition. Still, considering
the fact that they did not discuss these events with their parents, it is evident
that they were aware of what their parents' opinions might be. However, it was
clear that being consulted as experts in the "dark arts" of the Ouija board and
witchcraft by their peers served as an appealing aspect of the Wiccan religious
tradition for the Gardner teens.

Calling upon external supernatural powers was not something the Gardner
parents emphasized in their understanding of the Wiccan tradition's foregrounding of harmony with the earth. As Katie and Annae's mother had said of
people who seek out such powers or beings, "If [people] are not trying to help
themselves, then don't waste my time." Her understanding of Wicca seemed to
emphasize the religion's rational, human-centered side.

Reservations about the media representations and supernatural powers
aside, Katie's mother said that when she was a young teen herself, she experienced what she termed "metaphysical" events not completely distinct from the
popular practices of the supernatural, and also somewhat outside Wiccan religious beliefs. She described the experience:

I just started having strange dreams. What I think now, in retrospect, were
probably out-of-body experiences. But I'd never heard of them before. I
had no idea what was going on. I was taking everything in a religious context, you know, what I had believed as I grew up. Course then as I got
older, I started doing more reading. After I got through with looking at all

the churches and decided they weren't any help, I started doing more reading in the metaphysical area. It wasn't until we really moved out here [to the western part of the United States] that I started connecting with some of the people that kind of told me what was probably going on. Some of the books helped, too, because I'd read them and go, "So that's what was going on. Now I know."

Katie's mother did not attempt to explain these events of her early teen years within a framework of Wiccan religious beliefs. Instead, she relied upon the assistance of a therapist who specialized in past-life regression to analyze this experience of her childhood. As she noted, the religious traditions of her past had been unhelpful in providing a means to understand her experiences. Apparently, her current religious tradition of Wiccanism, while she felt it was more open to alternative explanations, similarly did not explicitly shape her interpretation of what she called the metaphysical aspect of her life.[13]

The experiences Katie and Annae's mother had and the practices in which she engaged to interpret them might have been outside the emphasis of Wiccan traditions. Yet they were consistent with a sensibility in Wicca, as described by her husband, as she relied upon emotional knowledge rather than looking specifically to her religious tradition for resources of interpretation: "You're encouraged in Wicca to use more of your feminine side, use more of that intuitive, feeling side, there's nothing that you are dogmatized to take on faith. You are encouraged to pay attention to what you feel, instead of what someone tells you to feel." This emotional knowledge forms the core of how the teens are aware of their place, and their power, within the universe as defined by Wicca, as he noted:

ANNAE AND KATIE'S FATHER: They [Annae and Katie] are very in tune to energies.

INTERVIEWER: [Their mother] mentioned Katie's abilities with animals.

ANNAE AND KATIE'S FATHER: With animals. That makes a lot of sense to them. Now, a Christian will tell you that a healing touch comes from God or from Christ, or something like that. It's a gift to you. [Katie] knows, not from having it drummed into her, but because she really wasn't dogmatized at all, but just from her own experience and what she can see and feel, that that power comes from within her. And so as being a part of the universe, being a part of those energies of the earth. A part of the divine.

Katie and Annae's father argued that in Wicca, supernatural powers do not arise from external sources such as God or Christ, but from within the self and in its relationship to the earth. Experiencing that power becomes a means of emotionally grounding and affirming the knowledge, central to the Wiccan religious tradition, of the harmonious relationship between humans and the earth. While this is rather distinct from the representations of witchcraft in the entertainment media, the emotional affirmation derived from personal reli-

gious experiences formed the bridge between Wiccan beliefs and experimentations with its more popularized forms among the teen Gardner daughters.

THE EXPERIMENTERS AND THEIR APPROACH
TO THE MEDIA AND THEIR BELIEFS

Lily attended a conservative Protestant church and occasionally went to
Catholic mass, and Annae and Katie were a pair of sisters who actively participated with their parents in the rituals of their city's Wiccan and pagan communities. Like the Resister and Mystical teens, these teens were unconcerned
about how the entertainment media might represent views or stories that differed from those of the religious traditions with which they were affiliated. Yet
unlike the Resisters and Mysticals, they directly related their supernatural encounters to their religious traditions. Katie and Annae employed Wiccan rituals at the beginning of the Ouija board play, ostensibly to make the séance a
more pleasant, perhaps "safer," or maybe even a more "authentic" experience.
Despite this ritual, however, most of the girls were "freaked out" by the end.
And this, after all, is the point of Ouija boards. As has been discussed in earlier
chapters, it is also the point of many of the teen experiences with the supernatural, from watching horror films, to visiting cemeteries, to telling scary stories late at night.

In many cases, these kinds of experiments are viewed as fairly innocuous
and unrelated to religion. What is interesting about the Gardner girls, however,
is that they did not seem particularly concerned about combining practices
from Wicca, even those designed to sacralize space and recognize harmony,
with the practices of witchcraft and Ouija boards, which are really about
"freaking" everybody out. Similarly, Lily did not interpret her father's musings
about the afterlife as a "different dimension," or her own paranormal experiences, as inconsistent with her Baptist beliefs. When her Sunday school teacher
suggested that such occurrences could have been related to the Devil, she was
largely unfazed: explanations of the paranormal from the entertainment
media, and those from Protestant Christianity, were interchangeable for her.

RELIGIOUS EXPERIENCES AND
THE AUTHORITY OF EMOTIONS

The experiences of these Experimenters had a few other things in common, as
well. First and most importantly, emotions were important in all of these cases.
What made it "real" for the teens was not that it was connected to a particular
tradition but that it *felt* real: they experienced fear or, in other cases, comfort.
They knew something had happened because they felt it. While some might
view this reliance on emotion as a superficial response to religious phenomena,
it is important to recognize that feelings have long been an important part of

what many consider authentic religious experience. In the eighteenth century, religious revivals echoed the rise of romanticism that had manifested itself in that era's poetry and fiction, drawing on feelings of fear and comfort for religious conversion. Emotions have always been an important part of the life of faith, providing a depth of commitment to religious belief, as William James had argued.[14] Furthermore, looking to the inward or emotional realm for validation of authentic spiritual experience had important precedents with the Protestant Great Awakenings. As historian Charles Lippy has noted, preachers of the eighteenth century placed a great emphasis upon the conversion experiences of individuals, making them—rather than traditions, doctrines, or beliefs—the locus for authentic religious experience.[15]

Discussions of the relationship between religious experiences, emotions, and a strengthened commitment to religious traditions usually center on religious experiences that people believe involve God or angels rather than contact with the dead. Yet as MacDonald has found, there is an association between traditionally religious practices such as prayer and the reporting of at least one paranormal experience, that of telepathy.[16] This may suggest that experiences of telepathy can strengthen commitments to religious traditions, or, as is suggested by the stories of this chapter, that people who experience paranormal occurrences such as telepathy do not see such events as in conflict with the beliefs and practices associated with their religious traditions. As noted before, consistency within a single tradition is not important to these families. This may explain, in part, why their teenage daughters were intrigued by the mystical realm they were acquainted with through popular film, books, practices of the Ouija board, and other places, and viewed experimenting with that mystical realm as not inconsistent with their religious traditions.[17]

MacDonald has also found that the proportion of people in the United States reporting experiences with spirits of the deceased—an aspect of the stories told by Lily, her father, and Annae Gardner—has dramatically increased over the past two decades.[18] This may be a result of an increase in the trauma associated with experiencing the death of a spouse or loved one. U.S. culture tends to provide few resources for coping with such occurrences, after all.

Moreover, the rise in the belief that one has been contacted by the dead may also be related to increasing religious pluralism in the United States. With increased religious diversity, people have more opportunities than ever to be familiar with religions, such as certain Judaic, Native American, and African traditions, where contact with one's ancestors is an important aspect of religious ceremony and belief. Moreover, as various religions have come into contact with the traditions of Protestantism, the dominant religion in the United States, that religion's central ideas about resurrection and a life in heaven after death have shaped how people conceive of the afterlife as a positive place.[19] And added to all of this are the Catholic traditions of intercessory and patron saints, who were called upon from beyond the material world to provide assistance in the present.[20] Some do not agree that all of these traditions are mixed in the beliefs of individuals. Sociologist Andrew Greeley, for instance, has argued that the competition for adherents between religious organizations in the United States has meant an increased awareness of one's own traditions regarding the afterlife because of the organizations' emphasis upon inculcating a certain orthodoxy of beliefs among their members.[21] Yet the examples of this chapter point to the need to further investigate people like the Gardners and Dearborns. Families like these are on the one hand very familiar with and committed to their religious traditions, and on the other, they find ideas and beliefs outside of those traditions appealing, explanatory, and not inconsistent with the religious traditions they claim.

SUPERNATURAL EXPERIMENTATIONS AS EMPOWERMENT

Second, in addition to really feeling something, these experiences gave the teens a sense of empowerment. Lily, Annae, and Katie, like most teens, often felt like they did not fit in with their peers. Added to that was the fact that, as with most teens, their parents had a lot of say over what they did in their day-to-day lives. Being able to tap into power from a realm beyond is particularly appealing during the teen years, when young people are stretching to embrace the independence of adulthood while often rebelling against its trappings. These activities allow girls to experience fear and horror in the safe contexts of their peer groups, among other young women who are experiencing the same real-world fears they are. Young teen girls too frequently live with the reality of high rates of violent crimes against women and abusive sexual relationships. Their familiarity with such real-life "horrors" adds to the appeal that supernatural events featuring the confrontation of (or working with) fear can lead to a sense of power that may otherwise be lacking. The sentimentality of religion and its overly sweet renderings of the supernatural in depictions of God and angels may be particularly unappealing to young women who have experienced suffering and a sense of powerlessness.[22]

EXPERIMENTATION, MIXING, AND GENDER

Are these kinds of supernatural experimentations more likely to happen among teen girls than among teen boys? Well, in the particular cases of Ouija boards and witchcraft, probably so. Both séances and spell-casting are deeply embedded in teen girl life. Moreover, each has a long historical connection to the traditions of women that were perceived as threats to the Christian tradition. This strengthens their relationship with rebellion. But teen boys have their own unique practices of the supernatural. These usually involve activities outside of the home, such as visits to cemeteries and other fear-inducing places, or challenges boys give to one another that involve fearsome or death-defying activities.

Religion, or spirituality, is for many people associated with feelings of being comforted or peaceful. So when girls bring religion into a mix with popular culture, they are doing two things. First, they are acknowledging, in a way, that just because they are engaging in supernatural experiments, they consider themselves to be fundamentally good people—people who are respectful of good and of God even if they are not overly involved in religious organizations. Second, they are adding a correction to religion's inability to deal with the horror in their lives. Contemporary religion, with its emphasis on sentimentality, may seem too removed from the darker facets of their own pain.

Mixing religious traditions and those of superstitions of teen life, therefore, is not really about confusion or postmodernism, or about not knowing enough about one's religious background. It is not about the power of the media to persuade young people to buy into beliefs that are dangerous or unorthodox. These young women sought out films, television programs, books, and popular practices of the supernatural, not as a tool to help them to decide what to believe, but because they enjoyed them as entertainment. Sometimes, of course, their interests moved beyond mere entertainment, and they did consciously seek out sources that they hoped would enable them to better engage the supernatural powers they believed were accessible to them. Then their entertainment pursuits became sources of information, particularly as those fictional accounts echoed stories they associated with their religious and familial traditions.

THE ROLE OF THE MEDIA
IN EXPERIMENTATION

So what is the role of the media in relation to the interpretations of the paranormal events for these young women and their families? As we have seen, the Dearborns and Gardners had somewhat different approaches to this question. Katie and Annae's parents struggled to assert their Wiccan identity as distinct from that which they saw in teen media culture, while Lily's father reflected few similar concerns regarding the separation of his Baptist beliefs from those seen in popular television programs and films. In the case of the Gardners, their religion has often been represented as folklore and has been delegitimated historically. Because witchcraft has long been a popular concept in the entertainment media and figured in parlor games and fiction long before television and film, distinctions between these representations and those of a more "orthodox" Wiccan tradition were difficult to maintain. This was particularly the case because Annae and Katie's mother seemed to have had her own experiences with paranormal phenomena that was not necessarily consistent with Wiccan traditions.

While they seemed to have differing approaches to the media, the Dearborns, like the Gardners, stressed the importance of emotional knowledge that had come from experience in interpreting and approaching the supernatural realm. In the case of the Dearborns, this emotional knowledge also influenced what they saw in the media. As Lily's father noted, "I don't think *Star Trek* is something that really pulls any weight on paranormal existence; I just think that it might offer some ideas on why it takes place." Referring to the way Lily's father approached his favorite television program as "trivial" or completely distinct from his beliefs concerning his experiences seems to miss the point, I think. The media, to use media and religion scholar Stewart Hoover's phrase, served as a "symbolic inventory" upon which Lily's father drew when putting together his own set of beliefs.[23] To use Lily's father's words, *Star Trek* was the source of the "what if" element of beliefs in the supernatural. It was not that *Star Trek* directly informed his *religious* beliefs, or even that he accepted all he saw in *Star Trek* as "religion." It was that *Star Trek*, particularly as it echoes certain ancient religious themes and comes clothed in the language and images of science, served as a source of information for what might be *possible* in the realm beyond the material world—an idea that seemed to resonate for Lily, Katie, and Annae, as well. This, it seems to me, is a key element of overlap between what we might consider to be legitimate expressions of religion and the stories of the supernatural that appear in the entertainment media. Each contains an element of the inexplicable and the mystical, pointing beyond the material world to something our tools of science cannot prove; thus it must be taken, to use religion's terminology, on faith. Both legitimate religion and the stories of the supernatural from the entertainment media are concerned with the question "*What if* these things are true?" The "what if" element unites some of our world religions' central questions with what some might call "superstition": What if there are good and evil forces beyond the control of individual humans (such as angels, demons, ghosts, or even aliens)? What if beings from the realm beyond can provide assistance to those on earth (such as God, angels, saints, or ghosts of the deceased)? What if humans can harness that power from the realm beyond (through prayer, séances, telepathy, or contact with aliens)? This is part of the appeal shared by late-twentieth- and early-twenty-first-century popular television and films as diverse as *Touched by an Angel*, *The X-Files*, and *The Sixth Sense*. Each addresses the mysteries of the realm beyond and presents a myth which, while fictional, draws upon these important questions in intriguing ways.

It is impossible to determine whether Lily, Katie, and Annae first learned of paranormal experiences from entertainment sources or from their parents, but both are important in how their own experiences with the realm beyond have come to be interpreted. Religious traditions have also played an important part in their interpretation. Lily, as noted, told her Sunday school teacher about the manifestations of evil that she experienced. She found the teacher's explanation of demon possession to be relevant and useful, and importantly, not contradictory with the interpretations informed by her father's experiences, horror films, documentaries on the paranormal, and numerous other sources. The fact that demon possession and "devil worship" is a topic that has been covered in stories of the entertainment media as well as in religion probably accounts for the fact that she does not see a need to separate the two. She sees the similarities between the dark stories of the supernatural and stories from the dark side of evangelicalism: both deal with evil, Satan, demon possession, and the like.

Similarly, Katie and Annae also interpreted what they saw in the entertainment media in light of their Wiccan traditions and its belief in the ability of individuals to access power within themselves when in harmony with the Earth. Of course, their interpretations were also importantly informed by how their friends viewed that tradition's relationship to its more popular, entertainment-inspired form of the "dark arts." Thus, while the beliefs of Wicca were key to their interpretations, so was the cultural position of Wicca as marginalized, historically delegitimized, and possibly dangerous, mysterious, or exciting.

To conclude, this is the first chapter that seems to directly address our initial question, "Do the stories of the entertainment media seem to replace those of religion for some teens?" On first glance, it seems that the answer is yes. Yet it is important to note the way in which the entertainment media provide key sources of information on the realm beyond, and how the interpretations of those stories were mediated by personal experience, parents, peers, and the cultural position of and beliefs concerning these teens' religions. This chapter has demonstrated that the persuasiveness of the media does not rest upon the images, music, or mythic story lines of the entertainment media alone. Instead, an approach to media like that articulated by Lily, Katie, and Annae seems to be supported in many different ways and from various important sources. Their interpretations of the supernatural may be limited by their cultural resources, but those resources are understood, importantly, in light of their experiences with religion.

In the next chapter, we turn to a group of young people who, quite frankly, would probably be appalled by the experiments of these teens and baffled by the seemingly casual way in which they mixed religious traditions with beliefs drawn from other aspects of U.S. culture. These next teens want to strengthen the boundaries between religion and the media, not blur them. Because they want to conserve their respective religious traditions in the face of what they see as a cultural incursion, I have termed them the Traditionalists.

THE TRADITIONALISTS

AFFIRMING THE BOUNDARY

BETWEEN RELIGION

AND THE MEDIA

"This generation of teens is more spiritual than their parents," wrote journalist Sharon Begley in a special report on teens that was published in a 2000 issue of *Newsweek* magazine.[1] Yet being spiritual, as we have seen in the previous chapters, does not necessarily mean being committed exclusively to one's religious tradition. Begley continues: "Many [teens] put together their own religious canon as they would a salad from a salad bar."

Not all teens are so comfortably eclectic, however, and in fact some place a great deal of importance in conserving and deepening their faith experience within a single tradition. This may represent an important position for a strong minority of young people. Indeed, one national poll found that more than three in ten teenagers in the United States describe themselves as strongly committed to their religious convictions.[2] Internationally, commitment to traditional faith groups has been on the rise, as documented in numerous studies on fundamentalisms around the world.[3] While highly committed teens may be found in every religious affiliation, it is worth noting that in the United States, almost the same percentage—three in ten—claim to be evangelical or "born-again" Christians, and there are reasons to suspect a high degree of overlap between these two categories.[4]

One of the characteristics of traditional religious identity is the presumed need to maintain values and practices that are separate from "secular" influence, notably those adherents believe can be found in the media. Therefore, Traditionalists tend to see a clear distinction between what they regard as stories that are a part of their religious tradition, and those stories that fall outside of, or even corrupt, religious tradition. We have discussed this presumed separation and its importance to evangelical Christian identity. Yet such a separation is not unique to that tradition. In fact, in the relatively small sample interviewed for this book, most people thought that there was a rather clear separation between traditional religion and the stories of the media—regardless of how they themselves related to religion.

This chapter highlights two teens who fall into the category of evangelical Protestantism and introduces two from other religious traditions who seek to draw distinct separations between their religious beliefs and their media practices: one a Mormon, and one an American Muslim. Their varying religious backgrounds, along with their unique life histories, lead to slightly different reasons for needing to separate themselves from the content and practices of the media. What these teens share in common is a strong commitment to conservative religious traditions that emphasize personal morality, and a resulting tendency to see the beliefs and practices of their religion as distinct from what they assume about the U.S. media. Additionally, while these teens all expressed a great deal of interest in their religion, their interest in the supernatural—even angels, the supernatural beings closest to their religious traditions—was marginal. I use the term "Traditionalist" not to highlight specific orientations to social or political choices made by these young people, but to note one desire that each teen shares in common: they are respectful of the religious traditions in which they participate, are in fact regular participants, and see themselves as continuing, or conserving, that tradition they hold dear. As we will see, their approaches to the media grow out of this commitment and out of their parents' shared commitment to it.

EVANGELICALS AND THE MEDIA:
SARA HANSEN AND SWEETIE BUCHANAN

Both fifteen-year-old Sara Hansen and eighteen-year-old Sweetie Buchanan described themselves as evangelical Christians.[5] Historian George Marsden has identified several common views shared by most people who identify themselves as evangelicals: "(1) The Reformation doctrine of the final authority of the Bible, (2) the real historical character of God's saving work recorded in Scripture, (3) salvation to eternal life based on the redemptive work of Christ, (4) the importance of evangelism and missions, and (5) the importance of a spiritually transformed life."[6] Evangelicalism is not the same as fundamentalism, as noted in chapter 1. In fact, evangelicalism formed in the 1930s and 1940s in response to what some viewed as the increasingly reactionary and separatist emphases within fundamentalism. In order to achieve the goals of evangelizing, or as Sara Hansen put it, "being a witness" to nonbelievers, evangelicals took three steps that have since defined the differences between fundamentalism and evangelicalism, as Christian Smith has argued:

first, evangelicals believed that the judgmental assumptions of fundamental-ism had to be abandoned in favor of greater openness toward those outside the tradition. Second, they believed that intellectual reasoning needed to be nurtured rather than eschewed, thus leading to the support of such institutional structures as evangelical schools of higher education and various academic journals and magazines. And third, evangelicals believed that social and political activism should be more central to church activities than they had been in the fundamentalist congregations.[7] While these differences seem to suggest a need for greater accommodation and negotiation with U.S. culture at large than had been the case among fundamentalists, Quentin Schultze argues that it has fostered two opposing views toward the media. On the one hand, the media are seen as a powerful force in the effort to introduce nonbelievers to the faith (most visibly employed in televangelism). On the other hand, popular culture is seen as a threat to the values and beliefs evangelicals hold dear. Well-known evangelical media critics such as Donald Wildmon and James Dobson exemplify this latter approach, employing what Schultze terms a "highly personalistic approach to morality."[8]

Other studies of evangelical approaches to the media affirm this distinction. Media researcher Todd Rendleman conducted a study of popular film reception among evangelical young adults. He found that they were primarily concerned with representations of nudity, bad language, and what they believed were negative and stereotypical characterizations of their faith.[9] In contrast to critiques of popular culture's encouragement of consumerism, sexism, or bad taste, evangelicals focus on media that they believe encourage or promote sexual promiscuity, improper language, violence, or an excessive and unproductive use of time.

These objections to the media, based upon personal morality, surfaced in many of the interviews with evangelical teens and their parents. To understand how these objections relate to the formation of teen beliefs, we turn first to the story of Sara Hansen.

Sara Hansen was an intense and athletic Anglo-American fifteen-year-old who competed in cross-country meets in her school and around her home state. Her father, a salesperson for the metals industry, and her mother, a nursing supervisor at a nearby hospital, strongly encouraged and supported the sports activities in which both Sara and her younger brother engaged. In fact, sports, God, and her family were the things Sara said were the most important in her life. She described herself and her mother, father, and younger brother as "strong Christians" who believed in the importance of being a "witness" to others. She viewed her drive to succeed athletically as a means to demonstrate the importance of a commitment that extended to her faith life. While she engaged in strenuous training for sports competitions, fulfilling the role of what she termed a "Christian witness" was what she considered the most difficult task of her life:

INTERVIEWER: What's the hardest thing you've faced in your life?
SARA: Probably just facing people who aren't Christian and trying to be a

witness to them. That's really hard. . . . Like, when people see [Sara and her family], we want them to see Jesus and stuff.

While the Hansen parents were both ex-Catholics, the family belonged at one time to a nondenominational "megachurch" in their area. Then they had begun to attend a relatively small church, most of whose members had at one time belonged to a large Baptist congregation.[10] In an interview with Sara's family, Sara's father noted his frustration at what he saw as the promotion of homosexuality in programs featuring the celebrity Ellen Degeneres. Sara's mother similarly objected to some of the programs on MTV because they were "too racy," and she expressed concern that some of the discussions on daytime talk shows were "inappropriate." When asked whether they ever watched any television programs or films with religious themes, Sara's mother noted that they had occasionally watched the WB program *7th Heaven*, which features a minister and his family encountering and triumphing in the face of moral problems that confront children and adolescents.

The Hansens encouraged the watching of programs like *7th Heaven*, as they believed this program, with its moral and upbeat messages, was consistent with their views. Unlike fundamentalist families who may have sought to shield their children from all media, the goal of these evangelical parents was to assist them in forming an understanding of how the views to which they adhered differed from those most frequently expressed in popular culture. In some cases, like the Hansens, this resulted in a family policy less structured by censorship or limitations than by implicit expectations of the parents and by the prioritizing of other activities over television, music, or film consumption. Sara's mother, for instance, insisted that the children did not watch enough television to warrant strict rules due to their own choices, which took up the majority of their leisure time (such as their avid participation in sports). She was confident that their choices were consistent with her own views, such as Sara's eleven-year-old brother's decision to not watch the popular Fox television program *The Simpsons* despite its popularity among his peers, because he felt it was "stupid."

While Sara's mother often voiced her opinion and encouraged the children to seek out other programming when she felt that what they were watching was inappropriate, Sara's father was more lenient. He noted that he occasionally even permitted his son to watch the NBC late-night television program *Saturday Night Live* with him because "he wants to see who the guest host might be or what the opening skit's gonna be." In contrast with the mother, this father did not recall discussing with either of his children instances he considered offensive that were portrayed in the media. This pattern of allowing the enforcement of media rules to fall to the mother is consistent with the view that child rearing and day-to-day preparation for adulthood is largely a woman's task, a socially conservative view generally supported or assumed among evangelical families.[11]

Despite the seeming lack of overt discussions about drawing distinctions between media and their religion within the family, Sara had adopted an approach to media that echoed the personalized, moralistic objections of other evangelical teens she most likely encountered through her church, sports, and school activities. When asked whether she thought about God when watching television, for example, she replied:

SARA: Yeah, like Jesus wouldn't want you to be watching this. Jesus wouldn't want you to be watching this 'cause it's not very Christian-like.
INTERVIEWER: What specifically?
SARA: Just like bad language and stuff, and sex stuff, all that stuff.

Interestingly, Sara described the problems of fictional television in terms of what she understood to be its moral message, using a framework popularized among evangelicals in the mid-1990s through bracelets, T-shirts, and other items bearing the slogan "WWJD," an abbreviation for "What Would Jesus Do?"[12] Although she occasionally felt pressure from her friends to attend R-rated films, she was uncomfortable with their themes because, as she said, "we know that's not right" according to the moral ideals of evangelical Christianity. In conversations with Sara, as was true with numerous other evangelical teens, discussions of the relationship between religion and media yielded comments about personal morality. Representations of beings or powers associated with the supernatural realm, such as angels, were not seen as relevant subjects to this discussion.

While Sara expressed concern that the practices of media consumption could distract her from her religiously defined goals, Sweetie Buchanan, like many teens, resisted the notion that the media could influence her in any way.[13] When she talked about this in her interview, Sweetie seemed anxious to assert that she was a critical thinker and viewer, despite what she assumed many seemed to believe about young people. While she expressed views that were largely consistent with the conservative evangelical Protestant traditions in which she grew up, Sweetie also saw herself as distinct from it because of a significant life experience: the divorce of her two evangelical parents.

Like a number of her contemporaries, Sweetie, an Anglo-American, spent a lot of time shuttling between two households. She lived in a middle-class neighborhood with her two younger half-siblings and her mother and stepfather, both of whom were professionals with college degrees. Her father and brother lived in a nearby town, and her stepfather's ex-wife and husband lived several blocks away with two of her stepfather's children (two other children are grown and have left the household). Sweetie's mother and stepfather reported that they often planned activities with all eight of the children related to the family.

Although more than a third of today's teens grow up in either blended or single-parent homes, making knowledge of such familial changes fairly commonplace, Sweetie said that she had always felt like an outsider at her Christian high school due to her parents' divorce.[14] During the interview with her family, her stepparents vehemently expressed the pain they felt as their two separate churches shunned each of them in response to the divorces. These experiences prompted both parents to leave organized religion in bitterness, and to strike up a relationship with each other out of their common concerns. Yet despite their lack of actual attendance or membership and their pain, Sweetie's mother and stepfather still viewed themselves as highly involved and committed to their evangelical religious traditions, making them what sociologists Hadaway and Marler have termed "mental affiliates" of organized religion.[15] This explains, in part, why Sweetie attended a Christian school and also partly explains her sense of discomfort within it. Sweetie could not accept the disapproval from her parents' churches and from her own colleagues, she explained, because she "always assumed that God knew what He was doing . . . my parents and God knew what they were doing." Thus, she did not judge the divorce as a reason to question the religious commitment of either her parents or stepparents, as her school colleagues had.

Sweetie, who was often told that she resembled the actress Cameron Diaz, attended the Christian school affiliated with her church until her junior year in high school. At that time, she switched to the public school in her area, primarily for its wider breadth of arts courses, but also because her best friend was changing schools at the same time and for the same reason. There is little doubt that her difference from those in her school also contributed to her desire to change locations.

Sweetie, like her parents, considered herself very committed to her evangelical Christian faith and by extension, to the conservative Baptist congregation she attended. She implicitly recognized that not all Baptist churches are as committed to Christianity, at least by her church's standards:

> They say [it's a] Baptist [church]. I don't even know exactly [what denomination it is]. They still have their name as Baptist, but actually we preach real Bible, real conservative or moderate conservative, I guess I could say.
> . . . Basically, what we believe is the Bible is a God-ordained book, and we believe everything in the Bible. We don't pick and choose different things. We believe that Jesus Christ is the Son of God [and] came to save everybody, so I think the best way to describe it, which separates us from other churches, is we believe everything that the Bible said is true, and happened.

In this statement, Sweetie described an approach to the Bible that is consistent with Christian fundamentalism. When asked if her church was fundamentalist, however, she refused that designation, noting that what distinguished her church from other Baptist churches was that they were "very music-oriented" and spent much of the weekly service in "praise and worship." Her youth minister wrote music and often the youth group performed when they traveled on mission trips. In addition to her involvement in youth group, Sweetie attended Sunday services, Sunday school, and a monthly prayer meeting regularly. While her distinctions between evangelicalism and fundamentalism were less clearly articulated than those of historians and sociologists of religion noted earlier, they reflect an important view of religiosity in the contemporary United States. While evangelicalism has become increasingly accepted as reflective of middle-class norms, fundamentalism is viewed as reactionary and, hence, less desirable as an identifier, particularly outside the fundamentalist strongholds in the southern United States.[16] With their commitment to evangelism, higher education, and activism, Sweetie's parents exemplify the evangelical approach described earlier.

In Sweetie's home, as was the case in Sara's, television and film were ostensibly regulated by time limits. Also like the Hansen parents, Sweetie's mother and stepfather valued their children's ability to form judgments of distinction between what they consumed in the media and what they believed with regard to their religious traditions. While the Hansens rarely seemed to engage in discussions about specifics regarding which television programs or films were objectionable and for what reasons, in Sweetie's family, such discussions seemed much more common and formed the basis for the parents' decisions to disallow the viewing of certain films or television programs. The NBC television program *Friends*, which during the time of this interview was achieving the highest ratings among teenagers of any television shows, was cited by Sweetie's mother as an example of a program they do not prefer to have their children watch because "intimacy between a man and a woman is to be held very sacred." The values on that program, she said, "open up things that [young people] should not be exposed to." This restriction related to the family's goal of raising children with discerning abilities, as stated by Sweetie's stepfather: "Our goal is to make our children different. Not odd. Not weird. Not some goofball. We want our children to be different, that they're not able to recite all of the rap words to a song. But to be able to tell you what a portion of the Constitution means. So we want them to be different, and we think part of that difference is that we don't give them full reign over what they watch on television, what they listen to, or what they read." While Sweetie's parents stressed that they preferred to have their children limit their media consumption, both Sweetie and her two stepsiblings were familiar with many programs that Sweetie's mother said she didn't "agree with." Sweetie, according to her parents, preferred reading classic fiction to watching television.

When interviewed on her own, Sweetie noted that she enjoyed movies and a few television programs, although she also stressed that her demanding schedule did not allow much free time for viewing. Her favorite television shows at the time of her interview were *The Practice* and *The Simpsons*, and she explained that she liked both for their satirical and witty writing. While these programs have little to do with her religious convictions, according to Sweetie, the programs she disliked were distinctly related to her beliefs about sex or appropriate gender roles for women. *Home Improvement; Grace under Fire; Dr. Quinn, Medicine Woman;* and *The Drew Carey Show* all feature women who, according to Sweetie and in keeping with the personal moralistic objections common among evangelicals as noted by Schultze, were either "masculine and selfish" or used language that is "very dirty." She recognized that some in her religious community might make similar criticisms of *The Simpsons,* but she enjoyed it nonetheless:

SWEETIE: They [her disapproving friends] make fun of [me]. "Oh yeah, she watches *The Simpsons* right before she does her devotions!" I'm like, "Hey! Doesn't say anything wrong!" I mean, intelligent TV watching I think is *very* important. To say, "Okay, these shows really go against what I believe, so I'm not going to watch them." And say, "This one certainly doesn't support what I believe, yet I can enjoy watching it and realize that it's funny to a point, but I just don't *believe* this." It's not like I would [laughing] in any way want to mimic their mentality or I support it, but I do think it's enjoyable to watch sometimes. It's nice humor.

INTERVIEWER: I find myself giggling through *The Simpsons*.

SWEETIE: Good! I'm not the only one. My mom thinks they're spawned by Satan. I would never let kids watch them [though].

In this exchange, Sweetie recognized the sanction among her church friends against her preferred programs and assertively justified her continued enjoyment by noting that she does not "support," "mimic," or "believe" in what is represented. She attempted to draw a distinction between the assumed persuasive influence of television and her own experience of the program by indirectly referring to television's realist codes (that is, the fact that they are believed to be persuasive because they present a believable representation of reality). Sweetie argued that because these programs do not represent reality as she understands it due to her religious convictions, she is not in danger of being negatively influenced by these programs. The point of critical viewing, according to Sweetie, is to affirm and maintain this distinction between realities, regardless of what is consumed in the media.

Another show that Sweetie enjoyed—despite the fact that it is "New Age," "socialistic," and "everything I disagree with"—was *Star Trek*. Like her experience with *The Simpsons,* those in her religious circles disapproved:

I remember my Bible teacher went off on that and *Home Improvement* and a couple other shows, saying, "If you watch these shows, knowing that they're not supporting biblical beliefs, then it is immoral." I told that to my dad [with whom she has watched the shows for years]. My dad's an ordained minister, and he's always worked with nonprofit or Christian organizations. He's like, "Everyone has a right to their own beliefs." I have to say, my dad's the most Christian man I know. If he can look at something—and he does point it out when we watch: "Oh, that's socialist, that's evolutionary. That's Gene Rodenberry's views coming through." And he points them out. Now I can spot those things. I probably watch it more intelligently than most Christians will watch Christian shows, or listen to [sermons] in church. They just take in everything. I don't take in anything unquestioningly. I think about everything. And so I say, it's not immoral.

It's not immoral to watch such programs, argued Sweetie, because she was able to view them critically, drawing distinctions between her own religious traditions and those she believed were supportive of socialism, evolutionary theory, or humanism, as she termed them. The importance of bringing "intelligence" to this project of discerning her religious beliefs from those she witnessed on television and in film was an outgrowth of the critical skills she felt were necessary to bring to all endeavors, including even her religious beliefs. Just as she had implicitly challenged Christians who "just take in everything," Sweetie felt that coming to a critical perspective on her religious tradition was an important part of both personal and spiritual growth: "In my junior year, I never questioned God or my faith, but I questioned Christians. And I questioned my beliefs, such things, I didn't believe in dating, I didn't believe in a lot of things. And last year was a real, real, tough year . . . and so that was when I finally decided, 'Okay, this is what I believe. And I'm going to build from here. These are not my parents' beliefs, these are my beliefs.' Because I questioned all my parents' beliefs." Sweetie noted that this period of questioning was marked by several events: first, her father was fired from his ministry job along with several other staff members of that church, leaving Sweetie bewildered and feeling betrayed. Second, when she switched to the public school, she found herself challenged by an English class that approached "the Bible as if it were just another piece of literature." In the latter context, she was confronted with the inconsistencies of the Bible and began to ask herself whether she was "taking this on faith or because I really just don't want to think about it anymore."

Despite the reservations that arose from her encounter with the information, new to her, that the Bible contained factual errors, Sweetie viewed herself as someone who was very concerned with behaving in a way that is consistent with her beliefs. This, again, was reflected in her media preferences. She disliked the film *Contact*, for example, because the character played by Matthew McConaughy, self-identified as a Christian, slept with the female character played by Jodie Foster after their first meeting. Sweetie was angered by the representation of Christianity she saw in this film: "They made everything about God look stupid. When her [Jodie Foster's character] dad died, she was sitting there, and the priest comes up and says, 'Oh, be comforted, my child' or something. She totally told him off. And so they made it seem like an eight-year-old was more intelligent than a man who devoted his life to God. It just seemed like a real uncomfortable mix of religion, science fiction, and philosophy." In keeping with her own emphasis on the importance of intelligence and critical thinking within her religious tradition as she understood it, Sweetie was upset that Christianity in this film, she believed, was equated with ignorance. In her criticism, she noted that in addition to the ignorance of the priest, the film portrayed Christianity as extremist, reactionary and violent—all stereotypes of the fundamentalism she eschewed. McConaughy's character, who was ostensibly portrayed as the moral and compassionate center of the film (indeed, he becomes a well-known minister in a moderate tradition), was objectionable to her due to the fact that he was not sexually abstinent.

While Sweetie attempted to draw a distinction between her own religious tradition and what she had seen in this film, what was interesting to me was that she seemed much less concerned about that movie's suggestion of the existence of alien life than about what she believed were the unfavorable portrayals of Christianity. The film pitted scientist against theologian as both use their own frames of reference to seek transcendence (Jodie Foster's character through her search for alien life, Matthew McConaughy's through a kind of New Age spiritualistic piety). Despite her verbal and analytical skills, Sweetie struggled to articulate why she was uncomfortable with the mix of aliens and Christianity she saw in this film. In the interview, she moved from the discussion of her dislike of this movie directly into a conversation about a male friend of hers who is an atheist. She noted that she finds it easier to respect persons with strong views and consistent actions than it is to respect those who are, like Matthew McConaughy's character, "neutral," or "kind of sort of believe in God." Although Sweetie believed that she could make judgments about what is consistent with her religious beliefs and what is not, her comments illustrate that such judgments are easier when representations of religion are either clearly in keeping with her own beliefs or clearly distinct from them.

Sweetie, like Sara and other evangelical teens interviewed, discerned whether a particular representation or story was consistent with her views by measuring it against the primary standard of personal morality: whether what was represented was what she considered "right" behavior. Sweetie desired consistency and clear boundaries, which suggests two explanations for why *Contact* was unappealing. First, as noted, was the conflict she saw between the coding of Matthew Conaughey's character as a Christian and as a positive moral leader, and his engagement in an act she considered inconsistent with behavior expected of Christians. Second, in the film's rather explicit suggestion that Christianity and the discovery of alien life might not be so incompatible after all, Sweetie was confronted with a blurring of boundaries that was outside her frame of reference. Yet her inability to clearly discuss why aliens might be problematic for a conservative Christian like herself was surprising to me. I had expected that she, like many other evangelicals interviewed, would equate aliens with other "evils," such as witchcraft and demon-possession, that are largely associated with transgressive behavior. Yet Sweetie had little interest in discussing aliens and their relevance (or irrelevance) to her Christian tradition. Her strong emphasis on right *behavior* overrode this concern. Like Sara, Sweetie said little about the supernatural realm in relation to media, which was consistent with other evangelical teens who, aside from the occasional labeling of certain entertainers or programs as evil or Satanic, never mentioned references to the realm beyond the material world in their interviews.

MEDIA AS DISTRACTING FROM HARD WORK AND SPIRITUALLY DEGRADING: ZEKE SCHWOCH

Some sociologists have argued that the prominence of the evangelical Protestant tradition has shaped other approaches to faith in the United States, notably Catholicism and reformed Judaism.[17] Mormonism, which foregrounds the Protestant emphasis on personal morality and individual choice and which has its originating roots in the United States, has been described as the prototypical American Protestant religion.[18] What Mormonism attempts to do, according to religious analyst Harold Bloom, is "to bring about in the spiritual realm what the American Revolution . . . inaugurated in the sociopolitical world," seeing humans as democratic actors rather than acquiescent subjects in their relation to God and the world.[19] This is similar to the democratization of religious choice observed among many in Protestant and Catholic traditions.[20]

Like their evangelical Protestant counterparts, Mormons hold two opposing views of the media. On the one hand, the Mormon Church owns a number of television and radio stations and other media outlets due to their belief in using the media to evangelize; on the other, many prominent Mormon authorities have encouraged families to avoid the alleged harmful effects of the media.[21] With its many similarities to the beliefs and approaches of evangelical Christianity, its adherents might be expected to share certain similarities with the evangelical teens described above. This is indeed the case for Zeke Schwoch.[22]

A confident Anglo-American young adult from a large middle-class family, Zeke was an older adolescent who was contemplating his imminent move out of his family's home at the time of his interview.[23] Zeke considered religion to be very important in his life, and in keeping with the Mormon emphasis on the family, he noted that after working in the construction business, he found being with his family "refreshing" due to values he shared with them that he believed differed markedly from those he observed in his work sites. Families are central in Mormon beliefs, as Mormons believe that families are eternal and live together in the afterlife. Thus, Zeke's emphasis on his family reflected both his own experience with them and his strong commitment to his religious beliefs.

Similar to the evangelical Hansen and Buchanan families, the Schwochs had relatively few restrictions on media use. Zeke's mother mentioned that they "buy all the Disney movies," enjoyed other PG-13 movies, and frequently watched the Fox television program *The Simpsons* together as a family, although (consistent with most of the families interviewed) she stressed that they devoted little of their family time to television or film viewing. Like the evangelical Hansen and Buchanan families, the Schwochs placed a premium on assisting their children in developing critical viewing skills, or the abilities to determine on their own which representations in television and film and on the Internet might be deemed inappropriate due to their religious convictions.

The Schwochs expressed concern about the misrepresentation of their religious traditions in U.S. television news programs and newsmagazines. Zeke specifically noted his frustration at discovering that Christian bookstores carried what he considered to be anti-Mormon literature. While some evangelicals and fundamentalist Christians relegate Mormonism to the status of a "cult," as Zeke and his father explained, this family, along with the majority of Mormons, viewed themselves as a part of the Christian tradition. The fact that Mormonism is marginalized by some evangelical Christians and misunderstood by many in the larger culture is an important point of commonality between Mormonism and American Islam, and by extension informs their somewhat similar stances in relation to mass media, as I will discuss further in a moment.

At the time of his interview, Zeke had recently returned from participation in the missionary trip that is required of all Mormon young men. One aspect of his experience as a missionary in the Philippines that he particularly enjoyed was the enforced separation from U.S. media. While serving as a missionary, he had been encouraged to avoid watching television, reading magazines or newspapers, or listening to popular music to better focus on his missionary work and its purpose. Looking back on the experience, he saw his media-free time as a missionary to be an ideal environment for his own religious development. The media, he discovered, were distracting to him: "Now that I've been home, I enjoy reading the newspaper in the morning, and I enjoy watching TV. There's a fine line. But as a missionary, there was no line. I realized when I was on my mission how much I could get done without a TV." This goal of productivity is an important aspect of how Zeke related to his own religious beliefs and identification, as he explained:

> I believe that we are happier when we are more conservative, when we are more righteous, when we follow. . . . As Latter-day Saints we use the term "Hold onto the iron rod," the "rod" being the word of God. And I believe when we keep the commandments, follow the word of God, and do what we're supposed to do, we will be happier. It will be harder, but I believe that we will be happier. It's just like somebody that works real hard, and somebody that's lazy. Sure it's nice to lay down and watch TV sometimes, but the most ambitious person, the hard worker out there, the one that seeks financial well-being, spiritual well-being, he is going to be the happier one.

Sounding a great deal like the Protestants Max Weber wrote of more than a century ago, in this statement Zeke affirmed the utility of conservativism and hard work for both spiritual and financial welfare.[24] Watching television was equated with "laziness," and because hard work and conservativism go together as its opposite, the laziness of television viewing is seen by Zeke to distract people from the goal of true happiness. Television also was "spiritually distracting," according to Zeke, another point that was brought home to him in the contrast he experienced between his media-free days as a missionary and upon his return to the United States:

> I remember I got home and my brother, we used to work together, and on the way to work and coming home and at work we listened to the radio and I remember [thinking], "Man, this music's evil." But then, the more I listened to it, you become a little bit desensitized. . . . As a missionary, spiritually I was up here [holds one hand above his head, indicating a higher level]. And, you know, music, now, me and music are kind of like here

[holds his hand lower, i.e., at a lower level]. And it's been more of a battle to me because I listen to music and I watch a little bit of TV, to get back up here [holds his hand back up in the higher position].

Zeke noted that after his missionary trip, he was more acutely aware of the "evil," as he termed it, in popular music such as that by Oasis, Marilyn Manson, Crash Test Dummies, and Nine Inch Nails. Not only was it distracting, but, in keeping with the hierarchy of religious well-being indicated earlier through his use of hand gestures, Zeke described this music as "spiritually degrading." Zeke equated television with "worldly" and hence what he saw as nonreligious or "secular" values. He affirmed that while it was a struggle, he felt compelled by his desire to remain true to his faith tradition to "stay out of the world," and thus to avoid the media as much as possible. In this sense, he sounded remarkably similar to Sara Hansen, the evangelical teen, as well as Hasan Ahmed, a Muslim teen.

DISTINCT FROM THE MEDIA: HASAN AHMED

In keeping with the conservative Muslim traditions of his biracial U.S. family, Hasan Ahmed[25] prayed five times a day and regularly participated in worship with his family in a mosque near their home. He also patterned his life around Muslim teachings as his family understood them, which included acting as a peacekeeper among his three siblings and avoiding sexual temptations by refusing to participate in one-on-one activities with members of the opposite sex. Hasan was an amiable soccer player with an easygoing and attractive smile. His mother was Anglo-American, and his father was an immigrant from Libya who described his racial/ethnic heritage as Arab American. While his father worked full-time in a technical computer position, his mother, who wore traditional Muslim dress, was employed part-time. She was also pursuing graduate studies in psychology to facilitate what she saw as an improvement to her career, for she was committed to the rights of women as well as to traditional Muslim beliefs. With three younger siblings and commitments to many school- and mosque-related activities, Hasan's middle-class Ahmed family kept a rigorous schedule.

As other researchers have noted and as has been painfully witnessed in the hate crime incidents in the aftermath of the World Trade Center bombings, individual Muslims often suffer prejudice due to tensions between the United States and predominantly Muslim countries.[26] This prejudice factors into people's responses to Hasan, as he explained in an interview conducted before 9/11/01: "Most of the time I'm not (discriminated against), but sometimes kids, they just like tease you, because they know you have to pray five times a day, or they tease you because, the uh, Israeli prime minister just died, and they're like, 'Did you kill him? Do you know Yasser Arafat?' And then they call you Aladdin, and camel jockey, and stuff like that. My friends do that, but they're just joking around. But some other people, they tease you for what's going on in the media and the news and stuff like that."

While many of the Christian participants in my research expressed incredulity at the idea that religion and the media might be intersecting topics of interest, the Ahmeds—parents and children alike—were eager to discuss misinformation and bias concerning representations of Islam in popular and news media. In addition to Edward Said's well-known indictment of Western media bias concerning Islam, several more recent research endeavors have pointed to the media misrepresentations that both influence and reflect the prejudices and stereotypes common throughout North American culture.[27] This pattern of bias led the local Muslim society of which the Ahmeds were a part to take a proactive stance. Hasan himself had demonstrated his commitment to standing up for what he understood to be his peaceful religious beliefs. In one of my first interviews with him, he told me about his reaction to a local controversy surrounding a Muslim basketball celebrity, who had been barred from the NBA for refusing to sing the national anthem. Apparently someone in his class made a snide remark to Hasan about his religion in response to the controversy, which led the teacher to conduct a current events discussion about it:

INTERVIEWER: What was it that made you want to stand up and speak about what you thought, when your whole class thought something different?

HASAN: I don't know. I guess I'm kinda different myself. I'm Muslim and there's not that many Muslims in my school, so when I'm around a Muslim, I kinda feel like we have to be friends 'cause we're the only people there. And so I have to like, shake their hands, and say hello, and also, I have to stand up because, if I don't say what I believe is right, then everybody else is gonna be wrong, and nobody else will learn. So if I try to teach them, then maybe somebody else will change and learn.

To say that Hasan's family had strict policies regarding media would be an understatement. This family kept two charts on their refrigerator: one for household chores, and the other for media use. The latter chart had the names of each family member in a column, with a row for each day of the week, so that each family member could keep track of his or her media use. They were not to exceed an hour of television viewing and a half-hour of video game playing a day. While the rules were not always faithfully followed (and the children were not punished for not following them), the strongly stated admonitions served an important function: they helped Hasan and his younger brothers and sister see the rules in relation to their morally conservative Muslim beliefs.[28]

The strictness toward media consumption reinforced for the Ahmed family that the prejudices against Muslims that they experienced and viewed in the news were unacceptable while also allowing the family to emphasize how their own beliefs—particularly those governing sexuality—were different from those of the media. There was evidence that the children had incorporated at least some of their parents' objections into their own approaches to the media.

In fact, in his individual interview with me, Hasan noted that he believed a part of his role as the oldest son in the family was to assist in the enforcement of the household rules, including those concerning the media.[29] A humorous example of this enforcement occurred one evening when I observed the children watching the Lawrence Olivier version of the movie *Robin Hood* on video. As I recorded in my notebook when I was observing them:

> Hasan asks Aziz to fast forward through the next section, but Aziz protests, saying that he hasn't seen this part. Hasan is getting somewhat agitated, and thus all of the kids' attention is directed to him as Sakinah asks excitedly if "they're gonna do it." Aziz replies with relish, "Four times!" as Hasan gets up and takes the remote control out of his hand. Then Sakinah says (to no one in particular) that the film's "not rated." Hasan tells her, "It would've been PG." Jemila asks, "Not G?" as Sakinah says, "PG, yeah," and returns to writing in her book (she was doing some schoolwork at the time). Hasan, who now has control of the remote control, fast forwards as soon as Robin Hood says to Maid Marian, "That's why I'm in love with you." During the silence as the tape fast forwards, Aziz says, "There's the first kiss." Hasan looks irritated, and Saleem comments with some irony, "We've seen it before anyway." "There they go again!" Sakinah exclaims as they kiss again. After the kissing scene ends, Hasan stops fast forwarding and they resume watching, Saleem turning back to the computer game he had been playing in the corner of the room.

Hasan's sense of self quite clearly drew upon both his family's Muslim beliefs and his role as the oldest child. Because of his interest in presenting himself to me as religiously committed, he tended to answer my questions about his beliefs in things of the supernatural realm with what he saw as the official stance of Islam. In other words, he explained his own beliefs by setting them in the context of "what Muslims believe." Hasan did not talk about ghosts, aliens, or other paranormal phenomena; he was convinced that such topics were outside the boundary of acceptable religion, and therefore it was unacceptable for him to consider them as potential beliefs.

There was room in his beliefs for one type of supernatural being in addition to Allah, and that was angels. However, Hasan, while acknowledging that Muslims believed in angels, was confident that what he saw of them in television and movies did not reflect his own tradition:

> INTERVIEWER: So, when you see these angels [on television and in movies], there is a tradition of angels in your religious background so that they make sense to you.
>
> HASAN: Yeah, except angels, a lot of shows deal with angels, but angels don't come down and appear. That doesn't happen in Islam. It happened to the prophet Muhammed when one angel came down and appeared as a man, but wasn't a man. The common belief, that I see from TV, is Christianity. When you die, if you're good, you go and become an

angel. But in Islam, those are two separate things. You can't become an angel. God made the angels specifically to serve him, and God made humans to—he wanted them to serve him, but he gave them the choice. Angels have to do it. Angels have to do that, whatever he says.

INTERVIEWER: So, are these Christian angels, then [in contemporary media]?

HASAN: Yeah.

INTERVIEWER: Okay. Some people I've talked with—especially people that are Christian—they told me that they think the show [*Touched by an Angel*] is open to a lot of religious beliefs and that lots of people from different backgrounds could find the show meaningful. That's one of the reasons I wanted to have you look at it [we had watched an episode together]. And I wondered if you thought that was true.

HASAN: Yeah, it's open to many different religious backgrounds. Um, I don't know how it could be related to my religion, though.

INTERVIEWER: So, you still think it's pretty specifically Christian? Or, maybe it could be open for people of different backgrounds, but not Muslim?

HASAN: It could be open to other religious backgrounds, but not Muslim.

Hasan affirmed that there might be some people who would find the angels in the popular television program appealing even if they were not religious or not Christian, yet he identified the angels he saw in the media as specifically Christian and thus distinct from his own tradition.

Although the family had strict rules governing the amount of hours devoted to media consumption, it was this ability to draw distinctions between their own religious tradition and what the family saw as the frequent representation of Christian views in the entertainment media that served as an important, guiding goal for the approach to media embraced in this family. Hasan echoed this concern in his comments to me:

INTERVIEWER: Do you think there's a relationship between the rules [that restrict viewing of television and film] and Muslim teachings?

HASAN: Mm-hmm, kind of. Because you're supposed to follow whatever your parents say and respect your parents, so whatever the parents say, you're supposed to do that. And you're supposed to read the Qur'an, which is like the Bible to us, so if you stay away from Nintendo, you'll read the Qur'an more.

For Hasan, rules regarding media use were part of the same continuum that also encompassed prohibitions on pork and restrictions concerning dating. Rather than seeing media restrictions as punitive, they became one aspect of an important project of maintaining and nurturing a distinct religious identity. Talking about these distinctions with a researcher such as myself afforded Hasan an opportunity to affirm a set of beliefs and practices that had been praised and encouraged by his parents and others in his Muslim community.

TRADITIONALISTS AND THE "IDEAL"
APPROACH TO RELIGION AND MEDIA

Hasan, Zeke, and Sara all fall into the category Carol Lytch has termed "conventionals": those young people who consider their family ties to be primary, who respect and obey their parents and other adults, and who accept the core beliefs of their religious tradition. It is important to note that, as Lytch argues, such acceptance comes as a result of thoughtful choice rather than unthinking conformity.[30] Each young person interviewed, both those described here and others in the study, asserted that they chose to live in harmony with their religious traditions.

The "conventionals" are also not uncritical in the rejection of popular culture. All of these young people, like the "conventionals" Lytch described, are careful to maintain a neat appearance while not stepping outside the fashions of their contemporaries; they chose not to look, as one teen noted, like "nerds."[31] This, as Smith notes, is a contrast between the evangelical and the fundamentalist approach to cultural trends and fashions, as fundamentalists are generally less concerned with the cultural standards of peers in defining codes of dress.[32]

Sweetie Buchanan, while perhaps at one time a "conventional" herself, has had to make more critical reflections on her relationship to her tradition based upon her parents' marginalization from it and her own experience in reconciling her views regarding her parents' divorce with those views embraced by her peers in her church and school. While this dissonance has not weakened her commitment to her parents and family, it has caused her to rethink her commitment to some aspects of her religious tradition. Sweetie is closer to what Lytch describes as a "classic" young person: one who identifies strongly with her religious tradition yet believes, in contrast to conventionals, that certain tenets of that tradition are more open to revision than others.[33] This openness to revision has included a willingness to question the "conventional" approach to the separation of media and religion. While she agrees that certain representations are not in agreement with her evangelical tradition (notably references to explicit sex and what she believes are less conservative gender roles), she believes that her ability to sort out these distinctions is more important than whether she completely abstains from viewing or consuming what her more "conventional" peers might otherwise term objectionable.

All of the teens described in this chapter believed that their approach to popular media was an extension of their understanding of distinctions between their religious tradition and the larger U.S. culture. Yet while evangelical teens Sara Hansen and Sweetie Buchanan wished to see their traditions as distinct in much the same ways as Hasan Ahmed and Zeke Schwoch, the history of evangelicalism and its current vitality in the larger culture suggest a different position with relation to that culture, and a more difficult task.

As Quentin Schultze notes in his analysis of evangelicals and their approach to the media, there are few distinguishing factors between evangelical critiques of the media and critiques emerging elsewhere. Indeed, parents from various (and from no) religious traditions who were interviewed for this study often voiced similar dismay at the promiscuity, violence, or bad language they believed was promoted in the mass media, and often their children echoed their sentiments. Perhaps, as Schultze argues, the primary distinction lies in the evangelical desire to employ the media to influence the religious direction of the entire country.[34] Yet I believe another distinction lies in the relationship of evangelicalism to increasingly dominant middle-class norms. While evangelical teens Sara Hansen and Sweetie Buchanan had little difficulty articulating views consistent with the personal moralistic tone of evangelical criticism, they had more difficulty articulating how this might be distinct from other critiques of popular culture. Both Hasan Ahmed and Zeke Schwoch, teens also committed to personal morality as a means by which to articulate their religion's influence on their media behavior, could adopt somewhat different strategies, as both came from traditions with fewer adherents that were often viewed as marginalized. With the increasing prominence of their faith tradition, evangelical teens are faced with a challenge that calls upon them to see themselves as distinct from dominant culture (a goal Sweetie Buchanan's parents articulated) even as those outside the evangelical tradition increasingly see them as representative of dominant values and norms (to which, especially in the case of Zeke, other traditions are deemed less significant or even apostasy).

Each of the teens asserts a separation between their religious tradition and what they believe are the differing values of the popular entertainment media. I term this view the "ideal" to signal that much of the traditions in both media criticism and religious formation have affirmed this approach as the one to which they believe young people should aspire.[35] I do not use the term to indicate my belief that this is the best response to this issue, nor, in particular, to point to a direct relationship between holding this view and maintaining a moral life that is superior to others. Some teens with different or no religious beliefs embrace morality with as much forthrightness as those described here, yet they do not maintain a distinction between religion and the media in quite the same way.

Interestingly, an element that seems to be missing in the primary language of these Traditionalists is that of the transcendent and experiential element in each of their traditions. It is interesting to note that none seemed particularly interested in, or capable of, engaging in critiques of representations of the supernatural realm that might be outside of their traditions. Hasan simply dismissed the angels depicted in popular entertainment media as outside his tradition, while Sweetie viewed such beings and phenomena as less than central to her faith traditions. In any case, such issues were clearly trumped by concerns with personal morality. This is despite the fact that each tradition examined here, and indeed all monotheistic religious traditions (which are dominant in the United States), embrace beliefs in God, angels, and a separation between these beings and humans that reflects the distinctions between material and immaterial, or natural and supernatural, realms.[36] It is also despite the fact that surveys demonstrate an increase in beliefs in angels and ghosts among persons of all ages, indicating that such beings may arise as taken for granted in conversations among peers.[37] While angels and demons have long been a part of popular culture and are particularly prevalent now, even these supernatural beings are not seen as interesting points for discussion in the relationship of religion and media among conservatively religious teens. Not all religiously committed teens find it so easy to sort out the distinctions between religious traditions and the stories of the media. Finally, therefore, we turn to the stories of teens who identify with religious traditions yet are intrigued by the stories of the supernatural they encounter in the entertainment media.

7

THE INTRIGUED TEENS (AND THE ISSUE OF ANGELS)

WISHING TO SEPARATE

RELIGION AND LEGEND,

BUT HAVING DIFFICULTY

DOING SO

A few years ago, an open-space park above the city of Boulder, Colorado, was witness to something suitably mystical for that city of New Agers: a scraggly tree not far from a hiking trail was found adorned with a single angel ornament. Then, months later, another angel appeared on the same tree, and then another. Soon hikers of all ages were making the "angel tree" a destination, hailing as "creative" and "magical" the acts of anonymous decorating that some claimed instilled a sense of community among Boulderites.[1] Not all were pleased with this seemingly mystical occurrence, however. In the fall of that year, Boulder city officials posted a sign on the tree, indicating that private expressions of any kind were not allowed on public land. The angels could remain until Christmas, a second note stated, but then should be removed to a more "appropriate private tree."[2] The American Civil Liberties Union got involved, stating that the Christmas deadline was inappropriate and the decorations should be removed immediately. The angels constituted a religious display in public, said the ACLU, and as such, they violated the First Amendment. Naturally, this piqued the interests of the national news outlets, most of whom, like syndicated columnist Jack Kisling, scoffed at the uproar.[3] The story was quickly framed as one of bureaucratic overkill in the face of benign positive expressions of individuals. Local residents voiced the appropriate protests to the government involvement. "The angels give you this feeling of peace and joy and happiness," stated one woman, identified by a newspaper reporter as the mother of a five-year-old. "I really don't think the angels have any connotation of religion," she continued. Another hiker, identified as an architect and the father of two children he frequently takes hiking, noted that the tree is "a bright spot for the kids. It's the parents who find it has some magic, then they point it out to the kids, who understand." Another father is quoted as saying that his three-year-old daughter believes the angels protect her when she is hiking.[4] Angels, as both those interviewed and the tone of reports covering the story suggested, are ubiquitous and harmless; moreover, they capture something of the magic of childhood. While the decorations on the tree seemed "drenched in personal significance," as one reporter wrote, there was little mention of formal religion and few officials of religious organizations were even interviewed. And why should they have been? Angels, at least in the current U.S. context, may be religious to some, but certainly they are not limited by the definitions and practices assigned them by formal religion.

While many of the previous chapters have discussed the dark side of evangelicalism, angels are clearly an example of evangelicalism's "light" side. And while supernatural evil has been a rather frequently used and effective narrative device in the popular culture of young people, angels appear with more regularity in the entertainment media aimed at adults. Angels do have a great appeal to teens, however; one national poll found that 75 percent of young people claimed to believe in them.[5] In fact, I believe that angels may emerge with special significance in this younger generation. Angels are an emblem of tolerance and goodness for many people and are related to religion in only the most generally accepted, least exclusive way. This makes them especially well suited to contemporary young people, who are part of the most religiously and culturally diverse generation ever, and who are interested in a spirituality that embodies their widely accepted standards of religious tolerance. As Elizabeth, a young woman who will be introduced in this chapter, noted approvingly, "You don't even have to believe in God" to believe in angels.

At the turn of the millennium, angels seemed to be everywhere in the United States: on our jewelry, stationery, T-shirts, and books, among other places.[6] Angels were a cornerstone to the rise and success of the profitable Christian retailing industry that is normally associated with conservative religion, but they were equally at home in New Age bookstores, as well as in commercial department stores and decorating catalogs. They could be found in programming on MTV and PBS. At one high point in 1994, there were eight books about angels on the *New York Times* best-seller list.[7] More than 5 million books on angels had been sold by that time, representing an exponential increase over the past few decades.[8] It is worth noting that this increase in sales parallels a shift in content, as well. While most of the books and materials about angels may have been written by theologians and authorities of Christian, Jewish, or Muslim faiths up until the 1980s, today's best-selling books and other materials about angels hail more frequently from creative writers, artists, former journalists, and even self-proclaimed mystics and psychics.[9]

In my interviews with teens and their families, I asked about many programs that contained some reference to the realm beyond this world. Given the time period of the study, I naturally wound up devoting a great deal of family interview time to the CBS program *Touched by an Angel*. In part, this was because the families often brought it up. The program, a regular in the top ten of the Nielsen ratings over the first three years of its airing (1997–2000), was immensely popular, especially with older adults.

I believe that part of the program's success can be attributed to its ability to give voice to certain taken-for-granted beliefs in the contemporary religion of the United States, as well as some of its unspoken yet widely accepted contradictions. On the one hand, the program drew upon religious imagery and narrative with its reference to angels and frequently placed words from Christian Scripture in the mouths of its protagonist angels. At the same time, the program placed itself at some distance from references to institutional religion (in the form of the church's building, clerical collars, and other markers) and doctrines of sin and salvation that are particularly important in conservative and evangelical beliefs.

While *Touched by an Angel* held only marginal appeal to the majority of teens, therefore, the program represents something important about the cultural context in which young people are growing into their own religious identity. Religious beliefs are not a regular subject of conversation among teens, but angels are found to be much less objectionable.[10] At the makeshift memorial that arose in the days following the Columbine High School shooting in the spring of 1999, several angels could be found in the artwork and words of young people struggling with grief and loss. For many, including young people, angels symbolize the presence of goodness from the realm beyond, regardless of how one feels about organized religion (figure 7.1).

Some teens, like those described as Traditionalists, seek out opportunities to discuss their religious faith and tradition with their friends. Others, however, choose to embrace their religious traditions modally; that is, they talk about religion when it seems appropriate to the situation and ignore it or even distance themselves from it when it is not.[11] The teens in this chapter do not distance themselves from their beliefs, but unlike the more Traditionalist religious teens of chapter 7, they are not likely to bring their beliefs into conversations without encouragement from others. In part, this is because their lives entwine various activities and commitments that make it impossible to maintain homogeneous relationships.[12] This, in turn, affects how and what they say about what they see as the relationship between their religious tradition and what they consume in the popular entertainment media. What the teens in this chapter share is a commitment to their religious tradition, a set of friends who come from religious traditions and levels of commitment that differ markedly from their own, and an interest in the mystical or supernatural realm—specifically, but not exclusively, an interest in angels. I use the term "intrigued" to point to this latter interest.

In this chapter, we will meet three teens: an Anglo-American young woman who regularly participates in a Lutheran (ELCA) congregation, a Mexican American young man who occasionally attends a Church of Christ congrega-

FIGURE 7.1
"Caution: Angels are working here. Watch out for wings." A fellow student's sign placed at the makeshift memorial, Columbine High School, April 20, 1999. Photo by author.

tion but who is surrounded by religious language in his home life, and a Latino young man who is a regular, if reluctant, participant in his Roman Catholic parish. While these young people were intrigued by beings and powers from the realm beyond, it's worth noting that none expressed interest in religious traditions other than their own. Unlike more Traditionalist teens, however, the "intrigued" teens expressed a greater amount of tolerance for those of other traditions and levels of commitment. They each expressed interest in the phenomena of the supernatural realm—especially those beings that seemed to be represented in both their religious beliefs and the entertainment media. We turn now to their stories.

TRADITIONAL, BUT QUESTIONING: ELIZABETH FARLEY

Responsible, articulate, and somewhat reserved until you get to know her, Elizabeth was the oldest child and only daughter in the Anglo-American, lower-middle-class Farley family.[13] When her parents divorced, Elizabeth, then a quiet fourteen-year-old, found solace in the youth group of the Lutheran (ELCA) church her grandmother attended, where she often talked with other young people who had experienced divorces in their family lives. Elizabeth's mother and brother never went to church as frequently as Elizabeth did. However, her mother was pleased that Elizabeth seemed to have found something "positive" in her life and thus made efforts to support her daughter's interests. Elizabeth was a frequent acolyte in the church, volunteered as a leader with the church's weekly after-school program, attended the church's infrequent events specifically designed for youth, and was known by many of the church members, most of whom were several decades older than she was.[14] Despite this difference in age and Elizabeth's sense that "the church's priorities are really with the older people," she enjoyed being a part of a smaller group of people who offered tremendous support during the time of her parents' divorce.

While Elizabeth's father had been raised in that same Lutheran church, her mother had been raised Southern Baptist, a tradition she rebelled against in her teen years. She never joined the Lutheran church to which her husband belonged (he was an infrequent attender), as she would have preferred instead a nondenominational "easygoing, New Age" church like the one she attended when she was in her early twenties. As Elizabeth became increasingly involved in the Lutheran church, both her mother and brother attended there rather than following her mother's preference.

While the Farleys lived in an affluent and gentrified suburb of a medium-sized urban area, Elizabeth's own family struggled financially after her parents' divorce. Elizabeth's mother supported Elizabeth and her younger brother with a part-time clerical job in a property management company, supplemented with child support funds, while attending a community college on a part-time basis. Because her church was located a few miles south of her house in what would be considered a "transitional" neighborhood (a mix of elderly middle- to lower-middle-income Anglo-American families and younger immigrant and Mexican American families of more modest means), the economic situation of Elizabeth's church friends more closely matched that of her own struggling single-parent family. Living between these two economic realities gave Elizabeth an added depth of perspective on her school friends' sometimes opulent lives (and some discomfort about the differences between them, as well). Elizabeth's involvement in her church was also bolstered through her relationships with her father's mother and their family. While her father had moved out of town following the divorce, the church afforded a way for her to be in regular contact with his family members and hence to maintain her connection to him.

In addition to her school and church friends, Elizabeth had some contact with young people she met through her mother's active involvement in a support group for single parents. This support group, like her church, was composed of mostly working- and lower-middle-class families, and thus had introduced Elizabeth to more peers who shared her family's financial struggles and experience of changed familial structure.

Due to her mother's busy work, school, and social schedule, Elizabeth often had responsibility for watching her younger brother, a task she accepted unquestioningly. Thus the siblings were usually home together alone in the afternoons and a few evenings each week. As Elizabeth was confined to her house during much of her free time, she spent a great deal of time on the telephone with her best friends. Usually, they talked about "cute boys" from school, although they also exchanged complaints about school, teachers, and parents. Sometimes, they shared music over the telephone or talked together while involved in online conversations in teen chat rooms. On only one occasion had her phone use been restricted by her mother. One of Elizabeth's former friends had joined a gang and began coming to Elizabeth's home in the afternoons when her mother wasn't home. Elizabeth believed her friend was visiting her primarily to use the telephone to be in contact with her fellow gang members. While Elizabeth was uncomfortable with this practice, she was unsure how to end it. Then one of the gang members called Elizabeth:

> ELIZABETH: Once, this guy called and he was sixteen and he's kind of involved in a gang, and my mom got kinda freaked out about that because she knew that he was in a gang. So she didn't give me his phone number and I didn't have it, so.
> INTERVIEWER: How did she know he was in a gang?
> ELIZABETH: His cousin was going out with my friend for a little while, and he got my number from a friend. He just called, and I was like, "Whoa." He just called to say "hi" and my mom had a fit. She thought I was gonna get involved in gangs or drugs and stuff.

Apparently, at some point Elizabeth had told her mother of the boy's involvement in a gang and had no doubt expressed her discomfort with this relationship. The occasion of the phone call allowed Elizabeth to reveal her friend's practices, thus giving her mother an opportunity to forbid her friend to come over to use their phone in the afternoons. Relating the story to me several months later, Elizabeth seemed relieved that her mother had intervened and ended this difficult situation. While she regretted that her friend had joined a gang, she did not regret the end of that relationship, as she felt that her friend was using her to gain access to a telephone and had gotten involved in a situation Elizabeth preferred to avoid.

Like a lot of teens, Elizabeth spent relatively less time watching television as a teen than she had a few years before as a preteen.[15] This is not to say she was not media-savvy, however; her free time was filled with reading teen magazines, chatting with other teens on the phone and the Internet, and of course, listening to popular music. Movies and television programs served to showcase the attractive male celebrities that were frequent topics of conversation in both mediated and interpersonal interactions with friends. This appeal of male celebrities goes a long way toward explaining the popularity of certain television shows and movies among Elizabeth and her teen friends. In fact, her preference for WB's *7th Heaven*, a popular television program that featured a minister and his family as they encountered various moral trials of childhood and adolescence, seemed to rest at least equally with its conservative moral values and its attractive male characters.[16] However, her conservative moral values prevented her from embracing some celebrities due to their alleged homosexuality:

ELIZABETH: I used to be kinda into Keanu Reeves. But, I don't know, after a while I started hearing rumors about him and it's like, okay, that's not cool. So I took down all his pictures.

INTERVIEWER: What wasn't cool?

ELIZABETH: I don't know why, but they said he was gay. I don't know why. They just did, and it was like, okay. He doesn't seem to be that interested in females, so I guess I'll just take this down now. [She chuckled and paused] But I think if it was that same thing with Devon Sawa, I don't think I'd care. He's too cute.

The joking nature of the last statement suggested that while Elizabeth preferred to avoid homosexuality, there might be occasions when such objections could be overruled: specifically, in the instance of a male celebrity deemed "too cute" to engender concern about his sexual preferences and their relationship to her own moral commitments.

Both Elizabeth and her mother spoke of television as a "bad habit" and a "waste of time," yet there were few restrictions placed on any kind of media consumption in the Farley household. This lack of restrictions was out of practicality. While Elizabeth's mother stated that she would prefer that Elizabeth watch an hour of television or less a day, and Elizabeth noted that she "tries" to follow this request, Elizabeth's limited options for entertainment in the home made viewing a more frequent practice.

Elizabeth's conversations about her religious tradition demonstrated the extent to which she understood religion as related to organized religion and religious institutions, and specifically to her church. When asked if she considered herself "spiritual," for instance, she replied:

ELIZABETH: Not really. I think of myself as religious, because if somebody's talking about religion, I'll usually jump in and say, "Well, at my church we do this." But I don't know about spiritual. I haven't really, really gotten into my religion yet. I haven't really found the spiritual part quite yet.

INTERVIEWER: Is that something that interests you?

ELIZABETH: Yeah. I really like getting into the church thing. It helped me a lot through the divorce.

In this statement, Elizabeth equated possible spiritual growth with a therapeutic understanding of how religion might be useful in times of stress.[17] Yet when I asked Elizabeth about whether she felt that religion influenced her media choices, she echoed the way in which the Traditionalist teen Sweetie Buchanan had related media choices to personal morality and her own ability to make decisions in this realm: "Not really. Sometimes if there's something that's religious on TV, that was like based on something that happened in some religion, sometimes I'll check it out. But I won't stop watching a program because it's like, something that's immoral or that wouldn't go by in our religion." Religion and moral issues as represented in the media were filtered through Elizabeth's sense of her own ability to judge those representations based on her grounding in her own religious tradition. Yet while she noted that she disliked negative portrayals of Christianity in television, she felt that she could watch even those and still appreciate the entertainment value of the program. Echoing the conversations with Traditionalists, her comments about religion and media tended to be framed around moral choices, yet unlike the Traditionalists, Elizabeth felt her own ability to make decisions overrode the preferences she equated with her religious tradition.

One of the earliest intriguing learnings from my research came from Elizabeth, and it surfaced in relation to something I asked all of the teens and their parents who participated in my research. The question was this: "Can you think of times when one of the television shows or movies you were watching dealt with religion?" People of various ages would sometimes respond to this question by mentioning programs and movies that used recognizably religious symbolism or references, such as the comedy *Angels in the Outfield* or television programs such as CBS's feel-good *Touched by an Angel* and WB's program *7th Heaven*. Some people would also mention programs where religion emerged as particular characters struggled with personal or moral issues, as in episodes of the popular NBC emergency room drama *ER*, when characters struggle with life-and-death issues, or the WB teen melodrama *Dawson's Creek,* in which one of the protagonists was a professed atheist living with her strict evangelical grandmother. Still others surprised me by mentioning programs that seemingly had nothing to do with religion as it is associated with the historical institutions of Christianity, Judaism, Islam, or other traditions. As noted in earlier chapters, sometimes *Star Trek,* the *Star Wars* movies, and *The X-Files,* among other sources, were mentioned as possibly religious in some sense.

Elizabeth took the second approach: she described the plot lines from several episodes of the syndicated teen melodrama *Beverly Hills 90210,* noting that a few of the lead characters in that program occasionally dealt with plot lines related to their Jewish backgrounds. Likewise, she mentioned a *Simpsons* episode in which Homer's lack of interest in religion is parodied as his daughter is whisked away by a neighbor for baptism. When I told Elizabeth that some people had also mentioned programs like *The X-Files* and *Star Trek* she hesitated, seeking the right words: "*The X-Files,* it's kinda, not really what you believe *religiously,* but what you *believe,* just, what you *believe in,* like ghosts and stuff. If you really believe that there's ghosts, or extraterrestrials. Same thing with *Early Edition* [a program in which the protagonist was miraculously delivered a newspaper a day early so that he could assist in the prevention of catastrophes reported there]." While *The X-Files* and *Early Edition* were more about "beliefs" than about "religion," according to Elizabeth, *Soul Man,* an ABC program with a brief run in the late 1990s that featured Dan Akroyd as an Episcopal priest and widowed single parent, was much more clearly religious to her. After all, it drew upon the traditional symbol of the clerical collar and scenes in the show often took place in the pastor's office or in the church's sanctuary. (The marker of the clerical collar, I should note, caused Elizabeth to assume that Akroyd's character was Roman Catholic, illustrating either her limited knowledge of that faith's vow of celibacy—or, more likely, the fact that characters wearing collars on television or in film are almost always Catholic.)[18]

Elizabeth's wish to divide television programming into categories of religion and beliefs reflects a similar division offered by media critic Horace Newcomb. Newcomb argued that religion on television can be divided into two distinct types: those programs that use such terms as "the man upstairs," or "the big guy,"[19] and those programs that use traditional and recognizable symbols of historical religion, such as the clerical collar or menorah, and often negative stereotypes, such as the hucksterish southern evangelical preacher or overexuberant and confused Hindi prophet. Yet while Newcomb suggested that there are two recognizable categories that are more and less related to what one might call authentic (i.e., related to the institution) religion, Elizabeth combined these two into the "authentic" camp. She distinguished these from a third category of programming: that which is about what she called "beliefs." These programs seem to fall somewhere between Newcomb's "man upstairs" and what others would simply call science fiction or fantasy.[20] Putting aside Elizabeth's limited knowledge of differing Protestant and Catholic faith traditions, what is interesting to me in her comment is that she clearly attempted to draw a firm boundary between religion as it is related to the historic institutions of Christianity, and beliefs that might fall outside of those traditions, such as belief in extraterrestrials or ghosts. Because she placed herself *inside* the traditions of established religion, these alternative beliefs were *outside* the realm of possibility. At least, she believed that they should be, as illustrated in the following comments. I had asked her whether her beliefs were similar to what she'd seen on *The X-Files*:

> Not really. Like, when they were saying there was a sighting of an alien. I can *sort of* believe it, but there's also something that could've been written off. "Oh well, somebody could've been faking it," or whatever. And same thing with ghosts. They're saying, "There's ghosts haunting my house." That could be anything, or it could just be in their mind. But when it gets into a thing like *The Exorcist*—which was this thing on television last week, about *The Exorcist*, and about people being possessed and stuff. That kinda weirded me out, because I have a Ouija board, and that's how the girl got possessed—it was through using the Ouija board by herself. And I was like, "Okay, put *that* away under my bed and never use it again!!"

Recognizing that such things as aliens and ghosts are outside of the realm of the beliefs associated with the historic institutions of religion, Elizabeth would go so far as to say that these phenomena probably do not exist. But she thought she would get rid of the Ouija board, just in case.

The conversation then took an interesting turn. Elizabeth, reflecting on experiences with the supernatural, related that one of her friends had told her of her experiences with a paranormal presence. This friend believed that she had been in contact with the spirit of her deceased younger brother. Pondering her friend's credibility, Elizabeth then confessed that she "sort of" believed in ghosts, although she quickly added that personally, she had never had an experience for which there was no other plausible explanation. Elizabeth acknowledged that this area of belief in the supernatural is in the realm of the possible. On the one hand, she recognized that these beliefs should be outside the boundary of "religion," while on the other, she acknowledged that she could not rule out the possibility that such phenomena could occur.

When it came to discussing her own beliefs, Elizabeth was even less clear on the boundaries that might distinguish religion from those beliefs in the supernatural that are much more central to the popular religiosity as seen in programs featuring "the man upstairs," to use Newcomb's phrase, than to the historic institutions of religion. When explaining her preference for *Touched by an Angel* over *Soul Man*, she spoke in terms of the angel program's "openness" to "beliefs" (as well as images and narratives), particularly those beliefs that she saw as beyond or outside formal religious institutions. When I asked her to compare the two programs, here is what emerged in our conversation:

ELIZABETH: I liked it [*Touched by an Angel*] a lot more, since it was more of a philosophy type, than kind of set out.

INTERVIEWER: Than set out? What do you mean?

ELIZABETH: Um, *Touched by an Angel*, it's kind of open on who God is, 'cause it can kinda be whatever your religion is, but with *Soul Man*, it's kinda set with, the guy's a priest, or minister, or whatever, so it's pretty much set that he's either Catholic or Christian. But with *Touched by an Angel*, I mean, angels, you don't even have to believe in God. You can just believe that there are angels.

INTERVIEWER: Did you think the show said anything about God?

ELIZABETH: They mentioned God, and there was kind of the impression that God existed, but it wasn't so set down like *Soul Man* was.

INTERVIEWER: You said *Soul Man* was more "set down" than *Touched by an Angel*?

ELIZABETH: Yeah. [*Soul Man*] is more based around the church, so it's got more of a structure than *Touched by an Angel*, because *Touched by an Angel*, they go everywhere. . . . And [*Touched by an Angel*] can kinda be, you know, it can be any religion, and it doesn't have to be religion, it can just be a belief, and stuff.

INTERVIEWER: Okay. Was [*Touched by an Angel*] similar to the way you think of God?

ELIZABETH: Yeah. I believe in angels and the supernatural, or whatever.

INTERVIEWER: Are the people [on *Touched by an Angel*] similar to people or things you've known in your church?

ELIZABETH: Not really, since it's kind of, um, not really religious.

Is *Touched by an Angel* religious or not? Is it about religion or "beliefs"? Are angels "religious"? Are they within her Christian tradition or "open" to other beliefs? In these statements Elizabeth noted that the program appealed to her because it was about "beliefs" as opposed to the "set down" imagery of the church building and clerical collar. Yet the program reflected her beliefs about God, presumably beliefs that open beyond the church building and experiences related to institutional religion. The program also allows for the possibility that a mystical, supernatural realm, one seemingly unexplained by her religious tradition (at least as she related it to me), could possibly exist.

MARGINALLY AFFILIATED YET RELIGIOUSLY SERIOUS: MICHAEL PEARSON

While Elizabeth had watched *Touched by an Angel* occasionally before our joint viewing and interview, Michael Pearson's African American single-parent family watched it faithfully, and both Michael and his mother expressed great enthusiasm for it. Of all of the families included in the study, Michael's was the only one that regularly watched what might be considered "religious" television or televangelism. Michael, his older sister, his mother, and Michael's twin toddler half-brothers enjoyed the TBN (Trinity Broadcasting Network) program *Praise the Lord,* which features evangelists and musicians such as the popular African American family group The Winans.

When I initially met Michael, I had no inkling that his enthusiasm for his religious tradition might be so strong. Within the first five minutes of my interview with his family, however, which was ostensibly primarily about media use, Michael's mother was emphatically thanking God for her promotions and the other benefits of her work. When asked about the family's religious commitments in response to these statements, however, Michael's mother clarified:

> Oh yes, I am, I am [religious]. Not *religious,* but I do have a relationship with God. And I don't consider it religion. I consider it a personal relationship with Christ. I don't—you know, I do attend a church, but my allegiance is not to a church or to organized religion, my allegiance is to God. . . . So I don't mind calling myself a Christian, but not in terms of religion, because you know, the scriptures tell us that religion is what caused so many wars and so much hatred. So I try to stay clear of even becoming in a tradition of men, you know what's I'm saying? The *relationship* is what I'm more interested in. And finding a way to really hear His voice in my life, and follow His word. . . . Anyway, my kids are whispering about me 'cause I'm talkin' about the Lord—
>
> MICHAEL [chuckles]: No.
>
> MICHAEL'S MOTHER: Oh, Michael, I know you better than that, sweetie! [Laughs] I know you havin' a fit, so I'm gonna leave it alone, but she asked me a question and I got to give the answer from my faith!

Like many baby boomers, Michael's mother drew a distinction between personal faith and participation in a religious institution, emphasizing her belief that the former is more important than the latter.[21] I then asked the family about the extent of their involvement with their Church of God in Christ congregation and learned that while they usually attend Sunday services, they don't often participate in other activities because their church is some distance from their home. As it is a large church and in a different school district, Michael did not have any friends who attended his church. He did note, however, that church came up in conversations when he was with his neighborhood friends:

> INTERVIEWER: Do you have some friends around here that you talk about church things with?
> MICHAEL: Yeah. We always talk about church.
> INTERVIEWER: What kinds of things do you talk about?
> MICHAEL: How God is good to us, and—I don't know, what she [his mother] just said! [Laughs]

During a later interview when he was not with his mother, Michael cautioned that while he is comfortable speaking with his friends about issues of faith, they do not do this frequently. When it did come up in their conversations, the talk of God's goodness was woven into life stories in a way that seemed to echo the God-language approach articulated by his mother.[22]

Michael had been introduced to me by a friend of mine who featured him in an educational television program about computer use among less affluent communities. As a young and articulate African American with remarkable competence in Web design, fifteen-year-old Michael had already received some attention from the media and was to receive more. After my initial two interviews with him Michael was selected to greet President Clinton when he visited Michael's home city to deliver a speech about educational initiatives in technology. Michael had high hopes that some of this publicity would help him to achieve his dream of becoming an actor in Hollywood. His mother, a hardworking and energetic single parent, relished the attention shown to Michael and also had great hopes that his talents would continue to be recognized and nurtured.

Mature for his age in terms of his commitment to hard work and respectful treatment of others, Michael looked younger than his fifteen years. His mother proudly told me that she considered him a "mama's boy," as she felt that having him close to home was preferable to the other alternatives pursued by his colleagues in their underprivileged area. Michael was uncomfortable with that designation, for obvious reasons. He preferred to describe his strong commitment to his mother, older sister, and two younger twin brothers in relation to his role as the oldest son in the family, noting that his career aspirations were closely tied to his desire to provide for his family someday.

This is not to say that his family was in a dire financial situation, however. While the absence of a college degree had limited his mother to lower-paying positions, she had been steadily promoted through university and government jobs due to her competence in accounting, her professionalism, and her strong interpersonal skills. Additionally, despite two divorces (the second of which came after her husband was released from the state penitentiary) and a lack of any child support, she had managed to purchase her own home, a well-maintained older brick bungalow in a neighborhood that, to her dismay, had fallen into hard economic times around her.

While the family did not have specific guidelines restricting media use, it was evident that they often talked together about interpretations of films they watched together. Michael's mother mentioned her frustration at the movies she believed glamorized gangs. She noted that even though the intention of some such films was to show the gritty and undesirable side of gang life, many in the audience preferred to adopt what she called the "surface" representations: "*Boyz in the Hood* had a wonderful message. But all the [audience members were instead] thinking about being strapped, selling their crack, making a wad of money in their pocket. . . . All they're gonna see is that side of the movie, 'cause that's all they want to see, you know what I'm saying? And [kids like my kids] that are looking for better things [than gang life], then they look at the movie and they see the story." Instead of focusing on restricting certain television programs or films, Michael's mother was most concerned that her children adopt interpretations that she believed were attuned to her hope that they would seek alternatives to the gang life so common among those in their neighborhood. In some ways, this strategy shared the focus of the Traditionalist parents mentioned in chapter 6. The family may have focused on discussions of interpretation rather than restrictions due to the older children's ages of fifteen and nineteen, an approach consistent with most families.[23] While there was little restriction of programs deemed inappropriate and virtually no critique of the representations of religious groups, Michael's mother, like other parents, wanted her children to be able to interpret what they see in the media in light of personal morality and their religious faith. Michael's mother also used this framework to explain what she believed were the problems with the black community at large. After noting that many of her white colleagues at work did not take an interest in television programs or films featuring African Americans (and one did not even know who the Academy Award–winning actor Denzel Washington was), Michael's mother equated this invisibility of African Americans from media representations with problems in the African American community:

> For a lot of blacks, that leaves them feeling like they don't belong. And that's why it's so easy for them to get involved in the stuff that they get involved in. If you feel like society's not paying attention to you, or they are paying attention when you kill or steal and destroy, then that's what you're gonna do, 'cause you still need to be noticed. And men especially, because that's their makeup. Men have to rule something, it's the truth. Like I tell my kids, I don't care how complicated things get, our basic makeup is not gonna change. We can switch roles, you can have tons of Mr. Moms. But that thing that God has placed in every man to be the head, and for every woman to be the nurturing person is gonna be there. And men want that

leadership. And when society says, "You [can't have it]," then they have to find some other way to fulfill it. And that's why you see so many black single women, is because a lot of the men, making the baby is what makes them the man, but the other part is too scary, 'cause society says they have to have a job, and then they don't feel capable to [get beyond] the slap in their face [from society]. So they go out and sell crack on the street. But I can't tolerate that, and he can't tolerate making minimum wage, so what do you do? You don't stay together.

In a statement that reflects both her beliefs and her painful experiences, Michael's mother weaves what might be considered a black feminist critique with an understanding of gender roles upheld by conservative religious traditions, all of which, as she argued, are implicated by the lack of acknowledgment of African Americans in the media and in society at large. To combat these problems, Michael's mother strives to help her children "seek out what you want to do in your life, don't live your life regretting." Relating this to her strategy guiding family media policies, she said: "I consider my job is to give my kids a really secure childhood as well as making them know that, no matter what, they are really loved. . . . And for them to learn to love themselves. Because life is hard. And so when we watch TV, and I know they get really sick of me, 'cause I'm one of the people who'll watch a program with them and try to bring out the positive points. So my whole thing is to give them self-esteem." The emphasis on self-esteem as a priority guiding this family's media interpretation practices was different from any of the other families discussed so far. It is important to note that none of the prior families discussed the difficulties of daily life to the extent that the Pearsons did, however. This suggests not only that media policies and interpretation strategies might be specific to race, as has been illustrated in the earlier comments of Michael's mother, but also to economic class position. Such a specificity of position is consistent with many arguments in media audience studies.[24] While a further exploration of these connections is warranted (particular with reference to the religious language commonly used among this and other African American families to discuss such issues of media interpretation), for the purposes of this project it is important to highlight the differences and similarities and position them in relation to the concern at hand: the intersection of legends, supernatural frameworks of religion, and the entertainment media.

Like my conversations with Elizabeth, some of the most illuminating things I learned from Michael emerged in the comparisons he drew between television programs that might seem to refer to religious themes. For example, he offered a distinction between CBS's *Touched by an Angel* and WB's *7th Heaven*, both of which might be considered to be in the same feel-good, moralistic, and family-oriented genre once exemplified by *The Waltons* or *Little House on the Prairie*. *7th Heaven* featured an Anglo-American middle-class minister and his family of seven, four of whom are adolescents and three younger (in the third season, the parents gave birth to twins, bringing the total number of siblings to seven). Although it is popular with teens, Michael described it as "fake," particularly when contrasted with *Touched by an Angel*: "*7th Heaven* is like a soap opera to me. They have soap opera problems. But I think . . . *Touched by an Angel* tells you really about God and how He feels about people, but *7th Heaven*, it just doesn't touch bases with that as much as *Touched by an Angel*." Michael's comparison of *Touched by an Angel* to *7th Heaven* provided me with an opportunity to explore how his views of the portrayal of organized religion might be similar to or different from Elizabeth's approach. I began by asking him why he felt that *7th Heaven* seemed fake, to which he replied:

> MICHAEL: All the problems in [*7th Heaven*] are just, out there. And then the ways they solve them are just like, "Oh, the family loves you, okay, I'm okay now." It just, doesn't get me.
>
> INTERVIEWER: Do you know some ministers, how they spend their time, in terms of how much time they spend in church and stuff?
>
> MICHAEL: Yeah. They spend a lot of time in church.
>
> INTERVIEWER: Do you think *Touched by an Angel* would be better if they spent time in church? 'Cause they didn't spend any time in church on the episode that we just watched.
>
> MICHAEL: Yeah, but—. See, what I'm saying, like, at least they say something about *God*. See, on *7th Heaven*, they don't say about God, they say about *the minister*. Like, "It would be better if you talked to me 'cause I'm a minister." But at least when they talk to an angel, they talk about God.

Like Elizabeth's contrast between *Soul Man* and *Touched by an Angel*, Michael discussed the differences between *7th Heaven* and *Touched by an Angel* in terms of the markings of organized religion in the form of the priest figure: if there is a recognizable clergyperson, it is somewhat "set," as Elizabeth said, or coded as a religious program. Michael's distinction, like Elizabeth's, also suggested that he found organized religion lacking. He, too, seemed to equate organized religion with the closing off of options rather than keeping open the possibility of God's (or angels') mysterious and inexplicable work in the real world. After all, although *7th Heaven* often features church life and in that sense references religion explicitly, the program, according to Michael, does not reveal anything about "God": *7th Heaven* does not "tell you really about God and how He feels about people."

Michael did not mention the fact that *Touched by an Angel* represented an understanding of divine power in the form of God's angels while *7th Heaven* never depicted supernatural and fantastical happenings. However, as both programs use the "God-language" of his family, it is possible that this difference in approaches to supernatural and powerful beings is at least part of what explains the appeal of the angel program in contrast to the pastor's family. Of course, there are also racial/ethnic and class implications in Michael's case. *7th Heaven*'s family lives in a large suburban house, and plotlines almost always center around the family's largely Anglo-American community. This would explain why the problems encountered by the adolescents and preteens on the program may seem "out there" to Michael. On the other hand, head angel Tess on *Touched by an Angel* is African American and this program did occasionally feature African Americans and other nonwhites in central roles in stories that did not always occur in the suburbs.[25] These differences explain the appeal in part, but they cannot fully account for why Michael sees God more in *Touched by an Angel* than in *7th Heaven*. The appeal of the supernatural over organized religion surfaced again when I asked him whether he would be interested in watching a program if he learned that it had something to do with religion:

> MICHAEL: It depends. I don't know, 'cause sometimes if it deals with reli-
> gion, I'll watch it. It depends on what religion they're talking about,
> 'cause some are not interesting.
> INTERVIEWER: Which ones are not interesting?
> MICHAEL: Like, Catholic. Because, it's kind of boring to me, since they just
> sit around and read devotions, and stuff. I don't know.
> INTERVIEWER: So, are there particular shows that you would be interested
> in watching? What would make you want to watch a show?
> MICHAEL: Angels are good. [Chuckles]

Touched by an Angel is indeed a regular favorite at Michael's house, although he and his family more often watch rented movies together. It's important to note, then, that programs like *Touched by an Angel* are only one of many genres this family enjoyed; in fact, they particularly liked action and comedies, naming Denzel Washington and Will Smith as favorite celebrities.

Like Elizabeth, Michael found angels appealing. Yet unlike Elizabeth, Michael was also interested in ghosts and fantastical occurrences, noting at one point that he believed a ghost lived in his house: "Every once in a while some-thing'll just come on while you're sitting there, it'll come on by itself or some-thing. Or like, you'll turn your head, and turn back and a chair's in a different place, or something." Michael saw no conflict between his Christian beliefs and his belief in the possibility of ghosts. Like Elizabeth, however, he drew the line at alien life, stating that he was not interested in programs about aliens and thought of aliens as "something I don't think could really happen."

RELUCTANTLY CATHOLIC:
JORDAN ORTIZ

At fourteen, Jordan was in his final year at a Catholic junior high, anticipating that he, like his older sister, would attend public high school the next year. While the choice to place both Jordan and his sister in Catholic schools through junior high had been expensive for the family, it reflected their interest in both better education and in raising their children Catholic, as both Jordan's parents had been raised. In fact, the family was very involved in their local parish and all of them considered themselves religiously conservative: "Church isn't a choice. It's just a matter of fact," as Jordan's mother explained. In addition to the family's faithful participation in weekly mass and the parents' weekly Bible study group, Jordan's father was on the Parish Council and also provided music for special masses with a musical group. Jordan's mother participated in service-oriented projects such as packing holiday boxes for the local food bank. In the past, both Jordan and his sister participated in sports programs through the parish. Despite this high level of involvement in the parish, however, Jordan elected to participate in a confirmation class through his school rather than his parish. When his mother, father, and sister emphasized that religion was "extremely important" to them and they all affirmed the importance of going to mass regularly, Jordan agreed nonchalantly that religion was "pretty important" to him. He said that he believed "you can go wherever you want [to other gatherings, religious or otherwise] and still be religious." Jordan had a great respect for his parents, however, noting that he agreed with them on most issues and appreciated the support they showed him when he was experiencing difficult times.

For most of his years in school, Jordan's mother and father had worked full time, he in a position as a technician and she in clerical and seasonal positions. Neither of them had college degrees, although Jordan's father had pursued coursework toward an associate's degree that was abandoned due to the family's financial needs. They spent a great deal of their free time with other members of their extended family, all of whom lived within a few miles of the Ortiz home.

When it came to the media, Jordan's parents had strong opinions about its negative effects, but they had no restrictions on television use or music listening. In fact, each of the children had their own television and stereo in their room. The parents explained this by saying that they did not appreciate their children's media preferences. Both Jordan and his sister liked horror films and science fiction, films that their mother refused to watch with them because, as she noted, she "doesn't approve" of them. Jordan's sister further explained, "They're devilish." Jordan's mother believed that it was important that her children understand which movies did not have her approval. I then asked about how discussions of approval took place:

> JORDAN'S SISTER, CARMEN: We mostly get [horror movies] at this video store. I used to bring home a lot of movies. And she'd go, "I don't like those."
>
> INTERVIEWER: And then you wouldn't be able to watch them?
>
> CARMEN: No, I'd watch them.
>
> INTERVIEWER: Oh, you would? You would just know that she didn't like them.
>
> CARMEN: Yeah.
>
> INTERVIEWER: What about you, Jordan? Have you ever had occasions when your mom or dad said that they didn't like different movies that you were seeing?

JORDAN: No, I usually go out to the movies with my cousin or something. They [his parents] tell me if it's good or not, but I just watch it.

Both Carmen and Jordan seemed to understand that their mother disapproved of their choices, yet while providing little elaboration, they both elected to follow their own preferences, giving no explanation for why they thought their mother objected to their selections.

Like Michael Pearson's mother, Jordan's mother was concerned about the absence of people in the media who were of her racial/ethnic background, noting that "there aren't enough Hispanic, Mexican programs on." What really bothered Jordan's parents, however, was the fact that television programming tended to reflect what they believed were moral values with which they disagreed. As Jordan's father noted: "You see a lot more programs now where gays are coming out, and they're promoting that lifestyle, they're making it comfortable, and so, they're not, I think they're going against traditional trends and attitudes. So in a way that's discrimination [against Catholicism and its values], because they're letting everybody just come in, do what they want." Jordan's parents believed that providing moral guidance to their children was a primary task of parenting. While they believed that their involvement in their parish and commitment to Catholicism assisted them in this, they viewed the popular entertainment media as directly undermining their efforts. To illustrate this point, Jordan's father and mother talked about a conversation on values that they had with Jordan after he had started at the public high school:

JORDAN'S FATHER: I mean, we're all media people, we were brought up with television, and believe it or not, we're influenced by television since we were children. . . . The reason I say this is, one time Jordan brought something home and he goes, "Here." And I go, "What is this?" And he said, "Oh, we did it during 7th hour." And it was sent home from a public school and it had to do with religion. And some of the things—I said, "Did you read this?" He said, "Yeah." And some of the things were off the wall! One of the things was—

JORDAN'S MOTHER: It was about living together without being married. Is that okay with you, is it not okay? It was okay with him. And in these situations, what would you do if your children had no food on the table? The only way to get money is by selling drugs. Would you go and sell the drugs? Well, he said yes, and we were floored! We said, "Wait a minute! We've been teaching religion in this house since the day you were born, you haven't missed mass unless you were sick! Where are these ideas—?" "Well, Mom, realistically, if your kids are starving and that's the only way you could get food, you've got to feed them!" That was his reasoning. And I said, "Nobody in America will ever starve because you can fall over and be at a church, and they'll open their doors and you get fed!" The process is to think about it, not to react to the situation but to think.

JORDAN'S FATHER: You see, so even though I think we've been teaching him, and doing this, [the media have an influence].

Jordan's parents were appalled that their son expressed views that differed from what they saw as values rooted in their Catholic faith, in this case that living together without marriage and selling drugs are always wrong no matter what the circumstances. They saw their son's regular participation in mass as a primary means by which he was to have learned those values. It is worth noting, also, that Jordan's mother pointed to the ability to rely upon the charity of the parish as a means of resisting the need to sell drugs for money. This illustrates again the central role of the Catholic parish in supporting what they perceive are its (and their) values. Yet for the current project, perhaps what is most interesting is the rather direct link Jordan's parents made between their son's failure to express their preferred values and the influence of the media. In this instance, neither the environments of peers or of school are considered, nor is the possibility that the church (or the parents) have somehow failed to convincingly socialize Jordan into what the parents perceive as desirable values rooted in Catholicism.

During the interviews, Jordan spoke little about how he perceived his own values as distinct from those of his parents or of Catholicism more generally. Yet while his parents seemed most interested in drawing distinctions between religion and the media, as the more conservative families of chapter 6 had done, an interesting change occurred when I asked Jordan's family about television programs or movies that dealt with religion. His mother and father began a list that included *Dr. Quinn, Medicine Woman; Touched by an Angel;* and *Little House on the Prairie.* Testing the genre limits of the family, I mentioned that I thought sometimes *The X-Files* dealt with religion. I was surprised when Jordan's mother responded enthusiastically:

JORDAN'S MOTHER: Yeah, they did! Just recently I remember seeing that. That's where they had Hispanics, on *The X-Files* the other night [this was a response to my earlier question about the representations of their racial/ethnic group on television].
INTERVIEWER: Yeah.
JORDAN'S MOTHER: They were talking about the—chicagua? The monster-guy, the alien?
JORDAN: El Chupacabra.
[Momentary silence; family seems stunned that Jordan has contributed.]
JORDAN'S FATHER: I'm impressed you remember that!
JORDAN'S MOTHER [to Jordan's father]: I know!
JORDAN'S FATHER: You know, another one is *Highway to Heaven.*

In this excerpt, Jordan mentioned the legend of the Chupacabras, featured in an *X-Files* episode. The legend is of the "goat-sucker," a monster who preys upon small animals and sucks blood from their necks in vampiric fashion (figure 7.2). After Jordan's brief contribution, the conversation continued, with

Jordan's parents listing more traditional fare with religious themes and Jordan again falling silent. During a separate interview with him, I attempted to talk with Jordan about his interest in this tale from Mexican folklore that had been the centerpiece of an *X-Files* episode on illegal aliens and an illness spawned from the space aliens among them. Jordan equated his enjoyment of this episode, and the program in general, with his love of horror and science fiction, but he said no more about it. It could be that he did not think much about the episode after viewing it, although his memory of the name of the legend, his parents' shocked response, and other comments he made concerning his questioning of his parents' beliefs might suggest otherwise. More likely, as is unfortunately the case in research of this kind, he could not—or did not wish to—find the words to express himself in the context either of an interview where his parents were present or in a one-to-one interview with a female adult. Thus, we cannot know whether this legend was discussed among his peers or what they made of it. The legend seems to have claims to recency (the first sighting was ostensibly in Puerto Rico in 1994) and makes connections with alien possibilities. Due to his parents' interests in encouraging a strict Catholic upbringing for both Jordan and his older sister, it was clear that Jordan's interest in such offbeat aspects of the supernatural as El Chupacabra would not be encouraged in the context of the family. His mother's enthusiastic mention of it in response to my question about examples of religion in television, however, demonstrates the practical difficulties even devout parents and their children encounter

FIGURE 7.2
The Chupacabras legend, featured in an *X-Files* episode, appealed to fourteen-year-old Jordan. The Chupacabras (Spanish for "goatsucker"), a mysterious creature responsible for killing animals in Puerto Rico and Mexico during the 1990s, based on eyewitness descriptions. Reprinted with permission from John Sibbick and Fortean Times/Fortean Picture Library.

when attempting to distinguish the beliefs that are deemed legitimate by the institution from those that appeal to other positions, such as, in this case, racial/ethnic background.

THE INTRIGUED TEENS AND THEIR APPROACH TO RELIGION AND MEDIA

The issue of the difficulties these teens encounter in making distinctions between religious tradition and the stories in the media are, of course, the point of this chapter. Part of this emerges because Elizabeth Farley and Michael Pearson both exhibit some similarities with the Traditionalists noted in chapter 6. Teens in both chapters embraced the beliefs of their religious tradition and relate this to their family's commitments to that tradition. Additionally, teens in both chapters exhibited a great deal of respect for other adults. However, Elizabeth, Michael, and Jordan have had to make accommodations with their religious tradition that some of the Traditionalist teens did not. In each case, this occurred because of the many and at times conflicting sources of information they encountered in their daily lives.[26]

Elizabeth elected to continue her participation in the Lutheran church her father's family attended, despite the fact that her mother expressed some alienation from that congregation due to her divorce from Elizabeth's father. As a result, although Elizabeth participated in many church-related activities, her mother and brother attended infrequently and mainly to support Elizabeth. Moreover, Elizabeth's church was in a different geographical community than that of her school, one that reflected her family's economic status more closely than the higher income status of her school friends. She described having two sets of friends, one from church and one from school, although in my interactions with her it was clear that the majority of her time and focus was devoted to the latter group. In addition to the economic differences, her school friends differed from those in her church in that they came from diverse religious backgrounds and commitments. Her friends included a conservative Protestant, a committed Catholic, and several who were either marginally or not at all involved in a religious community. These differences from the Traditionalist teens—in parental participation and support of the religious tradition, in the differing communities of friends, and in the differing economic situations—situated Elizabeth in a position in which choosing to continue her participation in the Lutheran congregation meant that while she identified with it, she did not always consider her religious tradition to be the central and only source for decision making. Despite her commitment to the personal moralistic approach of evangelical Protestantism that shaped her views on such things as intolerance for homosexuality and the need to evangelize unbelievers, Elizabeth, like some of her school friends, elected to experiment with excessive drinking and sexual intimacy—things Traditionalist teens would definitely eschew.

Michael, on the other hand, maintained strict codes of moral behavior, despite the fact that his own affiliation with his religious tradition was marginal. Unlike Elizabeth's family, Michael's mother strongly admonished Michael to adopt and continue the religious tradition and beliefs she had come to embrace, and this was frequently a subject of discussion in the family's home. Yet like Elizabeth, Michael did not base all of his decisions on his religious tradition; his commitment to success was based largely on culturally defined norms rather than strictly on a sense of mission or religiously defined purpose to his life. His experience as an African American male growing up in an economically disadvantaged neighborhood also informed his sense of being different from, and also suffering discrimination from, mainstream U.S. culture. Also, he had no friends from the church that he and his mother attended and exhibited few ties to that or any other specific congregation. However, Michael claimed that he found more commonalities than differences among his friends and their religious beliefs, despite their differing religious traditions (two of his best friends were Jehovah's Witness and several others attended Catholic and Protestant worship services infrequently). As both he and Elizabeth considered these religiously diverse school and neighborhood friends to be central in their lives, they also differed from more conservative teens who opted to maintain friendships primarily with persons who shared their level of commitment (and in some cases, even their specific religious tradition).

This pluralistic friendship environment and the somewhat detached connections to a specific religious tradition are important explanations for their approach to stories of the supernatural in the entertainment media. While both teens expressed intrigue with the nonmaterial realm as they saw it in the entertainment media, they did not automatically inscribe it within solely religious definitions, as more conservative teens may have done through talk about God and God's wishes for a moral life, heaven, and Satan. In addition to their interests in these "religious" supernatural beings, Elizabeth and Michael were also drawn to the realm of the unknown. Explanations for this realm that were offered by the entertainment media—that demon possession could occur through a Ouija board, and that ghosts might haunt houses—were not seen as dramatically inconsistent with what they considered their strong religious beliefs.

Jordan Ortiz is perhaps best described by the category which Carol Lytch, a sociologist of youth and religion, has termed "marginalizers": those young people who participate regularly in religious activities and whose families are highly committed to their religious traditions but for whom religion, their tradition, or even belief in God are not central to the ways in which they make lifestyle and career choices.[27] Jordan had a great respect for his parents and believed in living a life consistent with the moral choices he witnessed both through his immediate and extended family and their involvement in Catholic activities of their parish. Still, unlike the Traditionalist teens, Jordan considered his relationships with peers to be important, and in some ways more intimate, than his relationships with his parents or sister. Religion was important to him, but it was not to be seen as a "crutch" (as he might describe religion's role in the lives of more conservative teens); religion was viewed as useful in ways similar to the "utilitarian individualists" described by Robert Bellah in his book *Habits of the Heart*.[28] Jordan's Catholic parish provided for him a framework of beliefs, but as his parents' story demonstrated, he did not always find that framework to be the most useful or clear in solving particular moral problems he encountered or might encounter.

Jordan, like Elizabeth and Michael, expressed interest in the supernatural realm in ways that were markedly different from the Traditionalists. I do not believe that this difference can be explained fully by a lack of knowledge of their respective religious traditions, for both Elizabeth and Jordan in particular, after years of Sunday school, Bible studies, and confirmation classes, demonstrated a level of familiarity with their churches' beliefs on par with the Traditionalist teens. Rather, these differences in approaches to the supernatural realm point to the fact that when teens have many sources that influence their decision making, as is the case among what Giddens has termed the "post-traditional self," they also see many possible explanations as addressing their questions about the realm beyond the material world.[29] While I noted that the Traditionalists may have been a part of the most-studied group of religious adherents, I think that study of teens who find themselves at the crossroads of many interests, both religious and otherwise, warrants a great deal more research.

What is needed, in this approach, is a closer examination of different factors that can play a role in how individual young people make decisions about their religious lives and identities. The "culture as tool kit" approach advocated in the introduction suggests that we look not only at individual choices but also at how those options are limited, or preselected, by the associations young people have: how they are placed in terms of family structure, economics, political life, and geography, among other things. Continuing the case-study model of this section, we turn our attention to the group with the greatest interest in shaping and influencing the lives of today's young people: their parents.

Part III
CONTEXTS AND CONCLUSIONS

8

BABY BOOMERS AND THEIR MILLENNIAL KIDS

PARENTAL INTENTIONS

REGARDING THE MEDIA,

RELIGION, AND BELIEFS

IN THE SUPERNATURAL

In every generation, parents must consider how they are going to raise their children in the context of an environment that is largely beyond their control. The mass media, due to their overwhelming presence in the lives of young people, are usually viewed by parents (as well as other leaders in society) as one of the primary challenges parents confront in the home.[1] Some parents choose to carefully monitor their children's media input, some prefer to engage their young people in dialogue about the media, and others establish strict limitations on how much media, or what kind, may be consumed.[2] Media researchers have generally advocated talking with young people about their media choices, particularly as children enter their preteen and teen years.[3] However, it's also the case that in general, parents see more need to intervene when children are younger; once they've entered their teen years, most parents believe they can and should trust their children's judgment.[4]

In some ways, parental approaches to beliefs concerning religion and the supernatural realm mirror their approaches to the media. Most parents believe that their influence, particularly in the area of religious socialization, has largely taken place by the time their children reach their later high school years.[5] By the time teens reach the middle of their high school years, parents can no longer force their children to attend church.[6] If teens have not developed a commitment to their tradition by this point, forcing them to attend tends to give teens a negative experience both with religious institutions and with parents. Not surprisingly, most parents choose to avoid this. While this might indicate that parental views about the supernatural realm and about religion are more importantly conveyed in the early years, parents continue to play an important role in how teens interpret the stories and beliefs of their parents, as this book has demonstrated.[7]

In spite of the attention to peer influence among contemporary young people, most teens say that their parents are the greatest influence on their beliefs concerning religion and the supernatural.[8] Most teens also say that they believe that their ideas about various issues—from the specifics of drinking or premarital sex to more overarching ideas of values and beliefs—are very similar to their parents' views.[9] Some teens who stress that they make their own decisions rather than rely upon the input from parents note, in most cases, that their parent or parents were influential when they were younger, thus providing a foundation upon which they have since built.[10] For most teens, while peers are turned to most often for advice on how to behave in specific circumstances, parents remain an important source of support for underlying values.[11] Parents and teens today share views in a way that was not true between baby boomer parents and their own parents.[12] This suggests that while teen culture might look quite different from its earlier forms, there is a great deal of continuity in how both parents and teens make sense of their beliefs, including what they consume in the media that references the supernatural realm.

In previous chapters, the intentions and beliefs of parents have been highlighted with reference to the stories of young people. Here, I explore three related issues that underscore parental intentions. First, I consider what parents wish to teach their children about religion. Second, we will explore how their views of media relate to their beliefs about religion. The interaction of these two approaches—to beliefs and to the media—provide insight into how young people might interpret their parents' intentions. Finally, I examine how parents view the media: as a threat, a possible teaching aid, or a resource. I argue that an interesting difference emerges depending on how parents see themselves in relation to the values and norms of dominant, or elite, culture. This further extends our understandings of how young people come to evaluate the legends of the supernatural that they encounter in the entertainment media.

PARENTAL APPROACHES TO RELIGION AND BELIEFS

In my interviews with parents, I learned that there were basically six different but overlapping tendencies regarding how parents talked about what they wanted to teach their young people about religion and beliefs. The first, and probably the most widespread, was the tendency to equate religion with *morality,* or to view religion as a foundation providing the answers to what is "right" and "wrong," as I will illustrate in a moment. Other parents, however, defined religion as *identical to the institutions of organized religion* and then identified themselves as religious or not based upon their acceptance or rejection of the institutions. Still other parents talked about religion in *therapeutic* terms, in that it offered emotional support and positive feelings through small groups, a religious leader's emphasis, or individual relationships or experiences that may or may not have anything to do with formal religious organizations. Some talked about religion as *one category of a multidimensional life*, an activity that was a personal choice often based upon the pragmatic functions it fulfilled, and thus their definition of religion shared common ground with other social or civic organizations. Others saw religion as *integrally related to racial/ethnic identity* and thus asserted that it was impossible to define religion apart from the total cultural and social reality of being Jewish or Muslim, for example. A final few saw religion as *a source of ultimate meaning*, affirming a relationship with God, Allah, or another divinity as the "ground of all being" in a humanist or existentialist sense.[13]

Within each of these categories were parents who identified with a specific religious tradition (including a range of participation and commitment to it), as well as parents who did not. Also within each category were parents who offered clarifications that they were "spiritual" but not "religious," apparently meaning that they did not want to distance themselves from religion entirely, although they did not place great importance on the institutions of religion. This is a fairly common statement among baby boomers and relates to the fact that more adults now favor an approach to religious views based on personal choice rather than on institutional loyalty.[14] Not surprisingly, parents who emphasize the right of their teens to choose their own beliefs (rather than encouraging and modeling loyalty to a particular tradition) tend to have teens who do not participate regularly in formal or organized religion.[15]

While in some instances these definitions overlapped, it was clear that these six different approaches to religion were quite influential in how parents talked about religion and how they interpreted the relationship between religion and the media. Learning and accounting for how the parents I talked with defined religion became a key to understanding how parents expected the media to serve as a resource for (or detriment to) religious identity.

RELIGION, MORALITY, AND THE MEDIA

Regardless of the primary defining approach to religion taken by individuals throughout my study, the parents' conversations about teenagers, religious identity, and media often highlighted an understanding of religion as something that provides a moral foundation for their teens.[16] Thus while I often tried to guide the conversations on religious (or spiritual) identity toward issues of power, contestation, or negotiation with other aspects of identity, or toward existentialist questions of "meaning," it was often the moral issues that framed and shaped the parents' conversations. The following excerpt is from a discussion group that consisted of six Mexican American, Roman Catholic parents of middle to lower income and a seventh unmarried partner of a parent who is African American. Their comments illustrated this common approach to religion as a moral system:

> INTERVIEWER: Are there some things about religion that you try to teach your kids? And how do you try to do that?
>
> CONNIE: You know, what's right, and what's wrong, what's good and what's bad. You know, that there's just certain things that you do, you don't want to hurt people, you don't want to hurt yourself because you're a temple of God.
>
> JUDY: We always try to teach our children that it doesn't matter if we know what you've done, whether it's good or bad or whatever, because God always knows everything.
>
> CHERYL: God always knows.
>
> JUDY: And he's the one that matters, he always knows what you're doing.
>
> CONNIE: It's between you and him.
>
> JUDY: So, when you go out there, whatever you're doing in life, remember, consult God first.

In the comments of these women, there was no specific mention of the institution nor of racial/ethnic identity. There also was no reference to the ability of religion to provide shades of meaning to one's life. Religion was also not seen as one among many choices. Instead, religion was seen as the foundation upon which all other choices are made.

The discussions of religion and media in these womens' group, then, were not surprisingly colored by the perceived negative moral influences of the electronic media. When asked about whether the media have an influence on their teens, for instance, all but one parent emphatically agreed that it does. The couple who hosted the group mentioned above were the parents of Jordan, the Intrigued teen who, while nominally Catholic, was interested in legends of the supernatural such as the El Chupacabra story he saw in *The X-Files*. Jordan's parents expressed the belief that one of their primary parental tasks was to provide moral teaching to their two teenage children. They believed that their religion assisted them in this, and they saw the popular media as directly undermining their efforts. When Jordan expressed views that differed from what they saw as values rooted in their Catholic faith, they were outraged.[17] They saw their son's regular participation in mass as a primary means by which he was to have learned what they believed were their moral values, supported fully by the family's regular participation in Catholic mass and other parish-related activities. What was perhaps most interesting in the parents' conversation was the rather direct link they made between their son's failure to express their preferred values and the influence of the media. In their view, neither the environments of peers or of school were considered, nor was the possibility that the church (or the parents) had somehow failed to convincingly socialize Jordan into what the parents perceived as desirable values rooted in Catholicism. The emphasis on morality, then, continually led the conversation about media and religion in this discussion group back to issues of competing influences, which was the most common way of approaching the question of religion and media that I encountered among all my interviews.

RELIGION, THE INSTITUTION, AND THE MEDIA

While Jordan's parents emphasized the role of religion in providing a foundation for morality, they also saw the religious institution of their local parish as an important resource. Approaching religion as it is related to its organized/institutional form seems to be found not only among those who identify with the institutions, however, but also among both those who reject the institutions and those who are "marginal members."[18] While these latter individuals feel uncomfortable with the term "religion" because they associate it with the institution they have rejected, many do not wish to dismiss all of the other possible attributes of religion, such as its connection with a source of meaning or a foundation for morality. Thus they might identify themselves as "spiritual persons," as did Justine, a member of a discussion group of lower- to middle-income Anglo-American and biracial single parents from various religious backgrounds. When I asked Justine whether she believed that there was any relationship between religion and the teaching of values, she looked perplexed and embarrassed. One of her friends quickly interjected, "But you're a very spiritual person." Justine continued:

> JUSTINE: I grew up in a very strict Catholic family, and I think it kept me from growing spiritually. So, I found a different way. And that suits me better, and my daughter seems to be going that way too.
> INTERVIEWER: So when you teach your daughter about values, do you relate it in some way to your spirituality, or are there other bases?
> JUSTINE: I think I relate it more to, morals, you know, you have to have morals to live in society.

Justine saw religion as something antithetical to spirituality and not necessarily related to teaching her daughter about morals. She did not elaborate on how she could teach her daughter morality, for then the conversation turned to other members of her discussion group who were involved in religion and their experiences of how their involvement supported their beliefs. Yet some parents who did equate morality and organized religion were troubled by this issue when their teens expressed differences of opinion regarding religion. In an affluent and moderate-to-liberal Protestant group of Anglo-American parents, Tanya discussed her son Andy's reluctance concerning religion. Andy, incidentally, was the same age as Jordan:

> INTERVIEWER: Tanya, do you want to comment on your family's approach to religion, in terms of what you're trying to teach them?

TANYA: Well, I guess at this point Andy has rejected organized religion. He would not voluntarily go to church with me at this point.

INTERVIEWER: How old is he?

TANYA: He's fourteen. And he assures me that he has a spiritual nature, but it's not in church.

INTERVIEWER: So, how do you talk to him—

TANYA: Well, I hope he has a good foundation, if he ever wants to return to that, but then, you know, I think I observe his spiritual nature. So, just encourage him to explore. I'm certainly not going to force anything.

INTERVIEWER: Does he look at other religions?

TANYA: Not at this time. And that's something I think we'd be willing for him to do.

For Tanya, as for Justine, religion could not be defined primarily as the foundation of a "moral code" because they had to reconcile their belief that their children were moral with the fact that they were not affiliated with an institution of organized religion. Thus both Tanya and Justine asserted the "spiritual nature" of their teenage children. They believed their children were old enough—at fourteen and sixteen, respectively—to make up their own minds. While neither Tanya nor Justine's teenage children seemed interested in exploring other religions, it was perhaps the fact that they had a "spiritual nature" that reserved them from being "irreligious." It is also possible that having a spiritual nature was, according to their parents, another acceptable form of religion that may or may not be at all related to morality.

When religion was defined primarily in terms of the institution, it was perhaps not surprising that the relationship between religion and the media was conceived of in terms of how the institutions of religion were represented in the media. The most striking example of this occurred at the conclusion of an interview early in my research with a reformed Jewish family. After I had thanked the family for their participation and turned off my tape recorder, the father said with mild surprise, "I thought you were going to ask us about what we thought of televangelism and church services on television." In turn, I was surprised that a Jewish family would conceive of the question of how the media might be a resource in teaching their children about religion in terms of Protestant religiosity and its representation in the media. Yet this illustrated to me how widespread is the equation of this particular form of religion and the media. In subsequent interviews, I came armed with examples of how various religions are represented in popular culture and the news, which often elicited comments of recognition such as, "Oh yeah, I saw that episode of *ER* [when the character Dr. Benton prayed for his young son]," or they had seen religion referenced in post-9/11 programs such as PBS *Frontline*'s "Faith and Doubt at Ground Zero." Clearly, however, thinking of religion in its institutional form limited how people thought the media might have any relevance for their goals in teaching their children and teens about religion. After 9/11, religion became a concern of current events as well as piety and morality. In any case, none of the parents I interviewed mentioned televangelism or the broadcast of religious church services as resources they used in helping to communicate their religious beliefs to their children.

RELIGION AND MEDIA AS THERAPEUTIC

Unlike Jordan's parents, who related religion to both morality and organized religion, and Justine and Tanya, who were troubled by the implication that the two might be related, other persons seemed put off by what they saw as organized religion's emphasis on morality and its consequences. These parents emphasized religion and its therapeutic functions. In some ways, their approaches echoed the critiques of religion made by social theorists Spinoza, Hume, Marx, and Freud, among others: that the function of religion is to provide a means by which to cope with the fears and anxieties of everyday life. Cathy, a lower-income Anglo-American single parent who articulated this approach, felt that her teenage daughter had found in religion something she herself had missed when growing up:

> With my daughter, Brandy, she loves to go to church, and I think she just has that void. And for some reason, maybe it was the way I grew up, my parents' disinterest in religion, my yearning for it, we went to a church that was "hell and damnation," you're bad if you do this, you're bad if you do that, and I became kinda jaded and a little bit, not real sure of religion because that was the perception in my mind, all they want to do is pass the collection plate, take your money and tell you how horrible you are. Where Brandy hasn't been jaded in that way, and she's so open to just drinking in whatever she can get out of church . . . and it gives them hope, and something to put their faith in, that there is some purpose, that there is a reason for things, and that there's someone watching over you all the time. I think that gives her a lot of security, especially as a child of a single parent. She needs all the security she can get a hold of.

A feeling of security served as an important function of religion, according to Cathy. Other people I interviewed who seemed to define religion as therapeutic (both those affiliated with organized religion and those not) made much less specific statements, noting that religion was related to the pleasant feeling of knowing that "someone cares for you" or that "everything is going to work out in the end." Some people, like Jake Pickerington's family, introduced in chapters 5 and 7, mentioned guardian angels as such religious and therapeutic beings.

Not surprisingly, then, some of the popular prime-time dramas following in the genre of *Touched by an Angel* were mentioned as examples of how this approach to religion could be communicated to their teenage children via the media. Connie, a Mexican American, lower-income, Catholic single parent, commented on an episode of *Touched by an Angel* that she had watched with her son:[19] "What I got out of it was, you know, that she [the angel] was telling this kid that no matter how alone he felt and stuff, that God was always there, no matter how fast the car was, no matter how fast you go, God's gonna be right there with you, you know? And that's what I got out of it. And you know, I don't know what Shawn got out of it. I always try to teach him positive thinking, so I hope he got the same thing I did." This equation of religion with what makes one feel good or is "positive" sometimes led to the mention of programs that had fewer explicit religious references than *Touched by an Angel* has, but that were of the same television genre. One evangelical father mentioned *Early Edition* when asked which of the shows he watched had "religious themes." This program featured a man who received a copy of tomorrow's newspaper a day in advance so that he could avert tragedies that hadn't yet happened. When his wife quickly reminded him that the program didn't "really [have] any religion," he replied: "At least he's trying to be good. I don't have any problem with that."[20] *Early Edition* inevitably concluded happily as wrongs were righted and problems resolved. Thus it seemed that parents who embraced religion for its therapeutic benefits might also see media as a resource for encouraging such positive thinking—regardless of whether a particular program has explicitly religious themes or images.

RELIGION AND MEDIA AS ONE
AMONG MANY OPTIONS

Closely related to its therapeutic functions, religion was also viewed positively by some parents as one of many possible social and civic organizations that help young people to feel a sense of belonging. Some parents compared the religious and other social groups that were available to contemporary teens to those around when they were young people. While I had expected that the parents would see religion as more central to their home lives growing up than was perhaps the case now, several of the parents, such as Sandy and Donna, expressed the opposite position:

> SANDY: We have one of the largest teen groups in our church; it's huge. And they have a mass just for the teens. And that's on Sunday night at six, and they have a band for the music. And the parents were asked that if they come to sit way in the back. But I mean, that place was rocking, and I was absolutely shocked, and it used to be like fifteen years ago, the dorks went to this kind of stuff.
>
> DONNA: Maybe other things are coming in and taking the place of some of the things that we were used to. Since schools do seem kind of disconnected, they're getting bigger and bigger, and kids are working, and they're not using the school site as much as the family site, maybe they're going to the other stuff. You know? Maybe it's okay to go to Girl Scouts, maybe it's okay to go to church.

Rather than religion fading into irrelevance as might have been suggested by the "secularization thesis," these mothers saw a vitality and a role for religion in their teens' lives.[21] What emerged as a difference between the role of religion then and now, however, had to do with a perceived increase in the role of decision making among teens. Some parents discussed the teens' many possible sources of support as *relativized* or *flattened* to some extent: religion had become one among many *choices*. Regardless of the teens' position vis-à-vis the various social and religious groups available, some parents indicated that such choices are made with the same measure of pragmatism: how is affiliation here *useful* to me? These parents suggested that there was no longer a hierarchy of "acceptable" versus "dorky" activities in which teens may participate. Several teens echoed this sentiment in commenting on the sense that the boundaries between "cliques" were much less firm today that they were in their parents' day (not all agreed with this assertion, however). But perhaps more important, there are social forces that shape and subtly inform the choices teens can and do make; none of the Anglo-American teens "chose" to attend predominantly African American or Mexican churches, for example. Still, the perception among some teens and their parents was that the choices available to teens today are relative; each activity may be acceptable if it is found to fulfill the desired functions of providing security, meaning, social networks, activities, or a combination of all of these. It is thus not so much that organized religion either is or is not a viable avenue for meaning, but that it is on equal footing with several other options. It is to be judged for its effectiveness in meeting these needs.

Likewise, the entertainment media were seen as providing material that could be good or bad, helpful or not depending on the circumstances. It was good or "useful" when it opened opportunities to engage in interactions between parents and their teenage children. While media could be "bad" when it illustrated values that differed from the parents' preferences, it still could be marshaled into a "good" as it was useful for providing opportunities to discuss those different values, as Donna, an Anglo-American single parent stated:

> I'm pretty dismayed by the crap I see out there right now, and when [seventeen-year-old Bill] chooses a movie, I've said time and time again—. You know, he'll try to defend what he's going to see, and I'll just say, "Bill, remember if you're not against them, then you're basically with them. And it's your decision, you're seventeen, but whenever you spend your money to rent that video or to buy that book, or to buy that CD, whatever you're spending that money on, you're encouraging more of it, so just think about that." And usually, I'd have to say he argues with me and does what he wants to do anyway [laughs]. But I know he thinks about it, and there's been a couple times when he's come back and said, "Mom, you're right, I've got to think about that." Or he'll see a movie and say, "Mom, I know you'd approve of that movie," so I know it's sinking in.

Within this more relativized approach to religion and the practices associated with it, therefore, the media were not seen as undermining morality in the same way as we saw earlier. Nor were discussions of the media linked to expectations concerning religious institutions (either their representation in the media or their counterinfluence in the lives of young people). Media, like religion, could be made useful, depending on the situations and the goals of the parents.

RELIGION, MEDIA, AND RACIAL/ETHNIC IDENTITY

A relativistic approach to religion was not universal among my research participants, however, and survey research would be needed to demonstrate how widespread this, or the other approaches to religion mentioned, might be. Some families, rather than seeing religion as one of many facets of a multidimensional life, saw it instead as an umbrella so closely connected with racial/ethnic background that it was in a certain sense impossible to separate religion from other aspects of identity and practice. While parents drew distinctions, young people were likely to blur racial/ethnic and religious identity, as in the case of Sakinah, a preteen daughter in a conservative Muslim family who was biracial (Arab African/Anglo-American):

> INTERVIEWER: How about if you weren't Arab African/caucasian? If you were from a different racial background, how would your life be different?
>
> SAKINAH: I would like eat pork, and it wouldn't really matter if I ate any kind of meat. And I could listen to music. And I could probably watch MTV if we had cable.

In this statement Sakinah referred to the specific restrictions that her mother and father upheld due to their Muslim beliefs. While her older brothers, all in their teen years, were able to draw some distinctions between Arabs and the Muslim tradition, they noted that their school friends usually didn't recognize the difference. "Some people think we're terrorists," Sakinah's brother Aziz explained, "but when people get to know Muslims, they know that they're good."

Muslims were not the only ones equating religion and racial/ethnic identity, however. When I asked the Goldmans, a reformed Jewish family, what they considered their racial/ethnic background to be, the father looked at me incredulously and then said slowly, "Jewish." His three teen children laughed at the way he said it, as if to imply, "You already knew that," as I had been referred to them by a rabbi at their synagogue. They all concurred that their racial/ethnic heritage, too, was Jewish, despite the fact that I later learned that Ruth, the mother, is of Scandinavian heritage (and, incidentally, had grown up United Methodist).

In this family, religious activities overlapped with and were virtually indistinguishable from "family" activities, as the mother, Ruth, explained. She related their practices on Hanukkah to their attempts to resist the consumerism of the season: "I've tried to have Hanukkah be smaller presents, but spend that time doing an activity at least every night. . . . Sometimes it's something that may not seem that related, but it's a family activity, we're all gonna go see a movie. Or we make potato pancakes, or maybe there's a night when we play dreidel. . . . So I try to keep Hanukkah from being a Jewish Christmas." When they were unable to attend religious services on Friday nights during the school year, they conducted a brief prayer time followed by a movie or prerecorded television programming the family viewed together.

With this emphasis on racial/ethnic identity, it is not surprising that these families were aware of how persons of their racial/ethnic group were portrayed in the media. Jemila Ahmed, the mother of Hasan, who was introduced as a Traditionalist teen in chapter 6, was quite conscious of teaching her children about positive and negative portrayals of Muslims and Arabs in the media, as she noted:

> We're always excited if a Muslim in the news is presented positively. You know, if they present a side of a Muslim and you actually sympathize with the Muslim instead of becoming so angry. . . . Unfortunately, what usually happens is if it's a story or if it's a fantasy [i.e., not a news story], the Arab's the terrorist, the bad guy, and of course [sarcastically] an Arab is a Muslim. You know people don't get that Muslims are from all over the world, and so they always put it that way. And then it's a double whammy for my kids, because they are part Arab.

Because of their awareness of portrayals of Arabs and Muslims, this family had talked quite a bit about the Disney movie *Aladdin*. While the parents liked the fact that an Arab story was portrayed at all, they also had reservations about some of the negative stereotyping of the characters. During a participant observation, Sakinah viewed *Aladdin* intently; I wondered whether she recognized the negatives of the movie. They were not mentioned in this particular viewing, although I was aware that the movie had been frequently viewed in the household. Similarly, in the Goldman family, the parents mentioned many Jewish authors, producers, comedians, and films and television programs depicting Jewish characters. While Julie, the oldest daughter, named the TV program *Brooklyn Bridge* as one that had a "Jewish feel" to it, she also related this to her experiences with her relatives in New York City, who are Jewish by heritage but do not practice the faith. Her two teenage siblings could not think of any programs that had anything to do with practicing Judaism. Despite the fact that the family drew sharp distinctions between themselves as practicing Jews and their New York relatives as not at all "religious" or practicing, they did not identify Jewish representations in the media by the extent to which the characters, actors, or stories had to do with the practices of the faith.

While the connection between racial/ethnic identity and religion is perhaps clearest among those who are not white or not Christian, these examples raise implications for those who do fall into the latter categories. If Jews recognize a category of "cultural Jews" that are not practicing but are still Jewish, can the same be said of practicing Christians and their identification of and with "cultural Christians" they see in the media? It seems to me that the latter category is much more invisible due to the latent acceptance that to be Anglo-American and at least "vaguely Christian" is still the norm in the United States. This warrants further exploration for a greater understanding of the relationships between Christianity, hegemony, and religious representation in the media.[22]

RELIGION, MEANING, AND THE MEDIA

Despite the overwhelming frequency of the approaches to religion discussed earlier, I had expected that "religion" and "meaning" would be discussed simultaneously or possibly even interchangeably when people talked about their media experiences. Indeed, I had designed my questions with the expectation that I would be addressing the ways in which "meaning-making," a term from media reception studies, would overlap with the sense in which parents wanted to teach their children something of "ultimate meaning," or a search for truth.[23] Looking back, I'm sure my expectations were shaped by my own graduate education in a theological school. Perhaps it is telling, then, that two of the few parents who used this language in discussing what they hoped to teach their children about religion were a Presbyterian pastor and his wife. Lester explained his approach to religion as a "love/hate relationship with the Presbyterian church" and then continued:

> In our tradition, there's an encouragement to question and to search for truth and understanding which is integral to the system. Some people don't follow that, but it's integral to it. And so when I talk about our church to our kids, I talk about those kinds of values in our way of looking at things. Look at the Bible with a critical eye, try to understand. . . . And then if you pursue the strong questioning, searching for truth and your own understanding, then it really does take you beyond the denomination. And I think it takes you into the kind of realm that Don [a fellow group member and "seeker"] has entered into, where you start thinking, "What are the similarities? How can I synthesize this?" And that's an exciting dimension too, but then churches and denominations tend to want to reach out and grab you by the ass and say, "Come back here! You're thinking too much!" Because the system has to keep perpetuating itself.

Lester's comment helpfully broadens the analysis from the realm of individual parental choices concerning approaches to religion to the fact that this orientation is central to a tension in the moderate-to-liberal wings of American mainline religions today.[24] As young people are affirmed in their ability to make their own choices concerning religious identity and affiliation, it stands to reason that the distinctiveness of different denominations, and perhaps those between differing religions, would continue to decline. The "search" results in something like "cafeteria Catholicism," a term for the practice, not limited to Catholics, of picking and choosing the most personally meaningful aspects of the larger faith system while discarding those elements that are less desirable.[25]

Much like the relativistic approach to religion and to the role of the media to serve as a resource, then, Lester and his wife, Ellen, attempted to clarify the similarities and differences between the values the family viewed or heard in the media and what they believe. Yet more conscientiously than any other parents I interviewed, they also attempted to clarify differences between *specific religious representations* of the media and what they themselves believed. When Ellen noted that she believed her eighteen-year-old daughter Andrea would find *Touched by an Angel* appealing, Lester added:

> We talk about angels, 'cause Andrea's really interested in them. She has all the stereotypical angelic cherubim, seraphim, flying around her room.
> And I occasionally come from a biblical perspective and try to say, "Angels are messengers, and in the Bible, they don't look like that, they're people, almost human figures." So I don't really put it down, I don't think, but we haven't really discussed in depth why that's so attractive to her, the angelic hosts. Except that she does have a sense of the spiritual dimension of life, which that seems to catch onto.

Thus in his family practices around the use of media as a resource for religious identity, Lester echoed the stance of his church to some extent as he provided information of the family's specific religious identity while also allowing openness for further questioning. Andrea recognized and appreciated the search she had been encouraged to pursue in the realm of religion. Yet while she noted that she appreciated being able to talk with her parents about religion, she stated that it was in the discussions with her peers that she learned about and made her own decisions regarding religion. "We kind of make up our own religion," she said.

Andrea Gray's statement that she and her friends "make up their own religion" was certainly not one that would be made by all of the teens in my study (figure 8.1). Indeed, many teens were interested in preserving the religious traditions of the past, such as the Muslim children in the Ahmed family and Sweetie Buchanan in her evangelical family. Still, even teens with a conservative approach to religion sense that they have the power and right to make their own decisions regarding religion. In this way, the very Protestant notion of free will is very much alive in contemporary young American religion.[26] Young people have learned that regardless of whether their parents want them to be religious, ultimately they will have a right to choose how they will incorporate religion and other beliefs in the supernatural into their lives (or not, of course). Unlike family situations of the past, adolescence in the United States is generally understood to be a time of preparation for the ultimate and inevitable separation of the young person from his or her family of origin.[27] So part of the job of a teen's parent is to present the young person with the parents' views, but ultimately to stand back and hope that they choose to emulate them.

FIGURE 8.1
While some teens claim to "make up their own religion," many want to preserve the traditions of their families, occasionally talking these traditions and beliefs over with their friends. Photo by author.

While the way parents defined religion and the possible role of the media in teaching teens about religion might be related, as the previous analysis suggests, the categories are far from exclusive. Jemila, for example, the Anglo Muslim woman whose comments illustrated the connection between religion as racial/ethnic identity and media portrayals, spoke at least as strongly about religion as a foundation for moral living. When asked how she wanted to use either the media or the Qur'an to teach her children, for instance, she replied: "Morals, and think about what you're doing, and what is your purpose. I think my biggest thing—and not just with media, but with all of everything they do, is what's your intentions, and why are you doing this and how will it help you as an individual. . . . I mean, what are your intentions and goals? So that's the same with TV. Are we wasting our life here in front of the TV, in front of Nintendo?" She then noted that she believed it was all right to "waste time" some of the time, hence explaining what she believed was her lax attitude toward limiting media consumption (although their family media rules were among the strictest I encountered in my entire pool of research participants). Yet her goal was to give them "practice now in making choices that hopefully" will be morally admirable.

Ruth Goldman, who was also mentioned in the racial/ethnic identity section, seemed to share some common ground with Lester Gray's approach to religion as a search for truth: "With Reformed Judaism, there's a lot of choice, and a lot of individual responsibility. . . . There is no 'This is the answer' on many, many things. And I like that. I think I'd rather struggle with it than just have that package, that this is it because that's what's written, that's how it's supposed to be." Thus, despite her recognitions that what it meant to be Jewish encompassed both "practicing" and what she termed "culturally Jewish," she also embraced an approach to religion that encourages a search for ultimate meaning. She did not relate this to how she discussed media use, however. Like Lester's teen children, Ruth's take differing approaches to the faith: while the oldest is very observant, the youngest is largely indifferent and the middle teen falls somewhere in between. Instead of making up their "own religion," however, all three of the Goldman teens still identify themselves as Jewish, perhaps because of the primacy of the relationship they see between their religion and their racial/ethnic identity. Thus I believe that while the categories I listed are far from exclusive, they do tend to guide the ways parents approach religion and, in turn, how they expect the media or other cultural resources to serve or undermine their goals in teaching their teen children what it means to be religious.

THE MEDIA AND BELIEFS IN THE SUPERNATURAL: ROLE MODELING VERSUS "ISSUES" TELEVISION

As seen in the above examples, how parents view the media—whether as a threat or resource—is related to how they approach what they hope to teach their teens regarding religious beliefs and their relation to morality, organized religion, anxiety, social choices, racial/ethic identity, or the ultimate meaning of life. Aside from the special case of the Wiccan parents detailed in chapter 5, none of the parents interviewed talked about intentionally teaching their teens about beliefs in the supernatural realm. While religion is related to morality at least among some parents, none saw any relationship between beliefs in the supernatural realm and morality. In general, they also did not see any relation between supernatural beliefs and organized religion, anxiety, social choices, racial/ethnic identity, or ultimate meaning. The only supernatural being that seemed to bear any relationship to these categories were angels. Thus, it is worth considering how parents approach representations of angels in popular television and film. As I argued in the last chapter, we can see differences in how representations of the supernatural are approached when we consider how parents see themselves in relation to the values and norms of dominant, or elite, culture.

It is important to establish that any representations in the entertainment media appear within certain genre constraints: in other words, angels may appear in both horror movies and sentimental love stories, but they will be interpreted in different ways because of the associations we have with these genres.[28] I will discuss this issue in greater detail in the following chapter. Some of the criticisms I encountered when discussing angels in popular television related directly to the genre in which they appeared. During the time of this study, CBS's *Touched by an Angel* had been rated the second-most-watched drama of any television program for two years, and it would maintain its status for the following two years.[29] Because of its popularity, I chose to center my conversations about angels in reference to this television program and even watched an episode with several groups of parents.[30]

One of the most common criticisms I encountered when discussing *Touched by an Angel* was that the program was "unrealistic." After hearing elaborations on this comment, it became evident that parents from differing backgrounds defined realism in different ways. When watching the program, in fact, a few lower-income, mostly Anglo-American, single parents commented incredulously on the opening visual images: "He steals cars from a dealership?!" In contrast, a group of affluent Anglo-American parents indicated that it was what they called the lack of a reflection of the "complexity" they experienced in their own lives that made the realism problematic. The fact that the members of the more affluent group saw themselves as more distant from the story than the members of the other group was illustrated when Lester, a member of the affluent group, brought the subject up in relation to the complaint raised by several of the parents concerning the sexualized issues of early 1998 newscasts:

> JULIE [commenting on her reasons for censoring the popular teen program *Dawson's Creek*]: The one student had an affair with a teacher over the summer.
> MELANIE: Yeah, but that happens in the news! I mean, we heard about that teacher—
> JACK: We have our president and governor! [referring to the well-publicized accusations of sexual impropriety for both]
> MELANIE: I'm sorry, they just ran that story about that teacher, now she's pregnant again!
> LESTER: You're kidding!
> MELANIE: Six months pregnant! . . . But this is the stuff that comes on every day, and we have to discuss issues like oral sex, and what is adultery, and all of those issues because of our president and the media.
> LESTER: Yeah. And those are ethical issues that are much different than sitting in a car and saying, "Am I gonna steal this car?" They're much more complex, it seems like.

Lester is referring, I believe, to his conviction that the problems of the teen boy are solved simplistically in the particular episode that I asked the group to view together.

A second but related objection raised in this affluent group of parents was that their teenage sons and daughters did not know anyone like the troubled youth depicted on the program, and this would make the program "unrealistic" or implausible to their teens. As Don commented: "Well, see, I think our kids are fairly well sheltered. I don't think they've run into that particular characteristic of a teenager who really has no expectations of what his life is going to be like. I think all of my kids' friends expect to go to college, and grow up and have jobs, as opposed to the ghetto attitude of 'What difference does it make 'cause I'm never gonna get anywhere.' I just don't know how they'd respond. Amanda [fourteen] would not really understand where this comes from. Denny [sixteen] would think it's all too hokey." Perhaps rather than only being less "complex," therefore, the problems associated with car theft were also less frequently encountered in the trials of upper-middle-class life. They might seem implausible or unrealistic at least in part because they are so infrequently encountered.

The experiences reflected in the program seemed to resonate somewhat more with members of lower-income parents, however. Other parents expected that their teens would be familiar with the issue of car theft that was raised in the episode they viewed. Cheryl, a Mexican American Catholic, identified with the program's protagonist, for example:

CHERYL: I liked how it gave the message.

INTERVIEWER: What did you see as its message?

CHERYL: That he was saying that, nobody should love him. That—how can I say this?—you know, he was thinking that nobody cared, because maybe his mom was saying, "No, he couldn't do this, or he couldn't do that." He thought she was being strict so that's why he would go steal the cars and everything. And the surroundings, probably, where he grew up, it's like, you know, you're a man, you're supposed to do this and that, and a lot of peer pressure. He didn't really give it a chance. Like at the end he said, he started missing people. And he probably realized then that his mom was being right, and his friends were doing wrong. . . . I think when you get older, you realize, because, I know I was the black sheep of the family, and with my mom [starts to get choked up] I realize now what she did for me. And that makes it kinda hard. 'Cause then you start to say, "She was there for you." And when you have your kids, you see they tried their best. So that part of it got to me. When I see people, when they get older, they realize that this, you know, she was right.

She interpreted the show as affirming her mother's strict parenting practices, as well as her own. A lower-income, Anglo-American single parent interviewed at a different time agreed with Cheryl's interpretation, noting that she believed the episode highlighted her own approach to single parenting:

I thought the episode was good, I think as far as being a single parent— sometimes single parents, like that woman, get a bad rap that, if your kids don't turn out right, it's because you did something bad as a parent, and since you're a single parent, there's something dysfunctional about the home. And the most functional kids I know personally come from a one-parent home. . . . I'm not saying all the time, everybody makes mistakes, but just because you're a single parent doesn't mean that if your kid does-n't turn out the best, it's because you messed up as a single parent. Some kids are just, their environment around them, and their peers, it's just too strong. But I think sometimes single parents go the extra mile because the kid doesn't have two parents.

These parents, like others whose teen children encounter difficulties in their everyday lives, identified with characters or particular story lines in this and other popular entertainment programs. In contrast, the higher-income parents were reluctant to name such identifications if indeed they had them. This could be a result of their desire to distance themselves from the popular media and its "low-class" associations, as Ellen Seiter has argued in her analysis of affluent mothers and teachers.[31] Yet what is interesting is that the more affluent parents, while not mentioning identification with the characters or particular story lines, responded with appreciation and enthusiasm for this television program and its "uplifting" message, as one mother termed it. It was not identification, nor the program's "realistic" portrayal of life circumstances, then, that accounted for their enthusiasm.

An important distinction between the more and less affluent parents became evident in how they described what they see as the show's potential benefits to their children. Several members of the affluent Anglo-American parents' group liked the fact that the program highlighted important contemporary "issues." Julie, a somewhat regular viewer, and Jack, who had not seen the program before, stated:

> JULIE: In the past, [*Touched by an Angel*] has also brought in gang violence and things like that. I've seen them bring in issues from today's world that I am glad to see them handling on this show.
> INTERVIEWER: Did you want to add something?
> JACK: I think it's important for things like that to be on television, and I think that particular story is probably, something that needs to be talked more about. We do have, the black youth of America is almost an endangered species, with gang violence, and I don't know, that's a major, major problem in this country, and there are some good things being done, but it's a huge, huge problem.

Some of the lower-income parents saw the benefits of the program on a less abstract level. Rather than "important issues," they liked the way the show portrayed "real-life situations," as one Anglo-American single parent noted: "I like *Touched by an Angel* because it shows real-life situations that, it seems like there's no way that things could ever be better, and they get turned around." When Dick, an Anglo-American single parent, protested that expecting a troubled youth to change was "unrealistic," other members in his group of single parents responded:

> DONNA: Like Dick was saying, that's not reality, in reality a lot of kids would go off and [steal] the car. Yeah, probably, maybe most, but I think maybe some of them wouldn't.

JOE: I like to think that maybe there's one kid who wouldn't do it.

DONNA: Yeah, and I think that's the point of the show, that one of them didn't, and that's the hope you're talking about.

While one mother of the affluent group noted that "it is hard to comprehend that black youth have no hope," several members of a group of Anglo-American and biracial single parents seemed to understand this lack of hope among teens only too well. In fact, they commented on the importance of holding out hope for teens and thus pointed to this aspect of the episode as a worthwhile possible "effect" of the program. As Joe and Jean noted:

JOE: There's so much garbage on TV now that gives kids—I mean, kids are looking for a role model, or something to identify with, and there's so much stuff on TV that really takes them in the wrong direction, and this is more along the lines of giving the kids the sense that maybe there is some good left in the world. . . . The kids are goin', "What have I got to look forward to?" And these shows, they show that there's something.

JEAN: I think a show like this, it's kind of mushy, and not very realistic, but it's nice to know that there are shows out there that don't have the sex and the violence. It's nice to have shows like that once in a while that's just—fun.

Judy and Diane, from a lower-income group of Mexican American parents, made similar comments:

JUDY: We complain so much about what's on TV, but if we had more of that [shows like *Touched by an Angel*], maybe our kids would be tuned in with that.

DIANE: I try to look for the best in any kind of situation anyway, so it kinda went really good, and was a good ending. And whatever situations in the news or problems that happen during the day, I try to have that kind of hopeful outlook, you know, something good will come out of it.

Thus while more affluent parents hoped that such a program would acquaint their teens with important issues, it seems that the parents of teens who came from less privileged backgrounds hoped that positive role models—whether in television or elsewhere in their lives—might help them deal with the similarly difficult issues in their own lives.

The parents with comparatively less income and education viewed the episode of *Touched by an Angel* as possibly providing "role models" for their teens. They may have recognized that implausible details in the program, such as how a theft is staged or what language is used by purported gang members, can undermine the perceived ability of the program to be taken seriously by their teens as presenting a positive role model. Thus in part because the sentimentality may undermine the wish that "positive" programming be accepted and modeled by teens, and in part perhaps due to their own deeper knowledge of situations with similar problems, some of the lower-income parents had a bit more distance between themselves and the various television techniques (lighting, music, pacing, close-ups) designed to trigger an emotional response. The parents in the more affluent group, in contrast, saw television as providing "information" on lifestyles and choices that are distinct and distant from their own. Perhaps the details were of less concern to them, in part because they were less familiar; in any case, their main function was to symbolically represent the issues of importance rather than to present a plausible model for teens.

The factors influencing how the issues are resolved on the program then become important, perhaps especially because they are unconsciously accepted by the viewers and therefore not discussed in the groups. We turn, then, to a brief highlight of a few elements contained in the particular episode viewed by some parents for this research. First, the protagonist of the episode is depicted as having stolen a car from a dealership. While a dealership might be a familiar sight for those with economic means who have purchased cars at dealerships, and therefore it may function as a plausible symbol for the middle and upper classes of where car theft might occur, such thefts, as those from backgrounds of lesser means note, are rare. Second, it is worth noting that the particular episode featured an African American teen and his mother, who are poor and live in the inner city, and are depicted as having no support system. They thus are at the mercy of the compassion shown them by the angels, the protagonists of the television program. Third, the African American teen and his mother unquestioningly cooperate with and trust the criminal justice system—and it actually assists them. Fourth, the program is framed by Colin Powell's advocacy for volunteering (rather than, for instance, a call for economic justice or social change). Fifth and perhaps most central, it is up to the individual (with the encouragement of angels) rather than the social system to change. The program symbolically resolves social problems such as the high crime rate among black youths through the transformation of the individual. In other words, religion, as it is represented through the actions of the angels on this program, provides assistance for individual emotional and moral transformation. Considering these factors, then, it seems possible to argue that the middle-class parents are affirmed in their worldview. Their emotional responses are tapped not only by the codings of the television program, but also by the way in which religion functions in tandem with middle-class assumptions: the angels help individuals to make moral decisions that then help them to better live in the existing society. This, I believe, tells us something not only about the television program, but more broadly about the popular "guardian angels" and, by extension, the importance of morality and secondarily the supernatural in contemporary religion. The function of angels is to encourage individual moral behavior as it is defined by middle-class norms.

PARENTS, RELIGION, MEDIA, AND
REPRESENTATIONS OF THE SUPERNATURAL

Interestingly, while many parents criticized *Touched by an Angel* and other depictions of angels in television and film as "unrealistic," very few of these objections related to what one might call explicitly religious, "spiritual," or theological issues of the program. None of the parents questioned the existence of angels, and none questioned that God was the source of the angels' "assignments." Moreover, few questioned the lack of reference to organized religion or any other religious community in either *Touched by an Angel* or other popular television programs and films that feature angels. Among the parents, no one argued that the angels' role in the lives of individuals was "unrealistic" or "hokey"; instead, many parents commented, as one affluent Anglo-American father did, "Maybe I've got an angel that watches over me. I've been fairly amazed sometimes that the things that have happened to me have turned out." Angels may be role models, or they may serve to correct societal "issues." In either case, this chapter highlights the fact that parents from differing backgrounds and experiences can find common ground in representations of supernatural beings that play a role in goodness and morality. Angels, while related to morality and helpful in the process of coping with the anxieties of everyday life, are not necessarily seen as related to organized religion, nor are they related to a particular racial/ethnic approach to religion. While many saw angels as "open," non-Christians categorically identified the angels of television and film as "Christian," a point to which I will return in the next chapter. Thus angels cut across several of the definitions of religion addressed in this chapter, were able to articulate some of the differing approaches to media the parents had named, and even cut across lines of taste and economic background in their appeal. It is little wonder, then, that once Hollywood discovered this through the unlikely success of CBS's *Touched by an Angel,* a spate of television programs and films featuring angels soon followed in its wake. The entertainment media may provide powerful symbols, but their creators are particularly attuned to how better to reach a large audience. Angels, it seems, are sometimes able to do this quite successfully, as we will see in the next chapter.

9

RELIGION, CLASS, AND POLITICS

DISCUSSING ALIENS AND

ANGELS IN THE FAMILY

AND IN SOCIETY

Aliens have hit the big time: at the beginning of the twenty-first century, they were appearing in prime-time television programs such as Fox's *The X-Files* and WB's *Roswell* and in popular films like *Men in Black I* and *II*, Steven Spielberg's *AI*, and M. Night Shyamalan's *Signs*. Abduction stories often appeared in news stories, as well. Sometimes there seemed to be a blurred line separating news reports from science fiction. One reporter from *The Guardian* (London) investigated magnetic fields that allegedly caused some people to believe in aliens. An expert quoted in that story suggested that perhaps the magnetic fields are, rather, the way that aliens are in touch with us—an idea put forth in the popular film *Contact*. KABC-Radio in New York City told of a man who is suing the government for their alleged failure to investigate alien abductions, a story line that seems to overlap with Fox's *The X-Files*. Even *MacLean's* magazine offers reviews of nonfiction conspiracy theory books addressing the topic of aliens.[1] Appearances of aliens in such outlets attest to their publicness, raising the question of whether belief in aliens may have become more credible to mainstream U.S. society than it was—or has appeared to journalists and scholars.

According to several national polls, belief in aliens has indeed increased significantly over the past few decades.[2] Much to the chagrin of skeptics, researchers have found few connections between belief in alien abduction and mental illness or psychological disturbance, and no relation between belief in aliens and income, occupation, or level of education.[3] Some have even asserted

that those claiming alien abduction reflect a cross-section of the U.S. population that closely mirrors the country's demographics, with the population of
alien believers tilted toward a higher ratio of members of the Anglo-American
middle class.[4]

The Resister teens of chapter 3, both of whom were Anglo-American and
from impoverished backgrounds, showed that some young people see belief in
aliens as compatible with what they understand about religion. In fact, the stories of Resisters Jodie and Eric demonstrated that the stories of alien encounters and alien abductions could serve as substitutes for the meaning systems
they associated with organized religion. Both of those teens were also alienated
from elite culture and indeed from most forms of societal authority. One might
wonder, then, whether their belief in aliens and their taste for entertainment is
related to their class and economic background. As teens inherit both class and
economic situation from their parents, it is worth considering how these issues
intersect with beliefs in the supernatural that might be in the realm of the "possible" for contemporary persons of differing backgrounds.

In his study of French society in the 1960s, sociologist Pierre Bourdieu argued that people are educated into appreciating certain aspects of culture.
"Taste" thus tends to follow a hierarchy of privilege that is established through
either social origin or higher education (or, usually, the workings of both). [5]
Bourdieu's critique rests upon a culture that places more emphasis upon the
humanities and fine arts than that of the United States, which tends instead to
emphasize technological knowledge and materialism.[6] Still, many scholars
have found Bourdieu's ideas to be fertile ground for the consideration of taste
and preference and the relation of these to social location.

Several media scholars have been interested in the relationship between
class status and preference for certain forms of entertainment. Robert Allen,
Dorothy Hobson, Andrea Press, and Ellen Seiter and her collaborators have argued, for example, that soap operas have been considered "low class" not because of any recognizable aesthetic or plot-related factors but because the people who enjoy them—lower-income women—are themselves relegated to the
bottom of the social structure.[7] Viewers of talk shows such as *Jerry Springer* suffer the same associational labeling. *Roseanne, Grace under Fire,* and *Married
with Children* were routinely dismissed by some as "tacky" or "tasteless" for
much the same reasons.

There has been a long tradition of labeling some forms of entertainment as
higher class and, by extension, of greater worth to the culture at large.[8] Cultural
studies, an interdisciplinary field of research, arose in response to this type of
cultural critique.[9] Foregrounding works of popular appeal, cultural studies
scholars have advocated against dismissive attitudes toward popular culture
and instead have questioned why certain denigrated forms have the appeal that
they do. Henry Jenkins has explored the *Star Trek* fan community, while Janice
Radway has interviewed women who read romance novels.[10] In an important
sense, as this book has taken seriously the often delegitimated interest in legends of the supernatural, it continues in this tradition.

Marxist critic Antonio Gramsci argues that the ideas of the elite members of society are usually those ideas considered "legitimate" for public debate and consideration.[11] In the 1960s, scholars in media studies—in particular, those looking for the impact or effects of the media on audiences—came to recognize that rather than unproblematically influencing individuals directly, the media reinforced the values and norms that had already achieved consensual acceptance. The question to be asked, according to Hall, was "whether the consensus did indeed spontaneously simply arise or whether it was the result of a complex process of social construction and legitimation. . . . For if the media were not simply reflective or 'expressive' of an already achieved consensus, but instead tended to reproduce those very definitions of the situation which favoured and legitimated the existing structure of things, then what had seemed at first as merely a reinforcing role had now to be reconceptualized in terms of the media's role in the process of consensus-formation."[12] Hall argued that by naturalizing and legitimizing some viewpoints over others, the media play a key role in the maintenance of cultural power systems. They do not simply impact or convince a passive audience, but are subtly persuasive, as they echo a certain taken-for-granted perspective that, not coincidentally, happens to be that of the elite in a culture. Sociologist Todd Gitlin has noted that journalists, particularly those at the most prestigious publications, tend to have worldviews that echo those of the people who hold the greatest power and economic strength in a society. Thus, Gitlin argued, news tends to naturalize certain ways of looking at the world, giving a legitimacy and gravitas to the viewpoint closest to the elite classes.[13]

In the case of media representations of aliens, it is fairly clear that the "legitimate" approach is to dismiss them as false. News outlets such as the *Los Angeles Times* and the *Baltimore Sun* dismissively equate UFO "believers" with those who read the *National Enquirer,* a coded way of locating people in relation to working-class tastes, while other papers such as the *Denver Post* refer to such enthusiasts as the "flying saucer crowd."[14] NPR commentator Hallie Deaktor even goes so far as to equate alien enthusiasts with the mentally ill and deviant.[15] Many audience members are convinced by this "legitimate" approach, agreeing with the debunking of what some call UFOlogy.[16] Nevertheless, aliens remain interesting to a vast proportion of the audience. Why would this be the case, if everyone agreed that such interest was, as Philip Klass writes, a "craze" that all dates to a foolish mistake made by a low-ranking officer at Roswell Army Air Force Base, who identified a weather balloon as a "flying disk"?[17]

The answer to this seeming conundrum lies in the fact that the power to define reality is always contested. While many accept journalists and authors as credible authorities, others may wonder about the motives that underlie the ways in which they discuss certain events. These others may approach such reports with a certain skepticism. Thus the appeal of alien stories is related to a different consensually accepted idea: that of the importance of questioning certain forms of authority. Aliens have been the subject of conspiracy theories and questions of governmental cover-ups since they entered the public con- versation in the Cold War era. Thus, while many may be reluctant to an- nounce a firm belief in aliens, the idea that they may exist resonates well among those who are already questioning truth claims, particularly those of the U.S. government and its military who have been associated with their "cover-up."

Angels obviously occupy a less contradictory place in relation to the "legiti- mate" authority and consensus of the media and of the public. Yet what is legit- imized and consensually accepted in these realms is not what religious leaders consider to be "orthodox" ideas about angels. To some extent, therefore, the popular enthusiasm about angels likewise echoes the questioning of truth claims, this time as they relate to institutions of religion.

The association of aliens and angels may seem a bit strange at first. These beings, occupying very different positions in the minds of most people, pro- vide an interesting contrast with regard to the questions of class, religion, and politics in relation to beliefs concerning the supernatural realm. These con- trasts are examined here through the stories of two families from different backgrounds: the Donahues and the Pickeringtons. Teen members of these families have already been introduced. Both Jodie and Eric, the Resister teens, live in the Donahue house, as does Nancy Donahue, a Mystical teen. Jake Pick- erington was the Mystical teen who had no interest in religion yet was inter- ested in guardian angels and aliens. Here, we extend the earlier discussions, highlighting the issues that emerge at the intersection of religious identifica- tion, socioeconomic class, and politics.

ALIENS AND THE CHALLENGE TO GOVERNMENTAL AND RELIGIOUS AUTHORITY: THE DONAHUES

The people living in Nancy Donahue's house were, for the most part, not re- lated to one another by either blood or marriage. They had come together out of various situations of poverty and disenfranchisement. It is important to re- call four traits shared among members living in the household: First, everyone living in Nancy Donahue's house expressed quite a bit of cynicism toward in- stitutions of religion and government. Second, except for Nancy's mother, they were interested in distancing themselves from organized religion. Third, all of them expressed interest in aliens and other beings and powers related to the su- pernatural realm. They all felt largely left out of, even superfluous to, the work- ings of mainstream society. Fourth, they understood precisely that society un- dervalued them as humans because of their lowered economic position—and they were angry about it.

The views toward government expressed in this household were consistent with this sense that good people were often rendered powerless—or worse. When talking about why they didn't vote, Jodie, Eric, and Nancy's mother had this exchange:

INTERVIEWER: Do you vote in elections?

[Jodie laughs]

NANCY'S MOTHER: Well, she [Nancy] just registered.

NANCY: Yeah, but not for either one.

INTERVIEWER: So, you're independent?

NANCY: Yeah.

ERIC: That's what I registered for. But the last three times the election's come around, I've been in prison.

JODIE: There hasn't been anyone worth voting for. I mean, I wanted Clinton to win [during his election to a second term]. But he won, and he hasn't done nothin'.

NANCY'S MOTHER: Do you realize that they really cannot accomplish that much?

JODIE: Well they can accomplish at least something! He didn't do anything! [Nancy and Eric are nodding in agreement]

NANCY'S MOTHER: It's like, they're so governed by everybody else that they cannot do a lot!

JODIE: Yeah, that's true, 'cause if they want to do something they have to go through one person, and then they have to go through somebody else.

NANCY'S MOTHER: And they just can't. And anybody who tries to do something gets killed.

JODIE: Like Kennedy.

NANCY'S MOTHER: Kennedy. Lincoln. Almost Reagan.

Their comments here suggested a view of life that is deeply sinister: not only is public service ineffective, but pursuing social change can be fatal. No wonder they were reluctant to be more involved.

The young people in this household doubted their ability to transcend or change their circumstances. Yet their experiences also made them doubt, as Eric Day said, that humans are "the most intelligent life form." He and others in the house disputed what they felt was claimed by "them"—those people closer to the dominant culture and its legitimate ideas. The household members looked for ways they could demonstrate how "they" were wrong, and interest in aliens offered great potential for this.

Several of the people in the Donahue house were interested in the possibility that aliens might have played a role in the history of civilization, and among them there were varying degrees of commitment to this idea. One of the strongest appeals of the alien theory was in the "fact" that there was more "evidence" supporting the existence of aliens than these individuals believed there might be for other faith traditions. Mickey, the father of Nancy's children, also favored an alien explanation over traditional Christianity:

INTERVIEWER: Well, what about when people describe beliefs in aliens and it sort of sounds like religion? Like they'll talk about aliens coming and creating the world, for example.

MICKEY: Oh, like *Stargate*.

INTERVIEWER: Yeah, I guess so.

MICKEY: *Stargate* was the movie where they found the gate in Egypt, and when they went through it, they went all the way across the known universe to another planet that had another temple just like the one they went in. And the pyramids were nothing more than landing pads for the spacecrafts. And that, the procreation between the aliens and what would've been *Homo erectus* is what made *Homo sapiens*.

INTERVIEWER: So, some people believe something like that.

MICKEY: I do believe something like that happened.

INTERVIEWER: Okay. But you wouldn't call that religion?

MICKEY: No. I'd call that, a mistake. [We laugh] I don't think the aliens knew what they were getting into. They'd've left us alone a long time ago. I think they came down. I think there was something here that they needed, or they wouldn't've stopped. The way they perceive it, like on *Star Trek*, the prime directive is to never, ever mess with the society. If they don't have space flight capability, then you never let them know you exist. Don't change their society.

INTERVIEWER: What do you think of people who believe that aliens created the world, and they believe that as a religion?

MICKEY: I don't see how they could take it as a religion, unless they started worshiping aliens as their creator.

INTERVIEWER: Yeah.

MICKEY: Aliens were not our creator. We were here long before the aliens got here. The aliens just pointed us in a direction.

Mickey states his belief in aliens as something that is definitely not a religious belief. In fact, Mickey asserted several times in the interview that he was an atheist. Mickey used *Star Trek*'s prime directive as support for why he found plausibility in the story he had seen in the film *Stargate*. Obviously *Star Trek*'s writers were not aiming to provide support for such a belief system, but Mickey had woven together a belief system that was consistent enough for him. He believed the possibilities raised in *Stargate* at least merited serious consideration. Yet Mickey did not see the cosmology outlined in these popular fictional media as "religion," because the aliens did not "create" us. Religion was still something outside his belief system, he implied. This separation of religion and belief in the supernatural role of aliens echoes the rejection of legitimate and institutional authority witnessed in the Donahues' reservations about government. Among the Donahues, it was the legends of aliens that were accepted as more "legitimate," not the least because they were conceived to be "possible." Nancy's mother, the only one who actively embraced a "religious" identity, justified her belief in aliens in this way:

INTERVIEWER: So, you think that there's a relationship between these aliens that put us here and your religious beliefs?

NANCY'S MOTHER: Mm, well, that's possible. But it's just like with Noah's Ark. Everybody who has ever seen anything having to do with that is passed away or died. They're gone. Because you know why? Because we're not ready to know what's there yet, because we're not ready to accept it, 'cause most of 'em are still on that level, "Well, you know." Like the regular religious type.

The last statement draws a distinction between the Donahues' "openness" to what we are not ready to know yet and the tendency of the "regular religious type" to be uninterested in what might be possible. By separating the two, she was able to criticize those she saw as wanting to put the unknown into an explanation of some kind.

From their marginal position vis-à-vis dominant culture, the members of the Donahue household felt that they were able to evaluate the "blind spots" of establishment religion and also to lay bare the myth, inherited from modernity, that there is nothing "out there" that science cannot explain. Belief in aliens turned out to be consistent with the suspicion that there is something lurking just outside the gates that could overturn everything in the world as we know it. Therefore it could seem possible that in order to maintain their positions of power and influence, members of the dominant culture might have a vested interest in covering up aliens, along with any other secrets that might upset the status quo.

As Jodi Dean points out in her study of the relationships between alien abduction stories and political conspiracy theories, people who claim belief in aliens have chosen a marginal position relative to the rest of society: "To claim to have seen a UFO, to have been abducted by aliens, or even to believe those who say they have is a political act. It might not be a very big or revolutionary political act, but it contests the status quo. Immediately it installs the claimant at the margins of the social. . . . [Yet] abductees have to keep going; they have to continue relying on a system they don't trust, a system they fear, if they are to work, survive, and care for their families in whatever limited terrestrial way they can."[18] While claiming to believe in aliens automatically indicates identification with a marginalized position in society, therefore, it may not be surprising that some young people, like Jodie and Eric, mix these beliefs with other ideas that may be less marginalized. They realize that they must work within the system to some degree, even if they resent it. This is why Jodie contemplated a degree in computer science that would improve her economic state and also, possibly, draw approval from her father, who was employed in the computer industry. It also explains, in part, why both Jodie and Eric still retain some language and beliefs that draw upon the conservative Christianity of their upbringing.

Members of the Donahue household were interested in what was beyond the material world that science has never explained, even as they used the language of science to justify their own beliefs in aliens. In this way, a belief in aliens functions on a level that Bourdieu might call "rejection" of dominant culture.[19] As the Donahues embraced the alien theory, they recognized that it was not considered legitimate by dominant culture. Yet this very recognition allowed them to affirm themselves as more "open" to "the possible" than the "regular religious type." Thus by virtue of the theory's rejection (or "cover-up") within dominant culture and the "evidence" they have seen that supports it, the theories of aliens became a plausible, even legitimate alternative.

This notion of the possible should not be underestimated. When the Donahues talked about their beliefs in aliens, they did not consistently argue that these theories *are* true; they simply argued that they were *possible*. This also explains the appeal of the visual media they chose to watch. As Eric noted when describing why he sought out programs on the supernatural and on aliens:

ERIC: The reason I like them so much is because things they write about could actually happen.
INTERVIEWER: *Could,* or do you think they *did?*
ERIC: There's a possibility, I mean, it's *possible*. Theologically, scientifically, and everything else, it's *possible*.

Jodie, likewise, noted that she liked programs that provided a "new outlook on what *could* be happening," because, as she had stated earlier in the interview, "I think there's a lot more out there than we actually realize."

While the interest in aliens might seem bizarre to some, it is important to see it in the context of a culture that simultaneously embraces religious identity while regarding as optional the active participation in particular religious communities. This relates to the skepticism some have toward institutionalized Christianity and its leaders. At the same time, the increasing pluralism of the U.S. religious landscape has further undermined the organizations that formerly held religious authority in the United States. We as a society are less attracted to an orthodoxy that appeals to a centralized institutional authority. At the same time, however, we continue to be a society interested in scientific proof, and in the relationship between the material world and whatever lies beyond. So it is not the theological statements of elders or authorities that are important to us. What is important and interesting, to some of us at least, are the questions, the "what ifs," the possibilities—especially if there are "facts" that suggest that, as Jodie said, "there's more out there than we realize." As the institutions of religion are viewed by many in U.S. society as marginal to vital religious and spiritual beliefs, these institutions, and the orthodoxies they represent, have increasingly been called into question. In the Donahues' case, we can see that skepticism is not directed so much at God and supernatural beings, per se, as the theories of secularization had predicted. Instead, the skepticism is for the institutions and their historic beliefs.[20]

The questioning of these beliefs is not unique to persons of disadvantaged backgrounds like the Donahues; it cuts across the axes of socioeconomic background as well as age, gender, and race. Questioning the religious "givens" is an important aspect of the religious identity of the contemporary United States, a trend that historians say has its roots in the religious pluralism undergirding the country's beginnings.[21] As questioning has become foundational for what we might call religious beliefs, the media, in their ability to articulate and symbolize what might be "possible," then hold the potential for becoming more centrally important in how we think about religion, as well. Indeed, recent research in neighboring Canada suggests that greater religious belief is strongly associated with greater belief in the paranormal, affirming earlier research on the topic in the United States.[22]

It would be an overstatement to claim that the media are changing all of religion through depictions of the offbeat and unexplained. What we can argue instead is more subtle: it is not that the visual media themselves are so persuasive that viewers are "duped" into blithely accepting everything they see—even fictional representations—as the truth. We all know from our own experiences as television and film viewers that certain depictions fall flat while others seem to ring true. The question regarding the Donahues' interpretations then becomes not "Why are they so gullible?" or "What should be done about the persuasive powers of the visual media?" but "What factors make certain depictions of the visual media resonate with their experiences?" The answer to this question lies not in this household's economic background, but in their sense of alienation from middle-class and elite culture's norms. This relationship is highlighted in a review of the Pickerington family.

FROM THE COMFORTABLE SEAT OF THE NEW MIDDLE CLASS: THE PICKERINGTONS

"My biggest complaint with *The X-Files* is that they're too damned short," stated John, the stepfather of Jake Pickerington, introduced in chapter 5. The Pickeringtons were a family of teenage *X-Files* fans blended by a second marriage, which included Jake and his sister, Wendy, and three brothers from the stepfather's previous marriage, Don, Brad, and Curt. Like the Donahues, the Pickeringtons watched many programs on the supernatural, from *Unsolved Mysteries* to documentaries on Roswell, New Mexico. And like the Donahues, they too placed a value on remaining "open" to various possibilities when it came to the supernatural. Sounding a lot like Jodie Donahue, thirteen-year-old Curt Pickerington explained that he liked *The X-Files* because "I like to think there's stuff out there that we don't know about."

Yet the Pickeringtons occupied a much different place in the social stratum from the Donahues. With his lucrative construction job and her salary as a longtime teacher, the Pickerington parents earned a high income and lived in a desirable suburban section of their city. Despite their income and living situation, however, the Pickerington parents still found themselves at odds with what they considered the liberal norms of elite culture. In some ways, this revealed a particular dimension of the relationship of class and status in the United States, as their careers provided a lower social status than that of professionals who earn similar incomes.[23] Jake's stepfather was clearly troubled by the lower social status which he believed others assigned to his work, and he expressed this in relation to a perceived tension between small business owners like himself and policymakers that he assumed belonged to a higher-status profession. He rejected the perceived liberalism of policies that he believed undermined his interests as a small businessman. He belonged to a national organization that monitored political issues relating to small businesses, and he was angered by what he believed were the discriminatory ways that small businessmen were portrayed in the media: "Be a middle-aged white male business owner in this country today, and you are the greediest, evilest bastard that ever walked the face of this earth. I mean, you really are. When was the last time you saw something on TV that made corporate America out to be anything but evil? We're all bad guys, we're all greedy, you know, nothing is ever said about the fact that we employ about 70 percent of the nation's workers. I don't know, I really shouldn't go there, because I get fired up. But yes, there are a lot of things that offend me." Jake's stepfather saw himself as marginalized by such representations in the media and the beliefs about small businessmen that he felt were widespread throughout the society. He was angered by the things he saw in the news media that he believed were "totally made up," and frustrated when politicians and other leaders failed to take seriously either the needs or the contributions that he believed men like him made to society. He felt the news often veiled or misconstrued what was "actually" happening in favor of what he saw as a more "liberal," or anti–small business, viewpoint. In his view, the media reflected the prejudices of many governmental agency workers, which is why he felt it was so important to belong to a special-interest group that disseminated what he considered to be more objective information. Jake's stepfather's interest in aliens, like that of the Donahues, must be seen as in some ways related to a sense that the government and other culturally authoritative sources cannot be trusted to tell us the whole truth.

None of the Pickeringtons had been involved in organized religion for a long time. Much as we saw with the Donahue household, there was a relationship between what Jake's stepfather viewed in the visual media and what he believed regarding the realm beyond this world:

JAKE'S STEPFATHER: I do find that fascinating. Especially the alien thing. But for me, if these aliens have the ability to travel the billions of miles through space, if they wanted to own us, they'd own us already. So I think they're just observing. And you know, with as many spottings and unexplained things, there has to be something going on.

INTERVIEWER: Yeah, the whole Roswell thing's been really interesting.

CURT, JAKE, JAKE'S STEPFATHER: Oh, yeah!

JAKE'S STEPFATHER: Talk about having no explanation for something! And expecting us to buy into something that's flimsy at best! It's pretty amazing. But I'm not frightened by it. It doesn't—I don't know, maybe it should, but it doesn't make me nervous.

CURT: I'm not scared of it.

JAKE'S MOTHER: I don't want to be zapped up there!

JAKE'S STEPFATHER: No, I think when you get into the part where they might be inseminating women and inhabiting the planet that way, that's a little frightening, and that, you know, that would be the one reason that I would be nervous about it, but, I don't know.

When I was in the midst of this interview with the Pickeringtons, I have to admit to some surprise at hearing Jake's stepfather repeating some of the same science fiction legends articulated earlier by the Donahues. Furthermore, given what I had thought at the time was the low-culture status of alien legends in the wider culture and his aspirations toward an economic position within the upper middle class, I had expected that Jake's stepfather might attempt to draw a distinction between his own beliefs and those of the "fictional" programs of television. Yet instead of denying the plausibility of these stories, he denied that he was nervous about them—a quite different strategy. His statements demonstrate that there is more than "just" entertainment and the suspension of disbelief going on here. After all, why would he be nervous about it at all if it weren't possibly true, either for him or for those to whom he would defend himself?

Jake's stepfather demonstrates that at this point in history, it may be acceptable for some members of the middle class to include aliens in the list of what is possible beyond the material world. It also highlights the fact that despite certain economic and social resources, or a combination of cultural and social capital, people like Jake's stepfather may continue to feel alienated from certain legitimized positions and hence may find appealing the challenge to authority implicit in many of the programs and films about aliens.[24] Surprisingly, and not unlike the Donahues, the Pickeringtons were able to look to the media and find fictional stories about aliens that seemed plausible, or at least interesting to consider and not to be rejected outright.

Despite the similarities, there were some interesting differences between the Pickerington and Donahue families when it came to how they discussed issues of religion, the supernatural, and their representation in the media. As is no doubt often true with this kind of research, the most striking differences were probably evident as soon as I walked out their doors and they turned to talk to each other about their experiences.

I interviewed each of these families on two separate occasions, as I did with all the interviews conducted as a part of the larger research project that was foundational for this book. This two-stage method meant that upon my return, I sometimes could tell that the initial interview had prompted further conversation among the members of the households. While we had talked mostly about television programs, films, and viewing practices in my first visit with the Donahues, during my second visit I was regaled with stories of individual experiences with the supernatural. In separate interviews I heard about the ghosts, angels, and aliens that various members of the household had encountered or wished they would encounter. Clearly, they saw me as someone interested in their supernatural experiences and wanted to talk with me about these intriguing encounters.

Things were different with the Pickeringtons, however. Upon my return to their home, Jake's mother told me outright that my earlier visit had prompted a discussion about their lack of involvement in organized religion. Jake's step-father, who had been raised Catholic, had acknowledged to her that he felt he had failed his boys by not introducing them to religion. Jake's mother, having participated in evangelical Protestant churches up until her divorce when her children were quite young, agreed but had stressed to him that it was not too late. Adopting a confessional tone, she told me that she knew they should go to church and that my visit had prompted them to think about returning.

At the time I attributed this difference to the open-ended nature of the in-terviews I had conducted. Upon reflection I think perhaps these different re-sponses to the intervention of a researcher from the nearby university also say something about how the families conceived of themselves vis-à-vis "legiti-mate" culture. As persons experienced in this kind of qualitative research know, the "data" produced in an interview situation have everything to do with the re-lationship between the interviewer and person interviewed. When asked ques-tions about our lives and practices, we all present ourselves to others in a way that reflects the "truth" but also reflects what we want the asker to know about us. It is not that answers are not truthful; it is that every relationship, including that of a researcher and his or her "informant," takes place in a particular con-text, and that context plays a large role in how the content of a conversation is shared. I imagine that perhaps the Donahues, expecting that an educated per-son like me would be skeptical of supernatural claims, wanted to communicate the veracity of their experiences. They may have also interpreted my interest in such matters as a sign of support for beliefs similar to theirs. It is possible, of course, that they saw me as someone easily "duped" and therefore they wove these supernatural stories to shock me, for they may have seen me as a stand-in or representative of the middle class from which they felt alienated. The fact that the experiences were shared in a way that was meant to reveal something of themselves and their lives, however, demonstrated to me that these stories were a part of self-presentation, regardless of how I (or they) evaluated the experi-ences in relation to claims of "truth."

Thus while the Donahues were presenting themselves to me as persons rich in experiences with the "offbeat" supernatural that they believed offered legiti-mate challenges to institutional religion, the Pickeringtons presented them-selves as persons who had regrets about their self-distancing from these insti-tutions. Not coincidentally, organized religion is closer to that which has traditionally been conceived of as legitimate religion—just as the Pickering-tons themselves are closer to a dominant cultural position due to their income and education level.

While the Pickeringtons may feel that they should go to church, the fact is, they don't. But this fact is not explained by "the secularization hypothesis," which proposed that as scientific knowledge increased, the interest in and cul-tural authority of historic institutions of religion would decline.[25] This hy-pothesis might have predicted that a family like the Pickeringtons would not attend church because of its implausible claims about the realm beyond the natural world. But the Pickeringtons' lack of church attendance isn't due to the triumph of reason over faith in any simple way. This family remained fascinated with exactly that which we might have expected them to reject: the inexplicable, the possible, the "what if" beyond the material world. Science wasn't rejected either, of course; like the Donahues, the Pickeringtons were quite interested in the "scientific evidence" supporting what might be possible in the realm beyond the material world. Religious institutions do not hold exclusive claim to "legitimate" conversation about the supernatural; various thoughts about the unexplained can be legitimized through the marshaling of scientific evidence, whether it is presented in a convincing documentary form or even, as we saw with the Donahues, in a work of fiction that seems to ring true. As the narratives of *The X-Files* suggested, the "legitimate," acceptable posture toward beliefs in religion and the supernatural today is one of searching out possibilities, often outside the walls of organized religion: "The truth is out there."

It was interesting to me that in contrast to the Donahues' multiple experiences of supernatural occurrences, the Pickerington teens could not come up with a single personal experience with ghosts or demons, although some of the teens articulated "guardian angel" stories. This is not insignificant, given the fact that the Donahues' experiences with the world would be less positive than the Pickeringtons. The powerlessness they had experienced was reflected in their attraction to the supernatural and experiences with it. They had little vested interest in portraying themselves as aligned with the "legitimate" culture's respect for institutional religion or with its kinder, gentler supernatural experiences with guardian angels.

The Pickeringtons did, however.

ANGELS IN THE MEDIA: RESPONSES TO *TOUCHED BY AN ANGEL*

While belief in aliens is arguably at the margins of what is deemed acceptable or legitimate according to the norms of dominant culture, Judeo-Christian beliefs are so widely accepted as legitimate (and so strongly associated with the historic institutions of organized religion) that they are not perceived as a threat to the status quo. Angels, therefore, are acceptable to a variety of people, across lines of class, racial/ethnic background, gender, and within the various forms of Christianity in the United States. It is no surprise, therefore, that they have become a very popular and highly commodified object. As journalist Rita Ciolli notes, "There are angel cookbooks, angel perfume, angel champagne flutes, angel pasta, angel pins, even angel water."[26]

As was the case with aliens, recent decades have seen an increase in belief in angels. According to national polls, 72 percent of the general population and 76 percent of teens believe in angels. In 1978, only 56 percent of the general population and 64 percent of teens reported belief.[27] Like most in the United States, members of the Donahue and Pickerington households expressed interest in these guardians from the realm beyond.

As noted earlier, *Touched by an Angel* successfully popularized guardian angels in a way rarely seen on prime-time television in the last decade of the twentieth century and the beginning of the twenty-first. I therefore discussed it with many people and even viewed an episode with a few groups of parents and teens. Every week, *Touched by an Angel* articulated a story of ordinary people who were being cared for and guided by beings that they later discovered to be angels. And every week, those ordinary people were told, "God loves you." This heartwarming series was watched regularly by Sarah Donahue and occasionally by members of the Pickerington family. Jake Pickerington's mother said she wished she could have watched this program more frequently, because "I truly know that there are angels out there, I believe there are."

This television program's appeal crossed lines of income, class, racial/ethnic background, and to a lesser extent, age (while it occasionally won its time period with younger audiences, it was consistently successful in garnering audience members in the forty-five-plus age group).[28] Within some limits, therefore, it is clear that the program successfully articulated what many in the United States believed, or at least wished to believe, about angels.

Still, sometimes the responses to the program were surprising. While angels are widely accepted, television rarely is. This led me to expect that some would object to the program outright out of a belief that television always cheapens its subject matter or renders it superficial. When I watched an episode of *Touched by an Angel* with a group of well-educated parents whose household incomes were each well above $70,000, I had expected that they would be skeptical of the program because of its sentimentality, as sentimental melodrama is often a marker of "low culture" in television programs.[29] Yet after an episode was shown, the women asked for the tissue box to be passed around. Echoing the comments of the Pickeringtons, and also the narrative of the program, one high-income Anglo-American respondent said, "Maybe I've got an angel that watches over me. I've been fairly amazed sometimes that the things that have happened to me have turned out."

Parents from less affluent positions also affirmed this belief. As one lower-income Anglo-American single parent told me: "I'm religious, so I do believe in angels, and I do think there's always a reason, God always has a reason, even if it doesn't make sense at the time. You might say, 'Why am I given this cross to carry?' But it makes sense later in life." Another lower-income single parent, this one from a Mexican American Catholic background, agreed, equating the angels of the program with her belief that "God's always there, no matter what."

The most common response to the program was that parents of teens liked its "moral messages."[30] Not coincidentally, in a national survey *Touched by an Angel* was reportedly one of the top shows parents across the United States encouraged their teens to watch.[31] Despite negative initial reviews from television critics and CBS's plans to cancel the program after the first six episodes, the response to *Touched by an Angel* has been overwhelming. *Christianity Today* magazine reported that CBS had received more than 30,000 letters and phone calls asking that the show be continued after its initial run in 1994.[32] During the 1996–97 season and continuing for the next four television seasons, *Touched by an Angel* was the second-most-watched drama in the United States after *ER*, garnering an estimated weekly viewing audience of more than 20 million.[33] The program received more than two thousand fan letters a week, many of which were addressed to the program's angel characters rather than to the actors who played them.[34] Additionally, the unofficial *Touched by an Angel* Web site received nearly seven thousand visitors a month in 1997.[35] The program's ratings and popularity made it the centerpiece of CBS's financial success in the late 1990s and the early part of the new millennium. The success of this program, and the consensus that surrounds its acceptance, indicates that *Touched by an Angel* echoes a set of consensually agreed-upon ideas concerning religion and spirituality today.[36] This is consistent with recent polls that have found that somewhere between 50 and 70 percent of persons in the United States believe in angels.[37]

Despite their widespread acceptance, a few people interviewed saw these friendly and moral angels as a threat to organized religion and their own beliefs. For instance, John Hart, a conservative evangelical father of a teen and two preteens, expressed concern about *Touched by an Angel*, asserting that it was not "religious" according to his expectations:

INTERVIEWER: So, you wouldn't call [*Touched by an Angel*] a religious show?
JOHN: Well, it's . . . sort of a generalization of God. Looking for some
    higher power, or a New Age thing. To me, that's a dangerous thing, too,
    . . . It makes people think, "Oh, but it makes me feel good." . . . I think
    true religion, if it were broadcast on TV, and it was up front, not dis-
    guised in different ways, I think people would be offended.
INTERVIEWER: Because it wouldn't be their particular belief, or it's just
    hard to—
JOHN: Because part of religion is to face the truth that we're all sinners.
    People in general don't like to hear that.[38]

According to John, *Touched by an Angel* was not religious because it did not present the doctrine, key in evangelical Christian tradition, that individuals must recognize their sinfulness and seek forgiveness. Apparently, this must have been a fairly common objection to the program, for the official Web site of *Touched by an Angel* included a response to the question, "Why doesn't the program mention Jesus Christ or a plan for salvation?" in its answers to frequently asked questions. The Web page offered this reply: "While Martha Williamson [the television program's executive producer] shares your personal beliefs, CBS's mandate for our show is that we entertain on a GLOBAL scale. This is why you won't find the plan of salvation mentioned. Still, we hope you enjoy the show and will continue to support us. We appreciate your comments and concerns."[39] Despite John Hart's objection that *Touched by an Angel* did not articulate what he felt was an important aspect of his religious beliefs, he and his family still watched the television program regularly. His wife and teen son mentioned its "morals" and the fact that at least "it's got somebody looking to God for help" as two reasons why they believed that despite their reservations, it was a worthwhile program for family viewing.

Others in less conservatively oriented religious traditions expressed similar concerns about the program's "watering down" of Christianity and its appeal to sentimentality.[40] Some saw angels in general as dangerous distractions that have arisen because "people have trouble believing in God," as one seminary professor wrote.[41] Still, John's response to the program was relatively uncommon among evangelical Christians. The more common enthusiastic response to the program, found across classes, racial/ethnic groups, and religious affiliations, may have had its roots in the publication of Billy Graham's book *Angels*, which took flight on the best-seller lists in 1975, long before the television program appeared. Angels have held an important place in evangelical faith traditions at least since that time, although evidence suggests that their appeal to the faithful goes back much further and crosses many religious traditions.

Interestingly, others less committed to organized religion occasionally saw the angels in the popular television program as a challenge to, or improvement over, what they understood to be organized religion. At one point, I had asked one of my teen interviewees, Elizabeth Farley, to hold a discussion group about the angels in *Touched by an Angel* with her friends, some of whom were religiously affiliated but many of whom were not. Elizabeth herself was religiously affiliated but was not a Traditionalist; she was introduced earlier as a teen intrigued by the realm beyond this world. In the group discussion, Elizabeth was surprised to find that even some of those who were not involved in organized religion found the program appealing. She also found that angels seemed plausible to several of them:

ELIZABETH: Okay, how was [the program] different from what you think or believe?

ABBIE [no religious background]: It wasn't.

TRACY [no religious background]: I don't know. It just was.

VICKIE [marginally religious]: I don't think angels would be that—"I am an angel!" I don't think they'd do that.

LISA [religious]: They did for Mary.

VICKIE [marginally religious]: Well, I know, but. First of all, if they did that, who would believe them?

ELIZABETH [religious]: You know, Virgin Mary?

ABBIE [not religious]: When, like—

ELIZABETH: One person at a time [take turns speaking]!

TRACY [not religious, but regular viewer of the program]: I take it back. I think this show is more what I think God is like than like—the Bible. [laughter]

ABBIE [not religious]: Oh, I'd better scoot away from Lisa [a religious person] here!

TRACY [not religious, but a viewer]: No, but seriously! No, actually, I think this show's portrayal of God, and I think that's more true, that he just likes people, and he loves them, and stuff like that?

ABBIE [not religious, agreeing]: Rather than we have to be sin-free.

TRACY [not religious]: Yeah.

VICKIE [marginally religious]: I don't know.

TRACY [not religious]: 'Cause I think that like all religions are good.

The teens with some religious background seemed to struggle to articulate their belief in angels and to justify this belief with reference to their religious tradition (specifically, the claim that an angel appeared to Mary at the Annunciation). This reference may have been unclear to those with no religious background, but more likely it did not enhance the argument for the existence of angels for those who doubted this. It may also be that some of the girls were objecting to the program not based on its representation of angels, but based on their sense that it was overly sentimental or designed to appeal to an audience older than they were. Then Tracy, the young woman who never attended religious services but was a regular viewer *of Touched by an Angel*, made what her friends considered a strong statement of belief that validated the program's portrayal of angels and by extension, of God. She said, "I think this show is more what I think God is like than like—the Bible." The exchange that followed this declaration shows that the girls were able to recognize that her statement might be construed as a challenge to the organized religion of Christianity. The girls recognized the controversial nature of the statement by laughing and indicating that they would expect one of the church-attending group members to be angered or offended by the statement. Then Tracy continued, "Actually, I think this show's portrayal of God, and I think that's more true, that he just likes people, and he loves them, and stuff like that?" Abbie, a young woman who also had no religious background, agreed, adding, "Rather than we have to be sin-free." Chiming in with Tracy's statement, Abbie offered a more direct challenge to evangelical Christianity's emphasis on sin. Tracy then concluded with another statement related to this tradition, noting her belief that "all religions are good"—a direct challenge to evangelical Christianity's claims to exclusive religious authority.

Conflicting interpretations of angels and of the popular television program that featured them, as demonstrated in these examples, only occurred either when persons were aligned with religious institutions and saw the guardian angels depicted in the program as a threat to orthodoxy, or when persons with little vested interest in organized religion highlighted their skepticism regarding the right of religious organizations to define orthodoxy. Others—and there is reason to believe that this constitutes consensual opinion in the United States—saw angels, both in the popular television program and elsewhere, as benign and positive expressions of the role of goodness in the universe.

ANGELS, ALIENS, BELIEFS, AND THE MEDIA

We have seen that aliens and angels are, for the most part, discussed in very different ways. Aliens are discussed in the context of television programs, film plots, and entertainment in general. Angels, even when brought into the conversation in the context of entertainment, tend to be discussed in broader terms connected with the beliefs and practices of everyday life. Aliens were discussed in terms of science and government, focusing on issues of "proof," "evidence," or challenges to governmentally sanctioned explanations. Angels, on the other hand, were spoken of as "inspirational," "helpful," and, among most research participants at least, generally related to (rather than seen as a challenge to) organized religion.

Influential voices of governance and of religion, not surprisingly, treat the two phenomena quite differently. While governmental leaders see angels as strictly religious and therefore completely outside of their realms of interest and jurisdiction, the government has historically been quite concerned about the conspiracy theories that are abound with respect to aliens, which arose in the context of the Cold War and concerns about national security. Similarly, while religious leaders see aliens as perhaps politicized but definitely outside their realm of interest, religious leaders have historically been quite concerned about "angel worship" and what various groups might consider unorthodox beliefs concerning angels.[42]

Both the government and religious organizations see themselves as having an authoritative cultural voice, and both, in different ways, are threatened by patterns of belief about angels and aliens. The challenge arises from the fact that a large number of people from various walks of life in U.S. society are willing to consider the possibility that these beings exist. Sometimes, as in the case of those who live in Nancy Donahue's house, considering this possibility is closely related to a rejection of governmental authority and its claim to the right to lead, just as some statements concerning angels, such as those of the nonaffiliated girls in the teen discussion group, challenge the right of certain religious organizations to make exclusive claims to truth. Admittedly, the question of whether angels or aliens exist is often entertained not in serious or self-conscious pursuit of political or religious consciousness, but in the playful attitudes with which audiences approach the fictional stories of the entertainment media. As the entertainment media appeal to this desire for considering the "what if?" speculations about the realm beyond, they inadvertently contribute to these popularly expressed challenges to religious and governmental authority. In this sense, the entertainment media echo the culture's current "common sense" of questioning such authority, while also drawing upon and recasting historically potent legends of the supernatural into new and highly appealing forms.

The tendency, expressed among the Donahues, to see "official" religion as aligned with the elite is, as religious historian Vittorio Lanternari has argued, part of a response to the dominant culture from a disadvantaged position in the social strata.[43] Lanternari believes that such a position propels people toward participation in new religious movements that can be "a means of establishing a positive social identity for the oppressed."[44] On the other hand, not all persons are motivated to join movements. The teens in this and the preceding chapters were content to confine explorations of the supernatural to the realm of entertainment while going about the business of their everyday lives. This reflects a second possible alternative, one that has been argued by Max Weber, Ernst Troeltsch, and H. Richard Niebuhr: as time goes on and persons and their descendants move through differing social and economic positions relative to the society at large, certain beliefs once deemed delegitimated become associated increasingly with the dominant classes.[45] This occurs not because beliefs, such as those in aliens, suddenly become more plausible. Instead, conversations about aliens become more legitimated as more and more people question the right of certain societal organizations—namely, those of the government and religion—to authoritatively define the "truth" for everyone.

As the example of the Pickeringtons shows, contrary to popular characterizations of alien enthusiasts, there is no necessary connection between interest in these issues and income level or education. In fact, there is historical precedent for intellectuals in particular to be interested in the "offbeat" or delegitimated forms of the supernatural. Bradford Verter, a religious historian and expert on the rise of the occult, has pointed out that what we today call the occult traditions—such as tarot card reading, séances, and levitation—were first patronized by intellectuals.[46] Moreover, historian Herbert Leventhal makes the point that there is no evidence that ordinary people historically found beliefs and practices of occult incompatible with Christian teachings.[47] While we know that evangelical preachers in the eighteenth century (as today) equated occultic activities and witchcraft with the devil, most people saw such practices as evidence that ordinary people could draw upon supernatural power.

We have seen that taste does not predictably follow economic status with respect to the appeal of fictional stories of the supernatural and paranormal realms. Instead, these examples show that self-perception in relation to dominant culture is a significant factor of such appeal. If a person feels alienated from dominant ideas, stories presented by the entertainment media, such as those dealing with aliens and angels, may appeal to this sense of alienation. This does not necessarily mean that alienated persons are more likely to consider aliens or angels to be fact—although that is a point for future research. It does suggest, however, that persons who see themselves as alienated (even, as in the case of the Pickerington family, when they have higher income and education levels), may enjoy considering what is possible, as it offers an implicit challenge to the government or religion from which they feel alienated. The other side of this argument is that the people whom we might therefore expect to be least interested in the possibility that aliens exist are those most committed to either governance or religion. This makes for an interesting and ironic marriage of religionists, politicians, and scientific skeptics, as all dismiss aliens out of hand but from very different perspectives.

The implication of this for young people is that those who are not completely committed to religion, politics, or skeptical scientific inquiry—and there is reason to believe that this characterizes the majority of contemporary teens—may instead find resonance with the culturally acceptable position of questioning the status quo, in the realms of government and religion among others. Consequently, they are also likely to find "the possible" appealing in the entertainment media and may increasingly find media presentations to be not only entertaining, but also plausible. As these stories indirectly echo serious questions of societal institutions, they provide a symbolic means by which young people—and people of all ages—can cope with feelings of their own powerlessness within the society and beyond.

10

THE DARK SIDE

OF EVANGELICALISM

AND THE RELIGION

OF THE POSSIBLE

More than a century ago, Mark Twain wryly commented on the U.S. religious scene of his day: "The gospel of Christ came filtered down to nineteenth-century Americans through stage plays and through the despised novels and Christmas story, rather than from the drowsy pulpit."[1] Today, as then, central beliefs concerning the realm beyond this world and the afterlife come from many, often unexpected sources. Certainly, formal religious organizations continue to be one source of beliefs and values for some young people. But young people also derive their views from their parents and other family members, from their friends, from their associations with various groups, and from the media.[2] This is especially true, of course, for the young people with the least interest in formal religion, or those "marginal members" who claim some affiliation yet have limited exposure to religious traditions.

Historically, the mass media have been associated with religious change in at least two important ways. First, the invention of the printing press established an alternative center of power that challenged the church's authority to define the issues that were expressed to the public. This was the press's foundational role in the Reformation, as it contributed to diminishing the centralized cultural authority of the church. Eventually, this resulted in the emergence of the idea of "personal autonomy": the view, enshrined in the U.S. constitution, that individuals have the right and the freedom to decide for themselves what they will believe and practice in the realm of religion.[3]

Second, the media, and the entertainment media in particular, have played a role in religious change in a fundamental way, as well. Since fictional stories first achieved wide circulation in the Victorian era, those responsible for publishing these works have exercised the authority to determine which stories would be treated respectfully as "religious" and which were appropriately fictionalized as "superstitions." Since that time, the entertainment media have signaled that certain stories, notably those pertaining to the realm beyond this world, should not be taken seriously.

Twain's observation reminds us that what we have observed in this book is hardly new. I have attempted to illustrate, however, the contours of the specific "structure of feeling" in which today's young people are articulating their beliefs, colored as it is by a context of religious change defined by an increased public presence for conservative Protestant evangelicalism, an increasingly multicultural and religiously plural group of peers, and a sophisticated media system that seeks to appeal specifically to young people. These are only a few factors of the contemporary situation. Globalization, heightened concerns about terrorism, and increased immigration have placed concern about religious beliefs in the forefront of everyone's minds, including young people. Meanwhile, the spread of capitalist markets supported by the burgeoning advertising and media industries, as well as the human and civil rights movements associated with feminism, racial/ethnic identity, sexual orientation, and other previously unrecognized groups, have allowed for multiple "centers of value" with which young people might identify and from which they may glean insights into the realm beyond this world.[4]

I began this book by questioning the direction of media influence in relation to religion and supernatural beliefs. I noted that while it might seem that some young people find the images and stories of the entertainment media persuasive, the fact that such depictions belong to the realm of entertainment signal to most that such things should not be taken seriously at all. This theme runs through the five different approaches to the entertainment media, supernatural beliefs, and religion that emerged among the teens I talked with. Certainly, the young people I termed Traditionalists did not feel that the supernatural stories of the entertainment media were to be taken seriously in any way. The young people and their parents who were most closely related to religious traditions consistently said that they believed there was a great difference between their religious tradition and what they saw in the culture around them, including popular culture. Yet as we have seen, it is not always so easy to make such distinctions, since teen popular culture draws upon the stories of our shared culture and traditions, including those from the country's religious heritage. This, in part, explains why it was difficult for some of the teens I termed Intrigued to understand these supposed distinctions between the stories of religion and those of entertainment. Nevertheless, the Intrigued teens, too, recognized that stories of the supernatural in the media were supposed to be understood like fantasy.

The young people I termed Experimenters at first seem like they may be taking the supernatural stories more seriously than most, as they were interested in trying out different methods of contacting the realm beyond through spell-casting and séances. Yet these activities were pursued for fun and titillation for the most part, not necessarily out of a desire for spiritual transcendence or for the invocation of evil. Their practices of the supernatural related more to entertainment and fantasy than to religion (although, as we saw in those stories, the two are not unrelated and are articulated in relation to one another in the stories of these young people). The Mysticals, who weren't as proactive in seeking out such experiences as the Experimenters, similarly brought their religious beliefs into the context of leisure activities among their friends and family, such as in conversations about legend trips, guardian angels, and contact with deceased spirits. They were less interested in religion than the others, which seemingly made it possible for them to consider the stories and terms of religion and those of fantasy as interchangeable.

Finally, the Resisters also viewed the stories of the supernatural as fantastic. Like the Mysticals, they saw the stories of religion and fantasy as interchangeable. Yet unlike the laissez-faire attitude of the Mysticals, the Resisters seemed to recognize that claiming a relationship between God and aliens was a challenge to dominant culture and its ideology, which takes for granted religion's connection with goodness and justice.

If the message of media education and media literacy has been that young people need to learn to recognize the distinctions between reality and fantasy, we may safely conclude that young people from across a spectrum of beliefs seem to get it. Yet these issues are complicated by increasingly vocal concerns about what were once considered "harmless" teen slumber-party and drinking-related experiments with such things as Ouija boards, levitation, séances, and legend tripping. While not long ago these practices might have been dismissed as merely entertainment or "parlor games," today they are practiced in the shadow of evangelicalism's values. As a result, some teens may be intentionally participating in these activities as a direct challenge to that religious tradition's collusion with dominant positions in U.S. culture, as we saw among the Resisters.[5] Not that most teens engage in these practices to thumb their noses at that religious tradition, of course. They do these things because they are fun and titillating. But what makes them so is their association with danger and their flouting of conventional norms. As we saw in both the Experimenter and Resister teens, their interests in such dark or "funky" practices were often interpreted by teens as associated with rebellion. Recall the pleasure the Experimenter girls, Annae and Katie Gardner and Lily Dearborn, took in being viewed as dangerous by their peers. The practices and beliefs these girls engaged in were seen as an affront to religious traditions—and especially to conservative religious traditions.

The interpretation of formerly "harmless" teen practices as rebellious toward religious traditions in particular (as opposed to adult norms more generally) seems to me to be fairly new—or at least a recent recovery of a very old theme. It has become more common as evangelicalism has become more vocal in its condemnation of such activities as related to the "occult" or "dark arts." It may be that these practices will hold even more appeal for certain teens as the protests against them continue to accelerate. Rebelling against established traditions, after all, is practically a hallmark of teen behavior.

Still, based on the research reported in this book I wouldn't predict that many young people will decide to convert to Wiccan or neo-Pagan religions because of their interest in what they have seen in the television program *Charmed* or the Harry Potter films, among other such stories. There is a difference, as folklorist Bill Ellis has pointed out, between those practices that simply challenge the existing status quo, like the teen use of Ouija boards and spell-casting that appear in those entertainment stories, and practices that are grounded in a desire for an alternative worldview, such as joining a coven or the celebration of the equinox, to take the Wiccan example.[6] Because evangelicals are concerned about the "dark side" or the possibility that contacts with evil spirits might occur through means such as séances or Ouija boards, they may be less worried about whether teens approach those things out of a serious quest for religious meaning or simply out of play. The acts themselves, evangelicals believe, have consequences and mere participation puts the teens in serious danger, regardless of their attitudes. Yet ironically, by drawing attention to what they believe to be the consequences of such practices, evangelicals may actually be inciting *more* teens to engage in them. This is yet another example of how evangelicalism has been successful in introducing its definition of and concerns about evil into the public consciousness, and how it loses control of what happens once that definition gets woven into the culture. Young people may not be participating in such activities because they believe they are "evil," as evangelicals and more conservative Christian groups would define them; rather, they are participating as a way to protest the cultural authority that those groups lay claim to. Nevertheless, those who define such behaviors as connected to evil are bound to express their anxiety—thus continuing the cycle by setting themselves up in a position of cultural authority against which teens will choose to rebel. All of this calls into question the presumed persuasive or imitative "effects" of the media in this regard. To put it provocatively, it may be that the ascendance of evangelicalism in U.S. culture, rather than the entertainment media alone, has provided the incentive for teens like the Experimenters and Resisters to engage in these practices.

PLURALISM AND THE OPENNESS TO POSSIBILITY

The stories in this book demonstrate that young people bring to their media experiences certain beliefs regarding the realm beyond the material world. In most cases they do not consciously seek information about the supernatural from the media and are unlikely to have their minds changed about what they do believe based upon what they see there. Yet while there seem to be many differences in the specifics, many young audience members do seem to embrace one belief that may best be described as an openness to possibility.[7] Because many seem to accept the idea that beliefs about the supernatural are fluid rather than fixed and not particularly consequential in any case, possible contradictions are not viewed as a problem if they are noticed at all.

The entertainment media play upon this openness to and interest in possibilities: What if angels were to pose as humans, giving advice and support during difficult moments? What if aliens were to breed with humans, creating a hybrid race? What if humans could have supernatural powers that allowed them to fight evil? What if loved ones could return from the dead to bring peace and closure for those still living? What if ghosts could return to right the wrongs done them in their lifetimes? Each of these story lines addresses the realm beyond and presents a fantasy that, to varying degrees and whether consciously or not, draws upon issues traditionally considered religious. Stories of this sort enter today's plural religious landscape and compete or coexist with other stories, such as those from religious traditions, that may be viewed as equally possible and plausible—or equally fictional.

In the context of U.S. culture, where the taken-for-granted stance is one of openness to possibility, stories that tie the supernatural to a specific religious tradition are out of favor. The stories that explicitly embrace religious language and definitions are often rejected by persons who are not already members of those traditions.[8] Audiences, thus, do not approach the media completely open to all possibilities; those not greatly interested in religion are not interested in stories where the possibilities are limited to religion. While they may consider stories from the entertainment media in relation to their religious beliefs, most may be unlikely to abandon their commitment to an openness to possibilities.

The increasingly multicultural and religiously plural environment in which today's teens live influences their approach to religion and contributes to this openness to possibilities.[9] Tolerance for religious and racial difference is the encouraged ideal that young people encounter everywhere, from their schools to their parents to the media. And while many teens continue to form primary associations with those whose backgrounds are much like their own, most believe that all religions are equally good and have their own merit.[10]

Unfortunately, this tolerance of difference is not based in knowledge or a desire for understanding. While young people say that they believe all religions are equally good, they often know little about the tradition with which they identify themselves, let alone the traditions of others.[11] If the stories of their own tradition are largely seen to be about as relevant as folktales, then it would stand to reason that they are much more likely to view the stories of other traditions in this way. These stories from other traditions, like the stories of the entertainment media, are then open for "possible" consideration as viable beliefs concerning this world and its relationship to the realm beyond.[12]

A related issue arises in relation to the way in which adherence to beliefs has been evaluated in the past. While most of the people I interviewed, both teens and their parents, would not declare that they believed in aliens, ghosts, or the paranormal, many conceded that such events were possible. This is consistent with Roof's observation that when baby boomers were given an opportunity to express doubt about beliefs, they often did so.[13] An important direction in the future study of beliefs, therefore, lies in this exploration of uncertainty and openness to possibility.[14] Future research might benefit from the rephrasing of survey questions, asking not only "Do you believe in *X*?", but also "Do you believe that *Y* is possible?" This might enable us to better understand this emergent sense of uncertainty and how its appeal is upheld in relation to fictional stories of the supernatural.

"RELIGIOUS" AND "SECULAR" IDENTITIES

This, then, raises the question, Are young people taking the stories of religion less seriously today than they have in the past? This study was largely interpretive and based on a relatively small number of young people. It cannot speak to which approaches to religion and supernatural beliefs are most common among today's young people, or which might be bellwethers for the future. Certainly, the statistics suggest that many young people place themselves in the camp here identified as Traditionalist, whether they are evangelical Protestant, conservative or charismatic Roman Catholic, or affiliated with Sunni Muslim or conservative Jewish traditions, among others. Many young people who identify themselves with these groups take religion very seriously and celebrate its apparently growing influence in U.S. culture.

As we have seen, however, many people who do not embrace conservative religious practices and identities share in the critique that the media have a negative effect on culture. It is interesting, therefore, to note both the Traditionalists' emphasis upon morality as a distinction to which they hold special claim, and their self-presentation as a "subculture," which understates their position both numerically and with reference to the U.S. culture's historic relationship with religious values, particularly those of Protestantism.[15] Ironically, the distinctiveness of their perspective is not nearly as distinct as they might wish. This may explain why some, like those here termed the Intrigued teens, claim an identification with religious organizations yet have trouble drawing the strict lines of separation between mediated and religious stories that seem so clear to the Traditionalist teens. Separating out those I identify as Traditionalist and those who perhaps self-identify that way but also express intrigue with the realm beyond is an interesting question for the future. There are reasons to think that some young people might reveal either their more serious interest in the stuff of the supernatural realm or their less serious commitment to traditional religious beliefs, if offered those options. Whatever the case, it is clear that today's young people are not unilaterally "less" or "more" religious than previous generations, a fact more clearly illustrated in the national statistics on teen beliefs than anything that can be gleaned from a smaller, deeper study such as this.[16] What is interesting about these stories, however, is the blurring of boundaries between beliefs and understandings associated with traditional religions and those more popularly circulated elsewhere—which highlights the unsettled nature of religious life in the United States today.

By looking at how teens interpret stories of the supernatural from the entertainment media, this book has explored when and under what circumstances the boundaries seem to blur. While we have explored interesting areas of overlap from the perspective of the histories of both religion and popular representations in media culture geared for teens, we have not yet explored why all of these teens, even the Resisters, still choose to identify themselves as "religious" or "spiritual," or at least open to the supernatural realm, despite their disdain for organized religion and their recognition that what they see in entertainment media is fantasy. For an explanation, we need to return to the earlier discussion of the status of religion in relation to morality and ideology in the United States. What does it mean to define oneself as secular in the context of a culture in which religion is equated with morality? It seems plausible that teens, like those of other ages, associate secularism with immorality. The discourse of religion in the United States is limited by its prejudices, as those who espouse atheist views can attest.[17] Thus, teens who claim interest in beliefs that are not consistent with organized religion, as well as teens who claim no interest in organized religion, may identify themselves as religious or spiritual as a means of identifying themselves as moral and good people. Because religion and morality are closely entwined in U.S. culture, it may be impossible to separate the two in any discussion of self-identification with religion.

Because my own interest in religion grows out of its historical relation to the struggle against oppression, I was particularly interested, and perhaps even relieved, to find that teens from the worst circumstances seemed to recognize the importance of questioning the way certain views are legitimated through association with religion. Consistent with critical theory, these teens were aware of religion's role as a kind of guardian for ideological commitments that tended to favor the cultural elite. Yet aligning themselves with the "funky" side of religion and its mediated representations did not constitute a form of political resistance.[18] Instead, it was at least one aspect of a worldview that ultimately reinforces their lower social status by resulting in limited access to what sociologist Pierre Bourdieu has termed social and economic capital.[19] Their beliefs alone do not keep them from such attainment, certainly, but they provide reinforcement for their continuing desire to remain marginal to what they view as the unsavory relationship of (legitimated) religion to the "snobs" of suburbia, as one teen put it. Their ambiguity about their own position is again reflected in their reluctance to identify themselves as something other than religious or spiritual. I find this significant, as they are the teens in my study who should have been most likely to eschew those terms.

Religious organizations will, of course, always be about drawing and maintaining boundaries of identity, and in fact my research points to the importance of this project for the maintenance of religious organizations. But I also argue that such boundary-maintenance risks leaving unquestioned the issue of how certain aspects of religion come to be legitimated.

CHOOSING ONE'S BELIEFS AND
THE INDIVIDUALISM OF U.S. CULTURE

Today, parents and their teenage offspring seem to draw on a dizzying array of sources to form their beliefs about the world. But this is where a study of contemporary religion must confront the ideology of individualism that animates so much of American life today. How free are people to choose their own religious practices, from the media or from other locations? This book is ultimately not a celebration of some "semiotic democracy" or postmodern pluralism in which teens are free to make various meanings from the media texts that are available to them and in turn to construct their own religious beliefs.[20] Instead, I have attempted to demonstrate that the choices teens have are limited. The choices these young people made were influenced by their positions and their perceived relation to culture and its resources. Their socioeconomic status, racial/ethnic identity, and gender, along with their friendship circles and family structures, all played a role in how they approached the supernatural realm and what they expected from either it or religion. The young people who seemed most interested in initiating contact with the realm beyond this world were those whose parents had also experimented with things like séances or spent time thinking about visitations from deceased relatives. This consistency between parents and young people was a theme that ran through most of this book. Similarly, gender played a role in the kinds of explorations that seemed interesting, with witchcraft, séances, and angels for girls and hauntings and legend trips for boys. These apparent differences in preferences were seen to be breaking down, however, as gender roles have continued to undergo change. Racial/ethnic identity played a role, too, sometimes as a source of alternative stories (such as the discussion of ancestors among one African American teen and her dance teacher and peers) and at other times in the mention of preferences for certain representations in the media. These kinds of stories illustrated the plurality of religious belief and expression that young people bring to mediated stories, underscoring the fact of a religiously fragmented young population, committed to tolerance perhaps out of necessity while on the whole not all that interested in seeking out information about traditions that differ from their own.

Moreover, the "cultural tool kit" is limited by the taken-for-granted frameworks or hegemonies that each young person lives within, frameworks that reinforce the inequitable distribution of power and capital in U.S. society by favoring those views that privilege those in power over those who do not have it. Examples of this were particularly evident when we considered families at the margins of middle-class life and their different approaches to supernatural beings. While "guardian angels" were sensed by the relatively better-off Pickering-tons, the impoverished Donahues, who also hoped for angelic protection, blamed themselves for not having enough "faith," for example, to win big in the lottery. While the Pickeringtons were intrigued by the possibilities of alien life, the Donahues thought such visitations might be both possible and intrusive. They had experienced such invasive and unwelcome turns of events at other times in their lives, so, essentially, why couldn't they also be oppressed by aliens?

The taken-for-granted beliefs about the supernatural also echo an individualistic approach to the relationship of self, society, and the realm beyond. In each case, the individual experiences (or fears, or hopes for) a powerful intervention that is benign, malevolent, or positive *for the individual*. Elizabeth, for example, speculated that objects such as Ouija boards might be able to cause her to become possessed. Nancy was put at ease about an "evil presence" when she recognized the presence of a guardian angel whom she believed was sent to help her. Jake, the "secular" teen who expressed little interest in religion, also believed in guardian angels, such as on occasions when "you're about to get hit by a car or something" and an intervention of some kind prevents a personal tragedy. While Tammy's dance teacher and friends encouraged her to consider the idea that her ancestors offer similar personal support for her in her dancing, she was afraid that either they or the spirit of her deceased friend might cause her harm. Katie reveled in the idea that her Wiccan beliefs might give her access to personal power, while her sister, Annae, experienced power in a more material way as she was recognized by friends as an expert in the appealing dark arts. Eric, Jodie, and some of their friends at times expressed a wish that they could be participants in an alien abduction and on other occasions told stories of guardian angels they, too, had experienced. In all of these cases and many more not detailed here, teens seemed to equate the supernatural realm with a story line of intervention from somewhere else (whether heaven, hell, or outer space) that played out only in the lives of the individuals whom the occurrence touched.

Third, and perhaps most obviously, young people's choices with respect to religious beliefs were also limited by what the entertainment media did, and did not, have to offer them. Representations of the supernatural operate within the same constraints of individualism noted in the narratives of teens. The supernatural beings of television and film who "come down to help in some way," as one teen put it, are generally not represented in the media or described in phenomenological experience as effecting social change toward a less oppressive situation, for example. Their concern, too, is with the individual. These beings, when malevolent, return to (or never leave) earth to avenge wrongs or continue their rampage of terror, mental illness, or systematic colonization on unsuspecting individuals or coupled young people (as in the *Scream, Friday the 13th*, and the Freddie Krueger series, as well as in the television program and film *The X-Files*). When benevolent, they return to Earth from heaven (or stay on Earth rather than "moving on") in order to earn wings for themselves (as in

It's a Wonderful Life), to atone for past sins (as in the teen television series *Angel*), or to address unfinished business from life (as in *The Sixth Sense, Ghost,* and *Beetlejuice*); in each case the supernatural being must help individuals in their quest to live more fulfilled and meaningful lives. Individualism, the "dominant language" of U.S. society, as Bellah and his colleagues argued, upholds certain conservative beliefs that tend to negate the prospects for social and collective change.

Each of these things—personal experience, hegemony, and the media stories themselves—shapes and limits individual viewers' interpretations of the media and in turn informs their understandings of the stories of the supernatural they find there. I have tried to offer more than a mere description of how teens approach the media and supernatural beliefs. I wanted, as media theorist David Morley suggests, "to integrate the analysis of the broader questions of ideology, power and politics . . . with the analysis of the consumption, uses and functions of television in everyday life."[21]

I hope that this book has demonstrated that there are different ways to explain why the supernatural appeals to so many young people today. I do not claim that the five approaches I have outlined are the only approaches, or indeed that they cannot overlap. Yet these discussions of the relationship between religion and culture suggest that while many in the United States believe that the media have a negative influence on culture, no "one size fits all" response to this problem will be possible or even desirable. On the one hand, I believe that we need to engage young people in a conversation about their beliefs and their cultural preferences so that we can better know who they are and what they care about. On the other, I think it is important to see this study as one of many attempts to draw connections between religion, culture, belief, and ideology. In the aftermath of 9/11, many have begun to explore the serious questions of these relationships in terms of Middle Eastern cultures and Muslim countries. Religion plays a multifaceted role in our culture as well, and we owe it to ourselves and our young people to better understand its role—both good and bad—in relation to our own culture.

CONCLUSION

I began this book with a commitment to reflexive scholarship, and so it would be disingenuous to end it without finally answering the question, What do I think of all of this? To be honest, I have had different reactions at various points in the project. At times, I was intrigued and fascinated by what people told me, dimly aware during the interviews that what I was hearing and recording was challenging my own presuppositions about religion and secularism, about distinctions between formal and "lived" religion, about the differences I had assumed would exist between parents and their teenage children, and about how much people saw themselves as unaffected by media even as they uniformly assumed that the media had negative effects on other people.

At other times, especially when I was analyzing the patterns that emerged in what people had said, I felt incredibly frustrated and impatient by the individualism I heard in both the teen narratives and in the entertainment media's stories. I believe that the fascination with the supernatural realm, as it seems to transcend labels of "liberals" and "conservatives," is in fact an example of the loss of a middle ground on other issues. It is, of course, easier to talk of angels, aliens, and spirits of the deceased than of the increasing gap between the wealthy and the working poor in our own society, especially when there are such strongly held views regarding this gap and its causes and consequences. Agreeing with my Marxist colleagues at the university, I have wondered whether all of the talk of guardian angels and spirits of the deceased functions as a distraction from the real-life issues that define the world in which these young people are growing up. This is the world of decreased living wages, a growing gap between the rich and working poor, rising costs of health care and child care, deunionized work forces with jobs increasingly shipped to countries where workers' wages are lower, families that are weakened as parents must take multiple jobs in order to earn a living, and neighborhoods weakened as families are forced, due to the lack of affordable housing, to live at increasing distances from the places where parents work.[22] Looking for power from the realm beyond fits nicely with a population increasingly limited economically, socially, and politically in these ways. This is probably especially true in a culture where we all still profess to believe not only that things are getting better but also that we live in a country of equal opportunity where anyone can get ahead if he or she works hard enough. If it is up to each individual to improve his or her own lot, how can any of us blame those of us who, under the circumstances, look to the realm beyond for help in trying to do so?

On the other hand, when I thought about specific stories of the supernatural in the entertainment media, I was often struck by how much they were oriented toward collective approaches to change. Yes, supernatural beings like angels, and even psychics who contact spirits of the deceased, primarily act to help individuals. But this is not the full extent of the religious imagination. Buffy, Angel, and the young Charmed women, for instance, work together to address the various injustices of teen life. They work together to challenge racist practices and prejudiced views; they hold each other accountable for behaving with integrity toward others; they even unite with their classmates to confront corrupt administrators in their school. Rather than downplaying evil or viewing it individualistically, the fictional stories of the supernatural actually suggest that evil has the potential for large, social consequences. Young people who identify with Buffy, Angel, the young Superman, Spiderman, the Charmed women, or other supernatural heroes may be wishing that they could be a part of something bigger than themselves. As noted earlier, they want a destiny, a calling, a challenge that is ultimately worthy of their time and energy. They may or may not feel that religion is useful in this quest, and hence some may take a relativistic view toward religion, but most seem committed to justice and equality.

What does this study imply for those who live or work with young people? As I think is probably clear by now, my own view is that worrying about the "effects" of the entertainment media on young people, and efforts to control the media through censorship, are probably of limited usefulness. Focusing on what we as adults see as the negative aspects of the entertainment media runs the risk of increasing the generation gap and serving as a conversation stopper with young people. On the other hand, if we concede that artifacts of culture reflect many different facets of contemporary life and its contradictions, we can view even popular culture as a resource for conversation. Popular culture is neither wholly redemptive nor oppressive, and it is not the whole of young people's experiences, either. The point, then, may be to encourage young people to talk about how they evaluate what they see, hear, read, and view, remembering that they often find it easier to discuss their media than their life experiences. By knowing more about how the young people around us see the world, we can be better prepared to respond and, perhaps, even help them to find their own destiny.

I recognize that my own approach to this study of religious and social change has been informed by an orientation to economic circumstances, material consequences, and collective action. But I do not mean to imply that I feel that those who believe they have been in contact with the realm beyond are all being duped. That, too, would be disingenuous, for honestly, while working on this project I lay awake worrying about visitations from the realm beyond more nights than I'd care to admit! Who is to say, after all, that what the people here and throughout the United States (and around the world) believe they are experiencing is not real? It is certainly plausible that people are more attuned to contact with the realm beyond *because* the possibilities in "real life" are increasingly limited (even if that awareness, for many, is still beneath the surface). Maybe we in the United States did not feel the need to seek out such contacts until circumstances led so many to feel that they lacked power over their current material situations. Perhaps we find a high entertainment value in such matters because, in light of the questions many hold with regard to organized religion, we still enjoy thinking of what might be possible and what remains unexplained by scientific knowledge, whether those possibilities inspire fear or hope. Perhaps we should harken back to one of the great religious theorists of the last century, William James.[23] While asserting a rationalist approach to the study of religious beliefs, James advocated openness to the possibility that there might be supernatural reasons beyond that which can be explained rationally. Even in the cultural studies perspective I have advocated, we could argue that all ideas do have referents, and hence maybe there are expressions of the unknown and transcendent that are visited upon this world. Maybe there has always been a relationship between representations and real historical events; maybe the events have always occurred, and we have inherited—and are changing—the frameworks by which we interpret such things. While I believe that it is important to look at the appeal of the supernatural realm in relation to limited economic and political opportunities, I am not ready to simply explain everything away, although my training as a sociologist certainly tempts me to do so. Instead, like many of my informants and many, indeed, throughout U.S. society, I must leave all of the events explored and discussed here firmly in the realm of possibility.

Appendix A
COMMENTS ON METHODOLOGY

The multimethod research that formed the basis of this book was part of a larger research effort occurring between March 1996 and January 2002 at the University of Colorado's Center for Mass Media Research, titled "Symbolism, Meaning, and the Lifecourse." This project involved in-depth repeated interviewing and focus groups with a total of 269 individuals, 102 of whom were teens.[1] I served as associate director of the project, specializing in adolescents and the development of feminist qualitative research methods. Stewart Hoover was director, and Diane Alters, Joseph Champ, and Lee Hood conducted interviews and collaborated on analysis of transcripts and related issues.[2] Each of the interviewers was a former media professional and was pursuing a doctorate during participation in the project. During the project's first year, Henrik Boes, who was completing a thesis in religious studies, and Alf Linderman, a scholar-in-residence from Uppsala University in Sweden, also participated in the research. The Lilly Endowment, Inc., provided generous support for this research. The Louisville Institute provided support for a key year in the project's development, as well.[3]

There were three stages of ethnographic research that supported the arguments made in this book, followed by a final stage of critical/cultural history research. This multiple methodological approach was not part of my initial plan (as many a researcher will tell you, if I had known how long it would take to complete this project, I might not have undertaken it). The multiple methods arose as I attempted to address myself to the current methodological challenges in the fields of ethnographic media research and cultural studies. As media theorist Klaus Bruhn Jensen has pointed out, media researchers have foregrounded questions of media impact at the expense of a clearer understanding of how the media fit into people's everyday lives. Our methods cause us to make this mistake, Jensen has argued, as media audience researchers traditionally go about their work by selecting a media text, analyzing it, and then either playing it in a group setting or asking viewers, listeners, or readers to write to us with their responses. Too often, this approach has caused us to assume that there is a direct relationship between certain television programs, films, or popular songs and the impact they have on their audiences.

The turn to reader-response and cultural anthropological approaches in media studies has led researchers to pay more attention to the contexts that shape interpretations of the media.[4] Recent research has therefore included analysis of the ways in which interpretations relate to how friends talk about particular media, or how certain programs, films, or songs fit into and are understood in relation to particular genres.[5] Several media researchers have suggested that we think of our work less as media analysis and more generally as cultural analysis.[6] The problem with this approach, of course, is that it can become too broad. How are we to determine what is not in our field of study if we begin with culture? One promising direction has focused on cultural phenomena in which the media play some role, such as Elvis fandom or the formation of national identity in a global marketplace.[7] Cultural studies researchers have demonstrated the benefits of asking not only what people are doing and saying about their media use, but also why they are doing these things at this point in history. Thus, cultural studies work, based in a tradition of literary criticism and cultural history, has focused on the contextual analysis of media texts, exploring how particular texts express the ideas that often remain unspoken in a culture, yet shape its frameworks both in the processes of media creation and in their interpretation. The current study fits into this tradition as it explores the rise of interest in the supernatural in the United States, as well as what people actually say about these interests and how these interests seem to be related to media practices. I began with young people's narratives, asking questions about the various media they consumed and how they believed these related to their experiences and understandings of the religious or spiritual realm. I did not choose to focus on one particular horror movie, or indeed even on how audiences interpreted the television program I discuss at length, *Buffy the Vampire Slayer*, because I was less interested in how they might make sense of one media text than in how different media and cultural practices related to the broader question of how young people claim a religious identity in the increasingly mediated and plural religious context of U.S. culture. Moreover, there was a great deal of variety in media consumption patterns among the young people I interviewed, and focusing on the reception of one text, or even one media form, risked losing the dynamism of the identity process I wanted to understand.

I chose to focus on references to the supernatural realm because it was a recurring theme both in their narratives and in the media young people were consuming. It was also interesting to me that some young people seemed to see a seamless relationship between spirituality and supernaturalism, and I wanted to explore that further. As the interviewing went on, my focus on this issue then led to lengthier discussions of angels and their representations in film and television, conversations about the genres of horror and fantasy in film and television, and experiences with teen practices related to the supernatural, including things like Ouija boards and séances. I could not have arrived at this focus, and indeed at the argument at the heart of this book, without first participating in many fascinating conversations, both with those who participated in the ethnographic research of this project and those who responded to it at various stages along the way. I have analyzed the entertainment media as one contributor to the "cultural tool kit" that informs the options for religious identity narratives which include reference to the supernatural. But I have also argued that as the entertainment media express the culture's often unacknowledged and taken-for-granted perspectives, religious traditions have shaped the content of the entertainment media in ways that are quite interesting and unexpected.

In this research, I wanted to address three interrelated research questions: What do young people say and do about the supernatural in the entertainment media? How are these practices related to religious identity narratives? Why is the supernatural so prevalent in teen culture at this point in history? As ethnographic research often does, this project evolved as time went on, and I came to embrace multiple methods as the questions and focus of interest became clearer to me. Thus, although the research did not proceed neatly from phase I to II and so on, each stage offered a distinct set of insights, so it is worth considering them separately in greater detail.

RESEARCH PHASE I

The first stage of the ethnographic research consisted of a two-part interview: first, a group interview with all family members, followed a few weeks later by individual interviews with each family member and in some cases participant observations of family media practices. Participants for this first stage were recruited using what communication researcher Thomas Lindlof has termed "maximum variation sampling," in which each family was expected to add a contrasting element to the overall sample.[8] Thus, my research colleagues and I recruited participants based on an evolving sense of which groups might be under- or overrepresented in the sample, exploring such demographic variables as socioeconomic status, racial/ethnic background, marital status of the parent(s), geographic location, and religious affiliation or lack of it. None of these people had been known to me or the other interviewers in the project before the research. We located these participants through referrals from gatekeepers such as a leader of a support group for single parents, a school district media literacy expert, civic and religious leaders, and personal friends. The sample of teens was almost evenly divided by gender. While the majority of young people claimed an Anglo-American racial/ethnic background (69), 9 were African American, 3 were Mexican American, and the remaining 19 were biracial (see appendix B for racial/ethnic backgrounds of members of the sample). The young people came from families that were almost evenly divided between those earning an annual household income of less than $30,000, more than $70,000, or something in between. Most of the parents were college graduates, although 13 families had adults who had not completed college and 8 had no college background at all. The families lived in rural, urban, suburban, exurban, and small city environments within a midwestern/southwestern area of the United States. The largest number of teens claimed no religious affiliation (34), followed by those affiliated with Protestant (29), Roman Catholic (10), Jewish (4), Muslim (4), and other (17) traditions. All of the participants' interviews were tape-recorded and transcribed, and all of the names used in this study are pseudonyms.

RESEARCH PHASE II

As the research evolved and I read more about adolescent peer culture and developmental issues, it became clear that to address my research questions, two meetings with teens—one in the context of their families and one individual meeting—would not be sufficient. I came to realize that teens were easily "othered" in research situations, written about as a group collectively experiencing the universal challenges of "coming of age" in a way that could erase the differences of age and the context of the historical moment for the researcher and researched, rather than interrogating these differences. Feminist researchers have argued for the contextualization of such knowledge-gathering, advocating a dialogic approach: "When we construct texts collaboratively, self-consciously examining our relations with/for/despite those who have been contained as Others, we move against, we enable resistance to, Othering," as Fine has written.[9] Yet how might an overeducated researcher engage in "collaboration" with a person across the gulfs of age, embedment in history, socioeconomic background, ethnicity, and religious identity? Believing, with Bird, that acknowledging the limits of such relationships does not necessarily prevent us from learning something within them, I sought to develop relationships of mutual understanding and trust with a few teens over time, recognizing that such work could only reveal knowledge in limited ways.[10]

Thus, in the second stage of research I returned to some of the teens who had been most willing to talk with me about their experiences with religion and the supernatural realm, either those mediated or in "real life." As critical cases, these teens were not selected for their representativeness, but they were not exceptional, either.[11] They offered the best means by which to explore the seeming contradictions between the interpretations of mediated and religious stories of the supernatural. Although I originally referred to them as case-study subjects, the teens are better identified as peer interpreters. While I talked with them about their own experiences, I also asked their insights on responses I'd received from other teens, thus adding to the validity of my own evolving analysis. In this sense, I sought to involve participants in my research in a manner less "objective" and distant and more dialogical, following feminist critiques of positivist research.[12] From the original pool of participants, five teens (three males, two females) were asked to serve as the focus for "case studies" in this second phase of research. The case-study teens included a biracial Arab African/Anglo-American male (Hasan, a Traditionalist described in chapter 8), an Anglo-American female (Elizabeth, an Intrigued in chapter 9), an African American male (Michael, another Intrigued in chapter 9), a biracial Native American/Anglo-American female (Lily, an Experimenter described in chapter 6), and an Anglo-American male (Jake, a Mystical in chapter 7). Each of these teens participated in up to thirty hours of interview time, as well as informal social time that included activities such as going to the movies, attending parties, watching television, or talking over a meal. Contacts with these case-study teens took place over a period of between six months and more than three years.

The first teen who participated in this more in-depth, relational approach to research was Elizabeth. Actually, I began with a rather instrumentalist approach to my relationship with Elizabeth, viewing her as a paid "data-gatherer" for me. Initially, our relationship had been defined less by my interest in her own experiences, per se, than by my interest in the work she was doing to help me gain access to teen situations and discussions. It was not until I listened to the audiotape of the first group's gathering that I realized how valuable it had been to know so much about the context of her life before the group discussion. Gradually, I began to see Elizabeth more as a partner in an ongoing dialogue about both my research interests and her own life more generally. I trusted her enough to tell her about my research project and how its goals related to my personal life, and she in turn shared reflections on both her life and its relation to her media practices. In other words, we both "self-revealed," to use the language of constructivist research.[13] Over the course of the next two years we continued to see each other, sometimes informally for social outings and at other times for more formal interviews. We also communicated frequently by e-mail. My relationship with Elizabeth, while occasionally still related to my research, evolved into a mentorship: we now talk much more frequently about her homework assignments, friends, family issues, and other school challenges than about her media use. This, then, became a model for my relationships with the other four teens with whom I worked most intensively.

RESEARCH PHASE III

For the third and final stage of the qualitative interviewing research, three of the teens from the second stage (Hasan, Elizabeth, and Michael) were asked to recruit members of their social networks for discussion groups.[14] Additionally, three of the parents from the first stage were asked to recruit members of their friendship and family circles for similar discussion groups. These groups included a total of 18 teens (6 teens in each) and 21 parents of teens (7 parents in each).[15] I followed the work of Liebes and Katz, who employed a social group approach to simulate social occasions in which similar discussions about television programs might emerge.[16] Liebes and Katz, as well as Radway in her work on romance readers, were interested in approaching participants as members of a social group, rather than as individual representatives of certain subcultural groups.[17]

While I led the parents' groups, I decided to train the teen leaders so that they could hold the group with no adults present. It was media ethnographer Elizabeth Bird who suggested this approach to me.[18] I was aware that young people spent a great deal of time among their friends and that both media consumption and interpretations about the media often took place within the social networks of peers. I wondered whether the focus group setting might seem too much like a laboratory setting in which an adult (me) attempted to observe a social network discussion in action. Bird noted that it might help me to get a better reading of what teens would say if there were no adults present. In large part, this approach was possible because I could rely upon teens I knew fairly well to lead each of the groups. By the time I was ready to train these teens as leaders of a group, each of them had spent at least four hours of interview time with me and thus were familiar with the general goals of my research project.

The training of the teens involved watching at least one television program together and talking about both its interpretation and the challenges of engaging others in conversations of its interpretation. While I had offered several options to the first two leaders, they both chose to show an episode of *Touched by an Angel* to their friends, as the episode highlighted a teen in peril. Once those selections were made, I decided to ask the third leader to use the same program for consistency.[19] Each of the teens worked with me to modify an interview guide I designed, making it more accessible to teens, as they saw it. They also added or adjusted questions to suit what they believed were the biases of the particular group of friends they intended to include in the group discussion. The peer-led discussion group leaders recruited six of their friends and acquired permission slips from those friends and their parents.

On the night of each discussion group, the leader and his or her friends watched the previously agreed-upon episode and discussed it. They also answered a series of more general questions about media use in their homes and with their friends. The viewing and discussion took approximately two and a half hours. All of the group conversations were tape-recorded and took place in the homes of the leaders, and each had a pizza party upon completion of the interviews. The leaders then offered their initial reactions when I went to their homes to retrieve the tapes. I transcribed the tapes and then returned to the leaders' homes, getting more specific feedback as we listened to the tape again together and read through the group's transcript.

When I reflected on how much I had learned from the first training session with my first group leader (Elizabeth), I decided to audiotape and analyze these sessions with the other peer interpreters. These, along with the postgroup conversations, became key to my analytical work, again reinforcing the notion that the teens were working with me dialogically. Not only did they answer my preconceived questions, but they discussed my research goals and preliminary findings with me, providing insights ranging from how to ask questions to which categories of interpretation seemed most relevant to them.

The fact that the teens led the groups without any adults present is also worth discussing. By having the teens engage in the group without adults, I did not simply want to attempt to replicate an "actual" conversation among teens. Rather, I wanted to turn over some of the authority of ethnographic inquiry to the teens, and to my peer-group discussion leaders in particular. As I believe that teens are most comfortable conversing when they can control the terms of the conversation, I wanted to—in fact I felt I needed to—facilitate this control.[20] The results from the groups, therefore, were sometimes disappointing to me, as I did not learn exactly what I had anticipated. Upon first listening to the tapes, I felt disappointed with interruptions such as "She already answered that. Next question," or outbursts of uncontrollable laughter, or even the failure to ask what I believed were "obvious" follow-up questions. The young people frequently interrupted each other and talked over one another, and in the teen girls' group, during the entire fifty-minute discussion it was a rare moment when only one voice could be heard at a time. Despite these challenges, I grew to sense that the content of the conversations was guided to a much greater extent by the peer interpreters' (and group members') varied levels of comfort with and interest in the topics than would have been the case had I been present to moderate. This encouraged me to pay closer attention to the nuances that were present in the conversations, such as the various cues that caused embarrassment, a quick change of topic, or loud and repeated efforts at being heard by one or more participants.

I should note, too, that each of the peer interpreters handed over the tapes with some embarrassment, concerned that I would not be able to "get much out of it" because their group members "didn't take it very seriously." Yet I was surprised that this embarrassment was not present at all while we listened to the tapes and read through the transcripts together. I think this is evidence of the fact that the teens sensed the somewhat ambiguous nature of the research endeavor. They correctly surmised that as an adult researcher I would have some specific desires for coherence, clarity, and seriousness, yet they also sensed that the group's talk to some extent did represent "how teens talk about these things," which is exactly what I had expressed an interest in.

RESEARCH PHASE IV

By fall 1999, I realized that my project had grown beyond its initial inquiry into the relationship between religious identity formation and the media. A key consultation with Larry Grossberg helped me to realize my need to critically engage in analysis of the television and film cultures in which teens were immersed.[21] Grossberg also suggested the "media as resource" approach that I ultimately took in my analysis (I take it with some caveats, as noted in the introduction). A year later, a meeting with media theorist Horace Newcomb helped me to think about the role of genre in relation to the interpretation strategies I had observed.[22] After reading the first draft of this manuscript, Newcomb suggested that I organize the book with reference to identity narratives and encouraged me to pay particular attention to the intersection of religious identity narratives with narratives of race, gender, and class. He also encouraged me to focus on television, choosing one program to highlight that might underscore some of the things I was observing in my interviews.

I had actually begun to think about this during the fourth season of *Buffy the Vampire Slayer* (1999–2000). At that point, the program became more than a "guilty pleasure" for me (I had seen every episode of the first four seasons at least once, and most twice). Employing an analytical approach of social semiotics (which encompasses both visual and discourse analysis), I began to see connections between the data I was collecting and analyzing and what I was seeing in the then-popular teen phenomenon. I taped every episode of *Buffy* and *Angel* that year, adding them to the many tapes of the first three seasons that I had gathered. I explored each episode for religious allusions and imagery and chose three (and later a fourth) that I found particularly interesting in light of the argument developing in my book. I consulted fan sites, especially Buffyguide.com, for insights into how the program was being framed and interpreted by its young audience—especially in relation to beliefs about the supernatural realm and about religion. I read the growing academic literature on the program.[23] A flurry of e-mail exchanges with media scholar (and Buffy enthusiast) Lynne Edwards assisted in the analysis of these programs, as well.

I presented a preliminary analysis of these programs first in spring 2000, and a few months later to a different audience.[24] In response to the first presentation, art historian David Morgan helped me to think about the television program, teen entertainment, and indeed my entire project, from the perspective of cultural history, while theologians Mary Hess and Scott Carmode provided important insights into the formation of identity and its possible relation to the cultural resources of the media.[25]

For the better part of two years, I struggled with the question: "Why is the supernatural so prevalent now in popular culture and in teen life?" I read many theories on the subject, but few addressed the role I believed teen culture was playing, and in fact had been playing, in this development. It was in writing an encyclopedia entry on fundamentalists and the entertainment media that I was finally able to see the connection between evangelicalism's concerns with the End Times and evangelism, and the imagery of demons and hell that had been so prominent in the teen media I was observing.[26]

ANALYZING THE DATA

I brought to this study some fairly substantive experiences in work with young people. Specifically, this has included serving as a tutor in a mixed-race (primarily African American and Mexican American) juvenile detention center, in a small town primarily comprised of middle-income Anglo-Americans, and in a middle-income Anglo-American suburban neighborhood program. I volunteered at a community center in a racially mixed (primarily African American and Pacific Rim) lower-income urban area. I have also provided volunteer leadership to junior and senior high students at lower-income Anglo-American and racially mixed (African American and Anglo American) Presbyterian churches, tutoring some students in these groups, as well. For the most part, while my own experiences and biases influenced my interpretations of what I encountered and heard in the research, few of the teens or parents interviewed asked me questions about my own background, interests, or commitments. In general, people assumed that I shared their religious commitments (or lack thereof) and interests. While this was occasionally not the case, I did not challenge their assumptions.

Throughout the course of this study, I familiarized myself with the cultural environment in which teens live, reading about and discussing with teens issues of adolescent development, the high school experience, and the concerns of everyday life, including significant events such as the Columbine High School shootings and their aftermath.[27] I discussed my findings and raised questions among undergraduate students at my university. I also viewed many teen-oriented television programs and films, listened to the radio stations favored by the young people I had interviewed, and read books and magazines recommended by various young people. I sought out opportunities to talk with teens and their parents in their work environments, during travels, and through Internet list-serves and Web pages. In addition to involvement in my current "mainline" church and reflections on my past experiences with religious organizations, I also participated in a few practices of alternative spirituality with young adults (none of whom were a part of the research sample; these were graduate students in their late twenties and early thirties).[28] I also read extensively in areas related to adolescence and youth culture, especially cultural studies, media research, social psychology, cultural anthropology, and history.

Analysis of the data began with the first interview and continued concurrently with data collection, as a team of researchers carefully reviewed and discussed each transcript and collectively decided on appropriate follow-up questions. Mentions of religious and supernatural beliefs were coded and discussed in relation to stated self-identifications with religious organizations using a constant comparative method.[29] As more corroboration was found among subsequent cases, a possible theory of the negotiation between religious identity and supernatural legends was developed. Experts in the sociology of religion, drawing upon their own studies, offered confirmation for the evolving theory, thus strengthening this study's validity.[30] The analysis and writing was necessarily informed by the critical/cultural perspectives that framed it.[31]

My analysis focused on young people who identified with religious organizations or identified interests in either spirituality or the supernatural realm. There were teens in the sample who did not talk about any of these things, but it was difficult to draw conclusions about these teens. In part, this is due to the limits of the method. Many people know that the stories of the supernatural are delegitimated, and therefore they may not have considered such interests worth mentioning or may have opted not to share those interests with a researcher.

As the interviews were being conducted and upon their completion, to strengthen this study's reliability I compared my findings with that of statistically generalizable data generated through national surveys, as well as with other researchers conducting qualitative research on young people. This helped to triangulate my findings and to provide a depth of analysis, particularly when drawing upon varied sources from differing disciplines and traditions. I was fortunate to have opportunities to present sections of this book in both academic and more public settings, thus further enabling the comparison of my findings with those of others. I sought disconfirming evidence that might challenge my findings in order to strengthen the validity of this study.

I realize, as I noted in the preface, that the findings I describe are not necessarily reflective of a certain percentage of contemporary teens, and I make no claims to this study's generalizability across populations. As stated in the introduction, this study has not aimed to produce a comprehensive map of teen beliefs, but instead has attempted to analyze the constraints and creativities possible due to the historical moment and cultural context in which these teens live. I have suggested that we view the entertainment media and religion as parts of a whole, each contributing to and shaping the other. They are each part of a broader framework, participants in a culture defined by globalization, privatization, increasing economic disparities, and individualism. By providing an in-depth look at how a limited number of teens and parents of teens make sense of their beliefs and interpretations of the media, I hope that this methodology succeeds in suggesting further avenues for research into what people believe and the relation of these beliefs to the entertainment media.

Appendix B

Total sample size: 100
Total teens involved in in-depth interviewing and observation: 85
Total involved in focus groups: 15

GENDER

Teen boys: 51
Teen girls: 49

RACIAL/ETHNIC IDENTIFICATION

Anglo: 69
African American: 9
Mexican American: 3
Biracial: African American/Anglo: 8
Biracial: Arab/Anglo: 6
Biracial: Native American/Anglo: 2
Biracial: Mexican or South American/Anglo: 2
Biracial: Asian American (Korean)/Filipino: 1

RELIGIOUS AFFILIATION

[All but 3 of the teens share their parents' religious affiliations]
Protestants, total: 29
Nondenominational/Evangelical Protestant: 9

United Methodist: 3
Lutheran (ELCA): 3
Presbyterian (USA): 4
Assembly of God: 3
Church of Christ: 2
American Baptist: 1
Evangelical Baptist: 1
United Church of Christ: 1
Congregationalist: 1
Nazarene: 1
Roman Catholic: 10
Muslim: 6
Unitarian Universalist: 6
Mormon: 5
Jewish (Reformed): 4
Buddhist: 2
Wiccan: 2
Jehovah's Witness: 2
None/Nonpracticing: 34

FAMILY STRUCTURE

Two parent (no divorce): 60
Two parent (remarried, blended family): 15
Two parent (unmarried, gay/lesbian): 1
Single parent: 22
Nonparent guardian: 2

ANNUAL HOUSEHOLD INCOME

Below $30,000: 25
$30,000–70,000: 51
Above $70,000: 24

INTRODUCTION

1. Misty Snow, "Mindworks: What Would an Alien Think of Us?" *Star Tribune* (April 3, 2000), 1E.

2. James Fowler, *Stages of Faith: The Psychology of Human Development and the Quest for Meaning* (San Francisco: Harper and Row, 1981); David Gustafson, *Lutherans in Crisis: The Question of Identity in the American Republic* (Minneapolis: Fortress Press, 1993); Frans J. Beeck, *Catholic Identity after Vatican II: Three Types of Faith in One Church* (Chicago: Loyola University Press, 1985). The issue of bringing new young people in, or simply keeping them "in the fold," is significant and has been for a long time. When looking at the parents of today's teens, we find that Catholics lost about half of the young people raised in their traditions, evangelical Protestants lost 45 percent, and mainline Protestants lost more than 60 percent of the young people who had once been in their pews. These percentages are given in Wade Clark Roof, *A Generation of Seekers* (San Francisco: HarperSanFrancisco, 1993), and cited by Carol Lytch, "Choosing Faith across Generations: A Qualitative Study of Church-Affiliated High School Seniors and Their Parents" (Ph.D. diss., Emory University, 2000).

3. "Buffy Draws Children to Witchcraft," BBC News, Friday, August 4, 2000, available online at news.bbc.co.uk/hi/english/entertainment/newsid_864000.

4. George H. Gallup Institute, *The Spiritual Life of Young Americans: Approaching the Year 2000*, research report (Princeton, N.J.: George H. Gallup International Institute, 1999); George Gallup Jr. and Frank Newport, "Belief in Psychic and Paranormal Phenomena Widespread among Americans," *Gallup Poll Monthly* 299 (August 1990), 35–43.

5. The sales figure on angel books comes from Sebastian Smith, "Angel Mania Takes Flight in U.S.," *Agence France Press* (January 13, 1994), I. Cited in Robert Wuthnow, *After Heaven: Spirituality in America since the 1950s* (Berkeley: University of California Press, 1998), 121. *Touched by an Angel* was the second-highest-rated television drama (after *ER*) for much of the 1996–97, 1997–98, 1998–99, and 1999–2000 seasons, according to Nielsen Reports.

6. Gallup Institute, *The Spiritual Life of Young Americans*; Andrew M. Greeley, "Hallucinations among the Widowed," *Sociology and Social Research* 71 (1987): 258–65. Greeley notes that women experience contact with the dead more than men. Séances and contact with the dead are also a part of teen girl culture and have been for a long time. See Bill Ellis, *Raising the Devil: Satanism, New Religions, and the Media* (Lexington: University Press of Kentucky, 2000).

7. Gallup and Newport, "Belief in Psychic and Paranormal Phenomena."

8. Secularization theory predicted that scientific knowledge would continue to undermine both the mystical traditions of formal religion and the superstitions of folk religion, while societal institutions that had developed since early modernity—the nation-state, formal education, industry, and the market, among others—would eventually replace the functions of religion. The theory has been articulated by several theorists of early modernity, notably Comte, Weber, and Durkheim. They argued that secularization had its beginnings in early modernity, as the medieval church's powerful stronghold on Western society was increasingly challenged. Weber theorized that as scientific knowledge expanded and rational thinking became the norm throughout Western culture, religion—and particularly religion's worldviews regarding the supernatural—would decline. The world would become "disenchanted." Max Weber, "Religious Rejections of the World and Their Directions," in H. H. Gerth and C. Wright Mills, ed. and trans., *From Max Weber* (New York: Oxford University Press, 1946 [1920]), 323–59. Peter Berger popularized the most recent articulations of secularization, arguing that with modernization there would no longer be a place—or a need—for supernatural explanations. In turn, religion would retreat to a residual, marginal place in Western culture. See Peter Berger, *The Sacred Canopy* (Garden City, N.Y.: Anchor, Doubleday, 1967). Berger's theory is challenged by many within sociology-of-religion circles. See Rodney Stark and Laurence Iannaccone,"A Supply-Side Reinterpretation of the 'Secularization' of Europe," *Journal of the Scientific Study of Religion* 33 (1994): 230–52. An excellent overview of the secularization debate is found in Philip Gorski, "Historicizing the Secularization Debate: Church, State, and Society in Late Medieval and Early Modern Europe, ca. 1300 to 1700," *American Sociological Review* 65 (February 2000): 138–67.

9. See Steve Bruce, *Religion in the Modern World: From Cathedrals to Cults* (Oxford: Oxford University Press, 1996).

10. On the stability of religious involvement, see Roger Finke and Rodney Stark, *The Churching of America, 1776–1990: Winners and Losers in our Religious Economy* (New Brunswick, N.J.: Rutgers University Press, 1992). For more recent figures related to young people, see U.S. Census Bureau 2000 data, available at www.census.gov; Gallup Institute, *The Spiritual Life of Young Americans*.

11. See Stephen R. Warner, "Work in Progress toward a New Paradigm for the Sociological Study of Religion in the United States," *American Journal of Sociology* 98 (1993): 1044–93.

12. Gorski, "Historicizing the Secularization Debate."

13. Stolzenberg, Blair, and Waite found that family participation in worship

services declines after the child reaches the age of ten and does not rise again until the young people become parents themselves. R. Stolzenberg, M. Blair-Loy, and L. Waite, "Religious Participation in Early Adulthood: Age and Family Life Cycle Effects on Church Membership," *American Sociological Review* 60 (1995): 84–103. In their review of the data from the national Survey of Adolescent Health, Smith and his colleagues find a steady decline of participation with age. They note that weekly attendance drops 10 percent over the four years of high school. See Christian Smith, Melinda Lundquist Denton, Robert Faris, and Mark Regnerus, "Mapping American Adolescent Religious Participation," *Journal for the Scientific Study of Religion* 41 (2002): 597–612.

14. Smith, "Mapping American Adolescent Religious Participation"; Ram Cnaan, Richard Gelles, and Jill Sinha, "Youth and Religion: A Nation of Young Believers" (unpublished paper, 2002, available from cnaan@ssw.upenn.edu); Gallup Institute, *The Spiritual Life of Young Americans.* Johnson and Roberts point out that there is a great deal of continuity between generations, as in each generation, levels of belief, religious experience, and personal prayer are generally higher than regular levels of attendance at houses of worship. However, there are also declines from older to younger generations on all measures of religion—although the decline in attendance is steeper than that of other measures of religiosity. They analyzed data from the General Social Survey from 1972 to 2000 by dividing respondents into age groups according to cohorts and controlling for age in order to compare across cohorts. D. Paul Johnson and Alden E. Roberts, "Generational Continuity and Change in Religiosity" (paper presented to the Scientific Study of Religion conference, Columbus, Ohio, October 2001). This combination of declining attendance and enduring identification with religion suggests that a great many young people in the United States, despite their claim of a "religious" identity, might better be called "marginal members"—those who attend religious services several times a year or less yet are not hostile toward religion itself. The term "marginal members" is introduced in Penny Long Marler and Kirk Hadaway, "Toward a Typology of Protestant 'Marginal Members,'" *Review of Religious Research* 35 (1993): 35–54.

15. See, e.g., Diana L. Eck, *A New Religious America: How a "Christian Country" Has Now Become the World's Most Religiously Diverse Nation* (San Francisco: Harper-Collins, 2001); Wade Clark Roof, *Spiritual Marketplace* (Princeton, N.J.: Princeton University Press, 1999).

16. William MacDonald, "The Effects of Religiosity and Structural Strain on Reported Paranormal Experiences," *Journal for the Scientific Study of Religion* 34, no. 3 (1995): 366–76.

17. Toni Morrison's books, such as *Beloved,* are particularly well known examples of fictional works that contain supernatural elements. Recent successful films with supernatural elements include *The Sixth Sense* (1999) and *The Green Mile* (1999). An excellent collection of links, reviewing these and other films with supernatural elements, is available at www.projectsupernatural.net.

18. Bill Ellis, "Legend-Tripping in Ohio: A Behavioral Survey," *Papers in Comparative Studies* 3, no. 2 (1982): 65; S. Elizabeth Bird, "Playing with Fear: Interpreting the Adolescent Legend Trip," *Western Folklore* 53 (July 1994): 191–209.

19. Andrew Greeley, *The Sociology of the Paranormal: A Reconnaissance* (Beverly Hills, Calif.: Sage, 1975).

20. Miriam Lambouras, "The Marian Apparitions: Divine Intervention or Delusion?" *The Shepherd* 16, no. 12 (September 1996) to 18, no. 4 (December 1997).

21. Arnold Van Gennep, *The Rites of Passage*, trans. Monika B. Vizedom and Gabrielle L. Caffee (Chicago: University of Chicago Press, 1960).

22. Victor Turner, *The Ritual Process: Structure and Anti-Structure* (Ithaca, N.Y.: Cornell University Press, 1969).

23. A somewhat related argument, made in relation to gender-specific socialization and rituals related to gruesome or frightening stories, is made by Dolf Zillman and Rhonda Gibson, "Evolution of the Horror Genre," in James B. Weaver III and Ron Tamborini, eds., *Horror Films: Current Research on Audience Preferences and Reactions* (Mahwah, N.J.: Lawrence Erlbaum, 1996).

24. Ellis, "Legend-Tripping in Ohio"; Bird, "Playing with Fear."

25. J. G. Bachman, L. D. Johnston, and M. O'Malley, *Monitoring the Future: Questionnaire Responses from the Nation's High School Seniors, 1992* (Ann Arbor: Survey Research Center, Institute for Social Research, University of Michigan, 1992). Smith and his colleagues find that in more recent surveys, teens report similar beliefs to their parents, as well. Smith et al., "Mapping American Adolescent Religious Participation."

26. K. A. Moore, *National Commission on Children: 1990 Surveys of Parents and Children*, data set 19, in B. A. Chadwick and T. B. Heaton, eds., *Statistical Handbook on Adolescents in America* (Phoenix: Oryx Press, 1992).

27. See U.S. Census Bureau data, 2000.

28. Patricia Hersch, *A Tribe Apart: A Journey into the Heart of Adolescence* (New York: Fawcett Columbine, 1998).

29. J. Erickson, "Adolescent Religious Development and Commitment: A Structural Equation Model of the Role of Family, Peer Group, and Educational Influences," *Journal for the Scientific Study of Religion* 31, no. 2 (1992): 131–52. See also Marie Cornwall, "The Influence of Three Agents of Religious Socialization," in D. L. Thomas, ed., *The Religion and Family Connection* (Provo, Utah: Brigham Young University), 207–31.

30. Quote of Vanesa Vathansombat, seventeen, of Whittier, Calif. Cited in Sharon Begley, "A World of Their Own," Special Report on Teens, *Newsweek* (May 8, 2000), 53.

31. This idea is the basis of the "subcultural theory of religious socialization" as articulated by Erickson, "Adolescent Religious Development and Commitment." It has obvious connections with what is known as the "rational choice" approach to religious identification among adults. See Warner, "Work in Progress toward a New Paradigm"; Andrew Greeley, *Religious Change in America* (Cambridge, Mass.: Harvard University Press, 1989). For marginal members, see note 14.

32. Several have commented on the religious relativism of this generation. See Steve Rabey, *In Search of Authentic Faith: How Emerging Generations Are Transforming the Church* (Colorado Springs: Waterbrook Press). See also John Leland, "Searching for a Holy Spirit," *Newsweek* (May 8, 2000), 61–63.

33. Hammond, *Religion and Personal Autonomy*; Roof, *Spiritual Marketplace*, 10. Lytch suggests that personal autonomy is the defining characteristic of religious identity among contemporary teens. Lytch, "Choosing Faith across Generations."

34. Wuthnow, *After Heaven*. It was Wade Clark Roof who popularized the term "seekers," identifying the practice first with the baby boomer generation. Roof, *A Generation of Seekers*.

35. Mary Jo Neitz, *Charisma and Community* (New Brunswick, N.J.: Transaction).

36. Robert Bellah first identified this characteristic of religion, in Robert Bellah, *Beyond Belief: Essays on Religion in a Post-Traditional World* (New York: Harper and Row, 1970).

37. In one study, about half of the Catholics surveyed who regularly attend mass said that a person could be a "good Catholic" without going to mass every week. William V. D'Antonio, James D. Davidson, Dean R. Hoge, and Ruth A. Wallace, *Laity, American and Catholic: Transforming the Church* (Kansas City, Mo.: Sheed and Ward, 1996). Cited in Lytch, "Choosing Faith across Generations."

38. Research Services, Presbyterian Church (U.S.A.), *A Survey of Confirmands in Presbyterian Congregations*, research report (Louisville, Ky.: Presbyterian Church U.S.A., 1999).

39. Hammond, *Religion and Personal Autonomy*. Many have offered theories about why religious institutions have such a difficult time attracting the interest and loyalties of young people. One compelling argument notes that churches tend to orient their programs toward conventional families, and with the rise in divorce rates and single parenting, it's understandable that a shrinking number of families and their teenage children might feel comfortable in contexts that celebrate that arrangement. Penny Long Marler, "Lost in the Fifties: The Changing Family and the Nostalgic Church," in *Work, Family, and Religion in Contemporary Society*, ed. Nancy Ammerman and Wade Clark Roof (New York: Routledge, 1995). Another study confirms what many adults might recall about their own experiences with formal religion as teens: young people today say that religious services are "boring." Roger Dudley, *Why Our Teenagers Leave the Church* (Hagerstown, Md.: Review and Herald Publishing, 2000).

40. Christian Smith and colleagues make this claim. Smith et al., "Mapping American Adolescent Religious Participation." See also Leland, "Searching for a Holy Spirit," 61–63.

41. For an excellent analysis of the emergence of spirituality and its relationship to the emergence of a market-based economy in the nineteenth century, see Colin Campbell, *The Romantic Ethic and the Spirit of Modern Consumerism* (Oxford, U.K.: Basil Blackwell, 1987). See also David Morgan, *Protestants and Pictures* (New York: Oxford University Press, 1999). I am grateful to David for his suggestion of pursuing a historically informed understanding of spirituality.

42. Wuthnow, *After Heaven*.

43. David Morgan, *Visual Piety* (Berkeley: University of California Press, 1998); Lawrence Moore, *Selling God* (New York: Oxford University Press, 1994); Colleen McDannell, *Material Christianity* (New Haven, Conn.: Yale University Press, 1995).

44. Charles Fuller, *Spiritual, but Not Religious* (New York: Oxford University Press, 2001).

45. Anthony Giddens, *Modernity and Self-Identity: Self and Society in the Late Modern Age* (Stanford, Calif.: Stanford University Press, 1991), 28.

46. Ann Swidler, "Culture in Action: Symbols and Strategies," *American Sociological Review* 51 (April 1986): 273–86.

47. Ibid., 276ff.

48. This notion of the public nature of symbols draws upon Clifford Geertz, *The Interpretation of Cultures* (New York: Basic, 1973). The idea of culture as it is related to the taken-for-granted approaches to action, however, draws upon Antonio Gramsci's theory of hegemony, described in Antonio Gramsci, *Selections from the Prison Notebooks*, ed. and trans. Q. Hoare and G. N. Smith (New York: International Publishers, 1971).

49. Giddens, *Modernity and Self-Identity*, 54. I am thankful to my colleague Diane Alters for our ongoing discussions about Giddens's theories.

50. Nancy Ammerman, "Religious Identities and Religious Institutions," in *Hand-

book for the Sociology of Religion, ed. Michelle Dillon (Cambridge: Cambridge University Press, forthcoming).

51. Ammerman, "Religious Identities." Her use of the terms "public narratives" and "autobiographical narratives" references Margaret Somers's description of narratives as ontological (Ammerman modifies this to autobiographical), public, metanarratives, and conceptual narratives. See Margaret Somers, "The Narrative Constitution of Identity: A Relational and Network Approach," *Theory and Society* 23 (1994): 605–49.

52. Ammerman, "Religious Identities," 12.

53. Ibid.

54. Ibid., 22.

55. One would not expect transcendence to enter narratives of young people who affiliate with nontranscendental religious traditions, such as Buddhism or Hinduism.

56. As Swidler argues, the first shortcoming is one inherited from a rather simplistic reading of Marx's base/superstructure model, while the second is identified with Weber's rational/idealist argument that the ethos of Protestantism (the "Protestant work ethic") is what accounts for the success of capitalism.

57. The "culture as tool kit" idea draws upon Pierre Bourdieu's notion of practice as a set of skills one acquires due to one's location in relation to others in a culture (as opposed to being the result of a conscious effort). See Pierre Bourdieu, *Outline of a Theory of Practice*, trans. Richard Nice (Cambridge: Cambridge University Press, 1977). See also Pierre Bourdieu, *Distinction: A Social Critique of the Judgment of Taste*, trans. Richard Nice (Cambridge, Mass.: Harvard University Press, 1984).

58. Several theorists in the sociology of religion have argued that when religious traditions accommodate themselves to modernity through such processes as commodification, the accommodation weakens them. See Peter Berger, *The Sacred Canopy* (New York: Doubleday, 1967); James Hunter, *American Evangelicalism* (New Brunswick, N.J.: Rutgers University Press, 1983); Mark Shibley, *Resurgent Evangelicalism in the United States: Mapping Cultural Change since 1970* (Columbia: University of South Carolina Press, 1996). Smith argues instead that sometimes this adaptation to modern life can be a sign of religious strength rather than weakness. He notes that religious traditions are constantly forced to renegotiate their collective identities in relation to the contexts in which they find themselves. Christian Smith, *American Evangelicalism: Embattled and Thriving* (Chicago: University of Chicago Press, 1998).

59. Swidler, "Culture in Action." It is not Swidler, but those who have taken up her metaphor, who tend to overemphasize the agentive nature of individuals. Swidler has a more contradictory view of culture that seeks to embrace action and structure. She points out that "culture has an independent causal role because it shapes the capacities from which such strategies of action are constructed" (ibid., 177).

60. Raymond Williams, *The Long Revolution* (Harmondsworth, U.K.: Penguin, 1961), 46. See also Raymond Williams, *Marxism and Literature* (Oxford: Oxford University Press, 1977).

61. For an example of how racial/ethnic prejudices may be overlooked, see Stuart Hall, "Cultural Identity and Cinematic Representation," in *Exiles: Essays on Caribbean Cinema*, ed. Mbye Cham (London: Africa World Press), 220–36.

62. See Janice Peck, "Itinerary of a Thought: Stuart Hall, Cultural Studies, and the Unresolved Problem of the Relation of Culture to 'Not Culture,'" *Cultural Critique* 48 (spring 2001): 200–249.

63. The description of culture as a "structure of feeling" comes from Raymond

Williams, *The Long Revolution*. My description also draws upon Durkheim's concepts of culture as a collective unconscious, and religion as the form of its social identity that mystifies and ritualizes what its members value. Durkheim believed that religion functioned to manage society, in particular by keeping its less desirable impulses in check. Emile Durkheim, *The Elementary Forms of Religious Life* (New York: Free Press, 1965).

64. Walter Kendrick, *The Thrill of Fear: 250 Years of Scary Entertainment* (New York: Grove Press, 1991), cited in Edward J. Ingebretsen, *Maps of Heaven, Maps of Hell: Religious Terror as Memory from the Puritans to Stephen King* (Armonk, N.Y.: M. E. Sharpe, 1996), 202. Cultural critic Ingebretsen argues that with the rise of the horror genre in literature, film, and television, the fear of hell and damnation so central to the writings of Protestant theologians such as John Calvin and Jonathan Edwards have been "placed in the service of marketing just the emotions Kendrick identifies." Narratives of religious change and contact with the Sacred Other therefore share unlikely points of reference with stories often found in the "low culture" pulp fiction of horror, which has long been an important part of fictional supernatural stories in teen culture.

65. Judith Hess Wright, "Genre Films and the Status Quo," in *Film Genre Reader II*, ed. B. K. Grant (Austin: University of Texas Press, 1995).

66. Smith, "Mapping Adolescent Religious Participation."

67. U.S. Census data cited in Eleanor Chute, "Preteens, Teens Abound," *Pittsburgh Post-Gazette* (June 10, 2001), B1.

68. Victoria Rideout, Ulla Foehr, Donald Roberts, and Mollyann Brodie, *Kids and Media @ the New Millennium*, Kaiser Family Foundation Report, Executive Summary (November 1999).

69. A photo of Sarah Michelle Gellar, star of *Buffy the Vampire Slayer*, was on the cover of "Top of the Net," *Yahoo! Internet Live* (January 1, 2000), 106.

70. I'm thinking specifically of the concerts by Jennifer Lopez, Christina Aguilera, and others that have aired on network and cable channels, as well as network television programming like Fox's *American Idol* and *Making the Band*, the latter of which followed a group of teens aspiring to be participants in a constructed teen boy band, and *High School*, which followed several teens throughout a school year, giving them digital cameras to record their thoughts and experiences while also allowing documentary filmmakers to follow them. Popular reality programs *Survivor* and *Temptation Island* also had strong teen followings, although they were not targeted specifically to the teen audience.

71. David Buckingham, ed., *Reading Audiences: Young People and the Media* (Manchester, U.K.: Manchester University Press, 1993); George Lipsitz, *Time Passages: Collective Memory and American Popular Culture* (Minneapolis: University of Minnesota Press, 1990); Lawrence Grossberg, *We Gotta Get Out of This Place: Popular Conservativism and Postmodern Culture* (New York: Routledge, 1992); JoEllen Fisherkeller, "Learning about Power and Success: Young Urban Adolescents Interpret TV Culture," *Communication Review* 3, no. 3 (1999): 187–212; Jane Brown, Carol Reese Dykers, Jeanne Rogge Stele, and Anne Barton White, "Teenage Room Culture: Where Media and Identities Intersect," *Communication Research* 21, no. 6 (1994): 813–27.

72. Angela McRobbie, *Feminism and Youth Culture: From Jackie to Just Seventeen* (Boston: Unwin Hyman, 1991); David Morley, *Television, Audiences and Cultural Studies* (London: Routledge, 1992); Keith Roe, "Different Destinies—Different Melodies: School Achievement, Anticipated Status and Adolescents' Tastes in Music," *European Journal of Communication* 7 (1992): 335–57.

73. James Lull, "The Naturalistic Study of Media Use and Youth Culture," in *Media Gratifications Research: Current Perspectives*, ed. Karl Erik Rosengren, Lawrence Wenner, and Philip Palmgreen (Beverly Hills: Sage, 1985), 209–23; Dick Hebdige, *Hiding in the Light* (London: Routledge, 1988); Stuart Hall and Tony Jefferson, *Resistance through Rituals* (London: Hutchinson, 1976). The latter emphasize peer groups in a way that seems less true in the contemporary United States than it once was, as many young people affirm their ability and interest in moving between and among social groups, as opposed to finding a single group with which to identify. Nevertheless, friends from various circles suggest and share media as a way of expressing themselves. In cultural studies media scholarship, a lengthy debate exists concerning just how "active" audiences may be in constructing their own meanings and identities from media texts. While some focus on the agency of media consumers, others emphasize the extent to which media texts are able to exert and maintain cultural hegemony. I tend to be wary that an overemphasis upon audience "activity" obscures the ways in which media in conjunction with other social factors can frame and limit meaning-making. For an elaborated argument of this position, see David Morley, "Theoretical Orthodoxies: Textualism, Constructivism, and the 'New Ethnography' in Cultural Studies," in *Cultural Studies in Question,* ed. Marjorie Ferguson and Peter Golding (London: Sage, 1997), 121–37. Consistent with this position, renowned media audience researcher Sonia Livingstone writes, "[First,] audience interpretation is structured by textual factors . . . [such as] textual openness/closure, preferred readings, generic conventions, naturalizing discourses, or subject positioning. Second, audience interpretation is structured by psychosocial factors . . . [such as] sociodemographic position, cultural capital, interpretive community, contextual discourses, sociocognitive resources, national identity, even psychodynamic forces." Sonia Livingstone, "Relationships between Media and Audiences: Prospects for Audience Reception Studies," in *Media, Ritual and Identity,* ed. Tamar Liebes and James Curran (London and New York: Routledge, 2000), 237–55.

74. While there is little exploration based in fieldwork that has been published at this point, some provocative theories have emerged regarding the public at large. See Stewart Hoover, "Media and the Construction of the Religious Public Sphere," in *Rethinking Religion, Media, and Culture,* ed. Stewart Hoover and Knut Lundby (Thousand Oaks, Calif.: Sage, 1998), 283–97.

75. Hillary Warren, "Standing against the Tide: Conservative Protestant Families, Mainstream and Christian Media" (Ph.D. diss., University of Texas at Austin, 1998); Hillary Warren, "Southern Baptists and Disney," in *Religion and Popular Culture: Studies on the Interaction of Worldviews,* ed. Daniel A. Stout and Judith M. Buddenbaum (Ames: Iowa State University Press, 2001); Stewart Hoover, *Mass Media Religion* (Thousand Oaks, Calif.: Sage, 1988). For supporting evidence of this among adult news consumers, see Stewart Hoover, *Religion and the News* (Thousand Oaks, Calif.: Sage, 1998).

76. See, for example, Lynn Schofield Clark, "If You Stay Away from Nintendo, You'll Read the Qur'an More: Media, the Family, and Muslim Identity" (paper presented to the Second Public Media, Religion, and Culture Conference, Edinburgh, Scotland, 1999, available online at www.Colorado.edu/teens). Also in Stewart Hoover, Lynn Schofield Clark, and Diane Alters, with Joseph G. Champ and Lee Hood, *Media, Home, and the Family* (forthcoming).

77. Peck notes that a problem in much of cultural studies is the argument against the "autonomy" of culture. She writes: "Neither the 'superstructure' (cul-

ture) nor the 'base' ('not culture') are autonomous. Both are the materialization of human practical activity within a definite historical milieu and concrete ensemble of social relations. Signification is not the exclusive property of language nor the special province of culture, but is at once the practical activity (praxis) of human being and the material inscription of those multiple past and present activities 'in things and in the order of things' that necessarily escapes each of us, constitutes a field of objective imperatives for all of us, and inscribes every one of us within a system of social relations." Peck, "Itinerary of a Thought," 243. Cultural studies theorist Lawrence Grossberg introduces the concept of "articulation" to discuss the processes by which popular music industries, performers, texts, and audiences articulate with each other, bringing together production and consumption into the analysis of cultural products and social change. Lawrence Grossberg, *We Gotta Get Out of This Place.*

78. The data collected for this project were part of a larger ethnographic effort under the direction of Stewart M. Hoover at the University of Colorado. The project was titled "Symbolism, Meaning, and the Lifecourse." I served as the project's associate director and specialist on both adolescents and generational issues, and feminist/qualitative methodologies.

79. These interviews were conducted by a team of researchers, including Diane Alters, Joseph Champ, Lee Hood, and myself. Stewart Hoover was the director of this project. All members of the research team were affiliated with the University of Colorado at Boulder at the time of the study. None of the interviews took place within Boulder, however. Due to the high cost of living in Boulder, none of the persons conducting the interviews for this project reside there.

80. Because this study focused on teens residing in a home with their primary parents or guardians, I did not include teens who were living in juvenile detention centers or other locations emphasizing reform from or punishment of what might be considered deviant behaviors. Thus, the findings are necessarily skewed to nondelinquent teens.

81. Here, I am following the definition of adolescence offered in John Modell, *Into One's Own: From Youth to Adulthood in the United States 1920–1975* (Berkeley: University of California Press, 1989).

82. Barry A. Kosmin and Seymour Lachman, *One Nation under God: Religion in Contemporary American Society* (New York: Harmony Books, 1993).

83. Finke and Stark, *The Churching of America.*

84. While more young people in the Northeast claim religious affiliation, teens from the West nevertheless report more participation in religion than those from the Northeast. See Smith et al., "Mapping American Adolescent Religious Participation."

85. University of Colorado doctoral student Jin Park has referred to this as a "biblical" interpretation of the media in research team meetings. He will develop this concept further in a forthcoming work.

86. Media literacy experts and theorists speak of the importance of inoculation against the effects of the media, which some believe can be achieved through the development of a critical sensibility that guides media interpretation. See Rene Hobbs, "The Seven Great Debates in the Media Literacy Movement," *Journal of Communication* 48, no. 1 (winter 1998): 16–32. It is important to point out that most people believe that the media have a stronger and more negative impact on others than on themselves. This is called the "third person effect." See W. P. Davison, "The Third Person Effect in Communication," *Public Opinion Quarterly* 47 (1983): 1–15.

87. The subject of religion in *The Simpsons* has been the topic of several interesting analyses, including Mark Pinsky, *The Gospel according to the Simpsons* (Louisville, Ky.: Westminster John Knox Press, 2001).

CHAPTER 1

1. Headline from *The Hampton Roads Christian,* the student-produced monthly news magazine at Regent University. Cited in Marc Fisher, "Pat Robertson's J-School," *American Journalism Review* (July 7–13, 1998). Available at www.newslink.org/ajrfishermar98.html (July 8, 1998).

2. Jason Barker, "Youth Oriented TV and the Occult," *Watchman Expositor* 15, no. 6 (1998).

3. ChildCare Action Project (CAP): Christian Analysis of American Culture. Available at www.capalert.com/.

4. See materials on Pokemon and Harry Potter at www.jesus-is-lord.com/pokemon.html.

5. In fact, the boom in stories that draw upon supernatural themes in fantasy as well as in science fiction was observed three decades ago by noteworthy sociologists Mircea Eliade and Andrew Greeley. See the analysis of this in Nachman Ben-Yehuda, *Deviance and Moral Boundaries: Witchcraft, the Occult, Science Fiction, Deviant Sciences, and Scientists* (Chicago: University of Chicago Press, 1985).

6. The historical definition of occult is offered by Bradford Verter, "Dark Star Rising: The Emergence of Modern Occultism, 1800–1950" (Ph.D. diss., Princeton University, 1998). Folklorist Bill Ellis traces the change in the term in his analysis of satanic scares. See Bill Ellis, *Raising the Devil: Satanism, New Religions, and the Media* (Lexington: University Press of Kentucky, 2000).

7. Edward J. Ingebretsen, *Maps of Heaven, Maps of Hell: Religious Terror as Memory from the Puritans to Stephen King* (Armonk, N.Y.: M. E. Sharpe, 1996), xvi, 45.

8. An excellent groundbreaking work that demonstrates how religious groups in the past have lost control of their concerns once they entered the media is Diane Winston, *Red Hot and Righteous: The Urban Religion of the Salvation Army* (Cambridge, Mass.: Harvard University Press, 1999). That book has influenced my argument here.

9. Charles Lippy, *Being Religious, American Style* (Westport, Conn.: Greenwood Press, 1994).

10. Jon Butler, *Awash in a Sea of Faith: Christianizing the American People* (Cambridge, Mass.: Harvard University Press, 1990). Butler notes a range of magical practice that existed in New England, Virginia, and Pennyslvania, according to court records. Butler cites Darrett Rutman, who writes of magic between 1640 and 1700 in Virginia: "In sound mind and with clear conscience a Virginian could . . . hold that only the horseshoe over his door protect his sick wife from the evil intentions of a neighbor woman who perforce passed under it on her way to saying black prayers at his wife's bedside (1671), could attribute to a witch the death of his pigs and withering of his cotton (1698), and, in court, faced with suits for slander, could insist that 'to his thoughts, apprehension or best knowledge' two witches 'had rid him along the Seaside and home to his own house (again 1698)'" (ibid., 73–74). Darrett Rutman, "The Evolution of Religious Life of Early Virginia," *Lex et Scientia: The Journal of the American Academy of Law and Science* 14 (1978): 190–240.

11. I agree with Anthony Giddens's and Fredric Jameson's contention that the current period is better characterized as late capitalism, a form of modernism rather than a complete break, as is often articulated in postmodern theories. See Anthony Gid-

dens, *Modernity and Self-Identity: Self and Society in the Late Modern Age* (Stanford, Calif.: Stanford University Press, 1991); Fredric Jameson, "Postmodernism, or The Cultural Logic of Late Capitalism," *New Left Review* 146 (1984): 53–92.

12. This point in the analysis draws upon Bill Ellis's analysis of the folkloric nature of certain Pentecostal rituals. See Ellis, *Raising the Devil.*

13. Stewart Hoover and AnnaMaria Russo, "September 11 and the Visual Media" (presentation to the annual meeting of the American Academy of Religion, Denver, Colo., November 2001).

14. The "cultural tool kit" model of sociological analysis of culture was discussed in the introduction. Many have pointed to the connection between evangelicalism and the norms of U.S. society. See Linda Kintz, "Culture and the Religious Right," in *Media, Culture, and the Religious Right,* ed. Linda Kintz and Julia Lesage (Minneapolis: University of Minnesota Press, 1998), 3–20. See also cultural critic Wendy Kaminer, *Sleeping with Extra-Terrestrials: The Rise of Irrationalism and the Perils of Piety* (New York: Vintage, 1999). Unfortunately, Kaminer tends to paint all religious beliefs with the same brush, equating religious adherents with a lunatic fringe and therefore missing the power of religion in both individual lives and in U.S. ideology more broadly.

15. Winnifred Sullivan argues that despite Carter's argument from a liberal Protestant viewpoint, he largely supports a view that evangelicals would support: "Perhaps the reason that bringing God into the conversation is often viewed in certain liberal circles a social gaffe, is not because of a fear of religion but because of the accompanying implication that the believer stands over and against the nonbeliever. The believer, it is implied by such affirmations of faith, has access to a special revelation or truth," Winnifred Fallers Sullivan, "Diss-ing Religion: Is Religion Trivialized in American Public Discourse?" *Journal of Religion* (1995): 76.

16. *Touched by an Angel* and *7th Heaven* audience figures are measured by weekly Nielsen ratings. The conservative Media Research Center determined the fivefold increase in religion's representation in prime time. This is discussed by several journalists, including Diego Ribadeneira, "Viewers' Interest in Faith Prompts TV Networks to Get Religion," *Boston Globe* (April 25, 1998), 2B.

17. I am grateful to my colleague and friend Rebecca Sullivan for this anecdote. See article on chant in "They're Not Heavy, They're Brothers," *Newsweek* (February 14, 1994), 52.

18. Christian Smith gives the 20 million figure in *American Evangelicalism: Embattled and Thriving* (Chicago: University of Chicago Press, 1998). The other cite is from George Gallup and Jim Castelli, *The People's Religion: American Faith in the 1990s* (New York: Macmillan, 1989).

19. See www.cynet.com/Jesus/intro.htm.

20. Jim Brantlett, "When Will Jesus Return? Can We Know? Are We Close?" Available at www.virtualchurch.org (May 7, 2001).

21. www.discoverynet.com/~kurtz/TeensLivingforChrist.html (May 7, 2001).

22. Nancy Ammerman, "North American Fundamentalism," in Kintz and Lesage, *Media, Culture, and the Religious Right,* 55–114. See also Randall Balmer, *Mine Eyes Have Seen the Glory: A Journey into the Evangelical Subculture of America* (New York: Oxford University Press, 1989).

23. Johnson mentions the film's position in the top ten rental videos list for 1993 in Eithne Johnson, "The Emergence of Christian Video and the Cultivation of Videoevangelism," in Kintz and Lesage, *Media, Culture, and the Religious Right,* 191–210. Russ Doughten Films, distributors of *A Thief in the Night,* sent me a more complete

listing that noted the film's name in the top spot for sales for the years 1990–95, according to the *Christian Bookstore Journal*. It was also the number two rental. Sales remain strong, according to the film's distributor. Personal correspondence, August 29, 2001.

24. Lorenza Munoz, "Christian Movie Gains a Firm Toehold on Mainstream Circuit," *Los Angeles Times* (February 2, 2001), 1A.

25. Cited in Ellis, *Raising the Devil*, xv.

26. Albert Landry, quoted in Teresa Watanabe, "Exorcism Flourishing Once Again," *Los Angeles Times* (October 31, 2000), 1A.

27. www.boblarson.org (May 11, 2001).

28. Fuller Seminary's interest in exorcisms is related in Watanabe, "Exorcism Flourishing Once Again."

29. Maxine Sieleman, cited in Balmer, *Mine Eyes Have Seen the Glory*, 157.

30. This interview passage is from Christian Smith, *American Evangelicalism*, 143.

31. Wendy Murray Zoba, "Do You Believe in God? Columbine and the Stirring of America's Soul," *Christianity Today* (October 4, 1999), 33–43.

32. Bruce Nolan, "Otherworldly Unplugged: Multimedia Morality Play Is Based on Columbine," *Star Tribune* (March 18, 2000), 9B.

33. This anecdote is from Richard Flory, personal correspondence, November 1999.

34. William Lobdell, "Aiming to Scare the Devil Out of You: Conservative Christians Are Finding Alternatives to Halloween," *Los Angeles Times* (October 27, 2000), 1E.

35. Of course, this borrowing from religious traditions for entertainment purposes predates film. See William Leach, *Land of Desire: Merchants, Power, and the Rise of a New American Culture* (New York: Pantheon Books, 1993).

36. *From Max Weber: Essays in Sociology*, ed. H. H. Gerth and C. Wright Mills (London: Kegan Paul, 1947).

37. Schmidt details the nineteenth-century process by which the myth of Egyptian oracles was debunked through scientific investigation, its demystification becoming key to its entertainment value for an urban working class with leisure and money for amusement. Leigh E. Schmidt, "Visualizing God's Silence: Oracles, the Enlightenment, and Elihu Vedder's *Questioner of the Sphinx*," in *The Visual Culture of American Religion*, ed. David Morgan and Sally Promey (Berkeley: University of California Press, 2000), 211–28.

38. Margo Adler, "Diablo II Computer Game," *Morning Edition* (October 11, 2000, 11 A.M.).

39. www.battle.net/diablo2.

40. Steve Lohr, "It's Demons vs. Angels in Computer Game with a Religious Theme," *New York Times* (Monday, Oct. 18, 1999), B1, B8.

41. Christian Role Play Gamers Web site, available online at clubs.yahoo.com/clubs/christianrpgplayers.

42. www.cyberchristians.org.

43. For a longer discussion of the commercialization of Christianity, see Laurence Moore, *Selling God: American Religion in the Marketplace of Culture* (New York: Oxford University Press, 1994).

44. From the Media, Culture, and Religious Faith list-serve. Posting cited with permission. One woman responded to the specter of "witchcraft" with a plea that the evangelical protests against witchcraft be put in historical perspective. She noted simi-

larities between contemporary evangelical fears of witchcraft and the fears of women's powers that, in the fifteenth and sixteenth centuries, led to the persecution of many older women by state and religious authorities. She wrote, "I, who hung my head in shame at the many actions of the early church, particularly its brutal reactions against witchcraft, had hoped that we as a church had matured beyond the superstition and fear of our early church fathers. It appears not." This writer did not dispute the fact that the media may play a role in shaping audience interpretations; she was more concerned with the arguments evoked by the imagery and narratives than by the "influence" of those things on their own.

45. Marsha Witten, *All Is Forgiven: The Secular Message in American Protestantism* (Princeton, N.J.: Princeton University Press, 1993). Witten argues that pastors use "reframing," or referencing popular culture within sermons, as a way to make their messages more palatable for a "modern" audience. She sees this not as an accommodation to modernity that weakens religious traditions in the face of secular society but, rather, as a sign of vitality and creativity as a religious tradition grapples with and "reframes" modernity for the religious group's ends.

46. The review of religious games is available under "culture" at www.beliefnet.com.

CHAPTER 2

1. *Buffy the Vampire Slayer*, a midseason replacement for the WB Network in 1997, was based on a movie of the same name that received a lukewarm reception at the 1992 box office.

2. See, for example, the cover story, "God, Sex, Race and the Future: What Teens Believe," *Newsweek* (May 8, 2000), 52–75.

3. Ron Tamborini and James B. Weaver III, "Frightening Entertainment: A Historical Perspective of Fictional Horror," in *Horror Films: Current Research on Audience Preferences and Reactions*, ed. James B. Weaver III and Ron Tamborini (Mahwah, N.J.: Lawrence Erlbaum, 1996), 12.

4. The concept of religious identity as a function of "personal choice" was discussed in the introduction; see note 33.

5. *Teen Choice Awards*, Fox TV. Aired August 20, 2001.

6. The first episode of *Buffy the Vampire Slayer* was titled "Welcome to the Hellmouth" and aired on the WB Network on March 10, 1997.

7. See Rhonda V. Wilcox, "There Will Never Be a 'Very Special Buffy': Buffy and the Monsters of Teen Life," *Journal of Popular Film and Television* 27, no. 2 (1999): 16–23.

8. "Hot Summers," *Xpose* (September 1998): 28–33. Quoted in Rhonda Wilcox, "Who Died and Made Her the Boss?: Patterns of Mortality in *Buffy*," in *Fighting the Forces: What's at Stake in Buffy the Vampire Slayer*, ed. Rhonda Wilcox and David Lavery (Lanham, Mass.: Rowman and Littlefield, 2002), 3–17.

9. Wilcox, "There Will Never Be a 'Very Special Buffy.'"

10. Popular culture references appear so frequently on the program that fan sites such as www.Buffyguide.com devote weekly entries to them.

11. "Pangs," first aired November 23, 1999.

12. "The Harvest," first aired March 10, 1997. Cited in Patricia Pender, "I'm Buffy and You're . . . History: The Postmodern Politics of *Buffy*," in Wilcox and Lavery, *Fighting the Forces*, 40.

13. "Never Kill a Boy on a First Date," first aired March 31, 1997. Cited in Pender, "I'm Buffy," 40.

14. Kristina, "Believe at your own risk." Column, Much Ado about Buffy Web site. Available at www.chosentwo.com/buffy/columns/kristina/10believe.html. Retrieved September 1, 2002.

15. "Offspring," first aired November 1, 2001.

16. Pender, "I'm Buffy," 35–44.

17. Mark Dery, *The Pyrotechnic Insanitarium: American Culture on the Brink* (New York: Grove, 1999), 57. Cited in Pender, "I'm Buffy," 40.

18. Fredric Jameson's term as cited in Pender, "I'm Buffy," 40.

19. "Becoming," Part I, first aired May 12, 1998, cited in Pender, "I'm Buffy," 42.

20. Laurence Rickels, *The Vampire Lectures* (Minneapolis: University of Minnesota Press, 1999), cited in Gregory Erickson, "Sometimes You Need a Story: American Christianity, Vampires, and Buffy," in Wilcox and Lavery, *Fighting the Forces,* 108–19.

21. Many literary critics have noted this; see e.g., Diane DeKelb-Rittenhouse, "Sex and the Single Vampire: The Evolution of the Vampire Lothario and Its Representation in Buffy," in Wilcox and Lavery, *Fighting the Forces,* 143–52. Erickson also makes reference to this aspect of the vampire legend in "Sometimes You Need a Story."

22. Erickson, "Sometimes You Need a Story."

23. "Buffy vs. Dracula," first aired September 26, 2000.

24. Erickson, "Sometimes You Need a Story."

25. Joel N. Feimer, "Bram Stoker's *Dracula*: The Challenge of the Occult to Science, Reason, and Psychiatry," in *Contours of the Fantastic: Selected Essays from the Eighth International Conference on the Fantastic in the Arts,* ed. Michele K. Langford (Westport, Conn.: Greenwood Press, 1990), 165–71.

26. Jules Zanger, "Metaphor into Metonymy: The Vampire Next Door," in Joan Gordon and Veronica Hollinger, eds., *Blood Read: The Vampire as Metaphor in Contemporary Culture* (Philadelphia: University of Pennsylvania Press), 17–26. Cited in Erickson, "Sometimes You Need a Story," 111.

27. Erickson, "Sometimes You Need a Story."

28. Ibid., 114.

29. "Angel," first aired April 14, 1997.

30. On other film noir characters that Angel follows, see Raymond Chandler, *The Simple Art of Murder* (New York: Vintage, 1950). Chandler offers this description of a film noir protagonist: "But down these mean streets a man must go who is not himself mean, who is neither tarnished nor afraid. The detective in this kind of story must be such a man. He is the hero; he is everything. He must be a complete man and a common man and yet an unusual man. He must be, to use a rather weathered phrase, a man of honor—by instinct, by inevitability, without thought of it, and certainly without saying it. He must be the best man in his world and a good enough man for any world.... He is a lonely man and his pride is that you will treat him as a proud man or be very sorry you ever saw him.... The story is this man's adventure in search of a hidden truth, and it would be no adventure if it did not happen to a man fit for adventure. He has a range of awareness that startles you, but it belongs to him by right, because it belongs to the world he lives in. If there were enough like him, the world would be a very safe place to live in, without becoming too dull to be worth living in."

31. Buffy was one of several attractive teen postfeminist heroines on the WB Network. Others included *7th Heaven*'s Jessica Biel, sixteen; *Dawson's Creek*'s Katie Holmes, twenty, and Michelle Williams, eighteen; *Charmed*'s Shannen Doherty, twenty-seven, Alyssa Milano, twenty-six, and Holly Marie Combs, twenty-five; and *Felicity*'s Keri Russell, twenty-two. While the *Charmed* young women, like Buffy, rely on

supernatural powers, the others share with them an ability to know themselves, stand up to others, bond with female and male friends, and remain sexually alluring. On Buffy as postfeminist heroine, see A. Susan Owen, "Vampires, Postmodernity, and Postfeminism: *Buffy the Vampire Slayer*," *Journal of Popular Film and Television* 27, no. 2 (summer 1999): 24–31.

32. Elton E. Smith and Robert Haas, "Introduction: Victorian Literature and the Shifting Use of the Supernatural," in *The Haunted Mind: The Supernatural in Victorian Literature*, ed. Elton E. Smith and Robert Haas (Lanham, Md.: Scarecrow Press, 1999), vii.

33. Clover notes that in many of these films, evil enters the woman through the vagina, a fact sometimes illustrated in representations that depict women in standard rape posture. She notes, "The word vulva itself is related to valve—gate or entry to the body—and so it regularly serves for all manner of spirits, but the unclean one above all, in occult horror." Carol J. Clover, *Men, Women, and Chain Saws: Gender in the Modern Horror Film* (Princeton, N.J.: Princeton University Press, 1992), 76.

34. "Surprise," Part I, first aired January 19, 1998. "Innocence," Part II, first aired January 20, 1998.

35. "What's My Line?," Parts I and II, first aired November 17 and 24, 1997.

36. Like the differences between Buffy and Angel, Kendra serves as a foil to Buffy. Summoned to Sunnydale because Buffy temporarily died in an earlier episode ("There can only be one slayer"), Kendra is a well-read, militantly competent slayer who is appalled at Buffy's techniques, even as Buffy derides Kendra's in return. Unlike Buffy's circle of friends and her close relationship with her Watcher Giles, Kendra has few social connections as a result of her commitment to slaying. She is appalled to learn that Buffy has romantic feelings for a vampire. While Buffy epitomizes the clean-cut white southern California girl with her casual tank tops and long blond hair, Kendra is meant to appear as exotic: she is a light-skinned young woman of African descent who speaks in an Island accent and wears large hoop earrings, further coding her as a racial/ethnic "other," Her otherness is further accentuated by the fact that Kendra has always slayed on her own, while Buffy is supported in her planning and fighting by her friends. Lynne Edwards argues that Kendra's representations are consistent with the "tragic mulatto myth," in that she leaves her home, enters the white world, attempts assimilation, but ultimately fails to find acceptance and leaves in defeat. See Lynne Edwards, "Slaying in Black and White: Kendra as Tragic Mulatta in *Buffy*," in Wilcox and Lavery, *Fighting the Forces*, 85–97.

37. I am grateful to Lynne Edwards for suggesting this analysis to me (personal correspondence, June 8, 2001).

38. Tanya Kryzwinksa, "Hubble-Bubble, Herbs, and Grimoires: Magic, Manichaenism, and Witchcraft in Buffy," in Wilcox and Lavery, *Fighting the Forces*, 178–94.

39. Ibid., 185.

40. "Hush," first aired December 14, 1999. This episode received a 1999 Emmy nomination for Outstanding Writing in a Drama Series.

41. Christopher Golden and Nancy Holder, *Buffy the Vampire Slayer: The Watcher's Guide*, vol. 1 (New York: Pocket, 1998), 138–39. Cited in Mary Alice Money, "The Undemonization of Supporting Characters in Buffy," in Wilcox and Lavery, *Fighting the Forces*, 99–100.

42. "New Moon Rising," first aired May 2, 2000. Cited in Catherine Siemann, "Darkness Falls on the Endless Summer: Buffy as Gidget for the Fin de Siècle," in Wilcox and Lavery, *Fighting the Forces*, 120–29.

43. Jeffrey Cohen, ed., *Monster Theory: Reading Culture* (Minneapolis: University of Minnesota Press, 1996).

44. Ibid.

45. Clover, *Men, Women, and Chain Saws*.

46. Edward J. Ingebretsen, *Maps of Heaven, Maps of Hell* (Armonk, N.Y.: M. E. Sharpe, 1996), 214.

47. Genesis 6:2, 3; Ingebretsen, *Maps of Heaven*, 168.

48. Ingebretsen, *Maps of Heaven*.

49. Ibid.

50. Ibid., xvi.

51. Ibid., 45.

52. Gary Green, *The Language of Nightmare: A Theory of American Gothic Fiction* (Ann Arbor: University of Michigan Research Press, 1992). Cited in Ingebretsen, *Maps of Heaven*, 81.

53. Ingebretsen, *Maps of Heaven*.

54. "Sinners in the Hands of an Angry God," in *The Works of President Edwards*, vol. 6 (New York: Burt Franklin, 1968), 455. Cited in Ingebretsen, *Maps of Heaven*, 91.

55. Ingebretsen, *Maps of Heaven*, 96.

56. See, for example, Kirk Schneider, *Horror and the Holy: Wisdom Teachings of the Horror Tale* (Chicago: Open Court, 1993).

57. Lucy Fischer, "Birth Traumas: Parturition and Horror in Rosemary's Baby," in *The Dread of Difference: Gender and the Horror Film*, ed. Barry Keith Grant (Austin: University of Texas Press), 412–31.

58. Skal, *The Monster Show*.

59. Christopher Lee, quoted in Ellis, *Raising the Devil*.

60. Gardner, discussed in Verter, *Dark Star Rising*.

61. Ellis, *Raising the Devil*.

62. See, for example, Mircea Eliade, *Occultism, Witchcraft, and Cultural Fashions: Essays in Comparative Religions* (Chicago: University of Chicago Press, 1976); Andrew Greeley, *The Sociology of the Paranormal: A Reconnaissance* (Beverly Hills, Calif.: Sage, 1975).

63. Cohen, *Monster Theory*.

64. This point is made by Andrew Tudor, *Monsters and Mad Scientists: A Cultural History of the Horror Movie* (Oxford: Basil Blackwell, 1989).

65. For an interesting analysis of the theology of Oprah Winfrey and its relation to the esoteric traditions—formerly known as the occult—central to New Age spirituality, see Virginia S. Fink, "Oprah: Televangelism or New Millennial Spirituality" (paper presented at the annual conference of the Society for the Scientific Study of Religion, October 1999).

66. Martin Marty has argued that the appeal of things like healing, energies, and the affective, feeling-oriented aspects of religious practice lies in the perception that such things enhance their lives in practical ways. See Martin Marty, "Where the Energies Go," *Annals of the American Academy* 527 (May 1993): 11–26.

67. This is where the ideology of individualism still rears its head, for these stories do not suggest that social responsibility should be addressed as collective action but still rely on the power of individual to transform herself and those around her—echoing the beliefs of contemporary Protestant evangelicalism.

68. "Grave," first aired May 21, 2002.

69. Zinna, review of "Grave," in Episode Guide, Much Ado about Buffy Web site. Available at www.chosentwo.com/buffy. Retrieved August 29, 2002.

70. Thomas Hibbs, Buffy's War: Good and Evil 101. National Review Online. May 24, 2002. Available at www.nationalreview.com/comment/comment-hibbs052402.asp. Retrieved September 1, 2002.

71. According to www.Buffyguide.com, this song appears on Sarah McLachlan's bonus disc originally included with the limited edition double-CD release of *Surfacing* in 1997. The song itself can be heard, and the lyrics viewed, at home.att.net/~poofcatone/StFrancis.html. Retrieved August 30, 2002.

CHAPTER 3

1. See, for example, William Fore, *Television and Religion: The Shaping of Faith, Values, and Culture* (Minneapolis: Augsburg, 1987); Quentin Schultze et al. *Dancing in the Dark: Youth, Popular Culture, and the Electronic Media* (Grand Rapids, Mich.: William B. Eerdmans, 1991).

2. See, for example, Stewart Hoover, "Visual Religion in Media Culture," in *The Visual Culture of American Religion*, ed. David Morgan and Sally Promey (Berkeley: University of California Press, 2000).

3. The oft-discussed and debated separation of religion and secular realms has as an important source Emile Durkheim's *The Elementary Forms of Religious Life*, trans. Karen Fields (New York: Free Press, 1995).

4. The GED is the legal equivalent of a high school diploma, administered with the successful passing of a series of exams. It is available in the United States for those who fail to complete their high school education and enables them to pursue either higher education or jobs reserved for high school graduates.

5. Stuart Hall, "Encoding/Decoding in Television Discourse," reprinted in *Culture, Media, Language*, ed. Stuart Hall et al. (London: Hutchinson, 1981); John Fiske, *Television Culture* (London: Routledge, 1987). See the discussion in chapter 1, n. 48.

6. David M. Jacobs, *The UFO Controversy in America* (Bloomington: Indiana University Press, 1975), 232–33. Cited in Jodi Dean, *Aliens in America: Conspiracy Cultures from Outerspace to Cyberspace* (Ithaca, N.Y.: Cornell University Press, 1998).

7. George Gallup Jr. and Frank Newport, "Belief in Psychic and Paranormal Phenomena Widespread among Americans," *Gallup Poll Monthly* 299 (August 1990): 35–43; Budd Hopkins, "The Roper Poll on Unusual Experiences," in *Alien Discussions: Proceedings of the Abduction Study Conference*, ed. Andrea Prichard et al. (Cambridge, Mass.: North Cambridge Press, 1994), 215–16. Cited in Dean, *Aliens in America*.

8. Fund for UFO Research, *Final Report on the Psychological Testing of UFO Abductees* (Mt. Rainier, Md.: Fund for UFO Research, 1985). Cited in Dean, *Aliens in America*.

9. As an example, see James R. Lewis, ed., *The Gods Have Landed: New Religions from Other Worlds* (Albany: State University of New York Press, 1995).

10. See, for example, *Skeptical Inquirer* magazine, available online at www.csicop.org/si, as well as the Web site for urban legends at www.urbanlegends.com. Perhaps most influential has been Carl Sagan, *The Demon-Haunted World: Science as a Candle in the Dark* (New York: Random House, 1996).

11. I'm indebted to my colleague Janice Peck for this wry turn of phrase.

12. Bill Ellis, "The Varieties of Alien Experience," *Skeptical Inquirer* (spring 1988): 263–69.

13. Ellis, "The Varieties of Alien Experience," 266.

14. Peter M. Rojcewicz, "The 'Men in Black' Experience and Tradition: Analogies with the Traditional Devil Hypothesis," *Journal of American Folklore* 100 (1987): 148–60.

15. Richard Boylan, cited in Prichard et al., *Alien Discussions*, 542.

16. Clifford Wilson and John Weldon, *Close Encounters: A Better Explanation* (San Diego: Master Books, 1978).

17. Angels feature in Islam and some Jewish traditions, as well, but I was only able to find connections between Christian angels and aliens. This is related to Christianity's hegemonic status in the United States and to the prevalence of alien stories in the United States as compared with other parts of the world. There have been no reports of alien abductions in Asia or Africa, and few in continental Europe, for instance, according to Thomas E. Bullard, "UFO Abduction Reports: The Supernatural Kidnap Narrative Returns in Technological Guise," *Journal of American Folklore* 102 (1989): 147–70.

18. Geddes MacGregor, *Angels: Ministers of Grace* (New York: Paragon House, 1988), xxi.

19. John Mack, *Abduction: Human Encounters with Aliens* (New York: Scribner's, 1994).

20. Whitley Striber, *Communion* (New York: Beech Tree Books/Morrow, 1987).

21. Stephen Hawking, *A Brief History of Time* (New York: Bantam, 1988); Carl Sagan, *Contact: A Novel* (New York: Simon and Schuster, 1985).

22. Paul Davies, *The Mind of God* (New York: Simon and Schuster, 1992).

23. Michael Bugeja, "The Media Factor: Why God Has Gone Pop," *Word and World* 18 (winter 1998): 3–83.

24. Dean, *Aliens in America*.

25. Cited in ibid., 36.

26. Paul Willis, *Learning to Labor: How Working-Class Kids Get Working-Class Jobs* (London: Gower, 1977); S. Elizabeth Bird, *For Enquiring Minds* (Knoxville: University of Tennessee Press, 1992); Pierre Bourdieu, *Distinction: A Social Critique of the Judgment of Taste*, trans. R. Nice (Cambridge, Mass.: Harvard University Press, 1984).

27. Interview with Lily Dearborn, conducted by author, August 1996.

CHAPTER 4

1. "Murphy's Luck," first aired March 30, 2000. "Wrestling with Demons," first aired February 2, 2001.

2. Race, or "whiteness," is also an element of judgment applied here in collusion with taste and class. See Mike Hill, ed., *Whiteness: A Critical Reader* (New York: New York University Press, 1997).

3. More will be said about *Touched by an Angel* and other representations of religion in the media in subsequent chapters.

4. Robert Wuthnow cites a 1994 *Time* poll for this statistic in *After Heaven: Spirituality in America since the 1950s* (Berkeley: University of California Press, 1998).

5. Charles Earle Funk, ed., *Funk and Wagnall's New Practical Standard Dictionary of the English Language* (New York: Funk and Wagnall's, 1957). I learned of this from a colleague, Barbara Mastrolia, when I was asked to present research on television's representations of angels on a panel titled "Representations of Death."

6. I have analyzed the blurring of boundaries between representations of angels and ghosts in Hollywood film and television programs in "The Angels and Ghosts of

Hollywood: A Cultural Studies Analysis of the Guardian Angel," available online at www.mediameaning.org (under Publications at the Teens/Supernatural page).

7. See Bill Ellis, "Legend-Tripping in Ohio: A Behavioral Survey," *Papers in Comparative Studies* 3, no. 2 (1982): 65; S. Elizabeth Bird, "Playing with Fear: Interpreting the Adolescent Legend Trip," *Western Folklore* 53 (July 1994): 191–209.

8. See Bird, "Playing with Fear."

9. Ellis, "Legend-Tripping in Ohio."

10. Ibid., 61–73.

11. Bird, "Playing with Fear," 200.

12. Ibid., and Ellis, "Legend-Tripping in Ohio."

13. See Dolf Zillman and Rhonda Gibson, "Evolution of the Horror Genre," in *Horror Films: Current Research on Audience Preferences and Reactions*, ed. James B. Weaver III and Ron Tamborini (Mahwah, N.J.: Lawrence Erlbaum, 1996).

14. As noted in the introduction, Modell argues that the passage from adolescence to adulthood is marked by financial and social independence from parents. See John Modell, *Into One's Own: From Youth to Adulthood in the United States, 1920–1975* (Berkeley: University of California Press, 1989).

15. Nancy Tatom Ammerman, "Golden Rule Christianity: Lived Religion in the American Mainstream," in *Lived Religion in America: Toward a History of Practice*, ed. David Hall (Princeton, N.J.: Princeton University Press, 1997), 196–216.

16. MacDonald demonstrates that contact with spirits of the deceased are reported most frequently in relation to the death of a loved one. See William MacDonald, "Idionecrophanies: The Social Construction of Perceived Contact with the Dead," *Journal for the Scientific Study of Religion* 31, no. 2 (1992): 215–23.

17. Mbiti discusses the importance of ancestors in African religions in John Mbiti, *African Religious Philosophy* (Garden City, N.Y.: Doubleday, 1969).

18. Lippy highlights the importance of the slave experience in contemporary African American religion, noting the practice of conjuring central to that tradition. The conjuring of spirits was believed to enable people to tap into supernatural power through ritual, trance, or visionary experiences. See Charles Lippy, *Being Religious, American Style: A History of Popular Religiosity in the United States* (Westport, Conn.: Greenwood Press, 1994).

19. David Hall, *Worlds of Wonder, Days of Judgment: Popular Religious Belief in Early New England* (New York: Knopf, 1989).

20. The story of the Cock Lane Ghost circulated after two young women, Fanny and Elizabeth, reported hearing sounds of scratching and rattling that kept them awake. Elizabeth's father began to conduct public séances as a means of warding off the otherworldly spirits, and these séances became a public spectacle. Eventually, Elizabeth was found to be falsifying the spirits' visits, and her father was tried and convicted of fraud. Nevertheless, people continued to visit the sites of the Cock Lane hauntings and to ponder the possibility that, even if the visits to Elizabeth had been falsified, the original sounds might have been an actual ghost. Adam Woog, *Poltergeists: Opposing Viewpoints* (San Diego: Greenhaven Press, 1995).

21. See Lippy, *Being Religious, American Style.*

22. These teens also had some commonalties with what sociologist Carol Lytch has called "the Lost," those teens with little interest or incentive to engage in deeper explorations with religion. However, unlike the young people she described, the teens in this chapter were not distanced from family members or alienated from their environments at large. In particular, Tammy and Nancy's cases illustrate the importance of

racial and class positions relative to alienation from white middle-class norms and suggest the need for further exploration of these and other factors in how and why some teens are "lost" to conventional religion.

23. The debate over the "secularization hypothesis" is lively in religious studies. While many agree that religion has not dissolved with the emergence of modernity and rational thought, some question whether religion has declined in cultural authority and has hence become largely privatized in U.S. life. For a full discussion of the debate, see the introduction.

24. George H. Gallup Institute, *The Spiritual Life of Young Americans: Approaching the Year 2000*, research report (Princeton, N.J.: George H. Gallup International Institute, 1999).

25. Williams describes the sentimentality of religion in Peter Williams, *Popular Religion in America: Symbolic Change and the Modernization Process in Historical Perspective* (Englewood Cliffs, N.J.: Prentice-Hall, 1980).

26. MacDonald, "Idionecrephanies."

27. This is supported by William MacDonald, "The Effects of Religiosity and Structural Strain on Reported Paranormal Experiences," *Journal for the Scientific Study of Religion*, 34, no. 3 (1995): 366–76.

28. Nachman Ben-Yehuda, "The Revival of the Occult and of Science Fiction," *Journal of Popular Culture* 20, no. 2 (fall 1986): 1–16.

29. Geertz has argued that religion's role within cultures is to serve as the location for consideration of the 'ordering of existence', which includes beliefs about the supernatural and the afterlife, in Clifford Geertz, "Religion as a Cultural System," *The Interpretation of Cultures* (New York: Basic Books, 1973).

CHAPTER 5

1. George H. Gallup Institute, *The Spiritual Life of Young Americans: Approaching the Year 2000*, research report (Princeton, N.J.: George H. Gallup International Institute, 1999).

2. William MacDonald, "The Effects of Religiosity and Structural Strain on Reported Paranormal Experiences," *Journal for the Scientific Study of Religion* 34, no. 3 (1995): 366–76; David Yamane and Megan Polzer, "Ways of Seeing Ecstasy in Modern Society: Experiential-Expressive and Cultural-Linguistic Views," *Sociology of Religion* 55 (1994): 1–25.

3. Wade Clark Roof, *A Generation of Seekers* (San Francisco: HarperSanFrancisco, 1993); Carol Lytch, "Choosing Faith across Generations: A Qualitative Study of Church-Affiliated High School Seniors and Their Parents" (Ph.D. diss., Emory University, 2000).

4. Liminal moments are periods of dramatic ritualistic upheaval that mark transitions from one phase of life, that of an innocent child, to that of a mature adult, according to Victor Turner, *The Ritual Process: Structure and Anti-Structure* (Ithaca, N.Y.: Cornell University Press, 1969).

5. The contentiousness of the relationships in the Dearborn household eventually played a role in how my research contact with them was to come to an end. After six months of contact with Amber and her father, I received a phone call from the estranged mother, who demanded to view the transcripts of her daughter's conversations with me. She attempted to challenge the right to confidentiality that was a part of all research participants' agreements for this project. After a brief conversation, it

became clear that discontinuation of the research might be in the best interests of both the overall research project and the members of the Dearborn family.

6. American Baptist congregations are generally more liberal than their Southern Baptist counterparts.

7. For discussions of the rise in personal autonomy in contemporary U.S. religion, see Phillip Hammond, *Religion and Personal Autonomy: The Third Disestablishment in America* (Columbia: University of South Carolina Press, 1992); Wade Clark Roof and William McKinney, *American Mainline Religion: Its Changing Shape and Future* (New Brunswick, N.J.: Rutgers University Press, 1987); Roof, *A Generation of Seekers.*

8. Interviews with the Gardners conducted September 27, 1997, and October 10, 1997, by Diane Alters.

9. On the legitimization of Wiccanism among the U.S. military, see Mark Silk, "Something Wiccan This Way Comes," *Religion in the News* 2, no. 2 (1999): 9–10, 22; on the growth of contemporary Wiccanism and paganism, see Helen Berger, *A Community of Witches: Contemporary Paganism and Witchcraft in the United States* (Columbia: University of South Carolina Press, 1999).

10. Wicca is a particular set of beliefs related to but not identical with the pagan tradition, although the Gardner family often used the terms interchangeably. For more information on these religions, see Berger, *A Community of Witches.*

11. For an analysis of the perception that the Internet provides a protected space for pagan and Wiccan ritual, see Jan Fernback, "Neo-Pagan Ritual on the Internet," in *Practicing Religion in the Age of the Media: Explorations in Media, Religion, and Culture,* ed. Stewart Hoover and Lynn Schofield Clark (New York: Columbia University Press, 2002).

12. On the evolution of parlor games from practices of esoteric religions, see the discussion on the occult in chapter 2.

13. Passage cited and analyzed in Diane Alters, "Identity and Meaning: The Project of Self-Reflexivity in a Family" (unpublished paper, 1997), 13–15. Katie and Annae's mother echoes a "spiritual seeker" approach that Roof has argued is found among approximately 9 percent of the "baby boomer" population. Roof, *A Generation of Seekers.*

14. Religious experience is foundational to religious life and commitment, with commitment to doctrine and dogma of a tradition growing from it, according to William James, *The Varieties of Religious Experience: The Gifford Lectures, Delivered in 1901–1902 in Edinburgh* (New York: Vintage Books, 1990).

15. Charles Lippy, *Being Religious, American Style: A History of Popular Religiosity in the United States* (Westport, Conn.: Greenwood Press, 1994).

16. MacDonald makes this point using data from the 1984 General Social Survey in William L. MacDonald, "The Effects of Religiosity and Structural Strain on Reported Paranormal Experiences," *Journal for the Scientific Study of Religion* 34, no. 3 (1995): 366–76. He argues for the importance of separately analyzing types of paranormal experiences (clairvoyance, telepathy, contact with the dead) and their connections to social construction.

17. The influence of parental control on adolescent religious experiences is analyzed by Raymond Potvin and D. M. Sloane, "Parental Control, Age, and Religious Practice," *Review of Religious Research* 27 (1985): 3–14.

18. Citing data from the General Social Survey, MacDonald notes that while 25

percent of persons surveyed in 1972 agreed that they had been "really in touch with someone who had died," more than 40 percent agreed with the same statement in 1984. See MacDonald, "Effects of Religiosity and Structural Strain," For the statistic of more than 40 percent, MacDonald cites Andrew Greeley, "Hallucinations among the Widowed," *Sociology and Social Research* 71, no. 4 (1987): 258–65. MacDonald notes that the 1989 General Social Survey finds that 35.6 percent reported experiencing such contact, a dip from Greeley's finding yet still significantly above the 1972 date.

19. See, for example, Robert Bellah, "Is There a Common American Culture?" *Journal of the American Academy of Religion* 66 (1998): 613–25.

20. As an example, see Nicholas Orme, *The Saints of Cornwall* (Oxford: Oxford University Press, 2000).

21. Greeley and Hout use this statement to conclude their argument that religious organizations have a greater interest in maintaining orthodox positions when confronted with an increased competition with other sources of belief. Their research serves to offer an explanation for the increase in beliefs in life after death among Catholics and Jews in the United States over the past decades. Yet they seem to assume that survey respondents understand "life after death" as they do: with reference to heaven rather than with reference to perceived contact with the dead. Andrew M. Greeley and Michael Hout, "Americans' Increasing Belief in Life after Death: Religious Competition and Acculturation," *American Sociological Review* 64 (December 1999): 813–55.

22. Theologian Patricia Davis suggests that allowing young people to acknowledge the horrors in their own lives is a necessary aspect of religious and spiritual development that is currently neglected in most religious contexts. See Patricia Davis, "Horror and the Development of Girls' Spiritual Voices," in *In Her Own Time: Women and Developmental Issues in Pastoral Care*, ed. Jeanne Stevenson-Moessner (Minneapolis: Fortress Press, 2000), 103–13.

23. Stewart Hoover, "Media and the Construction of the Religious Public Sphere," in *Rethinking Media, Religion, and Culture*, ed. Stewart Hoover and Knut Lundby (Thousand Oaks, Calif.: Sage, 1997).

CHAPTER 6

1. Sharon Begley, "A World of Their Own," special report and cover story: "God, Sex, Race, and the Future: What Teens Believe," *Newsweek* (May 8, 2000), 53–56.

2. George H. Gallup International Institute, *The Spiritual Life of Young Americans: Approaching the Year 2000*, research report (Princeton, N.J.: George H. Gallup International Institute, 1999).

3. Martin Marty and Scott Appleby, eds., *Fundamentalisms Comprehended* (Chicago: University of Chicago Press, 1995); Jose Casanova, *Public Religions in the Modern World* (Chicago: University of Chicago Press, 1994).

4. Robert Wuthnow, *The Restructuring of American Religion: Society and Faith since World War II* (Princeton, N.J.: Princeton University Press, 1988).

5. Interviews with the Hansen family conducted by Lee Hood, November 2, 1997, and November 21, 1998. Interviews with Sweetie Buchanan and her family conducted by Diane Alters, January 11 and June 9, 1998.

6. George M. Marsden, *Understanding Fundamentalism and Evangelicalism* (Grand Rapids, Mich.: William B. Eerdmans, 1991), 4–5.

7. Christian Smith, *American Evangelicalism: Embattled and Thriving* (Chicago: University of Chicago Press, 1998).

8. Wildmon is the founder of the National Federation for Decency, the National Coalition for Better Television, and the better-known American Family Association, all three of which are watchdog groups that monitor sex, violence, and profanity in the media. Dobson is the author, radio host, and founder of the Focus on the Family ministry, which offers resources and exposés of what he purports are the negative influences of the media on contemporary teens, families, and young people. See Lynn Schofield Clark, "Fundamentalists and the Entertainment Media," in *Encyclopedia of Fundamentalism*, ed. Brenda Brasher (New York: Berkshire Publishing, 2001); Quentin Schultze, "Evangelicals' Uneasy Alliance with the Media," in *Religion and Mass Media: Audiences and Adaptations*, ed. Daniel Stout and Judith Buddenbaum (Thousand Oaks, Calif.: Sage, 1996), 61–73.

9. Todd Rendleman, "Evil Images in 'At Play in the Fields of the Lord': Evangelicals and Representations of Sexuality in Contemporary Film," *Velvet Light Trap: A Critical Journal of Film and Television* 46 (fall 2000): 12–26.

10. "Megachurch" is a term used to describe congregations of several thousand who draw their members from a wide geographic area. See John N. Vaughn, *Megachurches and America's Cities: How Churches Grow* (Grand Rapids, Mich.: Baker Books, 1993); Donald E. Miller, *Reinventing American Protestantism* (Berkeley: University of California Press, 1997).

11. For a historical overview of women's primary role in child-raising in the home, see Stephanie Coontz, *The Way We Never Were: American Families and the Nostalgia Trap* (New York: Basic Books, 1992). For a discussion of how this practice continues in the present, see Judith Stacey, *Brave New Families: Stories of Domestic Upheaval in Late-Twentieth-Century America* (New York: Basic Books, 1990).

12. In her dissertation on three church youth groups, Carol Lytch documents the use of these materials among evangelical youth. See Carol Lytch, "Choosing Faith across Generations: A Qualitative Study of Church-Affiliated High School Seniors and Their Parents" (Ph.D. diss., Emory University, 2000).

13. In media studies, adolescents, like older members of media audiences, generally assume that the media have no effect on them but probably have a deleterious impact on the lives and beliefs of others. This is called the "third person effect." See W. P. Davison, "The Third-Person Effect in Communication," *Public Opinion Quarterly* 47 (1983): 1–15.

14. U.S. Bureau of the Census, *Statistical Abstract of the United States: 1993*, 113th ed. (Washington, D.C.: GPO, 1993), 63. Available at www.census.gov. However, some have argued that due to measurement practices, the number of high school youth living with both parents of origin is actually lower than the census indicates, thus making blended and single-parent families closer to one-half than one-third. See Donald J. Hernandez, *America's Children: Resources from Family, Government, and the Economy* (New York: Russell Sage Foundation, 1993).

15. Kirk Hadaway and Penny Marler, "What the Polls Don't Show: A Closer Look at U.S. Church Attendance," *American Sociological Review* 58 (1993): 741–53.

16. Some estimate that as many as 40 percent of those in the United States now identify themselves as evangelical. See George H. Gallup and Jim Castelli, *The People's Religion: American Faith in the 90s* (New York: Macmillan, 1989).

17. On the Protestantization process as specifically related to U.S. Catholicism, see N. J. Demerath and Rhys Williams, *A Bridging of Faiths* (Princeton, N.J.: Princeton University Press, 1992). Wuthnow makes the more general argument in Robert Wuth-

now, *Christianity in the Twenty-First Century: Reflections on the Challenges Ahead* (New York: Oxford University Press, 1993).

18. Harold Bloom, *The American Religion* (New York: Touchstone, 1992).

19. Ibid., 107.

20. See Phillip Hammond, *Religion and Personal Autonomy: The Third Disestablishment in America* (Columbia: University of South Carolina Press, 1992).

21. Daniel A. Stout, "Protecting the Family: Mormon Teachings about Mass Media," in Stout and Buddenbaum, *Religion and Mass Media*, 85–99.

22. Ezekiel Schwoch was interviewed by Joseph Champ on February 26, 1998.

23. As noted in the introduction, Zeke and other teens who were over the age of 19 were included in this study if they met an important sociological criteria for consideration as adolescents: they were economically and socially dependent and still residing full-time in the home of their parents. This definition excludes students who are attending college, for they are no longer socially dependent on their parents and have entered the transitional phase of distancing from parents expected of adolescents in the United States.

24. Max Weber, *Protestant Ethic and the Spirit of Capitalism*, trans. Talcott Parsons (New York: Scribner, 1930).

25. Interviews and observations conducted with Hasan Ahmed and his family by the author on multiple occasions between June 1996 and March 1998.

26. See Omer Awass, "The Representation of Islam in the American Media," *Hamdard Islamicus* 19, no. 3 (1996): 87–102.

27. Edward Said, *Covering Islam* (New York: Pantheon Books, 1981).

28. For an in-depth analysis, see Lynn Schofield Clark, "If You Stay Away from Nintendo, You'll Read the Qur'an More: Media, the Family, and Muslim Identity" (paper presented to the Second Public Media, Religion, and Culture conference, Edinburgh, Scotland, July 1999). Available at www.Colorado.edu/Journalism/teens.

29. In fact, Hasan expressed exasperation that his parents didn't enforce the rules more strictly!

30. This argument, as Lytch points out, is in direct contrast to Giddens's assertion that certain people accept their religious tradition as a "given." My data further bear this out. See Lytch, "Choosing Faith across Generations."

31. Lytch, "Choosing Faith across Generations."

32. Smith, *American Evangelicalism*.

33. Lytch, "Choosing Faith across Generations."

34. Schultze, "Evangelicals and Mass Media."

35. See, e.g., Joshua Meyrowitz, *No Sense of Place: The Impact of Electronic Media on Social Behavior* (New York: Oxford University Press, 1985); Quentin Schultze, Roy Anker, James Bratt, William Romanowski, John Worst, and Lambert Zuidervaart, *Dancing in the Dark: Youth, Popular Culture, and the Media* (Grand Rapids, Mich.: William B. Eerdmans, 1991).

36. More liberal theological traditions, particularly feminists and process theologians, emphasize what is called the immanent, rather than transcendent, approaches to the human/divine relationship. See, e.g., Phyllis Trible, *God and the Rhetoric of Sexuality* (Philadelphia: Fortress Press, 1978); John B. Cobb and David Ray Griffin, *Process Theology: An Introductory Exposition* (Philadelphia: Westminster Press, 1972).

37. See Gallup Institute, *The Spiritual Life of Young Americans*; Robert Wuthnow, *After Heaven: Spirituality in America since the 1950s* (Berkeley: University of California Press, 1998).

CHAPTER 7

1. Mike McPhee, "Hark! Boulder Angels Reign," *Denver Post* (December 8, 1995), B1.

2. Karen Mitchell, Religion News Service, "Colorado Town Hung Up on Angels," *Cleveland Plain Dealer* (December 21, 1995), 28A.

3. Jack Kisling, "Two Cities with But a Single Thought," *Denver Post* (December 7, 1995), B11.

4. Mike McPhee, "Angels Stir Up a Flap: Boulder Debates Tree Ornaments," *Denver Post* (December 6, 1995), A1. It's worth noting that the journalists interviewed adult residents, unfortunately not talking with the unusually large population of college students and teens in that youthful city. Obviously, I think this says more about the biases of journalism than about the lack of discourse on angels among those who are still coming of age.

5. George H. Gallup International Institute, *The Spiritual Life of Young Americans: Approaching the Year 2000*, research report (Princeton, N.J.: George H. Gallup International Institute, 1999); see also Robert Wuthnow, *After Heaven: Spirituality in America since the 1950s* (Berkeley: University of California Press, 1998).

6. For a provocative analysis of the commodification of Christian symbols and the role of "stuff" in maintaining Christian culture, see Colleen McDannell, *Material Christianity* (New Haven, Conn.: Yale University Press, 1995).

7. Michael Rogness, "A Fascination with Angels," *Word and World* 18 (1998): 57–61.

8. The sales figure on angel books comes from Sebastian Smith, "Angel Mania Takes Flight in U.S.," *Agence France Press* (January 13, 1994), I. Cited in Wuthnow, *After Heaven*, 121.

9. See best-selling books by popular spirituality leader and frequent Oprah guest Marianne Williamson, as well as books by psychics Sylvia Browne (with Lindsay Harrison) and John Edwards.

10. Robert Wuthnow, *Learning to Care: Elementary Kindness in an Age of Indifference* (New York: Oxford University Press; 1999); Peter Benson, Dorothy Williams, and Arthur Johnson, *The Quicksilver Years: The Hopes and Fears of Young Adolescents* (San Francisco: Harper and Row, 1987).

11. Carol Lytch describes the "modal" practices of religiosity among what she refers to as marginalizing teens. See Carol Lytch, "Choosing Faith across Generations: A Qualitative Study of Church-Affiliated High School Seniors and Their Parents" (Ph.D. diss., Emory University, 2000).

12. For an analysis of the importance of homogeneity to intergroup relations in religious traditions, see Penny L. Marler, "Friendship Networks and Religious Marginality" (paper presented to the annual meeting of the American Sociological Association, August 2000, Washington, D.C.).

13. Interviewed multiple times by the author between March 1, 1996, and April 20, 2000. Between the time that she was fourteen and sixteen, Elizabeth served as what I called an "expert on teen life" for me. Elizabeth acted first as a formal research informant and interviewee and then as a leader and coanalyst of a few discussion groups she organized with her friends; later she spent time with me socializing on a more informal basis. She often patiently listened to and discussed my overall research interests and findings. More information on methodology is available in the appendix.

14. Like many white liberal Protestant churches, the most frequent attendees were

those of retirement age or older. For statistics on the demographics of mainline Protestant congregations and an argument about the approach to beliefs the members hold within them, see Wade C. Roof and William McKinney, *American Mainline Religion* (New Brunswick, N.J.: Rutgers University Press, 1987).

15. Television viewing declines throughout adolescence and never regains its prominence among many adults. See J. D. Klein, J. D. Brown, K. W. Childers, J. Oliveri, C. Porter, and C. Dykers, "Adolescents' Risky Behavior and Mass Media Use," *Pediatrics* 91 (1993): 281–86.

16. See in particular the homages to Matt Camden, the older teen male character in the *7th Heaven* family, portrayed by Barry Watson, available at www.filmkc.org/7thHeaven/menu.html.

17. This is similar to the "utilitarian individualism" noted in Robert Bellah, *Habits of the Heart: Individualism and Commitment in American Life* (Berkeley: University of California Press, 1985). It is also similar to the blending of spirituality and therapy noted in Catherine Albanese, "Fisher Kings and Public Places: The Old New Age in the 1990s," *Annals of the American Academy of Political and Social Science* 527 (May 1993): 131–43; see also Wade Clark Roof, *Spiritual Marketplace* (Princeton, N.J.: Princeton University Press, 1999).

18. Elizabeth's Lutheran pastor often wears a collar, so it is clear that she is familiar with the Protestant tradition of collar-wearing. I think this is suggestive of the fact that the clerical collar is usually associated with Catholicism in the media, and thus because she saw it in the media she assumed the consistency with other media rather than with her own experience. But this is not to rule out some confusion about Catholicism among Protestants. Coincidentally, when writing this chapter my husband and I met up with a man who was from my husband's home town. When my husband mentioned that his father had been a pastor in that town, the man asked, "Really? At the Catholic church?" We enjoyed kidding my father-in-law about that one!

19. I refer to this approach as "popular religiosity," borrowing the term and concept from Charles Lippy, *Being Religious, American Style: A History of Popular Religiosity in the United States* (Westport, Conn.: Greenwood Press, 1994).

20. See Horace Newcomb, "Religion on Television," in *Channels of Belief*, ed. John Ferre (Ames: Iowa University Press, 1990), 29–44.

21. The definitive work on baby boomers and spirituality is Wade Clark Roof, *A Generation of Seekers* (San Francisco: HarperCollins, 1993). See also Roof, *Spiritual Marketplace*.

22. Like Elizabeth, Michael led a peer discussion group with his friends for me and I was able to hear this. This kind of God-talk is not uncommon among Christian African Americans. See Cheryl Townsend Gilkes, "I Want to Know Where I Am: Framing the Sacred in African American Life and Culture" (paper presented to the annual meeting of the Society for the Scientific Study of Religion, Nashville, Tenn., November 1996).

23. C. A. Lin and D. J. Atkins, "Parental Mediation and Rule Making for Adolescent Use of Television and VCRs," *Journal of Broadcasting and Electronic Media* 33 (1989): 53–67.

24. See Sut Jhally and Lisa Lewis, *Enlightened Racism: The Cosby Show, Audiences, and the Myth of the American Dream* (Boulder, Colo.: Westview Press, 1992); Ella Shohat and Robert Stam, eds., *Unthinking Eurocentrism: Multiculturalism and the Media* (London and New York: Routledge, 1994); Hamid Naficy, *The Making of Exile*

Cultures: Iranian Television in Los Angeles (Minneapolis: University of Minnesota Press, 1993); Oscar Gandy, *Communication and Race: A Structural Perspective* (New York: Oxford University Press, 1998).

25. This is not to imply that *Touched by an Angel* is somehow free of ideology that would be appealing to the Anglo-American middle classes, however, as the ratings and an analysis of the program's appeal tell otherwise. See also "Religion, Ideology, and Class: A Case Study of *Touched by an Angel*" (paper presented at the annual meeting of the International Communication Association, San Francisco, May 1999). Available at www.Colorado.edu/Journalism/MEDIALYF.

26. In the sense that both encountered divorce and that this event proved a catalyst for rethinking that tradition, they were similar to Sweetie Buchanan, introduced in the previous chapter. However, unlike Sweetie, it was not the questioning of the religious colleagues that drove that rethinking, but rather Elizabeth's and Michael's reaction to the divorce and their efforts to deal with changed family situations.

27. Lytch, "Choosing Faith across Generations."

28. Bellah et al., *Habits of the Heart.*

29. Giddens argues that in contemporary modernity's situation of increased individual choice, for some persons, religious authority is one of several possible sources of "expert authority." Anthony Giddens, *Modernity and Self-Identity: Self and Society in the Late Modern Age* (Stanford, Calif.: Stanford University Press, 1991).

CHAPTER 8

1. C. Bybee, D. Robinson, and J. Turow, "Determinants of Parental Guidance of Children's Television Viewing for a Special Subgroup: Mass Media Scholars," *Journal of Broadcasting* 26 (1982): 697–710; J. L. Singer, D. G. Singer, and W. S. Rapaczynski, "Family Patterns and Television Viewing as Predictors of Children's Beliefs and Aggression," *Journal of Communication* 34, no. 2 (1984): 73–89; R. J. Desmond, J. L. Singer, D. G. Singer, R. Calam, and K. Colimore, "Family Mediation Patterns and Television Viewing: Young Children's Use and Grasp of the Medium," *Human Communication Research* 11 (1985): 461–80.

2. These three approaches have been investigated as active mediation (engaging young people in dialogue), restrictive mediation (rules governing content or time use), and coviewing (monitoring or sharing in the media consumption practices). See Amy Nathanson, "The Immediate and Cumulative Effects of Television Mediation on Children's Aggression" (Ph.D. diss., University of Wisconsin–Madison, 1998); Amy Nathanson, "Identifying and Explaining the Relationship Between Parental Mediation and Children's Aggression," *Communication Research* 26, no. 2 (1999): 124–43.

3. J. D. Brown, K. W. Childers, K. E. Bauman, and G. Koch, "The Influence of New Media and Family Structure on Young Adolescent Television and Radio Use," *Communication Research* 17 (1990): 65–82.

4. C. A. Lin and D. J. Adkins, "Parental Mediation and Rulemaking for Adolescent Use of Television and VCRs," *Journal of Broadcasting and Electronic Media* 33 (1989): 53–67.

5. This is the view supported in such noteworthy work on religious socialization as Robert Coles, *The Spiritual Life of Children* (Boston: Houghton Mifflin, 1990).

6. R. H. Potvin and D. M. Sloane, "Parental Control, Age, and Religious Practice," *Review of Religious Research* 27 (1985): 3–14. Cited in Carol Lytch, "Choosing Faith across Generations: A Qualitative Study of Church-Affiliated High School Seniors and Their Parents" (Ph.D. diss., Emory University, 2000).

7. Lytch, "Choosing Faith across Generations."

8. Jackson Carroll and Wade Clark Roof, "Family Disruption and Churchgoing Habits," *Christian Century* (January 7–14, 1998), 9; George H. Gallup International Institute, *The Spiritual Life of Young Americans: Approaching the Year 2000*, research report (Princeton, N.J.: George H. Gallup International Institute, 1999).

9. Jerald G. Bachman, Lloyd D. Johnston, and Patrick M. O'Malley, *Monitoring the Future: Questionnaire Responses from the Nation's High School Seniors, 1992* (Ann Arbor: Survey Research Center, Institute for Social Research, University of Michigan, 1993), 183–85.

10. Lytch, "Choosing Faith across Generations."

11. The Barna Reseach Group, *Third Millennium Teens: Research on the Minds, Hearts, and Souls of America's Teenagers*, research report (Barna Research Group, Ltd., 1999).

12. Lytch points out that the primary difference is that while baby boomers encountered increased choice as a result of the turbulent decade of the 1960s, their teenage children have inherited a tendency to emphasize personal choice. Lytch, "Choosing Faith across Generations."

13. The term and the existentialist approach to religion are represented in the writings of Paul Tillich, an influential twentieth-century theologian. Paul Tillich, *The Dynamics of Faith* (New York: Harper and Row, 1957). See also H. Richard Niebuhr, *The Responsible Self* (New York: Harper and Row, 1963).

14. Wade Clark Roof, *A Generation of Seekers: Spiritual Journeys of the Baby Boom Generation* (San Francisco: HarperSanFrancisco, 1993).

15. Wade Clark Roof and Lyn Gesch, "Boomers and the Culture of Choice," in *Work, Family, and Religion in Contemporary Society*, ed. Nancy Tatom Ammerman and Wade Clark Roof (New York: Routledge, 1995).

16. To a large extent this affirms Hoge, Johnson and Luidens's assertion that American baby boomers believe that an important function all religions share is the upholding of a "moral code," See Dean Hoge, Benton Johnson, and Donald Luidens, *Vanishing Boundaries: The Religion of Mainline Protestant Baby Boomers* (Louisville, Ky.: Westminster/John Knox Press, 1994); Nancy Tatom Ammerman, "Golden Rule Christianity: Lived Religion in the American Mainstream," in *Lived Religion in America: Toward a History of Practice*, ed. David Hall (Princeton, N.J.: Princeton University Press, 1997).

17. An excerpt of this conversation on values is found in chapter 7.

18. A term helpfully defined by Marler and Hadaway as those occasional church attenders who neverless seek to maintain some identification with institutional religion. See Penny Long Marler and C. Kirk Hadaway, "Toward a Typology of Protestant 'Marginal Members,'" *Review of Religious Research* 35, no. 1 (1993).

19. She viewed this episode in the context of a group discussion, as well. More information on methodology is available in appendix A.

20. Interview with John Hart conducted by Diane Alters, December 29, 1997.

21. Stephen R. Warner, "Work in Progress toward a New Paradigm for the Sociological Study of Religion in the United States," *American Journal of Sociology* 98 (1993): 1044–93.

22. See Linda Kintz and Julia Lesage, eds., *Media, Culture, and the Religious Right* (Minneapolis: University of Minnesota Press, 1998).

23. On meaning-making in media studies, see Klaus Bruhn Jensen, "When Is Meaning?," *Communication Yearbook* 14 (1990): 3–32. On meaning-making regarding

religion and regarding television, see Stewart Hoover, "Visual Religion in Media Culture," in *The Visual Culture of American Religion*, ed. David Morgan and Sally Promey (Berkeley: University of California Press, 2000).

24. Roof and Gesch, "Boomers and the Culture of Choice."

25. Reginald Bibby et al., "Religion and Identity: The Canadian, American, and Brazilian Cases," *International Journal of Comparative Sociology* 39, no. 2 (1998): 237–51.

26. N. Jay Demerath III, "Cultural Victory and Organizational Defeat in the Paradoxical Decline of Liberal Protestantism," *Journal for the Scientific Study of Religion* 34, no. 4 (1995): 458–69. The contemporary notion of "free will" relates to Calvin's idea that each individual is responsible for his or her own fate and therefore must choose to follow God on his or her own accord.

27. John Modell, *Into One's Own: From Youth to Adulthood in the United States, 1920–1975* (Berkeley: University of California Press, 1989).

28. On the importance of genre to the interpretation of the entertainment media, see Horace Newcomb, "Assessing the Violence Profile Studies of Gerbner and Gross: A Humanistic Critique and Suggestion," *Communication Research* 5, no. 3 (1978): 264–82.

29. *Touched by an Angel* was discussed in more detail in chapter 7.

30. For more information on group discussions and their role in the methodology of this project, see appendix A.

31. Ellen Seiter, *Television and New Media Audiences* (Oxford: Clarendon Press, 1998).

CHAPTER 9

1. David Hambling, "Online Science: Feel the Force, Luke: David Hambling Visits the Wider Shores of Magnetic Phenomena," *The Guardian* (August 21, 2000), 15; KABC-AM Radio (July 10, 2000); Brian Betmore, "Look Who's Paranoid Now," *MacLean's* (August 2000), 41. All stories and transcripts retrieved online using Lexis-Nexis on October 6, 2000.

2. Jodi Dean, *Aliens in America: Conspiracy Cultures from Outerspace to Cyberspace* (Ithaca, N.Y.: Cornell University Press, 1998).

3. Fund for UFO Research, "Final Report on the Psychological Testing of UFO Abductees" (Mt. Rainier, Md.: Fund for UFO Research, 1985). See also D. Lester and K. Monaghan, "Belief in Paranormal Phenomena and Personality," *Perceptual and Motor Skills* 81, no. 1 (1995): 114–15; C. A. Salter and L. M. Routledge, "Intelligence and Belief in the Supernatural," *Psychological Reports* 34, no. 1 (1974): 299–302; J. Royalty, "The Generalizability of Critical Thinking: Paranormal Beliefs versus Statistical Reasoning," *Journal of Genetic Psychology* 156, no. 4 (1995): 482. These sources were brought to my attention in Dean, *Aliens in America*.

4. Dean, *Aliens in America*, 18.

5. Pierre Bourdieu, *Distinction: A Social Critique of the Judgment of Taste*, trans. Richard Nice (Cambridge, Mass.: Harvard University Press, 1984).

6. Michele Lamont and Annette Lareau, "Cultural Capital: Allusions and Glissandos in Recent Theoretical Developments," *Sociological Theory* 6 (1988): 163.

7. Ellen Seiter, *Television and New Media Audiences* (Oxford: Clarendon Press, 1999).

8. In the United Kingdom, this tradition has been associated with F. R. Leavis. See, for example, F. R. Leavis and Denys Thompson, *Culture and Environment* (Lon-

don: Chatto and Windus, 1933). In the United States, the tradition of high culture vs. low culture is carried on in the writings of Neil Postman, among others. See Neil Postman, *Amusing Ourselves to Death: Public Discourse in the Age of Show Business* (New York: Viking, 1985).

9. For a history of cultural studies' intellectual development, see Graeme Turner, *British Cultural Studies: An Introduction* (New York and London: Routledge, 1990).

10. Henry Jenkins, *Textual Poachers: Television Fans and Participatory Culture* (New York: Routledge, 1992); Janice Radway, *Reading the Romance: Women, Patriarchy, and Popular Literature* (Chapel Hill: University of North Carolina Press, 1984).

11. Antonio Gramsci, *Selections from the Prison Notebooks*, ed. and trans. Q. Hoare and G. N. Smith (New York: International Publishers, 1971).

12. Stuart Hall, "The Rediscovery of 'Ideology': The Return of the Repressed in Media Studies," in *Culture, Society and the Media*, ed. Michael Gurevitch, Tony Bennett, James Curran, and Janet Woolacott (London: Methuen, 1982), 56–90, esp. 63–64.

13. Todd Gitlin, *Inside Prime Time* (New York: Pantheon, 1983); Todd Gitlin, *The Whole World Is Watching: Mass Media in the Making and Unmaking of the New Left* (Berkeley: University of California Press, 1980).

14. Laura Sullivan, "The Truth Is in There . . . They're Sure of It," *Los Angeles Times* (August 30, 2000), E2. Reprinted article from the *Baltimore Sun*, originally titled "UFO Theorists Mining NSA Site for X-Files," 1A. Bill Briggs, "Wyoming UFO Watch: Enthusiasts Scan Sky Every Year," *Denver Post* (June 27, 2000), E01. Articles retrieved online using Lexis-Nexis on October 6, 2000.

15. Hallie Deaktor, "Evidence on the Subway That Aliens Are Among Us," *All Things Considered*, National Public Radio (September 12, 2000). Transcript retrieved online using Lexis-Nexis on October 6, 2000.

16. The *Skeptical Inquirer* magazine, published by the Committee for the Scientific Investigation of Claims of the Paranormal, repeatedly uses this phrase derisively. See *Skeptical Inquirer* online at www.csicop.com.

17. Philip J. Klass, *The Real Roswell Crashed-Saucer Coverup* (Amherst, N.Y.: Prometheus, 1997).

18. Dean, *Aliens in America*, 6, 150.

19. Bourdieu, *Distinction*.

20. Most sociologists today dispute the idea that religious beliefs decrease as scientific knowledge increases, as once proposed by Weber (but it is important to note that this idea still holds wide public support in certain places that have great cultural legitimation, such as in institutions of higher education). Secularization theorists, however, debate whether institutions and historic beliefs are questioned to a greater degree in the present than they were in the past.

21. See Philip Hammond, *Religion and Personal Autonomy: The Third Disestablishment in America* (Columbia: University of South Carolina Press, 1992); R. Stephen Warner, "Work in Progress toward a New Paradigm for the Sociological Study of Religion in the United States," *American Journal of Sociology* 98, no. 5 (1993): 1044–93; William McKinney and Wade Clark Roof, *American Mainline Religion: Its Changing Shape and Future* (New Brunswick, N.J.: Rutgers University Press, 1987).

22. Alan Orenstein, "Religion and Paranormal Belief," *Journal for the Scientific Study of Religion* 41, no. 2 (2002): 301–11.

23. In the ranking of careers according to socioeconomic status, construction work ranks considerably lower in status than other positions.

24. Cultural and social capital are Bourdieu's terms for knowledge that has value in terms of its ability to relate a person to others in status positions and the relationships that, in turn, can build from these similarities and result in greater economic capital for persons. See Bourdieu, *Distinction*.

25. See note 20.

26. Rita Ciolli, "Angels among Us: Current Fascination Seems Boundless," *Pittsburgh Post-Gazette* (December 24, 1995), G2.

27. George H. Gallup Institute, *The Spiritual Life of Young Americans: Approaching the Year 2000*, research report (Princeton, N.J.: George H. Gallup International Institute, 1999); Robert Wuthnow, *After Heaven: Spirituality in America since the 1950s* (Berkeley: University of California Press, 1998).

28. Nielsen ratings, broken down by age groups, are usually not accessible to the general public. In this case, a media scholar with connections to a network affiliate was able to verify for me that *Touched by an Angel* did achieve some success among younger audiences.

29. On the relationship of sentimentality, kitsch, and the rejection of certain forms of popular fiction as "low culture," see Radway, *Reading the Romance*. See also her book, *A Feeling for Books: The Book-of-the-Month Club, Literary Taste, and Middle-Class Desire* (Chapel Hill: University of North Carolina Press, 1997).

30. In addition to the interviews conducted for the current project, I am indebted to Hillary Warren, a colleague in media and religion who shared some of her interview transcripts with me. In her dissertation research on Southern Baptists and their responses to news coverage of Disney, Warren found that people occasionally mentioned *Touched by an Angel* as an example of positive programming that depicted "uplifting" or "moral" values.

31. According to a national survey of teens, *Touched by an Angel* was rated one of the most encouraged shows among 10–17-year-olds for 1997, 1998, and 1999. Jeffrey Stanger and Natalia Gridina, *Media in the Home: The Fourth Annual Survey of Parents and Children* (Philadelphia: Annenberg Public Policy Center Survey Report, 1999).

32. "Television," *Christianity Today* (September 11, 1995), 58.

33. Based on weekly Nielsen television ratings research, 1996–2000.

34. Sandy Smith, "Heaven-Sent," *Aspire* (April 1996), 27–32.

35. Donald E. Piper, Jack Keeler, and William J. Brown, "Audience Involvement with *Touched by an Angel*" (paper presented to the annual conference of the Broadcast Education Association, Las Vegas, April 1997).

36. Lynn Schofield Clark, "How Audiences Talk about *Touched by an Angel*: Religion and Spirituality in Contemporary Public Discourse" (paper presented to the annual meeting of the Society for the Scientific Study of Religion, Nashville, Tenn., November 1997). Available at www.Colorado.edu/Journalism/teens. See also Lynn Schofield Clark, "Identity, Discourse, and Media Audiences: A Critical Ethnography of the Role of the Visual Media in Religious Identity-Construction among U.S. Teens" (Ph.D. diss., University of Colorado, 1998).

37. Gallup and Castelli, *People's Religion;* Gallup Institute, *The Spiritual Lives of Young Americans*; Wuthnow, *After Heaven*.

38. Interview with John Hart, conducted by Diane Alters, December 29, 1997.

39. www.angeltouch.com. Retrieved March 10, 1997.

40. Kevin Bradt, "Response to the Television Program *Nothing Sacred*" (keynote address presented to the Catholic Theological Society in America, Ottawa, Canada, June 1998).

41. Michael Rogness, "A Fascination with Angels," *Word and World* 18 (winter 1998): 3–83.

42. Harold Bloom, *Omens of Millennium: The Gnosis of Angels, Dreams, and Resurrection* (New York: Riverhead Books, 1996).

43. Vittorio Lanternari, "La Religion Populaire: Perspective Histoirque et Anthropologique," *Archives de Sciences Sociales des Religions* 53 (April 1996): 121–43. Cited in Charles Lippy, *Being Religious, American Style: A History of Popular Religiosity in the United States* (Westport, Conn.: Greenwood Press, 1994).

44. Lippy, *Being Religious, American Style*, 5.

45. Max Weber, "The Protestant Sects and the Spirit of Capitalism," in *From Max Weber: Essays in Sociology*, trans. Hans H. Gerth and C. Wright Mills (New York: Oxford University Press, 1946); Ernst Troeltsch, *The Social Teaching of the Christian Churches*, 2 vols., trans. Olive Wyon (New York: Macmillan, 1931); and H. Richard Niebuhr, *The Social Sources of Denominationalism* (New York; Henry Holt, 1929). Lippy, in *Being Religious, American Style*, also makes this argument.

46. Bradford Verter, "Dark Star Rising: The Emergence of Modern Occultism" (Ph.D. diss., Princeton University, 1998).

47. Herbert Leventhal, *In the Shadow of the Enlightenment: Occultism and Renaissance Science in Eighteenth-Century America* (New York: New York University Press, 1976).

CHAPTER 10

1. The quote is from Charles Lippy, *Being Religious, American Style: A History of Popular Religiosity in the United States* (Westport, Conn.: Greenwood Press, 1994), viii.

2. This point was made by Thomas Luckmann in *The Invisible Religion* (New York: Macmillan, 1967).

3. Philip Hammond, *Religion and Personal Autonomy: The Third Dissestablishment in America* (Columbia: University of South Carolina Press, 1992).

4. Wade Clark Roof, *Spiritual Marketplace* (Princeton, N.J.: Princeton University Press, 1999).

5. Kathleen S. Lowney, "Teenage Satanism as Oppositional Youth Culture," *Journal of Contemporary Ethnography* 23, no. 4 (January 1995): 453–84.

6. Bill Ellis, *Raising the Devil: Satanism, New Religions, and the Media* (Lexington: University Press of Kentucky, 2000).

7. This was true of all but the Traditionalist teens and of teens not at all interested in either religion or the supernatural realm. Respondents such as these comprise approximately 5 percent of the U.S. population. This suggests that while these 5 percent and the 30 percent or so of the young U.S. population who embrace conservative views may not hold this stance toward beliefs, a majority may. This is a subject for further research.

8. For insights into how religious programming oriented to adults is limited to audience members who already embrace those traditions depicted, see Stewart M. Hoover, *Mass Media Religion: Social Sources of the Electronic Church* (Thousand Oaks, Calif.: Sage, 1988).

9. Bruce A. Chadwick and Tim B. Heaton, eds., *Statistical Handbook on Adolescents in America* (Phoenix: Oryx Press, 1996).

10. George H. Gallup Institute, *The Spiritual Life of Young Americans: Approaching the Year 2000*, research report (Princeton, N.J.: George H. Gallup International Institute, 1999).

11. Carol Lytch, "Choosing Faith across Generations: A Qualitative Study of Church-Affiliated High School Seniors and Their Parents" (Ph.D. diss., Emory University, 2000).

12. Wade Clark Roof argues similarly that U.S. baby boomers are open to truth claims from various sources but are not unaware of the relationship between these claims and "power plays," See Roof, *Spiritual Marketplace.*

13. Wade Clark Roof, *A Generation of Seekers: The Spiritual Journeys of the Baby Boom Generation* (San Francisco: HarperSanFrancisco, 1993).

14. MacDonald makes a similar call for a reconsideration of uncertainty rather than implausibility as a means by which to explore secularization. William MacDonald, conversation during the annual meeting of the American Sociological Association, Washington, D.C. (August 2000).

15. The historical connection between Protestant religious values and the unfolding of U.S. history is analyzed in N. Jay Demerath III, "Cultural Victory and Organizational Defeat in the Paradoxical Decline of Liberal Protestantism." *Journal for the Scientific Study of Religion* 34, no. 4 (1995): 458–69.

16. Gallup Institute, *The Spiritual Life of Young Americans.*

17. See, for example, the argument about the prejudices concerning secularism's purported immorality in David Nash, "Religious Sensibilities in the Age of the Internet: Freethought Culture and the Historical Context of Communication Media," in *Practicing Religion in the Age of the Media: Explorations in Media, Religion, and Culture,* ed. Stewart Hoover and Lynn Schofield Clark (New York: Columbia University Press, 2002).

18. See, for example, the argument that taste effectively limits social opportunities in S. Elizabeth Bird, *For Enquiring Minds: A Cultural Study of Supermarket Tabloids* (Knoxville: University of Tennessee Press, 1992). This argument is related specifically to young people in the classic book by Paul Willis, *Learning to Labor: How Working-Class Kids Get Working-Class Jobs* (London: Saxon House, 1977).

19. Pierre Bourdieu, *Distinction: A Social Critique of the Judgment of Taste,* trans. Richard Nice (Cambridge, Mass.: Harvard University Press, 1984).

20. David Morley decries the "semiotic democracy" position in "Theoretical Orthodoxies: Textualism, Constructivism and the 'New Ethnography' in Cultural Studies," in *Cultural Studies in Question,* ed. Marjorie Ferguson and Peter Golding (London: Sage, 1997), 121–37.

21. Ibid., 127–28.

22. Barbara Ehrenreich has inspired me on this aspect of the conclusion. See her book *Nickel and Dimed: On (Not) Getting By in America* (New York: Metropolitan Books, Henry Holt, 2001).

23. William James, *The Varieties of Religious Experience: A Study in Human Nature* (Reprint, New Hyde Park, N.Y.: University Books, 1963).

APPENDIX A

1. I conducted interviews and observations with 94 persons (55 of whom were teens) and supervised other interviewers. Research team members, all well versed in both media studies and sociology of religion literature, read and interpreted each other's transcripts, thus triangulating and verifying data and analysis.

2. In addition to this book, a coauthored manuscript is being written out of the data from the project. This book is titled *Media, Home, and the Family,* by Stewart M. Hoover, Lynn Schofield Clark, and Diane F. Alters, with Joseph Champ and Lee Hood.

Stewart Hoover is writing a book that will draw upon this data as well. That book is tentatively titled *The Religion of the Media Age*.

3. Louisville Institute Dissertation Fellowship program in American Religion, 1997–98.

4. Perhaps the single most influential essay that led to a recentering of the study of interpretation strategies, moving it away from the text and toward the audience, was Stuart Hall, "Encoding/Decoding," in *Culture, Media, Language*, ed. Stuart Hall, Dorothy Hobson, Andrew Lowe, and Paul Willis (London: Hutchinson, 1980), 128–38. For a complete review of the turn to ethnographic inquiry and the importance of both critically informed cultural history (especially the Frankfurt School) and reader-response theories of literary criticism, see Graeme Turner, *British Cultural Studies: An Introduction*, 2nd ed. (New York: Routledge, 1996).

5. Simon Frith, *Performing Rites: On the Value of Popular Music* (Cambridge, Mass.: Harvard University Press, 1996); Horace Newcomb, "Assessing the Violence Profile Studies of Gerbner and Gross: A Humanistic Critique and Suggestion," *Communication Research* 5, no. 3 (1978): 264–82.

6. Stuart Hall discusses this in relation to the intentional naming of the Birmingham Center for Contemporary Cultural Studies. For recent calls for such research approaches, see David Morley, "Theoretical Orthodoxies: Textualism, Constructivism and the 'New Ethnography' in Cultural Studies," in *Cultural Studies in Question*, ed. Marjorie Ferguson and Peter Golding (London: Sage, 1997); Sonia Livingstone, introduction to *Children and Their Changing Media Environment: A European Comparative Study*, ed. Sonia Livingstone and Moira Bovill (Cresskill, N.J.: Lawrence Erlbaum, 2001).

7. Erika Doss, *Elvis Culture: Fans, Faith, and Image* (Lawrence: University of Kansas Press, 1999); David Morley and Kevin Robins, *Spaces of Identity: Global Media, Electronic Landscapes, and Cultural Boundaries* (London: Routledge, 1995).

8. Thomas R. Lindlof, *Qualitative Communication Research Methods* (Thousand Oaks, Calif.: Sage, 1995).

9. Michelle Fine, "Working the Hyphens: Self and Other in Qualitative Research," in *The Landscape of Qualitative Research: Theories and Issues*, ed. Norman Denzin and Yvonna S. Lincoln (Thousand Oaks, Calif.: Sage, 1998).

10. S. Elizabeth Bird, "Travels in Nowhere Land: Ethnography and the 'Impossible' Audience," *Critical Studies in Mass Communication* 9 (1992): 250–60.

11. Future study is needed to determine how many teens similarly are interested in or are capable of discussing both religious and mediated stories of the afterlife, and hence how representative are the teens analyzed here.

12. Egon Guba and Yvonna Lincoln offer a cogent description of what they call the four paradigms that have guided qualitative research: positivist (survey-based, designed with the assumption of scientific objectivity), postpositivist (interview- and observation-based, designed with the assumption of the need to get as close to the situation researched as possible while still maintaining some degree of objectivity), critical (based in Marxist, feminist, and postcolonial critiques), and constructivist (based in these critiques as well as the critiques of knowledge that challenges the very idea that unbiased, objective research is possible). My approach is a blend of what they term critical and constructivist research. See Egon C. Guba and Yvonna S. Lincoln, "Competing Paradigms in Qualitative Research," in *Handbook of Qualitative Research*, ed. Norman Denzin and Yvonna Lincoln (Thousand Oaks, Calif.: Sage, 1994), 105–17.

13. The Personal Narratives Group, eds., *Interpreting Women's Lives: Feminist Theory and Personal Narratives* (Bloomington: Indiana University Press, 1989).

14. Jake Pickerington was initially asked to serve as a group leader and in fact went through the training with me, but he was either unable to or uninterested in setting up a group among his peers.

15. The grant from the Louisville Institute provided the payment for focus group participants. Teen participants were paid $8 each ($25 for the peer interpreter), and parents were paid $25 each ($75 for the organizer). Pizza was purchased for each group, as well.

16. Tamar Liebes and Elihu Katz, *The Export of Meaning* (Oxford: Oxford University Press, 1990).

17. Janice Radway, *Reading the Romance: Women, Patriarchy, and Popular Literature* (Chapel Hill: University of North Carolina Press, 1984).

18. Personal conversation at the annual meeting of the International Communication Association, Albuquerque, N.M., May 1995.

19. Both Jake Pickerington and Hasan Ahmed agreed to use this program, although Jake ultimately did not host a group, as noted.

20. The phrase "controlling the terms of conversation" and the significance of this idea in relation to knowledge production is brilliantly analyzed in Jean and John Comaroff, *Of Revelation and Revolution: Christianity, Colonialism, and Consciousness in South Africa*, vol. 1 (Chicago: University of Chicago Press).

21. Personal conversation, Lawrence Grossberg, October 25, 1999.

22. Personal conversation, Horace Newcomb, June 4, 2000.

23. The edited volume *Fighting the Forces* was tremendously useful for my analysis, as was a special issue of the *Journal of Film and Television* devoted to vampires (see the notes in chapter 2). There is even an academic Web site devoted to analysis of *Buffy*, called *Slayage: An Online International Journal for* Buffy *Studies*, ed. Rhonda Wilcox and David Lavery. Available at www.middleenglish.org/slayage.

24. "Touched by a Vampire Named Angel" (paper presented at the Religious Communications Congress, Chicago, March 2000); "Religious Identity and the Supernatural in Popular Teen Media" (presented as part of a consultation with Stichting Porticus, Amsterdam, July 2000). I also presented some of this material at a colloquium at the Annenberg School of Communication, University of Pennsylvania, Philadelphia, January 2002.

25. I had several conversations with David Morgan and Mary Hess over the course of this project. David read drafts of several chapters, offering immensely detailed and helpful feedback, and Mary offered me opportunities to present my ideas among a variety of audiences I would not have met otherwise.

26. This entry was published in the *Encyclopedia of Fundamentalism*, ed. Brenda Brasher (New York: Routledge, 2002). My thanks to Brenda for inviting me to write on this topic.

27. Most of the formal interviewing I conducted was completed by the time of the Columbine incident, but I visited the memorial site, attended memorial services, and discussed this event and its aftermath with both teens who had been formally involved in my research and with other teens and their parents I knew from other, less formal contacts.

28. A few of my close friends who could be described as members of "Generation X" encouraged me to take seriously experiences with the supernatural realm, drawing a connection between the practices of channeling and the experience of profound

prayer. These friends remain anonymous to protect their privacy, but their views influenced me greatly.

29. Barry Glaser and Anselm Strauss, *The Discovery of Grounded Theory* (Chicago: Aldine Press, 1967).

30. Qualitative studies may posit theoretical possibilities, as Glaser and Strauss (1967) have argued. These possibilities may be tested further in survey research. Experts in related fields, reviewing their own data (collected both in surveys and in similarly ethnographic studies), found the arguments made here to be suggestive and consistent with their own findings.

31. J. Kincheloe and P. McLaren, "Rethinking Critical Theory and Qualitative Research," in *The Landscape of Qualitative Research: Theories and Issues*, ed. Norman Denzin and Yvonna S. Lincoln (Thousand Oaks, Calif.: Sage, 1998), 138–55.